50% Off

Online FSOT Test Prep Course!

By Mometrix

Dear Customer,

We consider it an honor and a privilege that you chose our FSOT Study Guide. As a way of showing our appreciation and to help us better serve you, we are offering **50% off our online FSOT Prep Course.** Many Foreign Service Officer Test courses are needlessly expensive and don't deliver enough value. With our course, you get access to the best FSOT prep material at half price.

We have structured our online course to perfectly complement your printed study guide. The FSOT Test Prep Course contains **in-depth lessons** that cover all the most important topics, over **1,700 practice questions** to ensure you feel prepared, more than **950 flashcards** for studying on the go, and over **180 instructional videos**.

Online FSOT Prep Course

Topics Covered:

- Writing
- Unites States Government
- United States History, Society, Customs, and Culture
- World History and Geography
- Economics
- Mathematics and Statistics
- Management Principles, Psychology, and Human Behavior
- Communications
- Computers and Internet
- And More!

Course Features:

- FSOT Study Guide
  - Get access to content from the best reviewed study guide available.
- Track Your Progress
  - Our customized course allows you to check off content you have studied or feel confident with.
- 5 Full-Length Practice Tests
  - With 1,700+ practice questions and lesson reviews, you can test yourself again and again to build confidence.
- FSOT Flashcards
  - Our course includes a flashcard mode consisting of over 950 content cards to help you study.

To receive this discount, visit us at mometrix.com/university/fsot/ or simply scan this QR code with your smartphone. At the checkout page, enter the discount code: **FSOT50OFF**

If you have any questions or concerns, please contact us at support@mometrix.com.

FREE Study Skills Videos/DVD Offer

Dear Customer,

Thank you for your purchase from Mometrix! We consider it an honor and a privilege that you have purchased our product and we want to ensure your satisfaction.

As part of our ongoing effort to meet the needs of test takers, we have developed a set of Study Skills Videos that we would like to give you for FREE. These videos cover our *best practices* for getting ready for your exam, from how to use our study materials to how to best prepare for the day of the test.

All that we ask is that you email us with feedback that would describe your experience so far with our product. Good, bad, or indifferent, we want to know what you think!

To get your FREE Study Skills Videos, you can use the **QR code** below, or send us an **email** at studyvideos@mometrix.com with *FREE VIDEOS* in the subject line and the following information in the body of the email:

- The name of the product you purchased.
- Your product rating on a scale of 1-5, with 5 being the highest rating.
- Your feedback. It can be long, short, or anything in between. We just want to know your impressions and experience so far with our product. (Good feedback might include how our study material met your needs and ways we might be able to make it even better. You could highlight features that you found helpful or features that you think we should add.)

If you have any questions or concerns, please don't hesitate to contact me directly.

Thanks again!

Sincerely,

Jay Willis
Vice President
jay.willis@mometrix.com
1-800-673-8175

FSOT Study Guide 2024-2025

FSOT Exam Prep Secrets

3 Full-Length Practice Tests

175+ Online Video Tutorials

6th Edition

Written and edited by Matthew Bowling

Printed in the United States of America

This paper meets the requirements of ANSI/NISO Z39.48-1992 (Permanence of Paper).

Mometrix offers volume discount pricing to institutions. For more information or a price quote, please contact our sales department at sales@mometrix.com or 888-248-1219.

Paperback
ISBN 13: 978-1-5167-2676-9
ISBN 10: 1-5167-2676-6

Dear Future Exam Success Story

First of all, **THANK YOU** for purchasing Mometrix study materials!

Second, congratulations! You are one of the few determined test-takers who are committed to doing whatever it takes to excel on your exam. **You have come to the right place.** We developed these study materials with one goal in mind: to deliver you the information you need in a format that's concise and easy to use.

In addition to optimizing your guide for the content of the test, we've outlined our recommended steps for breaking down the preparation process into small, attainable goals so you can make sure you stay on track.

We've also analyzed the entire test-taking process, identifying the most common pitfalls and showing how you can overcome them and be ready for any curveball the test throws you.

Standardized testing is one of the biggest obstacles on your road to success, which only increases the importance of doing well in the high-pressure, high-stakes environment of test day. Your results on this test could have a significant impact on your future, and this guide provides the information and practical advice to help you achieve your full potential on test day.

Your success is our success

We would love to hear from you! If you would like to share the story of your exam success or if you have any questions or comments in regard to our products, please contact us at **800-673-8175** or **support@mometrix.com**.

Thanks again for your business and we wish you continued success!

Sincerely,
The Mometrix Test Preparation Team

Need more help? Check out our flashcards at:
http://mometrixflashcards.com/FSOT

TABLE OF CONTENTS

Introduction

Thank you for purchasing this resource! You have made the choice to prepare yourself for a test that could have a huge impact on your future, and this guide is designed to help you be fully ready for test day. Obviously, it's important to have a solid understanding of the test material, but you also need to be prepared for the unique environment and stressors of the test, so that you can perform to the best of your abilities.

For this purpose, the first section that appears in this guide is the **Secret Keys**. We've devoted countless hours to meticulously researching what works and what doesn't, and we've boiled down our findings to the five most impactful steps you can take to improve your performance on the test. We start at the beginning with study planning and move through the preparation process, all the way to the testing strategies that will help you get the most out of what you know when you're finally sitting in front of the test.

We recommend that you start preparing for your test as far in advance as possible. However, if you've bought this guide as a last-minute study resource and only have a few days before your test, we recommend that you skip over the first two Secret Keys since they address a long-term study plan.

If you struggle with **test anxiety**, we strongly encourage you to check out our recommendations for how you can overcome it. Test anxiety is a formidable foe, but it can be beaten, and we want to make sure you have the tools you need to defeat it.

Review Video Directory

As you work your way through this guide, you will see numerous review video links interspersed with the written content. If you would like to access all of these review videos in one place, click on the video directory link found on the bonus page: **mometrix.com/bonus948/fsot**

Secret Key #1 – Plan Big, Study Small

There's a lot riding on your performance. If you want to ace this test, you're going to need to keep your skills sharp and the material fresh in your mind. You need a plan that lets you review everything you need to know while still fitting in your schedule. We'll break this strategy down into three categories.

Information Organization

Start with the information you already have: the official test outline. From this, you can make a complete list of all the concepts you need to cover before the test. Organize these concepts into groups that can be studied together, and create a list of any related vocabulary you need to learn so you can brush up on any difficult terms. You'll want to keep this vocabulary list handy once you actually start studying since you may need to add to it along the way.

Time Management

Once you have your set of study concepts, decide how to spread them out over the time you have left before the test. Break your study plan into small, clear goals so you have a manageable task for each day and know exactly what you're doing. Then just focus on one small step at a time. When you manage your time this way, you don't need to spend hours at a time studying. Studying a small block of content for a short period each day helps you retain information better and avoid stressing over how much you have left to do. You can relax knowing that you have a plan to cover everything in time. In order for this strategy to be effective though, you have to start studying early and stick to your schedule. Avoid the exhaustion and futility that comes from last-minute cramming!

Study Environment

The environment you study in has a big impact on your learning. Studying in a coffee shop, while probably more enjoyable, is not likely to be as fruitful as studying in a quiet room. It's important to keep distractions to a minimum. You're only planning to study for a short block of time, so make the most of it. Don't pause to check your phone or get up to find a snack. It's also important to **avoid multitasking**. Research has consistently shown that multitasking will make your studying dramatically less effective. Your study area should also be comfortable and well-lit so you don't have the distraction of straining your eyes or sitting on an uncomfortable chair.

The time of day you study is also important. You want to be rested and alert. Don't wait until just before bedtime. Study when you'll be most likely to comprehend and remember. Even better, if you know what time of day your test will be, set that time aside for study. That way your brain will be used to working on that subject at that specific time and you'll have a better chance of recalling information.

Finally, it can be helpful to team up with others who are studying for the same test. Your actual studying should be done in as isolated an environment as possible, but the work of organizing the information and setting up the study plan can be divided up. In between study sessions, you can discuss with your teammates the concepts that you're all studying and quiz each other on the details. Just be sure that your teammates are as serious about the test as you are. If you find that your study time is being replaced with social time, you might need to find a new team.

Secret Key #2 – Make Your Studying Count

You're devoting a lot of time and effort to preparing for this test, so you want to be absolutely certain it will pay off. This means doing more than just reading the content and hoping you can remember it on test day. It's important to make every minute of study count. There are two main areas you can focus on to make your studying count.

Retention

It doesn't matter how much time you study if you can't remember the material. You need to make sure you are retaining the concepts. To check your retention of the information you're learning, try recalling it at later times with minimal prompting. Try carrying around flashcards and glance at one or two from time to time or ask a friend who's also studying for the test to quiz you.

To enhance your retention, look for ways to put the information into practice so that you can apply it rather than simply recalling it. If you're using the information in practical ways, it will be much easier to remember. Similarly, it helps to solidify a concept in your mind if you're not only reading it to yourself but also explaining it to someone else. Ask a friend to let you teach them about a concept you're a little shaky on (or speak aloud to an imaginary audience if necessary). As you try to summarize, define, give examples, and answer your friend's questions, you'll understand the concepts better and they will stay with you longer. Finally, step back for a big picture view and ask yourself how each piece of information fits with the whole subject. When you link the different concepts together and see them working together as a whole, it's easier to remember the individual components.

Finally, practice showing your work on any multi-step problems, even if you're just studying. Writing out each step you take to solve a problem will help solidify the process in your mind, and you'll be more likely to remember it during the test.

Modality

Modality simply refers to the means or method by which you study. Choosing a study modality that fits your own individual learning style is crucial. No two people learn best in exactly the same way, so it's important to know your strengths and use them to your advantage.

For example, if you learn best by visualization, focus on visualizing a concept in your mind and draw an image or a diagram. Try color-coding your notes, illustrating them, or creating symbols that will trigger your mind to recall a learned concept. If you learn best by hearing or discussing information, find a study partner who learns the same way or read aloud to yourself. Think about how to put the information in your own words. Imagine that you are giving a lecture on the topic and record yourself so you can listen to it later.

For any learning style, flashcards can be helpful. Organize the information so you can take advantage of spare moments to review. Underline key words or phrases. Use different colors for different categories. Mnemonic devices (such as creating a short list in which every item starts with the same letter) can also help with retention. Find what works best for you and use it to store the information in your mind most effectively and easily.

Secret Key #3 – Practice the Right Way

Your success on test day depends not only on how many hours you put into preparing, but also on whether you prepared the right way. It's good to check along the way to see if your studying is paying off. One of the most effective ways to do this is by taking practice tests to evaluate your progress. Practice tests are useful because they show exactly where you need to improve. Every time you take a practice test, pay special attention to these three groups of questions:

- The questions you got wrong
- The questions you had to guess on, even if you guessed right
- The questions you found difficult or slow to work through

This will show you exactly what your weak areas are, and where you need to devote more study time. Ask yourself why each of these questions gave you trouble. Was it because you didn't understand the material? Was it because you didn't remember the vocabulary? Do you need more repetitions on this type of question to build speed and confidence? Dig into those questions and figure out how you can strengthen your weak areas as you go back to review the material.

Additionally, many practice tests have a section explaining the answer choices. It can be tempting to read the explanation and think that you now have a good understanding of the concept. However, an explanation likely only covers part of the question's broader context. Even if the explanation makes perfect sense, **go back and investigate** every concept related to the question until you're positive you have a thorough understanding.

As you go along, keep in mind that the practice test is just that: practice. Memorizing these questions and answers will not be very helpful on the actual test because it is unlikely to have any of the same exact questions. If you only know the right answers to the sample questions, you won't be prepared for the real thing. **Study the concepts** until you understand them fully, and then you'll be able to answer any question that shows up on the test.

It's important to wait on the practice tests until you're ready. If you take a test on your first day of study, you may be overwhelmed by the amount of material covered and how much you need to learn. Work up to it gradually.

On test day, you'll need to be prepared for answering questions, managing your time, and using the test-taking strategies you've learned. It's a lot to balance, like a mental marathon that will have a big impact on your future. Like training for a marathon, you'll need to start slowly and work your way up. When test day arrives, you'll be ready.

Start with the strategies you've read in the first two Secret Keys—plan your course and study in the way that works best for you. If you have time, consider using multiple study resources to get different approaches to the same concepts. It can be helpful to see difficult concepts from more than one angle. Then find a good source for practice tests. Many times, the test website will suggest potential study resources or provide sample tests.

Practice Test Strategy

If you're able to find at least three practice tests, we recommend this strategy:

Untimed and Open-Book Practice

Take the first test with no time constraints and with your notes and study guide handy. Take your time and focus on applying the strategies you've learned.

Timed and Open-Book Practice

Take the second practice test open-book as well, but set a timer and practice pacing yourself to finish in time.

Timed and Closed-Book Practice

Take any other practice tests as if it were test day. Set a timer and put away your study materials. Sit at a table or desk in a quiet room, imagine yourself at the testing center, and answer questions as quickly and accurately as possible.

Keep repeating timed and closed-book tests on a regular basis until you run out of practice tests or it's time for the actual test. Your mind will be ready for the schedule and stress of test day, and you'll be able to focus on recalling the material you've learned.

Secret Key #4 – Pace Yourself

Once you're fully prepared for the material on the test, your biggest challenge on test day will be managing your time. Just knowing that the clock is ticking can make you panic even if you have plenty of time left. Work on pacing yourself so you can build confidence against the time constraints of the exam. Pacing is a difficult skill to master, especially in a high-pressure environment, so **practice is vital**.

Set time expectations for your pace based on how much time is available. For example, if a section has 60 questions and the time limit is 30 minutes, you know you have to average 30 seconds or less per question in order to answer them all. Although 30 seconds is the hard limit, set 25 seconds per question as your goal, so you reserve extra time to spend on harder questions. When you budget extra time for the harder questions, you no longer have any reason to stress when those questions take longer to answer.

Don't let this time expectation distract you from working through the test at a calm, steady pace, but keep it in mind so you don't spend too much time on any one question. Recognize that taking extra time on one question you don't understand may keep you from answering two that you do understand later in the test. If your time limit for a question is up and you're still not sure of the answer, mark it and move on, and come back to it later if the time and the test format allow. If the testing format doesn't allow you to return to earlier questions, just make an educated guess; then put it out of your mind and move on.

On the easier questions, be careful not to rush. It may seem wise to hurry through them so you have more time for the challenging ones, but it's not worth missing one if you know the concept and just didn't take the time to read the question fully. Work efficiently but make sure you understand the question and have looked at all of the answer choices, since more than one may seem right at first.

Even if you're paying attention to the time, you may find yourself a little behind at some point. You should speed up to get back on track, but do so wisely. Don't panic; just take a few seconds less on each question until you're caught up. Don't guess without thinking, but do look through the answer choices and eliminate any you know are wrong. If you can get down to two choices, it is often worthwhile to guess from those. Once you've chosen an answer, move on and don't dwell on any that you skipped or had to hurry through. If a question was taking too long, chances are it was one of the harder ones, so you weren't as likely to get it right anyway.

On the other hand, if you find yourself getting ahead of schedule, it may be beneficial to slow down a little. The more quickly you work, the more likely you are to make a careless mistake that will affect your score. You've budgeted time for each question, so don't be afraid to spend that time. Practice an efficient but careful pace to get the most out of the time you have.

Secret Key #5 – Have a Plan for Guessing

When you're taking the test, you may find yourself stuck on a question. Some of the answer choices seem better than others, but you don't see the one answer choice that is obviously correct. What do you do?

The scenario described above is very common, yet most test takers have not effectively prepared for it. Developing and practicing a plan for guessing may be one of the single most effective uses of your time as you get ready for the exam.

In developing your plan for guessing, there are three questions to address:

- When should you start the guessing process?
- How should you narrow down the choices?
- Which answer should you choose?

When to Start the Guessing Process

Unless your plan for guessing is to select C every time (which, despite its merits, is not what we recommend), you need to leave yourself enough time to apply your answer elimination strategies. Since you have a limited amount of time for each question, that means that if you're going to give yourself the best shot at guessing correctly, you have to decide quickly whether or not you will guess.

Of course, the best-case scenario is that you don't have to guess at all, so first, see if you can answer the question based on your knowledge of the subject and basic reasoning skills. Focus on the key words in the question and try to jog your memory of related topics. Give yourself a chance to bring the knowledge to mind, but once you realize that you don't have (or you can't access) the knowledge you need to answer the question, it's time to start the guessing process.

It's almost always better to start the guessing process too early than too late. It only takes a few seconds to remember something and answer the question from knowledge. Carefully eliminating wrong answer choices takes longer. Plus, going through the process of eliminating answer choices can actually help jog your memory.

Summary: Start the guessing process as soon as you decide that you can't answer the question based on your knowledge.

How to Narrow Down the Choices

The next chapter in this book (**Test-Taking Strategies**) includes a wide range of strategies for how to approach questions and how to look for answer choices to eliminate. You will definitely want to read those carefully, practice them, and figure out which ones work best for you. Here though, we're going to address a mindset rather than a particular strategy.

Your odds of guessing an answer correctly depend on how many options you are choosing from.

Number of options left	5	4	3	2	1
Odds of guessing correctly	20%	25%	33%	50%	100%

You can see from this chart just how valuable it is to be able to eliminate incorrect answers and make an educated guess, but there are two things that many test takers do that cause them to miss out on the benefits of guessing:

- Accidentally eliminating the correct answer
- Selecting an answer based on an impression

We'll look at the first one here, and the second one in the next section.

To avoid accidentally eliminating the correct answer, we recommend a thought exercise called **the $5 challenge**. In this challenge, you only eliminate an answer choice from contention if you are willing to bet $5 on it being wrong. Why $5? Five dollars is a small but not insignificant amount of money. It's an amount you could afford to lose but wouldn't want to throw away. And while losing $5 once might not hurt too much, doing it twenty times will set you back $100. In the same way, each small decision you make—eliminating a choice here, guessing on a question there—won't by itself impact your score very much, but when you put them all together, they can make a big difference. By holding each answer choice elimination decision to a higher standard, you can reduce the risk of accidentally eliminating the correct answer.

The $5 challenge can also be applied in a positive sense: If you are willing to bet $5 that an answer choice *is* correct, go ahead and mark it as correct.

Summary: Only eliminate an answer choice if you are willing to bet $5 that it is wrong.

Which Answer to Choose

You're taking the test. You've run into a hard question and decided you'll have to guess. You've eliminated all the answer choices you're willing to bet $5 on. Now you have to pick an answer. Why do we even need to talk about this? Why can't you just pick whichever one you feel like when the time comes?

The answer to these questions is that if you don't come into the test with a plan, you'll rely on your impression to select an answer choice, and if you do that, you risk falling into a trap. The test writers know that everyone who takes their test will be guessing on some of the questions, so they intentionally write wrong answer choices to seem plausible. You still have to pick an answer though, and if the wrong answer choices are designed to look right, how can you ever be sure that you're not falling for their trap? The best solution we've found to this dilemma is to take the decision out of your hands entirely. Here is the process we recommend:

Once you've eliminated any choices that you are confident (willing to bet $5) are wrong, select the first remaining choice as your answer.

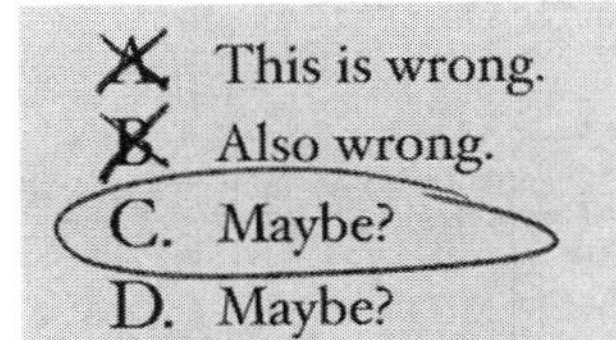

Whether you choose to select the first remaining choice, the second, or the last, the important thing is that you use some preselected standard. Using this approach guarantees that you will not be enticed into selecting an answer choice that looks right, because you are not basing your decision on how the answer choices look.

This is not meant to make you question your knowledge. Instead, it is to help you recognize the difference between your knowledge and your impressions. There's a huge difference between thinking an answer is right because of what you know, and thinking an answer is right because it looks or sounds like it should be right.

Summary: To ensure that your selection is appropriately random, make a predetermined selection from among all answer choices you have not eliminated.

Test-Taking Strategies

This section contains a list of test-taking strategies that you may find helpful as you work through the test. By taking what you know and applying logical thought, you can maximize your chances of answering any question correctly!

It is very important to realize that every question is different and every person is different: no single strategy will work on every question, and no single strategy will work for every person. That's why we've included all of them here, so you can try them out and determine which ones work best for different types of questions and which ones work best for you.

Question Strategies

✓ Read Carefully

Read the question and the answer choices carefully. Don't miss the question because you misread the terms. You have plenty of time to read each question thoroughly and make sure you understand what is being asked. Yet a happy medium must be attained, so don't waste too much time. You must read carefully and efficiently.

✓ Contextual Clues

Look for contextual clues. If the question includes a word you are not familiar with, look at the immediate context for some indication of what the word might mean. Contextual clues can often give you all the information you need to decipher the meaning of an unfamiliar word. Even if you can't determine the meaning, you may be able to narrow down the possibilities enough to make a solid guess at the answer to the question.

✓ Prefixes

If you're having trouble with a word in the question or answer choices, try dissecting it. Take advantage of every clue that the word might include. Prefixes can be a huge help. Usually, they allow you to determine a basic meaning. *Pre-* means before, *post-* means after, *pro-* is positive, *de-* is negative. From prefixes, you can get an idea of the general meaning of the word and try to put it into context.

✓ Hedge Words

Watch out for critical hedge words, such as *likely, may, can, sometimes, often, almost, mostly, usually, generally, rarely*, and *sometimes*. Question writers insert these hedge phrases to cover every possibility. Often an answer choice will be wrong simply because it leaves no room for exception. Be on guard for answer choices that have definitive words such as *exactly* and *always*.

✓ Switchback Words

Stay alert for *switchbacks*. These are the words and phrases frequently used to alert you to shifts in thought. The most common switchback words are *but, although*, and *however*. Others include *nevertheless, on the other hand, even though, while, in spite of, despite*, and *regardless of*. Switchback words are important to catch because they can change the direction of the question or an answer choice.

✓ Face Value

When in doubt, use common sense. Accept the situation in the problem at face value. Don't read too much into it. These problems will not require you to make wild assumptions. If you have to go beyond creativity and warp time or space in order to have an answer choice fit the question, then you should move on and consider the other answer choices. These are normal problems rooted in reality. The applicable relationship or explanation may not be readily apparent, but it is there for you to figure out. Use your common sense to interpret anything that isn't clear.

Answer Choice Strategies

ANSWER SELECTION

The most thorough way to pick an answer choice is to identify and eliminate wrong answers until only one is left, then confirm it is the correct answer. Sometimes an answer choice may immediately seem right, but be careful. The test writers will usually put more than one reasonable answer choice on each question, so take a second to read all of them and make sure that the other choices are not equally obvious. As long as you have time left, it is better to read every answer choice than to pick the first one that looks right without checking the others.

ANSWER CHOICE FAMILIES

An answer choice family consists of two (in rare cases, three) answer choices that are very similar in construction and cannot all be true at the same time. If you see two answer choices that are direct opposites or parallels, one of them is usually the correct answer. For instance, if one answer choice says that quantity x increases and another either says that quantity x decreases (opposite) or says that quantity y increases (parallel), then those answer choices would fall into the same family. An answer choice that doesn't match the construction of the answer choice family is more likely to be incorrect. Most questions will not have answer choice families, but when they do appear, you should be prepared to recognize them.

ELIMINATE ANSWERS

Eliminate answer choices as soon as you realize they are wrong, but make sure you consider all possibilities. If you are eliminating answer choices and realize that the last one you are left with is also wrong, don't panic. Start over and consider each choice again. There may be something you missed the first time that you will realize on the second pass.

AVOID FACT TRAPS

Don't be distracted by an answer choice that is factually true but doesn't answer the question. You are looking for the choice that answers the question. Stay focused on what the question is asking for so you don't accidentally pick an answer that is true but incorrect. Always go back to the question and make sure the answer choice you've selected actually answers the question and is not merely a true statement.

EXTREME STATEMENTS

In general, you should avoid answers that put forth extreme actions as standard practice or proclaim controversial ideas as established fact. An answer choice that states the "process should be used in certain situations, if..." is much more likely to be correct than one that states the "process should be discontinued completely." The first is a calm rational statement and doesn't even make a definitive, uncompromising stance, using a hedge word *if* to provide wiggle room, whereas the second choice is far more extreme.

BENCHMARK

As you read through the answer choices and you come across one that seems to answer the question well, mentally select that answer choice. This is not your final answer, but it's the one that will help you evaluate the other answer choices. The one that you selected is your benchmark or standard for judging each of the other answer choices. Every other answer choice must be compared to your benchmark. That choice is correct until proven otherwise by another answer choice beating it. If you find a better answer, then that one becomes your new benchmark. Once you've decided that no other choice answers the question as well as your benchmark, you have your final answer.

✓ Predict the Answer

Before you even start looking at the answer choices, it is often best to try to predict the answer. When you come up with the answer on your own, it is easier to avoid distractions and traps because you will know exactly what to look for. The right answer choice is unlikely to be word-for-word what you came up with, but it should be a close match. Even if you are confident that you have the right answer, you should still take the time to read each option before moving on.

General Strategies

✓ Tough Questions

If you are stumped on a problem or it appears too hard or too difficult, don't waste time. Move on! Remember though, if you can quickly check for obviously incorrect answer choices, your chances of guessing correctly are greatly improved. Before you completely give up, at least try to knock out a couple of possible answers. Eliminate what you can and then guess at the remaining answer choices before moving on.

✓ Check Your Work

Since you will probably not know every term listed and the answer to every question, it is important that you get credit for the ones that you do know. Don't miss any questions through careless mistakes. If at all possible, try to take a second to look back over your answer selection and make sure you've selected the correct answer choice and haven't made a costly careless mistake (such as marking an answer choice that you didn't mean to mark). This quick double check should more than pay for itself in caught mistakes for the time it costs.

✓ Pace Yourself

It's easy to be overwhelmed when you're looking at a page full of questions; your mind is confused and full of random thoughts, and the clock is ticking down faster than you would like. Calm down and maintain the pace that you have set for yourself. Especially as you get down to the last few minutes of the test, don't let the small numbers on the clock make you panic. As long as you are on track by monitoring your pace, you are guaranteed to have time for each question.

✓ Don't Rush

It is very easy to make errors when you are in a hurry. Maintaining a fast pace in answering questions is pointless if it makes you miss questions that you would have gotten right otherwise. Test writers like to include distracting information and wrong answers that seem right. Taking a little extra time to avoid careless mistakes can make all the difference in your test score. Find a pace that allows you to be confident in the answers that you select.

✓ Keep Moving

Panicking will not help you pass the test, so do your best to stay calm and keep moving. Taking deep breaths and going through the answer elimination steps you practiced can help to break through a stress barrier and keep your pace.

Final Notes

The combination of a solid foundation of content knowledge and the confidence that comes from practicing your plan for applying that knowledge is the key to maximizing your performance on test day. As your foundation of content knowledge is built up and strengthened, you'll find that the strategies included in this chapter become more and more effective in helping you quickly sift through the distractions and traps of the test to isolate the correct answer.

Now that you're preparing to move forward into the test content chapters of this book, be sure to keep your goal in mind. As you read, think about how you will be able to apply this information on the test. If you've already seen sample questions for the test and you have an idea of the question format and style, try to come up with questions of your own that you can answer based on what you're reading. This will give you valuable practice applying your knowledge in the same ways you can expect to on test day.

Good luck and good studying!

Writing

Transform passive reading into active learning! After immersing yourself in this chapter, put your comprehension to the test by taking a quiz. The insights you gained will stay with you longer this way. Scan the QR code to go directly to the chapter quiz interface for this study guide. If you're using a computer, simply visit the bonus page at **mometrix.com/bonus948/fsot** and click the Chapter Quizzes link.

Vocabulary

Word Roots and Prefixes and Suffixes

Affixes

Affixes in the English language are morphemes that are added to words to create related but different words. Derivational affixes form new words based on and related to the original words. For example, the affix *–ness* added to the end of the adjective *happy* forms the noun *happiness.* Inflectional affixes form different grammatical versions of words. For example, the plural affix *–s* changes the singular noun *book* to the plural noun *books*, and the past tense affix *–ed* changes the present tense verb *look* to the past tense *looked.* Prefixes are affixes placed in front of words. For example, *heat* means to make hot; *preheat* means to heat in advance. Suffixes are affixes placed at the ends of words. The *happiness* example above contains the suffix *–ness.* Circumfixes add parts both before and after words, such as how *light* becomes *enlighten* with the prefix *en-* and the suffix *–en.* Interfixes create compound words via central affixes: *speed* and *meter* become *speedometer* via the interfix *–o–*.

> **Review Video: Affixes**
> Visit mometrix.com/academy and enter code: 782422

Word Roots, Prefixes, and Suffixes to Help Determine Meanings of Words

Many English words were formed from combining multiple sources. For example, the Latin *habēre* means "to have," and the prefixes *in-* and *im-* mean a lack or prevention of something, as in *insufficient* and *imperfect.* Latin combined *in-* with *habēre* to form *inhibēre,* whose past participle was *inhibitus.* This is the origin of the English word *inhibit,* meaning to prevent from having. Hence by knowing the meanings of both the prefix and the root, one can decipher the word meaning. In Greek, the root *enkephalo-* refers to the brain. Many medical terms are based on this root, such as encephalitis and hydrocephalus. Understanding the prefix and suffix meanings (*-itis* means inflammation; *hydro-* means water) allows a person to deduce that encephalitis refers to brain inflammation and hydrocephalus refers to water (or other fluid) in the brain.

> **Review Video: Determining Word Meanings**
> Visit mometrix.com/academy and enter code: 894894

Prefixes

Knowing common prefixes is helpful for all readers as they try to determining meanings or definitions of unfamiliar words. For example, a common word used when cooking is *preheat.* Knowing that *pre-* means in advance can also inform them that *presume* means to assume in advance, that *prejudice* means advance judgment, and that this understanding can be applied to many other words beginning with *pre-*. Knowing that the prefix *dis-* indicates opposition informs the meanings of words like *disbar, disagree, disestablish,* and many more. Knowing *dys-* means bad, impaired, abnormal, or difficult informs *dyslogistic, dysfunctional, dysphagia,* and *dysplasia.*

SUFFIXES

In English, certain suffixes generally indicate both that a word is a noun, and that the noun represents a state of being or quality. For example, *-ness* is commonly used to change an adjective into its noun form, as with *happy* and *happiness, nice* and *niceness,* and so on. The suffix *–tion* is commonly used to transform a verb into its noun form, as with *converse* and *conversation or move* and *motion*. Thus, if readers are unfamiliar with the second form of a word, knowing the meaning of the transforming suffix can help them determine meaning.

PREFIXES FOR NUMBERS

Prefix	Definition	Examples
bi-	two	bisect, biennial
mono-	one, single	monogamy, monologue
poly-	many	polymorphous, polygamous
semi-	half, partly	semicircle, semicolon
uni-	one	uniform, unity

PREFIXES FOR TIME, DIRECTION, AND SPACE

Prefix	Definition	Examples
a-	in, on, of, up, to	abed, afoot
ab-	from, away, off	abdicate, abjure
ad-	to, toward	advance, adventure
ante-	before, previous	antecedent, antedate
anti-	against, opposing	antipathy, antidote
cata-	down, away, thoroughly	catastrophe, cataclysm
circum-	around	circumspect, circumference
com-	with, together, very	commotion, complicate
contra-	against, opposing	contradict, contravene
de-	from	depart
dia-	through, across, apart	diameter, diagnose
dis-	away, off, down, not	dissent, disappear
epi-	upon	epilogue
ex-	out	extract, excerpt
hypo-	under, beneath	hypodermic, hypothesis
inter-	among, between	intercede, interrupt
intra-	within	intramural, intrastate
ob-	against, opposing	objection
per-	through	perceive, permit
peri-	around	periscope, perimeter
post-	after, following	postpone, postscript
pre-	before, previous	prevent, preclude
pro-	forward, in place of	propel, pronoun
retro-	back, backward	retrospect, retrograde
sub-	under, beneath	subjugate, substitute
super-	above, extra	supersede, supernumerary
trans-	across, beyond, over	transact, transport
ultra-	beyond, excessively	ultramodern, ultrasonic

NEGATIVE PREFIXES

Prefix	Definition	Examples
a-	without, lacking	atheist, agnostic
in-	not, opposing	incapable, ineligible
non-	not	nonentity, nonsense
un-	not, reverse of	unhappy, unlock

EXTRA PREFIXES

Prefix	Definition	Examples
for-	away, off, from	forget, forswear
fore-	previous	foretell, forefathers
homo-	same, equal	homogenized, homonym
hyper-	excessive, over	hypercritical, hypertension
in-	in, into	intrude, invade
mal-	bad, poorly, not	malfunction, malpractice
mis-	bad, poorly, not	misspell, misfire
neo-	new	Neolithic, neoconservative
omni-	all, everywhere	omniscient, omnivore
ortho-	right, straight	orthogonal, orthodox
over-	above	overbearing, oversight
pan-	all, entire	panorama, pandemonium
para-	beside, beyond	parallel, paradox
re-	backward, again	revoke, recur
sym-	with, together	sympathy, symphony

Below is a list of common suffixes and their meanings:

ADJECTIVE SUFFIXES

Suffix	Definition	Examples
-able (-ible)	capable of being	toler*able*, ed*ible*
-esque	in the style of, like	picturesque, grotesque
-ful	filled with, marked by	thankful, zestful
-ific	make, cause	terrific, beatific
-ish	suggesting, like	churlish, childish
-less	lacking, without	hopeless, countless
-ous	marked by, given to	religious, riotous

Noun Suffixes

Suffix	Definition	Examples
-acy	state, condition	accuracy, privacy
-ance	act, condition, fact	acceptance, vigilance
-ard	one that does excessively	drunkard, sluggard
-ation	action, state, result	occupation, starvation
-dom	state, rank, condition	serfdom, wisdom
-er (-or)	office, action	teach*er*, elevat*or*, hon*or*
-ess	feminine	waitress, duchess
-hood	state, condition	manhood, statehood
-ion	action, result, state	union, fusion
-ism	act, manner, doctrine	barbarism, socialism
-ist	worker, follower	monopolist, socialist
-ity (-ty)	state, quality, condition	acid*ity*, civil*ity*, twen*ty*
-ment	result, action	Refreshment
-ness	quality, state	greatness, tallness
-ship	position	internship, statesmanship
-sion (-tion)	state, result	revi*sion*, expedi*tion*
-th	act, state, quality	warmth, width
-tude	quality, state, result	magnitude, fortitude

Verb Suffixes

Suffix	Definition	Examples
-ate	having, showing	separate, desolate
-en	cause to be, become	deepen, strengthen
-fy	make, cause to have	glorify, fortify
-ize	cause to be, treat with	sterilize, mechanize

Nuance and Word Meanings

Synonyms and Antonyms

When you understand how words relate to each other, you will discover more in a passage. This is explained by understanding **synonyms** (e.g., words that mean the same thing) and **antonyms** (e.g., words that mean the opposite of one another). As an example, *dry* and *arid* are synonyms, and *dry* and *wet* are antonyms.

There are many pairs of words in English that can be considered synonyms, despite having slightly different definitions. For instance, the words *friendly* and *collegial* can both be used to describe a warm interpersonal relationship, and one would be correct to call them synonyms. However, *collegial* (kin to *colleague*) is often used in reference to professional or academic relationships, and *friendly* has no such connotation.

If the difference between the two words is too great, then they should not be called synonyms. *Hot* and *warm* are not synonyms because their meanings are too distinct. A good way to determine whether two words are synonyms is to substitute one word for the other word and verify that the meaning of the sentence has not changed. Substituting *warm* for *hot* in a sentence would convey a different meaning. Although warm and hot may seem close in meaning, warm generally means that the temperature is moderate, and hot generally means that the temperature is excessively high.

Antonyms are words with opposite meanings. *Light* and *dark*, *up* and *down*, *right* and *left*, *good* and *bad*: these are all sets of antonyms. Be careful to distinguish between antonyms and pairs of words that are simply different. *Black* and *gray*, for instance, are not antonyms because gray is not the opposite of black. *Black* and *white*, on the other hand, are antonyms.

Not every word has an antonym. For instance, many nouns do not. What would be the antonym of *chair*? During your exam, the questions related to antonyms are more likely to concern adjectives. You will recall that adjectives are words that describe a noun. Some common adjectives include *purple*, *fast*, *skinny*, and *sweet*. From those four adjectives, *purple* is the item that lacks a group of obvious antonyms.

Review Video: Synonyms and Antonyms
Visit mometrix.com/academy and enter code: 105612

Denotative vs. Connotative Meaning

The **denotative** meaning of a word is the literal meaning. The **connotative** meaning goes beyond the denotative meaning to include the emotional reaction that a word may invoke. The connotative meaning often takes the denotative meaning a step further due to associations the reader makes with the denotative meaning. Readers can differentiate between the denotative and connotative meanings by first recognizing how authors use each meaning. Most non-fiction, for example, is fact-based and authors do not use flowery, figurative language. The reader can assume that the writer is using the denotative meaning of words. In fiction, the author may use the connotative meaning. Readers can determine whether the author is using the denotative or connotative meaning of a word by implementing context clues.

Review Video: Connotation and Denotation
Visit mometrix.com/academy and enter code: 310092

Nuances of Word Meaning Relative to Connotation, Denotation, Diction, and Usage

A word's denotation is simply its objective dictionary definition. However, its connotation refers to the subjective associations, often emotional, that specific words evoke in listeners and readers. Two or more words can have the same dictionary meaning, but very different connotations. Writers use diction (word choice) to convey various nuances of thought and emotion by selecting synonyms for other words that best communicate the associations they want to trigger for readers. For example, a car engine is naturally greasy; in this sense, "greasy" is a neutral term. But when a person's smile, appearance, or clothing is described as "greasy," it has a negative connotation. Some words have even gained additional or different meanings over time. For example, *awful* used to be used to describe things that evoked a sense of awe. When *awful* is separated into its root word, awe, and suffix, -ful, it can be understood to mean "full of awe." However, the word is now commonly used to describe things that evoke repulsion, terror, or another intense, negative reaction.

Review Video: Word Usage in Sentences
Visit mometrix.com/academy and enter code: 197863

Using Context to Determine Meaning

Context Clues

Readers of all levels will encounter words that they have either never seen or have encountered only on a limited basis. The best way to define a word in **context** is to look for nearby words that can assist in revealing the meaning of the word. For instance, unfamiliar nouns are often accompanied by examples that provide a definition. Consider the following sentence: *Dave arrived at the party in hilarious garb: a leopard-print shirt, buckskin trousers, and bright green sneakers.* If a reader was unfamiliar with the meaning of garb, he or she could read the examples (i.e., a leopard-print shirt, buckskin trousers, and bright green sneakers) and quickly determine that the word means *clothing*. Examples will not always be this obvious. Consider this sentence: *Parsley, lemon, and flowers were just a few of the items he used as garnishes.* Here, the word *garnishes* is exemplified by parsley, lemon, and flowers. Readers who have eaten in a variety of restaurants will probably be able to identify a garnish as something used to decorate a plate.

Review Video: Reading Comprehension: Using Context Clues
Visit mometrix.com/academy and enter code: 613660

Using Contrast in Context Clues

In addition to looking at the context of a passage, readers can use contrast to define an unfamiliar word in context. In many sentences, the author will not describe the unfamiliar word directly; instead, he or she will describe the opposite of the unfamiliar word. Thus, you are provided with some information that will bring you closer to defining the word. Consider the following example: *Despite his intelligence, Hector's low brow and bad posture made him look obtuse.* The author writes that Hector's appearance does not convey intelligence. Therefore, *obtuse* must mean unintelligent. Here is another example: *Despite the horrible weather, we were beatific about our trip to Alaska*. The word *despite* indicates that the speaker's feelings were at odds with the weather. Since the weather is described as *horrible*, then *beatific* must mean something positive.

Substitution to Find Meaning

In some cases, there will be very few contextual clues to help a reader define the meaning of an unfamiliar word. When this happens, one strategy that readers may employ is **substitution**. A good reader will brainstorm some possible synonyms for the given word, and he or she will substitute these words into the sentence. If the sentence and the surrounding passage continue to make sense, then the substitution has revealed at least some information about the unfamiliar word. Consider the sentence: *Frank's admonition rang in her ears as she climbed the mountain.* A reader unfamiliar with *admonition* might come up with some substitutions like *vow*, *promise*, *advice*, *complaint*, or *compliment*. All of these words make general sense of the sentence, though their meanings are diverse. However, this process has suggested that an admonition is some sort of message. The substitution strategy is rarely able to pinpoint a precise definition, but this process can be effective as a last resort.

Occasionally, you will be able to define an unfamiliar word by looking at the descriptive words in the context. Consider the following sentence: *Fred dragged the recalcitrant boy kicking and screaming up the stairs.* The words *dragged*, *kicking*, and *screaming* all suggest that the boy does not want to go up the stairs. The reader may assume that *recalcitrant* means something like unwilling or protesting. In this example, an unfamiliar adjective was identified.

Additionally, using description to define an unfamiliar noun is a common practice compared to unfamiliar adjectives, as in this sentence: *Don's wrinkled frown and constantly shaking fist identified him as a curmudgeon of the first order*. Don is described as having a *wrinkled frown and constantly shaking fist*, suggesting that a *curmudgeon* must be a grumpy person. Contrasts do not always provide detailed information about the unfamiliar word, but they at least give the reader some clues.

Words with Multiple Meanings

When a word has more than one meaning, readers can have difficulty determining how the word is being used in a given sentence. For instance, the verb *cleave*, can mean either *join* or *separate*. When readers come upon this word, they will have to select the definition that makes the most sense. Consider the following sentence: *Hermione's knife cleaved the bread cleanly*. Since a knife cannot join bread together, the word must indicate separation. A slightly more difficult example would be the sentence: *The birds cleaved to one another as they flew from the oak tree.* Immediately, the presence of the words *to one another* should suggest that in this sentence *cleave* is being used to mean *join*. Discovering the intent of a word with multiple meanings requires the same tricks as defining an unknown word: look for contextual clues and evaluate the substituted words.

Context Clues to Help Determine Meanings of Words

If readers simply bypass unknown words, they can reach unclear conclusions about what they read. However, looking for the definition of every unfamiliar word in the dictionary can slow their reading progress. Moreover, the dictionary may list multiple definitions for a word, so readers must search the word's context for meaning. Hence context is important to new vocabulary regardless of reader methods. Four types of context clues are examples, definitions, descriptive words, and opposites. Authors may use a certain word, and then follow it with several different examples of what it describes. Sometimes authors actually supply a definition of a word they use, which is especially true in informational and technical texts. Authors may use descriptive words that elaborate upon a vocabulary word they just used. Authors may also use opposites with negation that help define meaning.

Examples and Definitions

An author may use a word and then give examples that illustrate its meaning. Consider this text: "Teachers who do not know how to use sign language can help students who are deaf or hard of hearing understand certain instructions by using gestures instead, like pointing their fingers to indicate which direction to look or go; holding up a hand, palm outward, to indicate stopping; holding the hands flat, palms up, curling a finger toward oneself in a beckoning motion to indicate 'come here'; or curling all fingers toward oneself repeatedly to indicate 'come on', 'more', or 'continue.'" The author of this text has used the word "gestures" and then followed it with examples, so a reader unfamiliar with the word could deduce from the examples that "gestures" means "hand motions." Readers can find examples by looking for signal words "for example," "for instance," "like," "such as," and "e.g."

While readers sometimes have to look for definitions of unfamiliar words in a dictionary or do some work to determine a word's meaning from its surrounding context, at other times an author may make it easier for readers by defining certain words. For example, an author may write, "The company did not have sufficient capital, that is, available money, to continue operations." The author defined "capital" as "available money," and heralded the definition with the phrase "that is." Another way that authors supply word definitions is with appositives. Rather than being introduced by a signal phrase like "that is," "namely," or "meaning," an appositive comes after the vocabulary word it defines and is enclosed within two commas. For example, an author may write, "The Indians introduced the Pilgrims to pemmican, cakes they made of lean meat dried and mixed with fat, which proved greatly beneficial to keep settlers from starving while trapping." In this example, the appositive phrase following "pemmican" and preceding "which" defines the word "pemmican."

Descriptions

When readers encounter a word they do not recognize in a text, the author may expand on that word to illustrate it better. While the author may do this to make the prose more picturesque and vivid, the reader can also take advantage of this description to provide context clues to the meaning of the unfamiliar word. For example, an author may write, "The man sitting next to me on the airplane was obese. His shirt stretched across his vast expanse of flesh, strained almost to bursting." The descriptive second sentence elaborates on and helps to define the previous sentence's word "obese" to mean extremely fat. A reader unfamiliar with the word "repugnant" can decipher its meaning through an author's accompanying description: "The way the child grimaced and shuddered as he swallowed the medicine showed that its taste was particularly repugnant."

Opposites

Text authors sometimes introduce a contrasting or opposing idea before or after a concept they present. They may do this to emphasize or heighten the idea they present by contrasting it with something that is the reverse. However, readers can also use these context clues to understand familiar words. For example, an author may write, "Our conversation was not cheery. We sat and talked very solemnly about his experience and a number of similar events." The reader who is not familiar with the word "solemnly" can deduce by the author's preceding use of "not cheery" that "solemn" means the opposite of cheery or happy, so it must mean serious or sad. Or if someone writes, "Don't condemn his entire project because you couldn't find anything good to say about it," readers unfamiliar with "condemn" can understand from the sentence structure that it means the opposite of saying anything good, so it must mean reject, dismiss, or disapprove. "Entire" adds another context clue, meaning total or complete rejection.

Syntax to Determine Part of Speech and Meanings of Words

Syntax refers to sentence structure and word order. Suppose that a reader encounters an unfamiliar word when reading a text. To illustrate, consider an invented word like "splunch." If this word is used in a sentence like "Please splunch that ball to me," the reader can assume from syntactic context that "splunch" is a verb. We would not use a noun, adjective, adverb, or preposition with the object "that ball," and the prepositional phrase "to me" further indicates "splunch" represents an action. However, in the sentence, "Please hand that splunch to me," the reader can assume that "splunch" is a noun. Demonstrative adjectives like "that" modify nouns. Also, we hand someone some*thing*—a thing being a noun; we do not hand someone a verb, adjective, or adverb. Some sentences contain further clues. For example, from the sentence, "The princess wore the glittering splunch on her head," the reader can deduce that it is a crown, tiara, or something similar from the syntactic context, without knowing the word.

Syntax to Indicate Different Meanings of Similar Sentences

The syntax, or structure, of a sentence affords grammatical cues that aid readers in comprehending the meanings of words, phrases, and sentences in the texts that they read. Seemingly minor differences in how the words or phrases in a sentence are ordered can make major differences in meaning. For example, two sentences can use exactly the same words but have different meanings based on the word order:

- "The man with a broken arm sat in a chair."
- "The man sat in a chair with a broken arm."

While both sentences indicate that a man sat in a chair, differing syntax indicates whether the man's or chair's arm was broken.

Review Video: Syntax
Visit mometrix.com/academy and enter code: 242280

Determining Meaning of Phrases and Paragraphs

Like unknown words, the meanings of phrases, paragraphs, and entire works can also be difficult to discern. Each of these can be better understood with added context. However, for larger groups of words, more context is needed. Unclear phrases are similar to unclear words, and the same methods can be used to understand their meaning. However, it is also important to consider how the individual words in the phrase work together. Paragraphs are a bit more complicated. Just as words must be compared to other words in a sentence, paragraphs must be compared to other paragraphs in a composition or a section.

Determining Meaning in Various Types of Compositions

To understand the meaning of an entire composition, the type of composition must be considered. **Expository writing** is generally organized so that each paragraph focuses on explaining one idea, or part of an idea, and its relevance. **Persuasive writing** uses paragraphs for different purposes to organize the parts of the argument. **Unclear paragraphs** must be read in the context of the paragraphs around them for their meaning to be fully understood. The meaning of full texts can also be unclear at times. The purpose of composition is also important for understanding the meaning of a text. To quickly understand the broad meaning of a text, look to the introductory and concluding paragraphs. Fictional texts are different. Some fictional works have implicit meanings, but some do not. The target audience must be considered for understanding texts that do have an implicit meaning, as most children's fiction will clearly state any lessons or morals. For other fiction, the application of literary theories and criticism may be helpful for understanding the text.

RESOURCES FOR DETERMINING WORD MEANING AND USAGE

While these strategies are useful for determining the meaning of unknown words and phrases, sometimes additional resources are needed to properly use the terms in different contexts. Some words have multiple definitions, and some words are inappropriate in particular contexts or modes of writing. The following tools are helpful for understanding all meanings and proper uses for words and phrases.

- **Dictionaries** provide the meaning of a multitude of words in a language. Many dictionaries include additional information about each word, such as its etymology, its synonyms, or variations of the word.
- **Glossaries** are similar to dictionaries, as they provide the meanings of a variety of terms. However, while dictionaries typically feature an extensive list of words and comprise an entire publication, glossaries are often included at the end of a text and only include terms and definitions that are relevant to the text they follow.
- **Spell Checkers** are used to detect spelling errors in typed text. Some spell checkers may also detect the misuse of plural or singular nouns, verb tenses, or capitalization. While spell checkers are a helpful tool, they are not always reliable or attuned to the author's intent, so it is important to review the spell checker's suggestions before accepting them.
- **Style Manuals** are guidelines on the preferred punctuation, format, and grammar usage according to different fields or organizations. For example, the Associated Press Stylebook is a style guide often used for media writing. The guidelines within a style guide are not always applicable across different contexts and usages, as the guidelines often cover grammatical or formatting situations that are not objectively correct or incorrect.

Elements of Story

PLOT AND STORY STRUCTURE

PLOT AND STORY STRUCTURE

The **plot** includes the events that happen in a story and the order in which they are told to the reader. There are several types of plot structures, as stories can be told in many ways. The most common plot structure is the chronological plot, which presents the events to the reader in the same order they occur for the characters in the story. Chronological plots usually have five main parts, the **exposition**, **rising action**, the **climax**, **falling action**, and the **resolution**. This type of plot structure guides the reader through the story's events as the characters experience them and is the easiest structure to understand and identify. While this is the most common plot structure, many stories are nonlinear, which means the plot does not sequence events in the same order the characters experience them. Such stories might include elements like flashbacks that cause the story to be nonlinear.

> **Review Video: How to Make a Story Map**
> Visit mometrix.com/academy and enter code: 261719

EXPOSITION

The **exposition** is at the beginning of the story and generally takes place before the rising action begins. The purpose of the exposition is to give the reader context for the story, which the author may do by introducing one or more characters, describing the setting or world, or explaining the events leading up to the point where the story begins. The exposition may still include events that contribute to the plot, but the **rising action** and main conflict of the story are not part of the exposition. Some narratives skip the exposition and begin the story with the beginning of the rising action, which causes the reader to learn the context as the story intensifies.

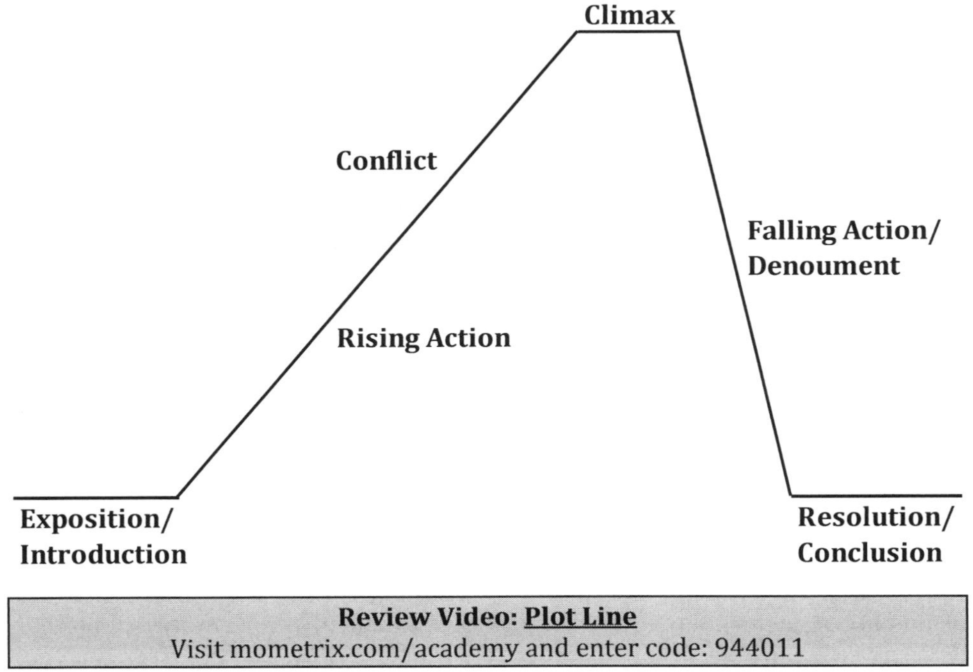

Review Video: Plot Line
Visit mometrix.com/academy and enter code: 944011

Conflict

A **conflict** is a problem to be solved. Literary plots typically include one conflict or more. Characters' attempts to resolve conflicts drive the narrative's forward movement. **Conflict resolution** is often the protagonist's primary occupation. Physical conflicts like exploring, wars, and escapes tend to make plots most suspenseful and exciting. Emotional, mental, or moral conflicts tend to make stories more personally gratifying or rewarding for many audiences. Conflicts can be external or internal. A major type of internal conflict is some inner personal battle, or **man versus self**. Major types of external conflicts include **man versus nature**, **man versus man**, and **man versus society**. Readers can identify conflicts in literary plots by identifying the protagonist and antagonist and asking why they conflict, what events develop the conflict, where the climax occurs, and how they identify with the characters.

Read the following paragraph and discuss the type of conflict present:

> Timothy was shocked out of sleep by the appearance of a bear just outside his tent. After panicking for a moment, he remembered some advice he had read in preparation for this trip: he should make noise so the bear would not be startled. As Timothy started to hum and sing, the bear wandered away.

There are three main types of conflict in literature: **man versus man**, **man versus nature**, and **man versus self**. This paragraph is an example of man versus nature. Timothy is in conflict with the bear. Even though no physical conflict like an attack exists, Timothy is pitted against the bear. Timothy uses his knowledge to "defeat" the bear and keep himself safe. The solution to the conflict is that Timothy makes noise, the bear wanders away, and Timothy is safe.

Review Video: Conflict
Visit mometrix.com/academy and enter code: 559550

Review Video: Determining Relationships in a Story
Visit mometrix.com/academy and enter code: 929925

Rising Action

The **rising action** is the part of the story where conflict **intensifies**. The rising action begins with an event that prompts the main conflict of the story. This may also be called the **inciting incident**. The main conflict generally occurs between the protagonist and an antagonist, but this is not the only type of conflict that may occur in a narrative. After this event, the protagonist works to resolve the main conflict by preparing for an altercation, pursuing a goal, fleeing an antagonist, or doing some other action that will end the conflict. The rising action is composed of several additional events that increase the story's tension. Most often, other developments will occur alongside the growth of the main conflict, such as character development or the development of minor conflicts. The rising action ends with the **climax**, which is the point of highest tension in the story.

Climax

The **climax** is the event in the narrative that marks the height of the story's conflict or tension. The event that takes place at the story's climax will end the rising action and bring about the results of the main conflict. If the conflict was between a good protagonist and an evil antagonist, the climax may be a final battle between the two characters. If the conflict is an adventurer looking for heavily guarded treasure, the climax may be the adventurer's encounter with the final obstacle that protects the treasure. The climax may be made of multiple scenes, but can usually be summarized as one event. Once the conflict and climax are complete, the **falling action** begins.

Falling Action

The **falling action** shows what happens in the story between the climax and the resolution. The falling action often composes a much smaller portion of the story than the rising action does. While the climax includes the end of the main conflict, the falling action may show the results of any minor conflicts in the story. For example, if the protagonist encountered a troll on the way to find some treasure, and the troll demanded the protagonist share the treasure after retrieving it, the falling action would include the protagonist returning to share the treasure with the troll. Similarly, any unexplained major events are usually made clear during the falling action. Once all significant elements of the story are resolved or addressed, the story's resolution will occur. The **resolution** is the end of the story, which shows the final result of the plot's events and shows what life is like for the main characters once they are no longer experiencing the story's conflicts.

Resolution

The way the conflict is **resolved** depends on the type of conflict. The plot of any book starts with the lead up to the conflict, then the conflict itself, and finally the solution, or **resolution**, to the conflict. In **man versus man** conflicts, the conflict is often resolved by two parties coming to some sort of agreement or by one party triumphing over the other party. In **man versus nature** conflicts, the conflict is often resolved by man coming to some realization about some aspect of nature. In **man versus self** conflicts, the conflict is often resolved by the character growing or coming to an understanding about part of himself.

Theme

A **theme** is a central idea demonstrated by a passage. Often, a theme is a lesson or moral contained in the text, but it does not have to be. It also is a unifying idea that is used throughout the text; it can take the form of a common setting, idea, symbol, design, or recurring event. A passage can have two or more themes that convey its overall idea. The theme or themes of a passage are often based on **universal themes**. They can frequently be expressed using well-known sayings about life, society, or human nature, such as "Hard work pays off" or "Good triumphs over evil." Themes are not usually stated **explicitly**. The reader must figure them out by carefully reading the passage. Themes are created through descriptive language or events in the plot. The events of a story help shape the themes of a passage.

Example

Explain why "if you care about something, you need to take care of it" accurately describes the theme of the following excerpt.

> Luca collected baseball cards, but he wasn't very careful with them. He left them around the house. His dog liked to chew. One day, Luca and his friend Bart were looking at his collection. Then they went outside. When Luca got home, he saw his dog chewing on his cards. They were ruined.

This excerpt tells the story of a boy who is careless with his baseball cards and leaves them lying around. His dog ends up chewing them and ruining them. The lesson is that if you care about something, you need to take care of it. This is the theme, or point, of the story. Some stories have more than one theme, but this is not really true of this excerpt. The reader needs to figure out the theme based on what happens in the story. Sometimes, as in the case of fables, the theme is stated directly in the text. However, this is not usually the case.

Review Video: Themes in Literature
Visit mometrix.com/academy and enter code: 732074

Character Development and Dialogue

Character Development

When depicting characters or figures in a written text, authors generally use actions, dialogue, and descriptions as characterization techniques. Characterization can occur in both fiction and nonfiction and is used to show a character or figure's personality, demeanor, and thoughts. This helps create a more engaging experience for the reader by providing a more concrete picture of a character or figure's tendencies and features. Characterizations also gives authors the opportunity to integrate elements such as dialects, activities, attire, and attitudes into their writing.

To understand the meaning of a story, it is vital to understand the characters as the author describes them. We can look for contradictions in what a character thinks, says, and does. We can notice whether the author's observations about a character differ from what other characters in the story say about that character. A character may be dynamic, meaning they change significantly during the story, or static, meaning they remain the same from beginning to end. Characters may be two-dimensional, not fully developed, or may be well developed with characteristics that stand out vividly. Characters may also symbolize universal properties. Additionally, readers can compare and contrast characters to analyze how each one developed.

A well-known example of character development can be found in Charles Dickens's *Great Expectations*. The novel's main character, Pip, is introduced as a young boy, and he is depicted as innocent, kind, and humble. However, as Pip grows up and is confronted with the social hierarchy of Victorian England, he becomes arrogant and rejects his loved ones in pursuit of his own social advancement. Once he achieves his social goals, he realizes the merits of his former lifestyle, and lives with the wisdom he gained in both environments and life stages. Dickens shows Pip's ever-changing character through his interactions with others and his inner thoughts, which evolve as his personal values and personality shift.

Dialogue

Effectively written dialogue serves at least one, but usually several, purposes. It advances the story and moves the plot, develops the characters, sheds light on the work's theme or meaning, and can, often subtly, account for the passage of time not otherwise indicated. It can alter the direction that the plot is taking, typically by introducing some new conflict or changing existing ones. **Dialogue** can establish a work's narrative voice and the characters' voices and set the tone of the story or of particular characters. When fictional characters display enlightenment or realization, dialogue can give readers an understanding of what those characters have discovered and how. Dialogue can illuminate the motivations and wishes of the story's characters. By using consistent thoughts and syntax, dialogue can support character development. Skillfully created, it can also represent real-life speech rhythms in written form. Via conflicts and ensuing action, dialogue also provides drama.

DIALOGUE IN FICTION

In fictional works, effectively written dialogue does more than just break up or interrupt sections of narrative. While **dialogue** may supply exposition for readers, it must nonetheless be believable. Dialogue should be dynamic, not static, and it should not resemble regular prose. Authors should not use dialogue to write clever similes or metaphors, or to inject their own opinions. Nor should they use dialogue at all when narrative would be better. Most importantly, dialogue should not slow the plot movement. Dialogue must seem natural, which means careful construction of phrases rather than actually duplicating natural speech, which does not necessarily translate well to the written word. Finally, all dialogue must be pertinent to the story, rather than just added conversation.

Writing Process

THE WRITING PROCESS

BRAINSTORMING

Brainstorming is a technique that is used to find a creative approach to a subject. This can be accomplished by simple **free-association** with a topic. For example, with paper and pen, write every thought that you have about the topic in a word or phrase. This is done without critical thinking. You should put everything that comes to your mind about the topic on your scratch paper. Then, you need to read the list over a few times. Next, look for patterns, repetitions, and clusters of ideas. This allows a variety of fresh ideas to come as you think about the topic.

FREE WRITING

Free writing is a more structured form of brainstorming. The method involves taking a limited amount of time (e.g., 2 to 3 minutes) to write everything that comes to mind about the topic in complete sentences. When time expires, review everything that has been written down. Many of your sentences may make little or no sense, but the insights and observations that can come from free writing make this method a valuable approach. Usually, free writing results in a fuller expression of ideas than brainstorming because thoughts and associations are written in complete sentences. However, both techniques can be used to complement each other.

PLANNING

Planning is the process of organizing a piece of writing before composing a draft. Planning can include creating an outline or a graphic organizer, such as a Venn diagram, a spider-map, or a flowchart. These methods should help the writer identify their topic, main ideas, and the general organization of the composition. Preliminary research can also take place during this stage. Planning helps writers organize all of their ideas and decide if they have enough material to begin their first draft. However, writers should remember that the decisions they make during this step will likely change later in the process, so their plan does not have to be perfect.

DRAFTING

Writers may then use their plan, outline, or graphic organizer to compose their first draft. They may write subsequent drafts to improve their writing. Writing multiple drafts can help writers consider different ways to communicate their ideas and address errors that may be difficult to correct without rewriting a section or the whole composition. Most writers will vary in how many drafts they choose to write, as there is no "right" number of drafts. Writing drafts also takes away the pressure to write perfectly on the first try, as writers can improve with each draft they write.

Revising, Editing, and Proofreading

Once a writer completes a draft, they can move on to the revising, editing, and proofreading steps to improve their draft. These steps begin with making broad changes that may apply to large sections of a composition and then making small, specific corrections. **Revising** is the first and broadest of these steps. Revising involves ensuring that the composition addresses an appropriate audience, includes all necessary material, maintains focus throughout, and is organized logically. Revising may occur after the first draft to ensure that the following drafts improve upon errors from the first draft. Some revision should occur between each draft to avoid repeating these errors. The **editing** phase of writing is narrower than the revising phase. Editing a composition should include steps such as improving transitions between paragraphs, ensuring each paragraph is on topic, and improving the flow of the text. The editing phase may also include correcting grammatical errors that cannot be fixed without significantly altering the text. **Proofreading** involves fixing misspelled words, typos, other grammatical errors, and any remaining surface-level flaws in the composition.

Recursive Writing Process

However you approach writing, you may find comfort in knowing that the revision process can occur in any order. The **recursive writing process** is not as difficult as the phrase may make it seem. Simply put, the recursive writing process means that you may need to revisit steps after completing other steps. It also implies that the steps are not required to take place in any certain order. Indeed, you may find that planning, drafting, and revising can all take place at about the same time. The writing process involves moving back and forth between planning, drafting, and revising, followed by more planning, more drafting, and more revising until the writing is satisfactory.

Review Video: Recursive Writing Process
Visit mometrix.com/academy and enter code: 951611

Outlining and Organizing Ideas

Essays

Essays usually focus on one topic, subject, or goal. There are several types of essays, including informative, persuasive, and narrative. An essay's structure and level of formality depend on the type of essay and its goal. While narrative essays typically do not include outside sources, other types of essays often require some research and the integration of primary and secondary sources.

The basic format of an essay typically has three major parts: the introduction, the body, and the conclusion. The body is further divided into the writer's main points. Short and simple essays may have three main points, while essays covering broader ranges and going into more depth can have almost any number of main points, depending on length.

An essay's introduction should answer three questions:

1. What is the **subject** of the essay?

   If a student writes an essay about a book, the answer would include the title and author of the book and any additional information needed—such as the subject or argument of the book.

2. How does the essay **address** the subject?

   To answer this, the writer identifies the essay's organization by briefly summarizing main points and the evidence supporting them.

3. What will the essay **prove**?

   This is the thesis statement, usually the opening paragraph's last sentence, clearly stating the writer's message.

The body elaborates on all the main points related to the thesis, introducing one main point at a time, and includes supporting evidence with each main point. Each body paragraph should state the point in a topic sentence, which is usually the first sentence in the paragraph. The paragraph should then explain the point's meaning, support it with quotations or other evidence, and then explain how this point and the evidence are related to the thesis. The writer should then repeat this procedure in a new paragraph for each additional main point.

The conclusion reiterates the content of the introduction, including the thesis, to remind the reader of the essay's main argument or subject. The essay writer may also summarize the highlights of the argument or description contained in the body of the essay, following the same sequence originally used in the body. For example, a conclusion might look like: Point 1 + Point 2 + Point 3 = Thesis, or Point 1 → Point 2 → Point 3 → Thesis Proof. Good organization makes essays easier for writers to compose and provides a guide for readers to follow. Well-organized essays hold attention better and are more likely to get readers to accept their theses as valid.

MAIN IDEAS, SUPPORTING DETAILS, AND OUTLINING A TOPIC

A writer often begins the first paragraph of a paper by stating the **main idea** or point, also known as the **topic sentence**. The rest of the paragraph supplies particular details that develop and support the main point. One way to visualize the relationship between the main point and supporting information is by considering a table: the tabletop is the main point, and each of the table's legs is a supporting detail or group of details. Both professional authors and students can benefit from planning their writing by first making an outline of the topic. Outlines facilitate quick identification of the main point and supporting details without having to wade through the additional language that will exist in the fully developed essay, article, or paper. Outlining can also help readers to analyze a piece of existing writing for the same reason. The outline first summarizes the main idea in one sentence. Then, below that, it summarizes the supporting details in a numbered list. Writing the paper then consists of filling in the outline with detail, writing a paragraph for each supporting point, and adding an introduction and conclusion.

INTRODUCTION

The purpose of the introduction is to capture the reader's attention and announce the essay's main idea. Normally, the introduction contains 50-80 words, or 3-5 sentences. An introduction can begin with an interesting quote, a question, or a strong opinion—something that will **engage** the reader's interest and prompt them to keep reading. If you are writing your essay to a specific prompt, your introduction should include a **restatement or summarization** of the prompt so that the reader will have some context for your essay. Finally, your introduction should briefly state your **thesis or main idea**: the primary thing you hope to communicate to the reader through your essay. Don't try to include all of the details and nuances of your thesis, or all of your reasons for it, in the introduction. That's what the rest of the essay is for!

Review Video: Introduction
Visit mometrix.com/academy and enter code: 961328

THESIS STATEMENT

The thesis is the main idea of the essay. A temporary thesis, or working thesis, should be established early in the writing process because it will serve to keep the writer focused as ideas develop. This temporary thesis is subject to change as you continue to write.

The temporary thesis has two parts: a **topic** (i.e., the focus of your essay based on the prompt) and a **comment**. The comment makes an important point about the topic. A temporary thesis should be interesting and specific.

Also, you need to limit the topic to a manageable scope. These three questions are useful tools to measure the effectiveness of any temporary thesis:

- Does the focus of my essay have enough interest to hold an audience?
- Is the focus of my essay specific enough to generate interest?
- Is the focus of my essay manageable for the time limit? Too broad? Too narrow?

The thesis should be a generalization rather than a fact because the thesis prepares readers for facts and details that support the thesis. The process of bringing the thesis into sharp focus may help in outlining major sections of the work. Once the thesis and introduction are complete, you can address the body of the work.

Review Video: Thesis Statements
Visit mometrix.com/academy and enter code: 691033

SUPPORTING THE THESIS

Throughout your essay, the thesis should be **explained clearly and supported** adequately by additional arguments. The thesis sentence needs to contain a clear statement of the purpose of your essay and a comment about the thesis. With the thesis statement, you have an opportunity to state what is noteworthy of this particular treatment of the prompt. Each sentence and paragraph should build on and support the thesis.

When you respond to the prompt, use parts of the passage to support your argument or defend your position. Using supporting evidence from the passage strengths your argument because readers can see your attention to the entire passage and your response to the details and facts within the passage. You can use facts, details, statistics, and direct quotations from the passage to uphold your position. Be sure to point out which information comes from the original passage and base your argument around that evidence.

BODY

In an essay's introduction, the writer establishes the thesis and may indicate how the rest of the piece will be structured. In the body of the piece, the writer **elaborates** upon, **illustrates**, and **explains** the **thesis statement**. How writers arrange supporting details and their choices of paragraph types are development techniques. Writers may give examples of the concept introduced in the thesis statement. If the subject includes a cause-and-effect relationship, the author may explain its causality. A writer will explain or analyze the main idea of the piece throughout the body, often by presenting arguments for the veracity or credibility of the thesis statement. Writers may use development to define or clarify ambiguous terms. Paragraphs within the body may be organized using natural sequences, like space and time. Writers may employ **inductive reasoning**, using multiple details to establish a generalization or causal relationship, or **deductive reasoning**, proving a generalized hypothesis or proposition through a specific example or case.

Review Video: Drafting Body Paragraphs
Visit mometrix.com/academy and enter code: 724590

PARAGRAPHS

After the introduction of a passage, a series of body paragraphs will carry a message through to the conclusion. Each paragraph should be **unified around a main point**. Normally, a good topic sentence summarizes the paragraph's main point. A topic sentence is a general sentence that gives an introduction to the paragraph.

The sentences that follow support the topic sentence. However, though it is usually the first sentence, the topic sentence can come as the final sentence to the paragraph if the earlier sentences give a clear explanation of the paragraph's topic. This allows the topic sentence to function as a concluding sentence. Overall, the paragraphs need to stay true to the main point. This means that any unnecessary sentences that do not advance the main point should be removed.

The main point of a paragraph requires adequate development (i.e., a substantial paragraph that covers the main point). A paragraph of two or three sentences does not cover a main point. This is especially true when the main point of the paragraph gives strong support to the argument of the thesis. An occasional short paragraph is fine as a transitional device. However, a well-developed argument will have paragraphs with more than a few sentences.

METHODS OF DEVELOPING PARAGRAPHS

Common methods of adding substance to paragraphs include examples, illustrations, analogies, and cause and effect.

- **Examples** are supporting details to the main idea of a paragraph or a passage. When authors write about something that their audience may not understand, they can provide an example to show their point. When authors write about something that is not easily accepted, they can give examples to prove their point.
- **Illustrations** are extended examples that require several sentences. Well-selected illustrations can be a great way for authors to develop a point that may not be familiar to their audience.
- **Analogies** make comparisons between items that appear to have nothing in common. Analogies are employed by writers to provoke fresh thoughts about a subject. These comparisons may be used to explain the unfamiliar, to clarify an abstract point, or to argue a point. Although analogies are effective literary devices, they should be used carefully in arguments. Two things may be alike in some respects but completely different in others.
- **Cause and effect** is an excellent device to explain the connection between an action or situation and a particular result. One way that authors can use cause and effect is to state the effect in the topic sentence of a paragraph and add the causes in the body of the paragraph. This method can give an author's paragraphs structure, which always strengthens writing.

TYPES OF PARAGRAPHS

A **paragraph of narration** tells a story or a part of a story. Normally, the sentences are arranged in chronological order (i.e., the order that the events happened). However, flashbacks (i.e., an anecdote from an earlier time) can be included.

A **descriptive paragraph** makes a verbal portrait of a person, place, or thing. When specific details are used that appeal to one or more of the senses (i.e., sight, sound, smell, taste, and touch), authors give readers a sense of being present in the moment.

A **process paragraph** is related to time order (i.e., First, you open the bottle. Second, you pour the liquid, etc.). Usually, this describes a process or teaches readers how to perform a process.

Comparing two things draws attention to their similarities and indicates a number of differences. When authors contrast, they focus only on differences. Both comparing and contrasting may be done point-by-point, noting both the similarities and differences of each point, or in sequential paragraphs, where you discuss all the similarities and then all the differences, or vice versa.

BREAKING TEXT INTO PARAGRAPHS

For most forms of writing, you will need to use multiple paragraphs. As such, determining when to start a new paragraph is very important. Reasons for starting a new paragraph include:

- To mark off the introduction and concluding paragraphs
- To signal a shift to a new idea or topic
- To indicate an important shift in time or place
- To explain a point in additional detail
- To highlight a comparison, contrast, or cause and effect relationship

PARAGRAPH LENGTH

Most readers find that their comfort level for a paragraph is between 100 and 200 words. Shorter paragraphs cause too much starting and stopping and give a choppy effect. Paragraphs that are too long often test the attention span of readers. Two notable exceptions to this rule exist. In scientific or scholarly papers, longer paragraphs suggest seriousness and depth. In journalistic writing, constraints are placed on paragraph size by the narrow columns in a newspaper format.

The first and last paragraphs of a text will usually be the introduction and conclusion. These special-purpose paragraphs are likely to be shorter than paragraphs in the body of the work. Paragraphs in the body of the essay follow the subject's outline (e.g., one paragraph per point in short essays and a group of paragraphs per point in longer works). Some ideas require more development than others, so it is good for a writer to remain flexible. A paragraph of excessive length may be divided, and shorter ones may be combined.

CONCLUSION

Two important principles to consider when writing a conclusion are strength and closure. A strong conclusion gives the reader a sense that the author's main points are meaningful and important, and that the supporting facts and arguments are convincing, solid, and well developed. When a conclusion achieves closure, it gives the impression that the writer has stated all necessary information and points and completed the work, rather than simply stopping after a specified length. Some things to avoid when writing concluding paragraphs include:

- Introducing a completely new idea
- Beginning with obvious or unoriginal phrases like "In conclusion" or "To summarize"
- Apologizing for one's opinions or writing
- Repeating the thesis word for word rather than rephrasing it
- Believing that the conclusion must always summarize the piece

Review Video: Drafting Conclusions
Visit mometrix.com/academy and enter code: 209408

COHERENCE IN WRITING

COHERENT PARAGRAPHS

A smooth flow of sentences and paragraphs without gaps, shifts, or bumps will lead to paragraph **coherence**. Ties between old and new information can be smoothed using several methods:

- **Linking ideas clearly**, from the topic sentence to the body of the paragraph, is essential for a smooth transition. The topic sentence states the main point, and this should be followed by specific details, examples, and illustrations that support the topic sentence. The support may be direct or indirect. In **indirect support**, the illustrations and examples may support a sentence that in turn supports the topic directly.
- The **repetition of key words** adds coherence to a paragraph. To avoid dull language, variations of the key words may be used.
- **Parallel structures** are often used within sentences to emphasize the similarity of ideas and connect sentences giving similar information.
- Maintaining a **consistent verb tense** throughout the paragraph helps. Shifting tenses affects the smooth flow of words and can disrupt the coherence of the paragraph.

Review Video: How to Write a Good Paragraph
Visit mometrix.com/academy and enter code: 682127

Sequence Words and Phrases

When a paragraph opens with the topic sentence, the second sentence may begin with a phrase like *first of all*, introducing the first supporting detail or example. The writer may introduce the second supporting item with words or phrases like *also*, *in addition*, and *besides*. The writer might introduce succeeding pieces of support with wording like, *another thing*, *moreover*, *furthermore*, or *not only that, but*. The writer may introduce the last piece of support with *lastly*, *finally*, or *last but not least*. Writers get off the point by presenting off-target items not supporting the main point. For example, a main point *my dog is not smart* is supported by the statement, *he's six years old and still doesn't answer to his name*. But *he cries when I leave for school* is not supportive, as it does not indicate lack of intelligence. Writers stay on point by presenting only supportive statements that are directly relevant to and illustrative of their main point.

Review Video: Sequence
Visit mometrix.com/academy and enter code: 489027

Transitions

Transitions between sentences and paragraphs guide readers from idea to idea and indicate relationships between sentences and paragraphs. Writers should be judicious in their use of transitions, inserting them sparingly. They should also be selected to fit the author's purpose—transitions can indicate time, comparison, and conclusion, among other purposes. Tone is also important to consider when using transitional phrases, varying the tone for different audiences. For example, in a scholarly essay, *in summary* would be preferable to the more informal *in short*.

When working with transitional words and phrases, writers usually find a natural flow that indicates when a transition is needed. In reading a draft of the text, it should become apparent where the flow is disrupted. At this point, the writer can add transitional elements during the revision process. Revising can also afford an opportunity to delete transitional devices that seem heavy handed or unnecessary.

Review Video: Transitions in Writing
Visit mometrix.com/academy and enter code: 233246

Types of Transitional Words

Time	afterward, immediately, earlier, meanwhile, recently, lately, now, since, soon, when, then, until, before, etc.
Sequence	too, first, second, further, moreover, also, again, and, next, still, besides, finally
Comparison	similarly, in the same way, likewise, also, again, once more
Contrasting	but, although, despite, however, instead, nevertheless, on the one hand... on the other hand, regardless, yet, in contrast
Cause and Effect	because, consequently, thus, therefore, then, to this end, since, so, as a result, if... then, accordingly
Examples	for example, for instance, such as, to illustrate, indeed, in fact, specifically
Place	near, far, here, there, to the left/right, next to, above, below, beyond, opposite, beside
Concession	granted that, naturally, of course, it may appear, although it is true that
Repetition, Summary, or Conclusion	as mentioned earlier, as noted, in other words, in short, on the whole, to summarize, therefore, as a result, to conclude, in conclusion
Addition	and, also, furthermore, moreover
Generalization	in broad terms, broadly speaking, in general

Review Video: Transition Words
Visit mometrix.com/academy and enter code: 707563

Review Video: How to Effectively Connect Sentences
Visit mometrix.com/academy and enter code: 948325

Writing Style and Form

Writing Style and Linguistic Form

Linguistic form encodes the literal meanings of words and sentences. It comes from the phonological, morphological, syntactic, and semantic parts of a language. **Writing style** consists of different ways of encoding the meaning and indicating figurative and stylistic meanings. An author's writing style can also be referred to as his or her **voice**.

Writers' stylistic choices accomplish three basic effects on their audiences:

- They **communicate meanings** beyond linguistically dictated meanings,
- They communicate the **author's attitude**, such as persuasive or argumentative effects accomplished through style, and
- They communicate or **express feelings**.

Within style, component areas include:

- Narrative structure
- Viewpoint
- Focus
- Sound patterns
- Meter and rhythm
- Lexical and syntactic repetition and parallelism
- Writing genre
- Representational, realistic, and mimetic effects
- Representation of thought and speech

- Meta-representation (representing representation)
- Irony
- Metaphor and other indirect meanings
- Representation and use of historical and dialectal variations
- Gender-specific and other group-specific speech styles, both real and fictitious
- Analysis of the processes for inferring meaning from writing

TONE

Tone may be defined as the writer's **attitude** toward the topic, and to the audience. This attitude is reflected in the language used in the writing. The tone of a work should be **appropriate to the topic** and to the intended audience. While it may be fine to use slang or jargon in some pieces, other texts should not contain such terms. Tone can range from humorous to serious and any level in between. It may be more or less formal, depending on the purpose of the writing and its intended audience. All these nuances in tone can flavor the entire writing and should be kept in mind as the work evolves.

Review Video: Style, Tone, and Mood
Visit mometrix.com/academy and enter code: 416961

WORD SELECTION

A writer's choice of words is a signature of their style. Careful thought about the use of words can improve a piece of writing. A passage can be an exciting piece to read when attention is given to the use of vivid or specific nouns rather than general ones.

Example:

General: His kindness will never be forgotten.

Specific: His thoughtful gifts and bear hugs will never be forgotten.

ACTIVE AND PASSIVE LANGUAGE

Attention should also be given to the kind of verbs that are used in sentences. Active verbs (e.g., run, swim) are about an action. Whenever possible, an **active verb should replace a linking verb** to provide clear examples for arguments and to strengthen a passage overall. When using an active verb, one should be sure that the verb is used in the active voice instead of the passive voice. Verbs are in the active voice when the subject is the one doing the action. A verb is in the passive voice when the subject is the recipient of an action.

Example:

Passive: The winners were called to the stage by the judges.

Active: The judges called the winners to the stage.

CONCISENESS

Conciseness is writing that communicates a message in the fewest words possible. Writing concisely is valuable because short, uncluttered messages allow the reader to understand the author's message more easily and efficiently. Planning is important in writing concise messages. If you have in mind what you need to write beforehand, it will be easier to make a message short and to the point. Do not state the obvious.

Revising is also important. After the message is written, make sure you have effective, pithy sentences that efficiently get your point across. When reviewing the information, imagine a conversation taking place, and concise writing will likely result.

Appropriate Kinds of Writing for Different Tasks, Purposes, and Audiences

When preparing to write a composition, consider the audience and purpose to choose the best type of writing. Four common types of writing are persuasive, expository, and narrative. **Persuasive**, or argumentative writing, is used to convince the audience to take action or agree with the author's claims. **Expository** writing is meant to inform the audience of the author's observations or research on a topic. **Narrative** writing is used to tell the audience a story and often allows more room for creativity. **Descriptive** writing is when a writer provides a substantial amount of detail to the reader so he or she can visualize the topic. While task, purpose, and audience inform a writer's mode of writing, these factors also impact elements such as tone, vocabulary, and formality.

For example, students who are writing to persuade their parents to grant them some additional privilege, such as permission for a more independent activity, should use more sophisticated vocabulary and diction that sounds more mature and serious to appeal to the parental audience. However, students who are writing for younger children should use simpler vocabulary and sentence structure, as well as choose words that are more vivid and entertaining. They should treat their topics more lightly, and include humor when appropriate. Students who are writing for their classmates may use language that is more informal, as well as age-appropriate.

Review Video: Writing Purpose and Audience
Visit mometrix.com/academy and enter code: 146627

Formality in Writing

Level of Formality

The relationship between writer and reader is important in choosing a **level of formality** as most writing requires some degree of formality. **Formal writing** is for addressing a superior in a school or work environment. Business letters, textbooks, and newspapers use a moderate to high level of formality. **Informal writing** is appropriate for private letters, personal emails, and business correspondence between close associates.

For your exam, you will want to be aware of informal and formal writing. One way that this can be accomplished is to watch for shifts in point of view in the essay. For example, unless writers are using a personal example, they will rarely refer to themselves (e.g., "*I* think that *my* point is very clear.") to avoid being informal when they need to be formal.

Also, be mindful of an author who addresses his or her audience **directly** in their writing (e.g., "Readers, *like you*, will understand this argument.") as this can be a sign of informal writing. Good writers understand the need to be consistent with their level of formality. Shifts in levels of formality or point of view can confuse readers and cause them to discount the message.

Clichés

Clichés are phrases that have been **overused** to the point that the phrase has no importance or has lost the original meaning. These phrases have no originality and add very little to a passage. Therefore, most writers will avoid the use of clichés. Another option is to make changes to a cliché so that it is not predictable and empty of meaning.

Examples:

> When life gives you lemons, make lemonade.
>
> Every cloud has a silver lining.

Jargon

Jargon is **specialized vocabulary** that is used among members of a certain trade or profession. Since jargon is understood by only a small audience, writers will use jargon in passages that will only be read by a specialized audience. For example, medical jargon should be used in a medical journal but not in a New York Times article. Jargon includes exaggerated language that tries to impress rather than inform. Sentences filled with jargon are not precise and are difficult to understand.

Examples:

> "He is going to *toenail* these frames for us." (Toenail is construction jargon for nailing at an angle.)

> "They brought in a *kip* of material today." (Kip refers to 1000 pounds in architecture and engineering.)

Slang

Slang is an **informal** and sometimes private language that is understood by some individuals. Slang terms have some usefulness, but they can have a small audience. So, most formal writing will not include this kind of language.

Examples:

> "Yes, the event was a blast!" (In this sentence, *blast* means that the event was a great experience.)

> "That attempt was an epic fail." (By *epic fail*, the speaker means that his or her attempt was not a success.)

Colloquialism

A colloquialism is a word or phrase that is found in informal writing. Unlike slang, **colloquial language** will be familiar to a greater range of people. However, colloquialisms are still considered inappropriate for formal writing. Colloquial language can include some slang, but these are limited to contractions for the most part.

Examples:

> "Can *y'all* come back another time?" (Y'all is a contraction of "you all.")

> "Will you stop him from building this *castle in the air*?" (A "castle in the air" is an improbable or unlikely event.)

Academic Language

In educational settings, students are often expected to use academic language in their schoolwork. Academic language is also commonly found in dissertations and theses, texts published by academic journals, and other forms of academic research. Academic language conventions may vary between fields, but general academic language is free of slang, regional terminology, and noticeable grammatical errors. Specific terms may also be used in academic language, and it is important to understand their proper usage. A writer's command of academic language impacts their ability to communicate in an academic or professional context. While it is acceptable to use colloquialisms, slang, improper grammar, or other forms of informal speech in social settings or at home, it is inappropriate to practice non-academic language in academic contexts.

Common Types of Writing

Autobiographical Narratives

Autobiographical narratives are narratives written by an author about an event or period in their life. Autobiographical narratives are written from one person's perspective, in first person, and often include the author's thoughts and feelings alongside their description of the event or period. Structure, style, or theme varies between different autobiographical narratives, since each narrative is personal and specific to its author and his or her experience.

Reflective Essay

A less common type of essay is the reflective essay. **Reflective essays** allow the author to reflect, or think back, on an experience and analyze what they recall. They should consider what they learned from the experience, what they could have done differently, what would have helped them during the experience, or anything else that they have realized from looking back on the experience. Reflection essays incorporate both objective reflection on one's own actions and subjective explanation of thoughts and feelings. These essays can be written for a number of experiences in a formal or informal context.

Journals and Diaries

A **journal** is a personal account of events, experiences, feelings, and thoughts. Many people write journals to express their feelings and thoughts or to help them process experiences they have had. Since journals are **private documents** not meant to be shared with others, writers may not be concerned with grammar, spelling, or other mechanics. However, authors may write journals that they expect or hope to publish someday; in this case, they not only express their thoughts and feelings and process their experiences, but they also attend to their craft in writing them. Some authors compose journals to record a particular time period or a series of related events, such as a cancer diagnosis, treatment, surviving the disease, and how these experiences have changed or affected them. Other experiences someone might include in a journal are recovering from addiction, journeys of spiritual exploration and discovery, time spent in another country, or anything else someone wants to personally document. Journaling can also be therapeutic, as some people use journals to work through feelings of grief over loss or to wrestle with big decisions.

Examples of Diaries in Literature

The Diary of a Young Girl by Dutch Jew Anne Frank (1947) contains her life-affirming, nonfictional diary entries from 1942-1944 while her family hid in an attic from World War II's genocidal Nazis. *Go Ask Alice* (1971) by Beatrice Sparks is a cautionary, fictional novel in the form of diary entries by Alice, an unhappy, rebellious teen who takes LSD, runs away from home and lives with hippies, and eventually returns home. Frank's writing reveals an intelligent, sensitive, insightful girl, raised by intellectual European parents—a girl who believes in the goodness of human nature despite surrounding atrocities. Alice, influenced by early 1970s counterculture, becomes less optimistic. However, similarities can be found between them: Frank dies in a Nazi concentration camp while the fictitious Alice dies from a drug overdose. Both young women are also unable to escape their surroundings. Additionally, adolescent searches for personal identity are evident in both books.

Review Video: Journals, Diaries, Letters, and Blogs
Visit mometrix.com/academy and enter code: 432845

Letters

Letters are messages written to other people. In addition to letters written between individuals, some writers compose letters to the editors of newspapers, magazines, and other publications, while some write "Open Letters" to be published and read by the general public. Open letters, while intended for everyone to read, may also identify a group of people or a single person whom the letter directly addresses. In everyday use, the most-used forms are business letters and personal or friendly letters. Both kinds share common elements: business or personal letterhead stationery; the writer's return address at the top; the addressee's address next; a salutation, such as "Dear [name]" or some similar opening greeting, followed by a colon in business letters or a comma in personal letters; the body of the letter, with paragraphs as indicated; and a closing, like "Sincerely/Cordially/Best regards/etc." or "Love," in intimate personal letters.

Early Letters

The Greek word for "letter" is *epistolē*, which became the English word "epistle." The earliest letters were called epistles, including the New Testament's epistles from the apostles to the Christians. In ancient Egypt, the writing curriculum in scribal schools included the epistolary genre. Epistolary novels frame a story in the form of letters. Examples of noteworthy epistolary novels include:

- *Pamela* (1740), by 18th-century English novelist Samuel Richardson
- *Shamela* (1741), Henry Fielding's satire of *Pamela* that mocked epistolary writing.
- *Lettres persanes* (1721) by French author Montesquieu
- *The Sorrows of Young Werther* (1774) by German author Johann Wolfgang von Goethe
- *The History of Emily Montague* (1769), the first Canadian novel, by Frances Brooke
- *Dracula* (1897) by Bram Stoker
- *Frankenstein* (1818) by Mary Shelley
- *The Color Purple* (1982) by Alice Walker

Blogs

The word "blog" is derived from "weblog" and refers to writing done exclusively on the internet. Readers of reputable newspapers expect quality content and layouts that enable easy reading. These expectations also apply to blogs. For example, readers can easily move visually from line to line when columns are narrow, while overly wide columns cause readers to lose their places. Blogs must also be posted with layouts enabling online readers to follow them easily. However, because the way people read on computer, tablet, and smartphone screens differs from how they read print on paper, formatting and writing blog content is more complex than writing newspaper articles. Two major principles are the bases for blog-writing rules: The first is while readers of print articles skim to estimate their length, online they must scroll down to scan; therefore, blog layouts need more subheadings, graphics, and other indications of what information follows. The second is onscreen reading can be harder on the eyes than reading printed paper, so legibility is crucial in blogs.

Rules and Rationales for Writing Blogs

1. Format all posts for smooth page layout and easy scanning.
2. Column width should not be too wide, as larger lines of text can be difficult to read
3. Headings and subheadings separate text visually, enable scanning or skimming, and encourage continued reading.
4. Bullet-pointed or numbered lists enable quick information location and scanning.
5. Punctuation is critical, so beginners should use shorter sentences until confident in their knowledge of punctuation rules.
6. Blog paragraphs should be far shorter—two to six sentences each—than paragraphs written on paper to enable "chunking" because reading onscreen is more difficult.
7. Sans-serif fonts are usually clearer than serif fonts, and larger font sizes are better.
8. Highlight important material and draw attention with **boldface**, but avoid overuse. Avoid hard-to-read *italics* and ALL CAPITALS.
9. Include enough blank spaces: overly busy blogs tire eyes and brains. Images not only break up text but also emphasize and enhance text and can attract initial reader attention.
10. Use background colors judiciously to avoid distracting the eye or making it difficult to read.
11. Be consistent throughout posts, since people read them in different orders.
12. Tell a story with a beginning, middle, and end.

Specialized Types of Writing

Editorials

Editorials are articles in newspapers, magazines, and other serial publications. Editorials express an opinion or belief belonging to the majority of the publication's leadership. This opinion or belief generally refers to a specific issue, topic, or event. These articles are authored by a member, or a small number of members, of the publication's leadership and are often written to affect their readers, such as persuading them to adopt a stance or take a particular action.

Resumes

Resumes are brief, but formal, documents that outline an individual's experience in a certain area. Resumes are most often used for job applications. Such resumes will list the applicant's work experience, certification, and achievements or qualifications related to the position. Resumes should only include the most pertinent information. They should also use strategic formatting to highlight the applicant's most impressive experiences and achievements, to ensure the document can be read quickly and easily, and to eliminate both visual clutter and excessive negative space.

Reports

Reports summarize the results of research, new methodology, or other developments in an academic or professional context. Reports often include details about methodology and outside influences and factors. However, a report should focus primarily on the results of the research or development. Reports are objective and deliver information efficiently, sacrificing style for clear and effective communication.

Memoranda

A memorandum, also called a memo, is a formal method of communication used in professional settings. Memoranda are printed documents that include a heading listing the sender and their job title, the recipient and their job title, the date, and a specific subject line. Memoranda often include an introductory section explaining the reason and context for the memorandum. Next, a memorandum includes a section with details relevant to the topic. Finally, the memorandum will conclude with a paragraph that politely and clearly defines the sender's expectations of the recipient.

Technology in the Writing Process

Modern technology has yielded several tools that can be used to make the writing process more convenient and organized. Word processors and online tools, such as databases and plagiarism detectors, allow much of the writing process to be completed in one place, using one device.

Technology for Planning and Drafting

For the planning and drafting stages of the writing process, word processors are a helpful tool. These programs also feature formatting tools, allowing users to create their own planning tools or create digital outlines that can be easily converted into sentences, paragraphs, or an entire essay draft. Online databases and references also complement the planning process by providing convenient access to information and sources for research. Word processors also allow users to keep up with their work and update it more easily than if they wrote their work by hand. Online word processors often allow users to collaborate, making group assignments more convenient. These programs also allow users to include illustrations or other supplemental media in their compositions.

Technology for Revising, Editing, and Proofreading

Word processors also benefit the revising, editing, and proofreading stages of the writing process. Most of these programs indicate errors in spelling and grammar, allowing users to catch minor errors and correct them quickly. There are also websites designed to help writers by analyzing text for deeper errors, such as poor sentence structure, inappropriate complexity, lack of sentence variety, and style issues. These websites can help users fix errors they may not know to look for or may have simply missed. As writers finish these steps, they may benefit from checking their work for any plagiarism. There are several websites and programs that compare text to other documents and publications across the internet and detect any similarities within the text. These websites show the source of the similar information, so users know whether or not they referenced the source and unintentionally plagiarized its contents.

Technology for Publishing

Technology also makes managing written work more convenient. Digitally storing documents keeps everything in one place and is easy to reference. Digital storage also makes sharing work easier, as documents can be attached to an email or stored online. This also allows writers to publish their work easily, as they can electronically submit it to other publications or freely post it to a personal blog, profile, or website.

Grammar and Usage

Parts of Speech

Nouns

A noun is a person, place, thing, or idea. The two main types of nouns are **common** and **proper** nouns. Nouns can also be categorized as abstract (i.e., general) or concrete (i.e., specific).

Common Nouns

Common nouns are generic names for people, places, and things. Common nouns are not usually capitalized.

Examples of common nouns:

People: boy, girl, worker, manager

Places: school, bank, library, home

Things: dog, cat, truck, car

Review Video: Nouns
Visit mometrix.com/academy and enter code: 344028

Proper Nouns

Proper nouns name specific people, places, or things. All proper nouns are capitalized.

Examples of proper nouns:

People: Abraham Lincoln, George Washington, Martin Luther King, Jr.

Places: Los Angeles, California; New York; Asia

Things: Statue of Liberty, Earth, Lincoln Memorial

Note: Some nouns can be either common or proper depending on their use. For example, when referring to the planet that we live on, *Earth* is a proper noun and is capitalized. When referring to the dirt, rocks, or land on our planet, *earth* is a common noun and is not capitalized.

General and Specific Nouns

General nouns are the names of conditions or ideas. **Specific nouns** name people, places, and things that are understood by using your senses.

General nouns:

Condition: beauty, strength

Idea: truth, peace

Specific nouns:

People: baby, friend, father

Places: town, park, city hall

Things: rainbow, cough, apple, silk, gasoline

COLLECTIVE NOUNS

Collective nouns are the names for a group of people, places, or things that may act as a whole. The following are examples of collective nouns: *class, company, dozen, group, herd, team,* and *public*. Collective nouns usually require an article, which denotes the noun as being a single unit. For instance, a choir is a group of singers. Even though there are many singers in a choir, the word choir is grammatically treated as a single unit. If we refer to the members of the group, and not the group itself, it is no longer a collective noun.

Incorrect: The *choir are* going to compete nationally this year.

Correct: The *choir is* going to compete nationally this year.

Incorrect: The *members* of the choir *is* competing nationally this year.

Correct: The *members* of the choir *are* competing nationally this year.

PRONOUNS

Pronouns are words that are used to stand in for nouns. A pronoun may be classified as personal, intensive, relative, interrogative, demonstrative, indefinite, and reciprocal.

Personal: *Nominative* is the case for nouns and pronouns that are the subject of a sentence. *Objective* is the case for nouns and pronouns that are an object in a sentence. *Possessive* is the case for nouns and pronouns that show possession or ownership.

Singular

	Nominative	Objective	Possessive
First Person	I	me	my, mine
Second Person	you	you	your, yours
Third Person	he, she, it	him, her, it	his, her, hers, its

Plural

	Nominative	Objective	Possessive
First Person	we	us	our, ours
Second Person	you	you	your, yours
Third Person	they	them	their, theirs

Intensive: I myself, you yourself, he himself, she herself, the (thing) itself, we ourselves, you yourselves, they themselves

Relative: which, who, whom, whose

Interrogative: what, which, who, whom, whose

Demonstrative: this, that, these, those

Indefinite: all, any, each, everyone, either/neither, one, some, several

Reciprocal: each other, one another

Review Video: Nouns and Pronouns
Visit mometrix.com/academy and enter code: 312073

Verbs

A verb is a word or group of words that indicates action or being. In other words, the verb shows something's action or state of being or the action that has been done to something. If you want to write a sentence, then you need a verb. Without a verb, you have no sentence.

Transitive and Intransitive Verbs

A **transitive verb** is a verb whose action indicates a receiver. **Intransitive verbs** do not indicate a receiver of an action. In other words, the action of the verb does not point to an object.

Transitive: He drives a car. | She feeds the dog.

Intransitive: He runs every day. | She voted in the last election.

A dictionary will tell you whether a verb is transitive or intransitive. Some verbs can be transitive or intransitive.

Action Verbs and Linking Verbs

Action verbs show what the subject is doing. In other words, an action verb shows action. Unlike most types of words, a single action verb, in the right context, can be an entire sentence. **Linking verbs** link the subject of a sentence to a noun or pronoun, or they link a subject with an adjective. You always need a verb if you want a complete sentence. However, linking verbs on their own cannot be a complete sentence.

Common linking verbs include *appear, be, become, feel, grow, look, seem, smell, sound,* and *taste*. However, any verb that shows a condition and connects to a noun, pronoun, or adjective that describes the subject of a sentence is a linking verb.

Action: He sings. | Run! | Go! | I talk with him every day. | She reads.

Linking:

Incorrect: I am.

Correct: I am John. | The roses smell lovely. | I feel tired.

Note: Some verbs are followed by words that look like prepositions, but they are a part of the verb and a part of the verb's meaning. These are known as phrasal verbs, and examples include *call off*, *look up*, and *drop off*.

Review Video: Action Verbs and Linking Verbs
Visit mometrix.com/academy and enter code: 743142

Voice

Transitive verbs may be in active voice or passive voice. The difference between active voice and passive voice is whether the subject is acting or being acted upon. When the subject of the sentence is doing the action, the verb is in **active voice**. When the subject is being acted upon, the verb is in **passive voice**.

Active: Jon drew the picture. (The subject *Jon* is doing the action of *drawing a picture*.)

Passive: The picture is drawn by Jon. (The subject *picture* is receiving the action from Jon.)

VERB TENSES

Verb **tense** is a property of a verb that indicates when the action being described takes place (past, present, or future) and whether or not the action is completed (simple or perfect). Describing an action taking place in the present (*I talk*) requires a different verb tense than describing an action that took place in the past (*I talked*). Some verb tenses require an auxiliary (helping) verb. These helping verbs include *am, are, is* | *have, has, had* | *was, were, will* (or *shall*).

Present: I talk	Present perfect: I have talked
Past: I talked	Past perfect: I had talked
Future: I will talk	Future perfect: I will have talked

Present: The action is happening at the current time.

Example: He *walks* to the store every morning.

To show that something is happening right now, use the progressive present tense: I *am walking*.

Past: The action happened in the past.

Example: She *walked* to the store an hour ago.

Future: The action will happen later.

Example: I *will walk* to the store tomorrow.

Present perfect: The action started in the past and continues into the present or took place previously at an unspecified time.

Example: I *have walked* to the store three times today.

Past perfect: The action was completed at some point in the past. This tense is usually used to describe an action that was completed before some other reference time or event.

Example: I *had eaten* already before they arrived.

Future perfect: The action will be completed before some point in the future. This tense may be used to describe an action that has already begun or has yet to begin.

Example: The project *will have been completed* by the deadline.

Review Video: Present Perfect, Past Perfect, and Future Perfect Verb Tenses
Visit mometrix.com/academy and enter code: 269472

Conjugating Verbs

When you need to change the form of a verb, you are **conjugating** a verb. The key forms of a verb are present tense (sing/sings), past tense (sang), present participle (singing), and past participle (sung). By combining these forms with helping verbs, you can make almost any verb tense. The following table demonstrate some of the different ways to conjugate a verb:

Tense	First Person	Second Person	Third Person Singular	Third Person Plural
Simple Present	I sing	You sing	He, she, it sings	They sing
Simple Past	I sang	You sang	He, she, it sang	They sang
Simple Future	I will sing	You will sing	He, she, it will sing	They will sing
Present Progressive	I am singing	You are singing	He, she, it is singing	They are singing
Past Progressive	I was singing	You were singing	He, she, it was singing	They were singing
Present Perfect	I have sung	You have sung	He, she, it has sung	They have sung
Past Perfect	I had sung	You had sung	He, she, it had sung	They had sung

Mood

There are three **moods** in English: the indicative, the imperative, and the subjunctive.

The **indicative mood** is used for facts, opinions, and questions.

Fact: You can do this.

Opinion: I think that you can do this.

Question: Do you know that you can do this?

The **imperative** is used for orders or requests.

Order: You are going to do this!

Request: Will you do this for me?

The **subjunctive mood** is for wishes and statements that go against fact.

Wish: I wish that I were famous.

Statement against fact: If I were you, I would do this. (This goes against fact because I am not you. You have the chance to do this, and I do not have the chance.)

ADJECTIVES

An **adjective** is a word that is used to modify a noun or pronoun. An adjective answers a question: *Which one? What kind?* or *How many?* Usually, adjectives come before the words that they modify, but they may also come after a linking verb.

Which one? The *third* suit is my favorite.

What kind? This suit is *navy blue*.

How many? I am going to buy *four* pairs of socks to match the suit.

> **Review Video: Descriptive Text**
> Visit mometrix.com/academy and enter code: 174903

ARTICLES

Articles are adjectives that are used to distinguish nouns as definite or indefinite. *A*, *an*, and *the* are the only articles. **Definite** nouns are preceded by *the* and indicate a specific person, place, thing, or idea. **Indefinite** nouns are preceded by *a* or *an* and do not indicate a specific person, place, thing, or idea.

Note: *An* comes before words that start with a vowel sound. For example, "Are you going to get an **u**mbrella?"

Definite: I lost *the* bottle that belongs to me.

Indefinite: Does anyone have *a* bottle to share?

> **Review Video: Function of Articles in a Sentence**
> Visit mometrix.com/academy and enter code: 449383

COMPARISON WITH ADJECTIVES

Some adjectives are relative and other adjectives are absolute. Adjectives that are **relative** can show the comparison between things. **Absolute** adjectives can also show comparison, but they do so in a different way. Let's say that you are reading two books. You think that one book is perfect, and the other book is not exactly perfect. It is not possible for one book to be more perfect than the other. Either you think that the book is perfect, or you think that the book is imperfect. In this case, perfect and imperfect are absolute adjectives.

Relative adjectives will show the different **degrees** of something or someone to something else or someone else. The three degrees of adjectives include positive, comparative, and superlative.

The **positive** degree is the normal form of an adjective.

Example: This work is *difficult*. | She is *smart*.

The **comparative** degree compares one person or thing to another person or thing.

Example: This work is *more difficult* than your work. | She is *smarter* than me.

The **superlative** degree compares more than two people or things.

Example: This is the *most difficult* work of my life. | She is the *smartest* lady in school.

> **Review Video: Adjectives**
> Visit mometrix.com/academy and enter code: 470154

ADVERBS

An **adverb** is a word that is used to **modify** a verb, an adjective, or another adverb. Usually, adverbs answer one of these questions: *When? Where? How?* and *Why?* The negatives *not* and *never* are considered adverbs. Adverbs that modify adjectives or other adverbs **strengthen** or **weaken** the words that they modify.

Examples:

He walks *quickly* through the crowd.

The water flows *smoothly* on the rocks.

Note: Adverbs are usually indicated by the morpheme *-ly*, which has been added to the root word. For instance, *quick* can be made into an adverb by adding *-ly* to construct *quickly*. Some words that end in *-ly* do not follow this rule and can behave as other parts of speech. Examples of adjectives ending in *-ly* include: *early, friendly, holy, lonely, silly*, and *ugly*. To know if a word that ends in *-ly* is an adjective or adverb, check your dictionary. Also, while many adverbs end in *-ly*, you need to remember that not all adverbs end in *-ly*.

Examples:

He is *never* angry.

You are *too* irresponsible to travel alone.

Review Video: Adverbs
Visit mometrix.com/academy and enter code: 713951

Review Video: Adverbs that Modify Adjectives
Visit mometrix.com/academy and enter code: 122570

COMPARISON WITH ADVERBS

The rules for comparing adverbs are the same as the rules for adjectives.

The **positive** degree is the standard form of an adverb.

Example: He arrives *soon*. | She speaks *softly* to her friends.

The **comparative** degree compares one person or thing to another person or thing.

Example: He arrives *sooner* than Sarah. | She speaks *more softly* than him.

The **superlative** degree compares more than two people or things.

Example: He arrives *soonest* of the group. | She speaks the *most softly* of any of her friends.

Prepositions

A **preposition** is a word placed before a noun or pronoun that shows the relationship between that noun or pronoun and another word in the sentence.

Common prepositions:

about	before	during	on	under
after	beneath	for	over	until
against	between	from	past	up
among	beyond	in	through	with
around	by	of	to	within
at	down	off	toward	without

Examples:

The napkin is *in* the drawer.

The Earth rotates *around* the Sun.

The needle is *beneath* the haystack.

Can you find "me" *among* the words?

> **Review Video: Prepositions**
> Visit mometrix.com/academy and enter code: 946763

Conjunctions

Conjunctions join words, phrases, or clauses and they show the connection between the joined pieces. **Coordinating conjunctions** connect equal parts of sentences. **Correlative conjunctions** show the connection between pairs. **Subordinating conjunctions** join subordinate (i.e., dependent) clauses with independent clauses.

Coordinating Conjunctions

The **coordinating conjunctions** include: *and, but, yet, or, nor, for,* and *so*

Examples:

The rock was small, *but* it was heavy.

She drove in the night, *and* he drove in the day.

Correlative Conjunctions

The **correlative conjunctions** are: *either...or* | *neither...nor* | *not only...but also*

Examples:

Either you are coming *or* you are staying.

He *not only* ran three miles *but also* swam 200 yards.

Review Video: Coordinating and Correlative Conjunctions
Visit mometrix.com/academy and enter code: 390329

Review Video: Adverb Equal Comparisons
Visit mometrix.com/academy and enter code: 231291

Subordinating Conjunctions

Common **subordinating conjunctions** include:

after	since	whenever
although	so that	where
because	unless	wherever
before	until	whether
in order that	when	while

Examples:

I am hungry *because* I did not eat breakfast.

He went home *when* everyone left.

Review Video: Subordinating Conjunctions
Visit mometrix.com/academy and enter code: 958913

Interjections

Interjections are words of exclamation (i.e., audible expression of great feeling) that are used alone or as a part of a sentence. Often, they are used at the beginning of a sentence for an introduction. Sometimes, they can be used in the middle of a sentence to show a change in thought or attitude.

Common Interjections: Hey! | Oh, | Ouch! | Please! | Wow!

Agreement and Sentence Structure

Subjects and Predicates

Subjects

The **subject** of a sentence names who or what the sentence is about. The subject may be directly stated in a sentence, or the subject may be the implied *you*. The **complete subject** includes the simple subject and all of its modifiers. To find the complete subject, ask *Who* or *What* and insert the verb to complete the question. The answer, including any modifiers (adjectives, prepositional phrases, etc.), is the complete subject. To find the **simple subject**, remove all of the modifiers in the complete subject. Being able to locate the subject of a sentence helps with many problems, such as those involving sentence fragments and subject-verb agreement.

Examples:

simple subject

The small, red car is the one that he wants for Christmas.

complete subject

simple subject

The young artist is coming over for dinner.

complete subject

Review Video: Subjects in English
Visit mometrix.com/academy and enter code: 444771

In **imperative** sentences, the verb's subject is understood (e.g., [You] Run to the store), but is not actually present in the sentence. Normally, the subject comes before the verb. However, the subject comes after the verb in sentences that begin with *There are* or *There was.*

Direct:

John knows the way to the park.	Who knows the way to the park?	John
The cookies need ten more minutes.	What needs ten minutes?	The cookies
By five o'clock, Bill will need to leave.	Who needs to leave?	Bill
There are five letters on the table for him.	What is on the table?	Five letters
There were coffee and doughnuts in the house.	What was in the house?	Coffee and doughnuts

Implied:

Go to the post office for me.	Who is going to the post office?	You
Come and sit with me, please?	Who needs to come and sit?	You

PREDICATES

In a sentence, you always have a predicate and a subject. The subject tells who or what the sentence is about, and the **predicate** explains or describes the subject. The predicate includes the verb or verb phrase and any direct or indirect objects of the verb, as well as any words or phrases modifying these.

Think about the sentence *He sings.* In this sentence, we have a subject (He) and a predicate (sings). This is all that is needed for a sentence to be complete. Most sentences contain more information, but if this is all the information that you are given, then you have a complete sentence.

Now, let's look at another sentence: *John and Jane sing on Tuesday nights at the dance hall.*

subject predicate

John and Jane sing on Tuesday nights at the dance hall.

Review Video: Complete Predicate
Visit mometrix.com/academy and enter code: 293942

SUBJECT-VERB AGREEMENT

Verbs must **agree** with their subjects in number and in person. To agree in number, singular subjects need singular verbs and plural subjects need plural verbs. A **singular** noun refers to **one** person, place, or thing. A

plural noun refers to **more than one** person, place, or thing. To agree in person, the correct verb form must be chosen to match the first, second, or third person subject. The present tense ending *-s* or *-es* is used on a verb if its subject is third person singular; otherwise, the verb's ending is not modified.

Review Video: Subject-Verb Agreement
Visit mometrix.com/academy and enter code: 479190

Number Agreement Examples:

Single Subject and Verb: Dan (singular subject) calls (singular verb) home.

Dan is one person. So, the singular verb *calls* is needed.

Plural Subject and Verb: Dan and Bob (plural subject) call (plural verb) home.

More than one person needs the plural verb *call.*

Person Agreement Examples:

First Person: I *am* walking.

Second Person: You *are* walking.

Third Person: He *is* walking.

Complications with Subject-Verb Agreement

Words Between Subject and Verb

Words that come between the simple subject and the verb have no bearing on subject-verb agreement.

Examples:

The joy (singular subject) of my life returns (singular verb) home tonight.

The phrase *of my life* does not influence the verb *returns.*

The question (singular subject) that still remains unanswered is (singular verb) "Who are you?"

Don't let the phrase "*that still remains...*" trouble you. The subject *question* goes with *is.*

Compound Subjects

A compound subject is formed when two or more nouns joined by *and*, *or*, or *nor* jointly act as the subject of the sentence.

Joined by And

When a compound subject is joined by *and*, it is treated as a plural subject and requires a plural verb.

Examples:

plural subject — plural verb

You and Jon are invited to come to my house.

plural subject — plural verb

The pencil and paper belong to me.

Joined by Or/Nor

For a compound subject joined by *or* or *nor*, the verb must agree in number with the part of the subject that is closest to the verb (italicized in the examples below).

Examples:

subject — verb

Today or tomorrow is the day.

subject — verb

Stan or Phil wants to read the book.

subject — verb

Neither the pen nor the book is on the desk.

subject — verb

Either the blanket or pillows arrive this afternoon.

Indefinite Pronouns as Subject

An indefinite pronoun is a pronoun that does not refer to a specific noun. Some indefinite pronouns function as only singular, some function as only plural, and some can function as either singular or plural depending on how they are used.

Always Singular

Pronouns such as *each*, *either*, *everybody*, *anybody*, *somebody*, and *nobody* are always singular.

Examples:

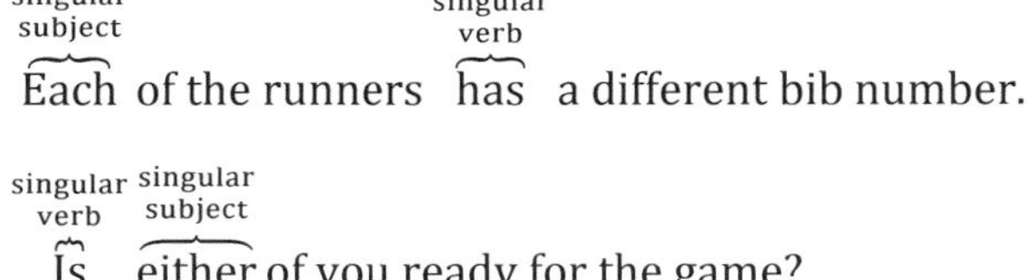

singular subject
singular verb
Each of the runners has a different bib number.
singular verb
singular subject
Is either of you ready for the game?

Note: The words *each* and *either* can also be used as adjectives (e.g., *each* person is unique). When one of these adjectives modifies the subject of a sentence, it is always a singular subject.

singular subject: Everybody; singular verb: grows

Everybody grows a day older every day.

singular subject: Anybody; singular verb: is

Anybody is welcome to bring a tent.

Always Plural

Pronouns such as *both*, *several*, and *many* are always plural.

Examples:

plural subject: Both; plural verb: were

Both of the siblings were too tired to argue.

plural subject: Many; plural verb: have tried

Many have tried, but none have succeeded.

Depend on Context

Pronouns such as *some*, *any*, *all*, *none*, *more*, and *most* can be either singular or plural depending on what they are representing in the context of the sentence.

Examples:

singular subject: All; singular verb: was

All of my dog's food was still there in his bowl.

plural subject: all; plural verb: were

By the end of the night, all of my guests were already excited about coming to my next party.

Other Cases Involving Plural or Irregular Form

Some nouns are **singular in meaning but plural in form**: news, mathematics, physics, and economics.

The *news is* coming on now.

Mathematics is my favorite class.

Some nouns are plural in form and meaning, and have **no singular equivalent**: scissors and pants.

Do these *pants come* with a shirt?

The *scissors are* for my project.

Mathematical operations are **irregular** in their construction, but are normally considered to be **singular in meaning**.

One plus one is two.

Three times three is nine.

Writing

Note: Look to your **dictionary** for help when you aren't sure whether a noun with a plural form has a singular or plural meaning.

COMPLEMENTS

A complement is a noun, pronoun, or adjective that is used to give more information about the subject or object in the sentence.

DIRECT OBJECTS

A direct object is a noun or pronoun that tells who or what **receives** the action of the verb. A sentence will only include a direct object if the verb is a transitive verb. If the verb is an intransitive verb or a linking verb, there will be no direct object. When you are looking for a direct object, find the verb and ask *who* or *what.*

Examples:

I took *the blanket.*

Jane read *books.*

INDIRECT OBJECTS

An indirect object is a noun or pronoun that indicates what or whom the action had an **influence** on. If there is an indirect object in a sentence, then there will also be a direct object. When you are looking for the indirect object, find the verb and ask *to/for whom or what.*

Examples:

We taught [the old dog]$_{\text{indirect object}}$ [a new trick]$_{\text{direct object}}$.

I gave [them]$_{\text{indirect object}}$ [a math lesson]$_{\text{direct object}}$.

Review Video: Direct and Indirect Objects
Visit mometrix.com/academy and enter code: 817385

PREDICATE NOMINATIVES AND PREDICATE ADJECTIVES

As we looked at previously, verbs may be classified as either action verbs or linking verbs. A linking verb is so named because it links the subject to words in the predicate that describe or define the subject. These words are called predicate nominatives (if nouns or pronouns) or predicate adjectives (if adjectives).

Examples:

My [father]$_{\text{subject}}$ is a [lawyer]$_{\text{predicate nominative}}$.

Your [mother]$_{\text{subject}}$ is [patient]$_{\text{predicate adjective}}$.

PRONOUN USAGE

The **antecedent** is the noun that has been replaced by a pronoun. A pronoun and its antecedent **agree** when they have the same number (singular or plural) and gender (male, female, or neutral).

Examples:

Singular agreement: John (antecedent) came into town, and he (pronoun) played for us.

Plural agreement: John and Rick (antecedent) came into town, and they (pronoun) played for us.

To determine which is the correct pronoun to use in a compound subject or object, try each pronoun **alone** in place of the compound in the sentence. Your knowledge of pronouns will tell you which one is correct.

Example:

Bob and (I, me) will be going.

Test: (1) *I will be going* or (2) *Me will be going*. The second choice cannot be correct because *me* cannot be used as the subject of a sentence. Instead, *me* is used as an object.

Answer: Bob and I will be going.

When a pronoun is used with a noun immediately following (as in "we boys"), try the sentence **without the added noun**.

Example:

(We/Us) boys played football last year.

Test: (1) *We played football last ye*ar or (2) *Us played football last year*. Again, the second choice cannot be correct because *us* cannot be used as a subject of a sentence. Instead, *us* is used as an object.

Answer: We boys played football last year.

Review Video: Pronoun Usage
Visit mometrix.com/academy and enter code: 666500

Review Video: Pronoun-Antecedent Agreement
Visit mometrix.com/academy and enter code: 919704

A pronoun should point clearly to the **antecedent**. Here is how a pronoun reference can be unhelpful if it is puzzling or not directly stated.

Unhelpful: Ron and Jim (antecedent) went to the store, and he (pronoun) bought soda.

Who bought soda? Ron or Jim?

Helpful: Jim (antecedent) went to the store, and he (pronoun) bought soda.

The sentence is clear. Jim bought the soda.

Some pronouns change their form by their placement in a sentence. A pronoun that is a **subject** in a sentence comes in the **subjective case**. Pronouns that serve as **objects** appear in the **objective case**. Finally, the pronouns that are used as **possessives** appear in the **possessive case**.

Examples:

Subjective case: *He* is coming to the show.

The pronoun *He* is the subject of the sentence.

Objective case: Josh drove *him* to the airport.

The pronoun *him* is the object of the sentence.

Possessive case: The flowers are *mine*.

The pronoun *mine* shows ownership of the flowers.

The word *who* is a subjective-case pronoun that can be used as a **subject**. The word *whom* is an objective-case pronoun that can be used as an **object**. The words *who* and *whom* are common in subordinate clauses or in questions.

Examples:

He knows who (subject) wants (verb) to come.

He knows the man whom (object) we want (verb) at the party.

CLAUSES

A clause is a group of words that contains both a subject and a predicate (verb). There are two types of clauses: independent and dependent. An **independent clause** contains a complete thought, while a **dependent (or subordinate) clause** does not. A dependent clause includes a subject and a verb, and may also contain objects or complements, but it cannot stand as a complete thought without being joined to an independent clause. Dependent clauses function within sentences as adjectives, adverbs, or nouns.

Example:

I am running (independent clause) because I want to stay in shape. (dependent clause)

The clause *I am running* is an independent clause: it has a subject and a verb, and it gives a complete thought. The clause *because I want to stay in shape* is a dependent clause: it has a subject and a verb, but it does not express a complete thought. It adds detail to the independent clause to which it is attached.

Review Video: Clauses
Visit mometrix.com/academy and enter code: 940170

Review Video: Independent and Dependent Clauses
Visit mometrix.com/academy and enter code: 556903

TYPES OF DEPENDENT CLAUSES

ADJECTIVE CLAUSES

An **adjective clause** is a dependent clause that modifies a noun or a pronoun. Adjective clauses begin with a relative pronoun (*who, whose, whom, which,* and *that*) or a relative adverb (*where, when,* and *why*).

Also, adjective clauses usually come immediately after the noun that the clause needs to explain or rename. This is done to ensure that it is clear which noun or pronoun the clause is modifying.

Examples:

I learned the reason (independent clause) why I won the award. (adjective clause)

This is the place (independent clause) where I started my first job. (adjective clause)

An adjective clause can be an essential or nonessential clause. An essential clause is very important to the sentence. **Essential clauses** explain or define a person or thing. **Nonessential clauses** give more information about a person or thing but are not necessary to define them. Nonessential clauses are set off with commas while essential clauses are not.

Examples:

A person who works hard at first (essential clause) can often rest later in life.

Neil Armstrong, who walked on the moon, (nonessential clause) is my hero.

Review Video: Adjective Clauses and Phrases
Visit mometrix.com/academy and enter code: 520888

Adverb Clauses

An **adverb clause** is a dependent clause that modifies a verb, adjective, or adverb. In sentences with multiple dependent clauses, adverb clauses are usually placed immediately before or after the independent clause. An adverb clause is introduced with words such as *after, although, as, before, because, if, since, so, unless, when, where*, and *while*.

Examples:

When you walked outside, (adverb clause) I called the manager.

I will go with you unless you want to stay. (adverb clause)

Noun Clauses

A **noun clause** is a dependent clause that can be used as a subject, object, or complement. Noun clauses begin with words such as *how, that, what, whether, which, who,* and *why*. These words can also come with an adjective clause. Unless the noun clause is being used as the subject of the sentence, it should come after the verb of the independent clause.

Examples:

The real mystery is how you avoided serious injury. (noun clause: "how you avoided serious injury")

What you learn from each other depends on your honesty with others. (noun clause: "What you learn from each other")

SUBORDINATION

When two related ideas are not of equal importance, the ideal way to combine them is to make the more important idea an independent clause and the less important idea a dependent or subordinate clause. This is called **subordination**.

Example:

Separate ideas: The team had a perfect regular season. The team lost the championship.

Subordinated: Despite having a perfect regular season, *the team lost the championship*.

PHRASES

A phrase is a group of words that functions as a single part of speech, usually a noun, adjective, or adverb. A **phrase** is not a complete thought and does not contain a subject and predicate, but it adds detail or explanation to a sentence, or renames something within the sentence.

PREPOSITIONAL PHRASES

One of the most common types of phrases is the prepositional phrase. A **prepositional phrase** begins with a preposition and ends with a noun or pronoun that is the object of the preposition. Normally, the prepositional phrase functions as an **adjective** or an **adverb** within the sentence.

Examples:

The picnic is on the blanket. (prepositional phrase: "on the blanket")

I am sick with a fever today. (prepositional phrase: "with a fever")

Among the many flowers, John found a four-leaf clover. (prepositional phrase: "Among the many flowers")

VERBAL PHRASES

A **verbal** is a word or phrase that is formed from a verb but does not function as a verb. Depending on its particular form, it may be used as a noun, adjective, or adverb. A verbal does **not** replace a verb in a sentence.

Examples:

Correct: Walk a mile daily. (verb: "Walk")

This is a complete sentence with the implied subject *you*.

Incorrect: To walk (verbal) a mile.

This is not a sentence since there is no functional verb.

There are three types of verbal: **participles**, **gerunds**, and **infinitives**. Each type of verbal has a corresponding **phrase** that consists of the verbal itself along with any complements or modifiers.

PARTICIPLES

A **participle** is a type of verbal that always functions as an adjective. The present participle always ends with *-ing*. Past participles end with *-d, -ed, -n,* or *-t*. Participles are combined with helping verbs to form certain verb tenses, but a participle by itself cannot function as a verb.

Examples: dance (verb) | dancing (present participle) | danced (past participle)

Participial phrases most often come right before or right after the noun or pronoun that they modify.

Examples:

Shipwrecked on an island (participial phrase), the boys started to fish for food.

Having been seated for five hours (participial phrase), we got out of the car to stretch our legs.

Praised for their work (participial phrase), the group accepted the first-place trophy.

GERUNDS

A **gerund** is a type of verbal that always functions as a **noun**. Like present participles, gerunds always end with *-ing*, but they can be easily distinguished from participles by the part of speech they represent (participles always function as adjectives). Since a gerund or gerund phrase always functions as a noun, it can be used as the subject of a sentence, the predicate nominative, or the object of a verb or preposition.

Examples:

We want to be known for teaching (gerund) the poor (object of preposition: teaching the poor).

Coaching (gerund) this team (subject: Coaching this team) is the best job of my life.

We like practicing (gerund) our songs (object of verb: practicing our songs) in the basement.

INFINITIVES

An **infinitive** is a type of verbal that can function as a noun, an adjective, or an adverb. An infinitive is made of the word *to* and the basic form of the verb. As with all other types of verbal phrases, an infinitive phrase includes the verbal itself and all of its complements or modifiers.

Examples:

infinitive
To join the team is my goal in life.
noun

infinitive
The animals have enough food to eat for the night.
adjective

infinitive
People lift weights to exercise their muscles.
adverb

Review Video: Verbals
Visit mometrix.com/academy and enter code: 915480

Appositive Phrases

An **appositive** is a word or phrase that is used to explain or rename nouns or pronouns. Noun phrases, gerund phrases, and infinitive phrases can all be used as appositives.

Examples:

appositive
Terriers, hunters at heart, have been dressed up to look like lap dogs.

The noun phrase *hunters at heart* renames the noun *terriers.*

appositive
His plan, to save and invest his money, was proven as a safe approach.

The infinitive phrase explains what the plan is.

Appositive phrases can be **essential** or **nonessential**. An appositive phrase is essential if the person, place, or thing being described or renamed is too general for its meaning to be understood without the appositive.

Examples:

essential
Two of America's Founding Fathers, George Washington and Thomas Jefferson, served as presidents.

nonessential
George Washington and Thomas Jefferson, two Founding Fathers, served as presidents.

Absolute Phrases

An absolute phrase is a phrase that consists of **a noun followed by a participle**. An absolute phrase provides **context** to what is being described in the sentence, but it does not modify or explain any particular word; it is essentially independent.

Examples:

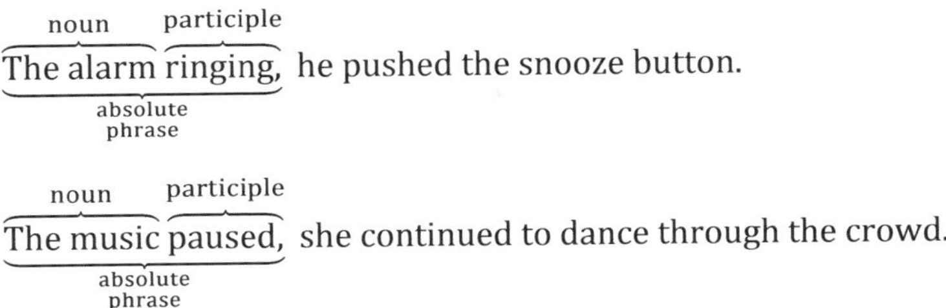

PARALLELISM

When multiple items or ideas are presented in a sentence in series, such as in a list, the items or ideas must be stated in grammatically equivalent ways. For example, if two ideas are listed in parallel and the first is stated in gerund form, the second cannot be stated in infinitive form. (e.g., *I enjoy reading and to study.* [incorrect]) An infinitive and a gerund are not grammatically equivalent. Instead, you should write *I enjoy reading and studying* OR *I like to read and to study*. In lists of more than two, all items must be parallel.

Example:

Incorrect: He stopped at the office, grocery store, and the pharmacy before heading home.

The first and third items in the list of places include the article *the*, so the second item needs it as well.

Correct: He stopped at the office, *the* grocery store, and the pharmacy before heading home.

Example:

Incorrect: While vacationing in Europe, she went biking, skiing, and climbed mountains.

The first and second items in the list are gerunds, so the third item must be as well.

Correct: While vacationing in Europe, she went biking, skiing, and *mountain climbing*.

Review Video: Parallel Sentence Construction
Visit mometrix.com/academy and enter code: 831988

SENTENCE PURPOSE

There are four types of sentences: declarative, imperative, interrogative, and exclamatory.

A **declarative** sentence states a fact and ends with a period.

The football game starts at seven o'clock.

An **imperative** sentence tells someone to do something and generally ends with a period. An urgent command might end with an exclamation point instead.

Don't forget to buy your ticket.

An **interrogative** sentence asks a question and ends with a question mark.

Are you going to the game on Friday?

An **exclamatory** sentence shows strong emotion and ends with an exclamation point.

I can't believe we won the game!

SENTENCE STRUCTURE

Sentences are classified by structure based on the type and number of clauses present. The four classifications of sentence structure are the following:

Simple: A simple sentence has one independent clause with no dependent clauses. A simple sentence may have **compound elements** (i.e., compound subject or verb).

Examples:

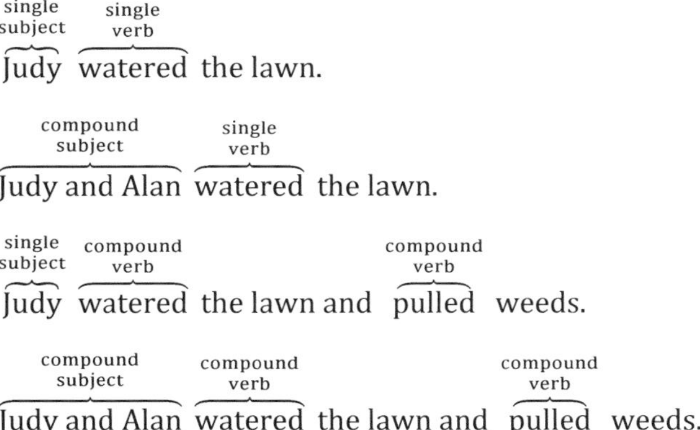

Compound: A compound sentence has two or more independent clauses with no dependent clauses. Usually, the independent clauses are joined with a comma and a coordinating conjunction or with a semicolon.

Examples:

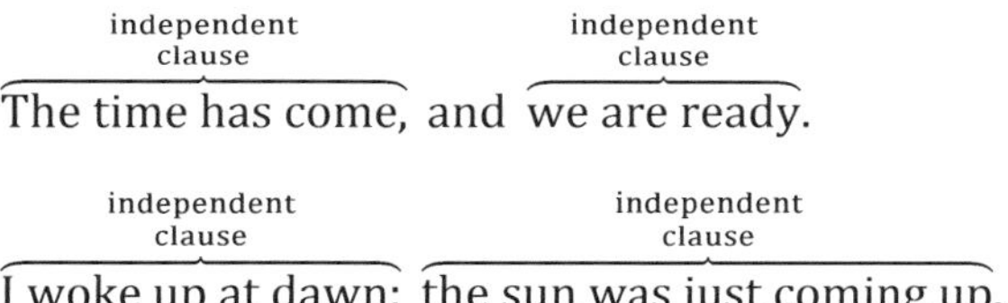

Complex: A complex sentence has one independent clause and at least one dependent clause.

Examples:

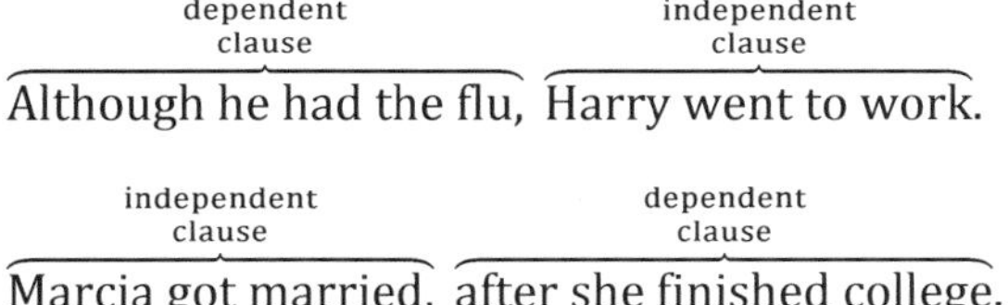

Compound-Complex: A compound-complex sentence has at least two independent clauses and at least one dependent clause.

Examples:

John is my friend (independent clause) who went to India, (dependent clause) and he brought back souvenirs. (independent clause)

You may not realize this, (independent clause) but we heard the music (independent clause) that you played last night. (dependent clause)

> **Review Video: Sentence Structure**
> Visit mometrix.com/academy and enter code: 700478

Sentence variety is important to consider when writing an essay or speech. A variety of sentence lengths and types creates rhythm, makes a passage more engaging, and gives writers an opportunity to demonstrate their writing style. Writing that uses the same length or type of sentence without variation can be boring or difficult to read. To evaluate a passage for effective sentence variety, it is helpful to note whether the passage contains diverse sentence structures and lengths. It is also important to pay attention to the way each sentence starts and avoid beginning with the same words or phrases.

Sentence Fragments

Recall that a group of words must contain at least one **independent clause** in order to be considered a sentence. If it doesn't contain even one independent clause, it is called a **sentence fragment**.

The appropriate process for **repairing** a sentence fragment depends on what type of fragment it is. If the fragment is a dependent clause, it can sometimes be as simple as removing a subordinating word (e.g., when, because, if) from the beginning of the fragment. Alternatively, a dependent clause can be incorporated into a closely related neighboring sentence. If the fragment is missing some required part, like a subject or a verb, the fix might be as simple as adding the missing part.

Examples:

> **Fragment**: Because he wanted to sail the Mediterranean.
>
> **Removed subordinating word**: He wanted to sail the Mediterranean.
>
> **Combined with another sentence**: Because he wanted to sail the Mediterranean, he booked a Greek island cruise.

Run-on Sentences

Run-on sentences consist of multiple independent clauses that have not been joined together properly. Run-on sentences can be corrected in several different ways:

Join clauses properly: This can be done with a comma and coordinating conjunction, with a semicolon, or with a colon or dash if the second clause is explaining something in the first.

Example:

> **Incorrect**: I went on the trip, we visited lots of castles.
>
> **Corrected**: I went on the trip, and we visited lots of castles.

Split into separate sentences: This correction is most effective when the independent clauses are very long or when they are not closely related.

Example:

> **Incorrect**: The drive to New York takes ten hours, my uncle lives in Boston.
>
> **Corrected**: The drive to New York takes ten hours. My uncle lives in Boston.

Make one clause dependent: This is the easiest way to make the sentence correct and more interesting at the same time. It's often as simple as adding a subordinating word between the two clauses or before the first clause.

Example:

> **Incorrect**: I finally made it to the store and I bought some eggs.
>
> **Corrected**: When I finally made it to the store, I bought some eggs.

Reduce to one clause with a compound verb: If both clauses have the same subject, remove the subject from the second clause, and you now have just one clause with a compound verb.

Example:

> **Incorrect**: The drive to New York takes ten hours, it makes me very tired.
>
> **Corrected**: The drive to New York takes ten hours and makes me very tired.

Note: While these are the simplest ways to correct a run-on sentence, often the best way is to completely reorganize the thoughts in the sentence and rewrite it.

Review Video: Fragments and Run-on Sentences
Visit mometrix.com/academy and enter code: 541989

DANGLING AND MISPLACED MODIFIERS

DANGLING MODIFIERS

A dangling modifier is a dependent clause or verbal phrase that does not have a clear logical connection to a word in the sentence.

Example:

> dangling modifier
>
> **Incorrect**: Reading each magazine article, the stories caught my attention.
>
> The word *stories* cannot be modified by *Reading each magazine article*. People can read, but stories cannot read. Therefore, the subject of the sentence must be a person.
>
> gerund phrase
>
> **Corrected**: Reading each magazine article, I was entertained by the stories.

Example:

dangling modifier

Incorrect: Ever since childhood, my grandparents have visited me for Christmas.

The speaker in this sentence can't have been visited by her grandparents when *they* were children, since she wouldn't have been born yet. Either the modifier should be clarified or the sentence should be rearranged to specify whose childhood is being referenced.

dependent clause

Clarified: Ever since I was a child, my grandparents have visited for Christmas.

adverb phrase

Rearranged: Ever since childhood, I have enjoyed my grandparents visiting for Christmas.

Misplaced Modifiers

Because modifiers are grammatically versatile, they can be put in many different places within the structure of a sentence. The danger of this versatility is that a modifier can accidentally be placed where it is modifying the wrong word or where it is not clear which word it is modifying.

Example:

modifier

Incorrect: She read the book to a crowd that was filled with beautiful pictures.

The book was filled with beautiful pictures, not the crowd.

modifier

Corrected: She read the book that was filled with beautiful pictures to a crowd.

Example:

modifier

Ambiguous: Derek saw a bus nearly hit a man on his way to work.

Was Derek on his way to work or was the other man?

modifier

Derek: On his way to work, Derek saw a bus nearly hit a man.

modifier

The other man: Derek saw a bus nearly hit a man who was on his way to work.

Split Infinitives

A split infinitive occurs when a modifying word comes between the word *to* and the verb that pairs with *to*.

Example: To *clearly* explain vs. *To explain* clearly | To *softly* sing vs. *To sing* softly

Though considered improper by some, split infinitives may provide better clarity and simplicity in some cases than the alternatives. As such, avoiding them should not be considered a universal rule.

Double Negatives

Standard English allows **two negatives** only when a **positive** meaning is intended. (e.g., The team was *not displeased* with their performance.) Double negatives to emphasize negation are not used in standard English.

Negative modifiers (e.g., never, no, and not) should not be paired with other negative modifiers or negative words (e.g., none, nobody, nothing, or neither). The modifiers *hardly, barely*, and *scarcely* are also considered negatives in standard English, so they should not be used with other negatives.

PUNCTUATION

END PUNCTUATION

PERIODS

Use a period to end all sentences except direct questions and exclamations. Periods are also used for abbreviations.

Examples: 3 p.m. | 2 a.m. | Mr. Jones | Mrs. Stevens | Dr. Smith | Bill, Jr. | Pennsylvania Ave.

Note: An abbreviation is a shortened form of a word or phrase.

QUESTION MARKS

Question marks should be used following a **direct question**. A polite request can be followed by a period instead of a question mark.

Direct Question: What is for lunch today? | How are you? | Why is that the answer?

Polite Requests: Can you please send me the item tomorrow. | Will you please walk with me on the track.

Review Video: Question Marks
Visit mometrix.com/academy and enter code: 118471

EXCLAMATION MARKS

Exclamation marks are used after a word group or sentence that shows much feeling or has special importance. Exclamation marks should not be overused. They are saved for proper **exclamatory interjections**.

Example: We're going to the finals! | You have a beautiful car! | "That's crazy!" she yelled.

Review Video: Exclamation Points
Visit mometrix.com/academy and enter code: 199367

COMMAS

The comma is a punctuation mark that can help you understand connections in a sentence. Not every sentence needs a comma. However, if a sentence needs a comma, you need to put it in the right place. A comma in the wrong place (or an absent comma) will make a sentence's meaning unclear.

These are some of the rules for commas:

Use Case	Example
Before a **coordinating conjunction** joining independent clauses	Bob caught three fish, and I caught two fish.
After an **introductory phrase**	After the final out, we went to a restaurant to celebrate.
After an **adverbial clause**	Studying the stars, I was awed by the beauty of the sky.
Between **items in a series**	I will bring the turkey, the pie, and the coffee.
For **interjections**	Wow, you know how to play this game.
After ***yes* and *no* responses**	No, I cannot come tomorrow.
Separate **nonessential modifiers**	John Frank, who coaches the team, was promoted today.
Separate **nonessential appositives**	Thomas Edison, an American inventor, was born in Ohio.
Separate **nouns of direct address**	You, John, are my only hope in this moment.
Separate **interrogative tags**	This is the last time, correct?
Separate **contrasts**	You are my friend, not my enemy.
Writing **dates**	July 4, 1776, is an important date to remember.
Writing **addresses**	He is meeting me at 456 Delaware Avenue, Washington, D.C., tomorrow morning.
Writing **geographical names**	Paris, France, is my favorite city.
Writing **titles**	John Smith, PhD, will be visiting your class today.
Separate **expressions like *he said***	"You can start," she said, "with an apology."

A comma is also used **between coordinate adjectives** not joined with *and*. However, not all adjectives are coordinate (i.e., equal or parallel). To determine if your adjectives are coordinate, try connecting them with *and* or reversing their order. If it still sounds right, they are coordinate.

Incorrect: The kind, brown dog followed me home.

Correct: The kind, loyal dog followed me home.

Review Video: When to Use a Comma
Visit mometrix.com/academy and enter code: 786797

SEMICOLONS

The semicolon is used to join closely related independent clauses without the need for a coordinating conjunction. Semicolons are also used in place of commas to separate list elements that have internal commas. Some rules for semicolons include:

Use Case	Example
Between closely connected independent clauses **not connected with a coordinating conjunction**	You are right; we should go with your plan.
Between independent clauses **linked with a transitional word**	I think that we can agree on this; however, I am not sure about my friends.
Between items in a **series that has internal punctuation**	I have visited New York, New York; Augusta, Maine; and Baltimore, Maryland.

Review Video: How to Use Semicolons
Visit mometrix.com/academy and enter code: 370605

COLONS

The colon is used to call attention to the words that follow it. When used in a sentence, a colon should only come at the **end** of a **complete sentence**. The rules for colons are as follows:

Use Case	Example
After an independent clause to **make a list**	I want to learn many languages: Spanish, German, and Italian.
For **explanations**	There is one thing that stands out on your resume: responsibility.
To give a **quote**	He started with an idea: "We are able to do more than we imagine."
After the **greeting in a formal letter**	To Whom It May Concern:
Show **hours and minutes**	It is 3:14 p.m.
Separate a **title and subtitle**	The essay is titled "America: A Short Introduction to a Modern Country."

Review Video: Using Colons
Visit mometrix.com/academy and enter code: 868673

PARENTHESES

Parentheses are used for additional information. Also, they can be used to put labels for letters or numbers in a series. Parentheses should be not be used very often. If they are overused, parentheses can be a distraction instead of a help.

Examples:

Extra Information: The rattlesnake (see Image 2) is a dangerous snake of North and South America.

Series: Include in the email (1) your name, (2) your address, and (3) your question for the author.

Review Video: Parentheses
Visit mometrix.com/academy and enter code: 947743

QUOTATION MARKS

Use quotation marks to close off **direct quotations** of a person's spoken or written words. Do not use quotation marks around indirect quotations. An indirect quotation gives someone's message without using the person's exact words. Use **single quotation marks** to close off a quotation inside a quotation.

Direct Quote: Nancy said, "I am waiting for Henry to arrive."

Indirect Quote: Henry said that he is going to be late to the meeting.

Quote inside a Quote: The teacher asked, "Has everyone read 'The Gift of the Magi'?"

Quotation marks should be used around the titles of **short works**: newspaper and magazine articles, poems, short stories, songs, television episodes, radio programs, and subdivisions of books or websites.

Examples:

"Rip Van Winkle" (short story by Washington Irving)

"O Captain! My Captain!" (poem by Walt Whitman)

Although it is not standard usage, quotation marks are sometimes used to highlight **irony** or the use of words to mean something other than their dictionary definition. This type of usage should be employed sparingly, if at all.

Examples:

The boss warned Frank that he was walking on "thin ice."	Frank is not walking on real ice. Instead, he is being warned to avoid mistakes.
The teacher thanked the young man for his "honesty."	The quotation marks around *honesty* show that the teacher does not believe the young man's explanation.

Review Video: Quotation Marks
Visit mometrix.com/academy and enter code: 884918

Periods and commas are put **inside** quotation marks. Colons and semicolons are put **outside** the quotation marks. Question marks and exclamation points are placed inside quotation marks when they are part of a quote. When the question or exclamation mark goes with the whole sentence, the mark is left outside of the quotation marks.

Examples:

Period and comma	We read "The Gift of the Magi," "The Skylight Room," and "The Cactus."
Semicolon	They watched "The Nutcracker"; then, they went home.
Exclamation mark that is a part of a quote	The crowd cheered, "Victory!"
Question mark that goes with the whole sentence	Is your favorite short story "The Tell-Tale Heart"?

Apostrophes

An apostrophe is used to show **possession** or the **deletion of letters in contractions**. An apostrophe is not needed with the possessive pronouns *his, hers, its, ours, theirs, whose*, and *yours*.

Singular Nouns: David's car | a book's theme | my brother's board game

Plural Nouns that end with ***-s***: the scissors' handle | boys' basketball

Plural Nouns that end without ***-s***: Men's department | the people's adventure

Review Video: When to Use an Apostrophe
Visit mometrix.com/academy and enter code: 213068

Review Video: Punctuation Errors in Possessive Pronouns
Visit mometrix.com/academy and enter code: 221438

Hyphens

Hyphens are used to **separate compound words**. Use hyphens in the following cases:

Use Case	Example
Compound numbers from 21 to 99 when written out in words	This team needs twenty-five points to win the game.
Written-out fractions that are used as adjectives	The recipe says that we need a three-fourths cup of butter.
Compound adjectives that come before a noun	The well-fed dog took a nap.
Unusual compound words that would be hard to read or easily confused with other words	This is the best anti-itch cream on the market.

Note: This is not a complete set of the rules for hyphens. A dictionary is the best tool for knowing if a compound word needs a hyphen.

Review Video: Hyphens
Visit mometrix.com/academy and enter code: 981632

Dashes

Dashes are used to show a **break** or a **change in thought** in a sentence or to act as parentheses in a sentence. When typing, use two hyphens to make a dash. Do not put a space before or after the dash. The following are the functions of dashes:

Use Case	Example
Set off parenthetical statements or an **appositive with internal punctuation**	The three trees—oak, pine, and magnolia—are coming on a truck tomorrow.
Show a **break or change in tone or thought**	The first question—how silly of me—does not have a correct answer.

Ellipsis Marks

The ellipsis mark has **three** periods (...) to show when **words have been removed** from a quotation. If a **full sentence or more** is removed from a quoted passage, you need to use **four** periods to show the removed text and the end punctuation mark. The ellipsis mark should not be used at the beginning of a quotation. The ellipsis mark should also not be used at the end of a quotation unless some words have been deleted from the end of the final quoted sentence.

Example:

> "Then he picked up the groceries...paid for them...later he went home."

Brackets

There are two main reasons to use brackets:

Use Case	Example
Placing **parentheses inside of parentheses**	The hero of this story, Paul Revere (a silversmith and industrialist [see Ch. 4]), rode through towns of Massachusetts to warn of advancing British troops.
Adding **clarification or detail to a quotation** that is not part of the quotation	The father explained, "My children are planning to attend my alma mater [State University]."

Review Video: Brackets
Visit mometrix.com/academy and enter code: 727546

Common Usage Mistakes

Word Confusion

Which, That, and Who

The words *which*, *that*, and *who* can act as **relative pronouns** to help clarify or describe a noun.

Which is used for things only.

Example: Andrew's car, *which is old and rusty,* broke down last week.

That is used for people or things. *That* is usually informal when used to describe people.

Example: Is this the only book *that Louis L'Amour wrote?*

Example: Is Louis L'Amour the author *that wrote Western novels?*

Who is used for people or for animals that have an identity or personality.

Example: Mozart was the composer *who wrote those operas.*

Example: John's dog, *who is called Max,* is large and fierce.

Homophones

Homophones are words that sound alike (or similar) but have different **spellings** and **definitions**. A homophone is a type of **homonym**, which is a pair or group of words that are pronounced or spelled the same, but do not mean the same thing.

To, Too, and Two

To can be an adverb or a preposition for showing direction, purpose, and relationship. See your dictionary for the many other ways to use *to* in a sentence.

Examples: I went to the store. | I want to go with you.

Too is an adverb that means *also, as well, very,* or *in excess.*

Examples: I can walk a mile too. | You have eaten too much.

Two is a number.

Example: You have two minutes left.

There, Their, and They're

There can be an adjective, adverb, or pronoun. Often, *there* is used to show a place or to start a sentence.

Examples: I went there yesterday. | There is something in his pocket.

Their is a pronoun that is used to show ownership.

Examples: He is their father. | This is their fourth apology this week.

They're is a contraction of *they are.*

Example: Did you know that they're in town?

Knew and New

Knew is the past tense of *know*.

> Example: I knew the answer.

New is an adjective that means something is current, has not been used, or is modern.

> Example: This is my new phone.

Then and Than

Then is an adverb that indicates sequence or order:

> Example: I'm going to run to the library and then come home.

Than is special-purpose word used only for comparisons:

> Example: Susie likes chips more than candy.

Its and It's

Its is a pronoun that shows ownership.

> Example: The guitar is in its case.

It's is a contraction of *it is*.

> Example: It's an honor and a privilege to meet you.

Note: The *h* in honor is silent, so *honor* starts with the vowel sound *o*, which must have the article *an*.

Your and You're

Your is a pronoun that shows ownership.

> Example: This is your moment to shine.

You're is a contraction of *you are*.

> Example: Yes, you're correct.

Saw and Seen

Saw is the past-tense form of *see*.

> Example: I saw a turtle on my walk this morning.

Seen is the past participle of *see*.

> Example: I have seen this movie before.

Affect and Effect

There are two main reasons that *affect* and *effect* are so often confused: 1) both words can be used as either a noun or a verb, and 2) unlike most homophones, their usage and meanings are closely related to each other. Here is a quick rundown of the four usage options:

Affect (n): feeling, emotion, or mood that is displayed

> Example: The patient had a flat *affect*. (i.e., his face showed little or no emotion)

Affect (v): to alter, to change, to influence

Example: The sunshine *affects* the plant's growth.

Effect (n): a result, a consequence

Example: What *effect* will this weather have on our schedule?

Effect (v): to bring about, to cause to be

Example: These new rules will *effect* order in the office.

The noun form of *affect* is rarely used outside of technical medical descriptions, so if a noun form is needed on the test, you can safely select *effect*. The verb form of *effect* is not as rare as the noun form of *affect*, but it's still not all that likely to show up on your test. If you need a verb and you can't decide which to use based on the definitions, choosing *affect* is your best bet.

HOMOGRAPHS

Homographs are words that share the same spelling, but have different meanings and sometimes different pronunciations. To figure out which meaning is being used, you should be looking for context clues. The context clues give hints to the meaning of the word. For example, the word *spot* has many meanings. It can mean "a place" or "a stain or blot." In the sentence "After my lunch, I saw a spot on my shirt," the word *spot* means "a stain or blot." The context clues of "After my lunch" and "on my shirt" guide you to this decision. A homograph is another type of homonym.

BANK

(noun): an establishment where money is held for savings or lending

(verb): to collect or pile up

CONTENT

(noun): the topics that will be addressed within a book

(adjective): pleased or satisfied

(verb): to make someone pleased or satisfied

FINE

(noun): an amount of money that acts a penalty for an offense

(adjective): very small or thin

(adverb): in an acceptable way

(verb): to make someone pay money as a punishment

INCENSE

(noun): a material that is burned in religious settings and makes a pleasant aroma

(verb): to frustrate or anger

LEAD

(noun): the first or highest position

(noun): a heavy metallic element

(verb): to direct a person or group of followers

(adjective): containing lead

Object

(noun): a lifeless item that can be held and observed

(verb): to disagree

Produce

(noun): fruits and vegetables

(verb): to make or create something

Refuse

(noun): garbage or debris that has been thrown away

(verb): to not allow

Subject

(noun): an area of study

(verb): to force or subdue

Tear

(noun): a fluid secreted by the eyes

(verb): to separate or pull apart

Commonly Misused Words and Phrases

A Lot

The phrase *a lot* should always be written as two words; never as *alot.*

Correct: That's a lot of chocolate!

Incorrect: He does that alot.

Can

The word *can* is used to describe things that are possible occurrences; the word *may* is used to described things that are allowed to happen.

Correct: May I have another piece of pie?

Correct: I can lift three of these bags of mulch at a time.

Incorrect: Mom said we can stay up thirty minutes later tonight.

Could Have

The phrase *could of* is often incorrectly substituted for the phrase *could have*. Similarly, *could of, may of,* and *might of* are sometimes used in place of the correct phrases *could have, may have,* and *might have.*

Correct: If I had known, I would have helped out.

Incorrect: Well, that could of gone much worse than it did.

Myself

The word *myself* is a reflexive pronoun, often incorrectly used in place of *I* or *me*.

> **Correct**: He let me do it myself.
>
> **Incorrect**: The job was given to Dave and myself.

Off

The phrase *off of* is a redundant expression that should be avoided. In most cases, it can be corrected simply by removing *of*.

> **Correct**: My dog chased the squirrel off its perch on the fence.
>
> **Incorrect**: He finally moved his plate off of the table.

Supposed To

The phrase *suppose to* is sometimes used incorrectly in place of the phrase *supposed to*.

> **Correct**: I was supposed to go to the store this afternoon.
>
> **Incorrect**: When are we suppose to get our grades?

Try To

The phrase *try and* is often used in informal writing and conversation to replace the correct phrase *try to*.

> **Correct**: It's a good policy to try to satisfy every customer who walks in the door.
>
> **Incorrect**: Don't try and do too much.

Chapter Quiz

Ready to see how well you retained what you just read? Scan the QR code to go directly to the chapter quiz interface for this study guide. If you're using a computer, simply visit the bonus page at **mometrix.com/bonus948/fsot** and click the Chapter Quizzes link.

United States Government

Transform passive reading into active learning! After immersing yourself in this chapter, put your comprehension to the test by taking a quiz. The insights you gained will stay with you longer this way. Scan the QR code to go directly to the chapter quiz interface for this study guide. If you're using a computer, simply visit the bonus page at **mometrix.com/bonus948/fsot** and click the Chapter Quizzes link.

US Government and Citizenship

Political Science and Its Ties to Other Major Disciplines

Political science focuses on studying different governments and how they compare to each other, general political theory, ways political theory is put into action, how nations and governments interact with each other, and a general study of governmental structure and function. Other elements of **political science** include the study of elections, governmental administration at various levels, development and action of political parties, and how values such as freedom, power, justice, and equality are expressed in different political cultures. Political science also encompasses elements of other disciplines, including:

- **History**—how historical events have shaped political thought and process
- **Sociology**—the effects of various stages of social development on the growth and development of government and politics
- **Anthropology**—the effects of governmental process on the culture of an individual group and its relationships with other groups
- **Economics**—how government policies regulate the distribution of products and how they can control and/or influence the economy in general

General Political Theory

Based on general political theory, the four major purposes of any given government are:

- **Ensuring national security**—the government protects against international, domestic, and terrorist attacks and also ensures ongoing security through negotiating and establishing relationships with other governments.
- **Providing public services**—the government should "promote the general welfare," as stated in the Preamble to the US Constitution, by providing whatever is needed to its citizens.
- **Ensuring social order**—the government supplies means of settling conflicts among citizens as well as making laws to govern the nation, state, or city.
- **Making decisions regarding the economy**—laws help form the economic policy of the country, regarding both domestic and international trade and related issues. The government also has the ability to distribute goods and wealth to some extent among its citizens.

Main Theories Regarding the Origin of the State

There are four main theories regarding the origin of the state:

- **Evolutionary**—the state evolved from the family, with the head of state the equivalent of the family's patriarch or matriarch.
- **Force**—one person or group of people brought everyone in an area under their control, forming the first government.

- **Divine Right**—certain people were chosen by the prevailing deity to be the rulers of the nation, which is itself created by the deity or deities.
- **Social Contract**—there is no natural order. The people allow themselves to be governed to maintain social order, while the state, in turn, promises to protect the people they govern. If the government fails to protect its people, the people have the right to seek new leaders.

INFLUENCES OF PHILOSOPHERS ON POLITICAL STUDY

Ancient Greek philosophers **Aristotle** and **Plato** believed political science would lead to order in political matters and that this scientifically organized order would create stable, just societies.

Thomas Aquinas adapted the ideas of Aristotle to a Christian perspective. His ideas stated that individuals should have certain rights but also certain duties, and that these rights and duties should determine the type and extent of government rule. In stating that laws should limit the role of government, he laid the groundwork for ideas that would eventually become modern constitutionalism.

Niccolò Machiavelli, author of *The Prince*, was a proponent of politics based on power. He is often considered the founder of modern political science.

Thomas Hobbes, author of *Leviathan* (1651), believed that individuals' lives were focused solely on a quest for power and that the state must work to control this urge. Hobbes felt that people were completely unable to live harmoniously without the intervention of a powerful, undivided government.

CONTRIBUTIONS OF JOHN LOCKE, MONTESQUIEU, AND ROUSSEAU TO POLITICAL SCIENCE

John Locke published *Two Treatises of Government* in 1689. This work argued against the ideas of Thomas Hobbes. He put forth the theory of *tabula rasa*—that people are born with minds like blank slates. Individual minds are molded by experience, not innate knowledge or intuition. He also believed that all men should be independent and equal. Many of Locke's ideas found their way into the Constitution of the United States.

The two French philosophers, **Montesquieu** and **Rousseau**, heavily influenced the French Revolution (1789-1799). They believed government policies and ideas should change to alleviate existing problems, an idea referred to as "liberalism." Rousseau, in particular, directly influenced the Revolution with writings such as *The Social Contract* (1762) and *Declaration of the Rights of Man and of the Citizen* (1789). Other ideas Rousseau and Montesquieu espoused included:

- Individual freedom and community welfare are of equal importance
- Man's innate goodness leads to natural harmony
- Reason develops with the rise of civilized society
- Individual citizens carry certain obligations to the existing government

POLITICAL IDEOLOGIES OF DAVID HUME, JEREMY BENTHAM, JOHN STUART MILL, JOHANN GOTTLIEB FICHTE, AND GEORG HEGEL

David Hume and **Jeremy Bentham** believed politics should have as its main goal maintaining "the greatest happiness for the greatest number." Hume also believed in empiricism, or that ideas should not be believed until the proof has been observed. He was a natural skeptic and always sought out the truth of matters rather than believing what he was told.

John Stuart Mill, a British philosopher and economist, made significant contributions to the fields of social and economic theory. A majorly influential thinker in the realm of classical liberalism, Mill believed in progressive policies such as women's suffrage, emancipation, and the development of labor unions and farming cooperatives. His ideas on free speech and the harm principle were the basis for the "clear and present danger" test outlined by Oliver Wendell Holmes Jr. when determining if speech is protected by the First Amendment of the US Constitution.

Johann Fichte and **Georg Hegel**, German philosophers in the late 18th and early 19th centuries, supported a form of liberalism grounded largely in socialism and a sense of nationalism.

Main Political Orientations

The four main political orientations are:

- **Liberal**—liberals believe that government should work to increase equality, even at the expense of some freedoms. Government should assist those in need, focusing on enforced social justice and free basic services for everyone.
- **Conservative**—a conservative believes that government should be limited in most cases. The government should allow its citizens to help one another and solve their own problems rather than enforcing solutions. Business should not be overregulated, allowing a free market.
- **Moderate**—this ideology incorporates some liberal and some conservative values, generally falling somewhere between in overall belief.
- **Libertarian**—libertarians believe that the government's role should be limited to protecting the life and liberty of citizens. Government should not be involved in any citizen's life unless that citizen is encroaching upon the rights of another.

Major Principles of Government as Outlined in the United States Constitution

The six major principles of government as outlined in the United States Constitution are:

- **Federalism**—the power of the government does not belong entirely to the national government but is divided between federal and state governments.
- **Popular sovereignty**—the government is determined by the people and gains its authority and power from the people.
- **Separation of powers**—the government is divided into three branches (executive, legislative, and judicial) with each having its own set of powers.
- **Judicial review**—courts at all levels of government can declare laws invalid if they contradict the constitutions of individual states, or the US Constitution, with the Supreme Court serving as the final judicial authority on decisions of this kind.
- **Checks and balances**—no single branch can act without input from another, and each branch has the power to "check" any other, as well as balance other branches' powers.
- **Limited government**—governmental powers are limited, and certain individual rights are defined as inviolable by the government.

Types of Powers Delegated to the National Government by the US Constitution

The structure of the US government divides power between national and state governments. Powers delegated to the federal government by the Constitution are:

- **Expressed powers**—powers directly defined in the Constitution, including power to declare war, regulate commerce, make money, and collect taxes
- **Implied powers**—powers the national government must have in order to carry out the expressed powers
- **Inherent powers**—powers inherent to any government, not expressly defined in the Constitution

Some of these powers, such as collection and levying of taxes, are also granted to the individual state governments.

Primary Positions of Federalism and Development through the Years in the US

The way federalism should be practiced has been the subject of debate since the writing of the Constitution. There were—and still are—two main factions regarding this issue:

- **States' rights**—those favoring the states' rights position feel that the state governments should take the lead in performing local actions to manage various problems.
- **Nationalist**—those favoring a nationalist position feel the national government should take the lead to deal with those same matters.

The flexibility of the Constitution has allowed the US government to shift and adapt as the needs of the country have changed. Power has often shifted from the state governments to the national government and back again, and both levels of government have developed various ways to influence each other.

Effects of Federalism on Policy-Making and the Balance of Politics in the US

Federalism has three major effects on **public policy** in the US:

- Determining whether the local, state, or national government originates policy
- Affecting how policies are made
- Ensuring policy-making functions under a set of limitations

Federalism also influences the **political balance of power** in the US by:

- Making it difficult, if not impossible, for a single political party to seize total power
- Ensuring that individuals can participate in the political system at various levels
- Making it possible for individuals working within the system to be able to affect policy at some level, whether local or more widespread

Three Branches of the US Federal Government

The following are the three branches of the US Federal government and the individuals that belong to each branch:

- **Legislative Branch**—this consists of the two houses of Congress: the House of Representatives and the Senate. All members of the Legislative Branch are elected officials.
- **Executive Branch**—this branch is made up of the president, vice president, presidential advisors, and other various cabinet members. Advisors and cabinet members are appointed by the president, but they must be approved by Congress.
- **Judicial Branch**—the federal court system, headed by the Supreme Court.

Review Video: Three Branches of Government
Visit mometrix.com/academy and enter code: 718704

Major Responsibilities of the Three Branches of the Federal Government

The three branches of the federal government each have specific roles and responsibilities:

- The **Legislative Branch** is largely concerned with lawmaking. All laws must be approved by Congress before they go into effect. They are also responsible for regulating money and trade, approving presidential appointments, and establishing organizations like the postal service and federal courts. Congress can also propose amendments to the Constitution, and can impeach, or bring charges against, the president. Only Congress can declare war.

- The **Executive Branch** carries out laws, treaties, and war declarations enacted by Congress. The president can also veto bills approved by Congress, and serves as commander in chief of the US military. The president appoints cabinet members, ambassadors to foreign countries, and federal judges.
- The **Judicial Branch** makes decisions on challenges as to whether laws passed by Congress meet the requirements of the US Constitution. The Supreme Court may also choose to review decisions made by lower courts to determine their constitutionality.

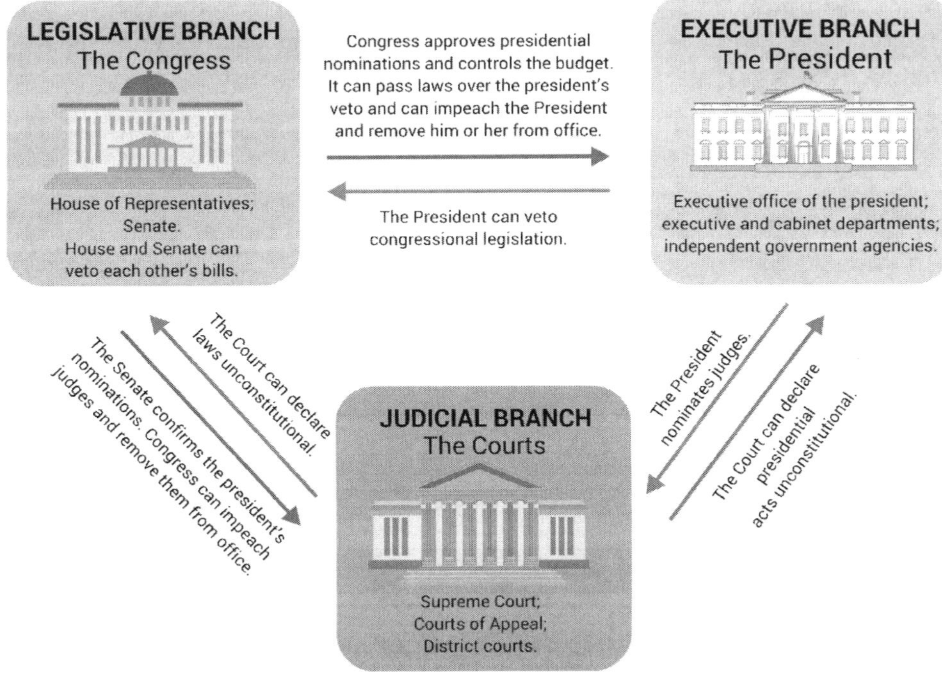

US Citizenship

Qualifications of a US citizen/How Citizenship May Be Lost

Anyone born in the US, born abroad to a US citizen, or who has gone through a process of naturalization is considered a **citizen** of the United States. It is possible to lose US citizenship as a result of conviction of certain crimes such as treason. Citizenship may also be lost if a citizen pledges an oath to another country or serves in the military of a country engaged in hostilities with the US. A US citizen can also choose to hold dual citizenship, work as an expatriate in another country without losing US citizenship, or even to renounce citizenship if he or she so chooses.

Rights, Duties, and Responsibilities Granted to or Expected from Citizens

Citizens are granted certain rights under the US government. The most important of these are defined in the **Bill of Rights**, and include freedom of speech, religion, assembly, and a variety of other rights the government is not allowed to remove. A US citizen also has a number of **duties**:

- Paying taxes
- Loyalty to the government (though the US does not prosecute those who criticize or seek to change the government)
- Support and defense of the Constitution

- Serving in the Armed Forces when required by law
- Obeying laws as set forth by the various levels of government.

Responsibilities of a US citizen include:

- Voting in elections
- Respecting one another's rights and not infringing on them
- Staying informed about various political and national issues
- Respecting one another's beliefs

BILL OF RIGHTS

IMPORTANCE OF THE BILL OF RIGHTS

The first ten amendments of the US Constitution are known as the **Bill of Rights**. These amendments prevent the government from infringing upon certain freedoms that the Founding Fathers felt were natural rights that already belonged to all people. These rights included freedom of speech, freedom of religion, freedom of assembly, and the right to bear arms. Many of the rights were formulated in direct response to the way the colonists felt they had been mistreated by the British government.

RIGHTS GRANTED IN THE BILL OF RIGHTS

The first ten amendments were passed by Congress in 1789. Three-fourths of the existing thirteen states had ratified them by December of 1791, making them official additions to the Constitution. The rights granted in the Bill of Rights are:

- **First Amendment**—freedom of religion, speech, freedom of the press, and the right to assemble and to petition the government
- **Second Amendment**—the right to bear arms
- **Third Amendment**—Congress cannot force individuals to house troops
- **Fourth Amendment**—protection from unreasonable search and seizure
- **Fifth Amendment**—no individual is required to testify against himself, and no individual may be tried twice for the same crime
- **Sixth Amendment**—the right to criminal trial by jury and the right to legal counsel
- **Seventh Amendment**—the right to civil trial by jury
- **Eighth Amendment**—protection from excessive bail or cruel and unusual punishment
- **Ninth Amendment**—prevents rights not explicitly named in the Constitution from being taken away because they are not named
- **Tenth Amendment**—any rights not directly delegated to the national government, or not directly prohibited by the government from the states, belong to the states or to the people

Review Video: Bill of Rights
Visit mometrix.com/academy and enter code: 585149

SITUATIONS WHERE THE GOVERNMENT RESTRICTS OR REGULATES FIRST AMENDMENT FREEDOMS

In some cases, the government restricts certain elements of First Amendment rights. Some examples include:

- **Freedom of religion**—when a religion espouses illegal activities, the government often restricts these forms of religious expression. Examples include polygamy, animal sacrifice, and use of illicit drugs or illegal substances.
- **Freedom of speech**—this can be restricted if exercise of free speech endangers other people.
- **Freedom of the press**—laws prevent the press from publishing falsehoods.

In **emergency situations** such as wartime, stricter restrictions are sometimes placed on these rights, especially rights to free speech and assembly, and freedom of the press, in order to protect national security.

Constitution's Address of the Rights of Those Accused of Crimes

The US Constitution makes allowances for the **rights of criminals**, or anyone who has transgressed established laws. There must be laws to protect citizens from criminals, but those accused of crimes must also be protected and their basic rights as individuals preserved. In addition, the Constitution protects individuals from the power of authorities to prevent police forces and other enforcement organizations from becoming oppressive. The fourth, fifth, sixth, and eighth amendments specifically address these rights.

Supreme Court's Provision of Equal Protection Under the Law for All Individuals

When the Founding Fathers wrote in the Declaration of Independence that "all men are created equal," they actually were referring to men, and, in fact, defined citizens as white men who owned land. However, as the country has developed and changed, the definition has expanded to more wholly include all people.

"**Equality**" does not mean all people are inherently the same, but it does mean they all should be granted the same rights and should be treated the same by the government. Amendments to the Constitution have granted citizenship and voting rights to all Americans regardless of race or gender. The Supreme Court evaluates various laws and court decisions to determine if they properly represent the idea of **equal protection**. One sample case was Brown v. Board of Education in 1954, which declared separate-but-equal treatment to be unconstitutional.

Civil Liberty Challenges Addressed in Current Political Discussions

The **civil rights movements** of the 1960s and the ongoing struggle for the rights of women and other minorities have sparked **challenges to existing law**. In addition, debate has raged over how much information the government should be required to divulge to the public. Major issues in the 21st century political climate include:

- Continued debate over women's rights, especially regarding equal pay for equal work
- Debate over affirmative action to encourage hiring of minorities
- Debate over civil rights of homosexuals, including marriage and military service
- Decisions as to whether minorities should be compensated for past discriminatory practices
- Balance between the public's right to know and the government's need to maintain national security
- Balance between the public's right to privacy and national security

Civil Liberties vs. Civil Rights

While the terms *civil liberties* and *civil rights* are often used interchangeably, in actuality, their definitions are slightly different. The two concepts work together, however, to define the basics of a free state:

- **"Civil liberties"** define the constitutional freedoms guaranteed to citizens. Examples include freedoms such as free speech, privacy, or free thought.
- **"Civil rights"** are guarantees of or protections of civil liberties. One comparison can be found in the case of freedom of religion. The civil liberty is that one has the freedom to practice the religion of his or her choice, whereas the civil right would protect that individual from being denied a job on the basis of their religion.

Suffrage, Franchise, and the Change of Voting Rights Over the Course of American History

Suffrage and franchise both refer to the right to **vote**. As the US developed as a nation, there was much debate over which individuals should hold this right. In the early years, only white male landowners were granted suffrage. By the 19th century, most states had franchised, or granted the right to vote, to all adult white males. The **Fifteenth Amendment** of 1870 granted suffrage to formerly enslaved men. The **Nineteenth Amendment** gave women the right to vote in 1920, and in 1971 the **Twenty-sixth Amendment** expanded voting rights to include any US citizen over the age of eighteen. However, those who have not been granted full citizenship and citizens who have committed certain crimes do not have voting rights.

Ways in Which the Voting Process Has Changed Over the Years

The first elections in the US were held by **public ballot**. However, election abuses soon became common, since public ballot made it easy to intimidate, threaten, or otherwise influence the votes of individuals or groups of individuals. New practices were put into play, including **registering voters** before elections took place and using a **secret or Australian ballot**. In 1892, the introduction of the **voting machine** further privatized the voting process, since it allowed complete privacy for voting. Today, debate continues about the accuracy of various voting methods, including high-tech voting machines and even low-tech punch cards.

Effect of Political Parties on the Functioning of an Individual Government

Different types and numbers of political parties can have a significant effect on how a government is run. If there is a **single party**, or a one-party system, the government is defined by that one party, and all policy is based on that party's beliefs. In a **two-party system**, two parties with different viewpoints compete for power and influence. The US is basically a two-party system, with checks and balances to make it difficult for one party to gain complete power over the other. There are also **multiparty systems**, with three or more parties. In multiparty systems, various parties will often come to agreements in order to form a majority and shift the balance of power.

Development of Political Parties in the US.

George Washington was adamantly against the establishment of **political parties**, based on the abuses perpetrated by such parties in Britain. However, political parties developed in US politics almost from the beginning. Major parties throughout US history have included:

- **Federalists and Democratic-Republicans**—these parties formed in the late 1700s and disagreed on the balance of power between national and state government.
- **Democrats and Whigs**—these developed in the 1830s, and many political topics of the time centered on national economic issues.
- **Democrats and Republicans**—the Republican Party developed before the Civil War, after the collapse of the Whig party, and the two parties debated issues centering on slavery and economic issues, such as taxation.

While third parties sometimes enter the picture in US politics, the government is basically a two-party system, dominated by the Democrats and Republicans.

Functions of Political Parties

Political parties form organizations at all levels of government. Activities of individual parties include:

- Recruiting and backing candidates for offices
- Discussing various issues with the public, increasing public awareness
- Working toward compromise on difficult issues
- Staffing government offices and providing administrative support

At the administrative level, parties work to ensure that viable candidates are available for elections and that offices and staff are in place to support candidates as they run for office and afterward, when they are elected.

Processes of Selecting Political Candidates

Historically, in the quest for political office, a potential candidate has followed one of the following four processes:

- **Nominating convention**—an official meeting of the members of a party for the express purpose of nominating candidates for upcoming elections. The Democratic National Convention and the Republican National Convention, convened to announce candidates for the presidency, are examples of this kind of gathering.
- **Caucus**—a meeting, usually attended by a party's leaders. Some states still use caucuses, but not all.
- **Primary election**—the most common method of choosing candidates today, the primary is a publicly held election to choose candidates.
- **Petition**—signatures gathered to place a candidate on the ballot. Petitions can also be used to place legislation on a ballot.

Ways the Average Citizen Participates in the Political Process

In addition to voting for elected officials, American citizens are able to participate in the political process through several other avenues. These include:

- Participating in local government
- Participating in caucuses for large elections
- Volunteering to help political parties
- Running for election to local, state, or national offices

Individuals can also donate money to political causes or support political groups that focus on specific causes such as abortion, wildlife conservation, or women's rights. These groups often make use of **representatives** who lobby legislators to act in support of their efforts.

Ways in Which Political Campaign Gains Funding

Political campaigns are very expensive. In addition to the basic necessities of a campaign office, including office supplies, office space, etc., a large quantity of the money that funds a political campaign goes toward **advertising**. Money to fund a political campaign can come from several sources, including:

- The candidate's personal funds
- Donations by individuals
- Special interest groups

The most significant source of campaign funding is **special interest groups**. Groups in favor of certain policies will donate money to candidates they believe will support those policies. Special interest groups also do their own advertising in support of candidates they endorse.

Importance of Free Press and the Media

The right to free speech guaranteed in the first amendment to the Constitution allows the media to report on **government and political activities** without fear of retribution. Because the media has access to information about the government, the government's policies and actions, and debates and discussions that occur in Congress, it can keep the public informed about the inner workings of the government. The media can also draw attention to injustices, imbalances of power, and other transgressions the government or government officials might commit. However, media outlets may, like special interest groups, align themselves with certain political viewpoints and skew their reports to fit that viewpoint. The rise of the **internet** has made media reporting even more complex, as news can be found from an infinite variety of sources, both reliable and unreliable.

Forms of Government

Anarchism, Communism, and Dictatorship

Anarchists believe that all government should be eliminated and that individuals should rule themselves. Historically, anarchists have used violence and assassination to further their beliefs.

Communism is based on class conflict, revolution, and a one-party state. Ideally, a communist government would involve a single government for the entire world. Communist government controls the production and flow of goods and services rather than leaving this to companies or individuals.

Dictatorship involves rule by a single individual. If rule is enforced by a small group, this is referred to as an oligarchy. Dictators tend to rule with a violent hand, using a highly repressive police force to ensure control over the populace.

Fascism and Monarchy

Fascism centers on a single leader and is, ideologically, an oppositional belief to communism. **Fascism** includes a single-party state and centralized control. The power of the fascist leader lies in the "cult of personality," and the fascist state often focuses on expansion and conquering of other nations. **Monarchy** was the major form of government for Europe through most of its history.

A monarchy is led by a king or a queen. This position is hereditary, and the rulers are not elected. In modern times, constitutional monarchy has developed, where the king and queen still exist, but most of the governmental decisions are made by democratic institutions such as a parliament.

Presidential System and Socialism

A presidential system, like a parliamentary system, has a legislature and political parties, but there is no difference between the head of state and the head of government. Instead of separating these functions, an elected president performs both. Election of the president can be direct or indirect, and the president may not necessarily belong to the largest political party. In **socialism**, the state controls the production of goods, though it does not necessarily own all means of production. The state also provides a variety of social services to citizens and helps guide the economy. A democratic form of government often exists in socialist countries.

Review Video: Communism vs. Socialism
Visit mometrix.com/academy and enter code: 917677

Totalitarian and Authoritarian Systems

A totalitarian system believes everything should be under the control of the government—from resource production, to the press, to religion, and other social institutions. All aspects of life under a totalitarian system must conform to the ideals of the government. **Authoritarian** governments practice widespread state authority but do not necessarily dismantle all public institutions. If a church, for example, exists as an organization but poses no threat to the authority of the state, an authoritarian government might leave it as it is. While all totalitarian governments are by definition authoritarian, a government can be authoritarian without becoming totalitarian.

Review Video: Totalitarianism vs. Authoritarianism
Visit mometrix.com/academy and enter code: 104046

Parliamentary and Democratic Systems

In a parliamentary system, government involves a legislature and a variety of political parties. The head of government, usually a prime minister, is typically the head of the dominant party. A head of state can be elected, or this position can be taken by a monarch, as in Great Britain's constitutional monarchy system.

In a **democratic system** of government, the people elect their government representatives. The word *democracy* is a Greek term that means "rule of the people." There are two forms of democracy: direct and indirect. In a direct democracy, each issue or election is decided by a vote where each individual is counted separately. An indirect democracy employs a legislature that votes on issues that affect large numbers of people whom the legislative members represent. Democracy can exist as a parliamentary system or a presidential system. The US is a presidential, indirect democracy.

Realism, Liberalism, Institutionalism, and Constructivism in International Relations

The theory of realism states that nations are by nature aggressive and work in their own self-interest. Relations between nations are determined by military and economic strength. The nation is seen as the highest authority. **Liberalism** believes states can cooperate and that they act based on capability rather than power. This term was originally coined to describe Woodrow Wilson's theories on international cooperation. In **institutionalism**, institutions provide structure and incentive for cooperation among nations. Institutions are defined as a set of rules used to make international decisions. These institutions also help distribute power and determine how nations will interact. **Constructivism**, like liberalism, is based on international cooperation but recognizes that perceptions countries have of each other can affect their relations.

Review Video: Social Liberalism
Visit mometrix.com/academy and enter code: 624507

Effects of Foreign Policy on a Country's Position in World Affairs

Foreign policy is a set of goals, policies, and strategies that determine how an individual nation will interact with other countries. These strategies shift, sometimes quickly and drastically, according to actions or changes occurring in the other countries. However, a nation's **foreign policy** is often based on a certain set of ideals and national needs. Examples of US foreign policy include isolationism versus internationalism. In the 1800s, the US leaned more toward isolationism, exhibiting a reluctance to become involved in foreign affairs. The World Wars led to a period of internationalism, as the US entered these wars in support of other countries and joined the United Nations. Today's foreign policy tends more toward **interdependence**, or **globalism**, recognizing the widespread effects of issues like economic health.

Major Figures Involved in Determining and Enacting US Foreign Policy

US foreign policy is largely determined by Congress and the president, influenced by the secretary of state, secretary of defense, and the national security adviser. Executive officials carry out policies. The main departments in charge of these day-to-day issues are the **US Department of State**, also referred to as the State Department. The Department of State carries out policy, negotiates treaties, maintains diplomatic relations, assists citizens traveling in foreign countries, and ensures that the president is properly informed of any international issues. The **Department of Defense**, the largest executive department in the US, supervises the armed forces and provides assistance to the president in his role as commander-in-chief.

Major Types of International Organizations

Two types of international organizations are:

- **Intergovernmental organizations (IGOs)**. These organizations are made up of members from various national governments. The UN is an example of an intergovernmental organization. Treaties among the member nations determine the functions and powers of these groups.

- **Nongovernmental organizations (NGOs)**. An NGO lies outside the scope of any government and is usually supported through private donations. An example of an NGO is the International Red Cross, which works with governments all over the world when their countries are in crisis but is formally affiliated with no particular country or government.

Role of Diplomats in International Relations

Diplomats are individuals who reside in foreign countries in order to maintain communications between that country and their home country. They help negotiate trade agreements and environmental policies, as well as conveying official information to foreign governments. They also help to resolve conflicts between the countries, often working to sort out issues without making the conflicts official in any way. **Diplomats**, or **ambassadors**, are appointed in the US by the president. Appointments must be approved by Congress.

Role of the United Nations in International Relations and Diplomacy

The United Nations (**UN**) helps form international policies by hosting representatives of various countries who then provide input into policy decisions. Countries that are members of the UN must agree to abide by all final UN resolutions, but this is not always the case in practice, as dissent is not uncommon. If countries do not follow UN resolutions, the UN can decide on sanctions against those countries, often economic sanctions, such as trade restriction. The UN can also send military forces to problem areas, with "peacekeeping" troops brought in from member nations. An example of this function is the Korean War, the first war in which an international organization played a major role.

Civil Rights and Supreme Court Cases

The Civil Rights Act of 1871

The Civil Rights Act of 1871 was a statute passed following the Civil War. It was comprised of the **1870 Force Act** and the **1871 Ku Klux Klan Act**, and was passed primarily with the intention of protecting Southern black people from the Ku Klux Klan. Since it was passed in 1871, the statute has only undergone small changes. It has, however, been interpreted widely by the courts. In 1882, some parts of the Civil Rights Act of 1871 were found unconstitutional, but the Force Act and the Klan Act continued to be applied in civil rights cases in subsequent years.

Plessy v. Ferguson

Plessy v. Ferguson was an 1896 Supreme Court case. The case resulted in the decision that **de jure racial segregation** in **public facilities** was legal in the United States, and permitted states to restrict black people from using public facilities. The case originated when, in 1890, a black man named Homer Plessy decided to challenge a Louisiana law that segregated black and white people on trains by sitting in the white section of a train. Plessy was convicted of breaking the law in a Louisiana court, and the case was appealed to the US Supreme Court, where the Supreme Court upheld the Louisiana decision. The case established the legality of the doctrine of separate but equal, thereby allowing racial segregation. The decision was later overturned by **Brown v. the Board of Education of Topeka**.

The Fair Employment Act

The Fair Employment Act was signed by President Franklin Roosevelt in 1941. The purpose of the act was to **ban racial discrimination** in industries related to **national defense**, and it represented the very first federal law to ban discrimination in employment. The **Fair Employment Act** mandated that all federal government agencies and departments concerned with national defense, as well as private defense contractors, guaranteed that professional training would be conducted without discrimination based on race, creed, color, or national origin. The Fair Employment Act was followed by **Title VII of the 1964 Civil Rights Act**, which banned discrimination by private employers, and by **Executive Order 11246** in 1965, which concerned federal contractors and subcontractors.

Brown v. Board of Education

Brown versus the Board of Education of Topeka was a Supreme Court case that was decided in 1954. The case made it illegal for **racial segregation** to exist within **public education facilities.** This decision was based on the finding that separate but equal public educational facilities would not provide black and white students with the same standard of facilities. The case originated in 1951, when a lawsuit was filed by Topeka parents, who were recruited by the NAACP, against the Board of Education of the City of Topeka, Kansas in a US district court. The parents, one of whom was named Oliver Brown, wanted the Topeka Board of Education to eliminate racial segregation. The district court agreed that segregation had negative effects, but did not force the schools to desegregate because it found that black and white school facilities in the District were generally equal in standards. The case was appealed to the Supreme Court, where the finding was that separate educational facilities are unequal.

Bolling v. Sharpe

Bolling v. Sharpe was a 1954 Supreme Court case. Like Brown v. Board of Education, this case addressed issues concerning **segregation in public schools**. The case originated in 1949, when parents from Anacostia, an area in Washington, DC, petitioned the Board of Education of the District of Columbia to allow all races to attend a new school. The request was denied. A lawsuit was brought before the District Court for the District of Columbia on behalf of a student named Bolling and other students to admit them to the all-white school. The case was dismissed by the district court and taken to the Supreme Court. The Supreme Court ruled that the school had to be desegregated based on the Fifth Amendment.

Civil Rights Act of 1964

The Civil Rights Act of 1964 was passed to protect the rights of both **black men** and **women**. It served as part of the foundation for the women's rights movement. The act was a catalyst for change in the United States, as it made it illegal to engage in acts of **discrimination** in public facilities, in government, and in employment. The Civil Rights Act prohibited unequal voter registration, prohibited discrimination in all public facilities involved in interstate commerce, supported desegregating public schools, ensured equal protection for black people in federally funded programs, and banned employment discrimination.

The Pregnancy Discrimination Act

The Pregnancy Discrimination Act was passed in 1978 as an amendment to the sex discrimination clause of the Civil Rights Act of 1964. The **Pregnancy Discrimination Act** stipulated that people cannot be discriminated against due to pregnancy, childbirth, or medical issues related to pregnancy or childbirth. If a person becomes pregnant, gives birth, or has related medical conditions, they must receive treatment that is equivalent to that received by other employees and also receive equal benefits as other employees. The **Family and Medical Leave Act** was passed in 1993 to advance protections under the Pregnancy Discrimination Act.

Civil Rights Act of 1968

The Civil Rights Act of 1968 was passed following the passing of the Civil Rights Act of 1964. The act made it illegal to **discriminate** against individuals during the sale, rental, or financing of **housing**. Therefore, the act is also referred to as the **Fair Housing Act of 1968**. The act made it illegal to refuse to sell or rent housing based on race, color, religion, or national origin. It also made it illegal to advertise housing for sale or rent and to specify a preference to rent or sell the property to an individual of a particular race, color, religion, or national origin. In addition, the act ensured protection for civil rights workers.

Age Discrimination in Employment Act

The Age Discrimination in Employment Act of 1967 made it illegal for employers to discriminate against people who are **forty years old** or greater in age. The act establishes standards for employer-provided pensions and benefits, and mandates that information regarding the needs of older workers be made publicly available. In addition to generally banning age discrimination, the **ADEA** specifies particular actions that are illegal. Employers may not specify that individuals of a certain age are preferred or are conversely restricted from applying to job ads. Age limits are only permitted to be mentioned in job ads if age has been shown to be a bona fide occupational qualification. The act stipulates that it is illegal to discriminate against age through apprenticeship programs and that it is illegal to restrict benefits to older employees. However, employers are permitted to lower the benefits provided to older employees based on age if the expense of providing fewer or lesser benefits is equivalent to the expense of providing benefits to younger employees.

Loving v. Virginia

Loving v. Virginia was a 1967 Supreme Court case that ruled that a particular law in Virginia known as the **Racial Integrity Act of 1924** was unconstitutional, as the law had prohibited interracial marriage. The Supreme Court ruling would put an end to **race-based restrictions on marriage**. The case originated when Mildred Jeter and Richard Loving, an interracial Virginia couple that was married in Washington, DC due to the Virginia state law prohibiting interracial marriage, returned to Virginia and received charges of violating the interracial marriage ban. After pleading guilty, the couple was forced to move to DC to avoid a jail sentence, where they brought their case to the Supreme Court on the premise that their Fourteenth Amendment rights had been violated. The Supreme Court found that the Virginia law was unconstitutional and overturned the conviction that the couple had been charged with.

Jones v. Mayer

Jones v. Mayer was a 1968 Supreme Court case that ruled that Congress has the authority to **regulate the sale of private property** for the purpose of preventing racial discrimination. This United States Supreme Court ruling was based on a legal statute that stipulates that it is illegal in the United States to commit acts of racial discrimination, both privately and publicly when selling or renting property. The United States Supreme Court ruled that the congressional power to uphold the statute extends from the power of Congress to uphold the Thirteenth Amendment.

Roe v. Wade

Roe v. Wade was a controversial 1973 US Supreme Court case. The case originated in 1970 in Texas, which had an **anti-abortion law**. The plaintiff was an unmarried pregnant woman who was assigned the name "Jane Roe" to protect her identity. Texas anti-abortion law characterized the acts of having or attempting to perform an abortion as crimes, with the exception of cases in which an abortion could save the life of a mother. The lawsuit argued that the Texas law was unconstitutionally vague and was not consistent with the rights guaranteed by the First, Fourth, Fifth, Ninth, and Fourteenth Amendments. While the Texas court ruled in favor of Roe, it did not rule that Texas had to discontinue the enforcement of its anti-abortion law. Roe appealed to the Supreme Court in 1971, and the court's decision in 1973 struck down Texas's abortion laws. The case overturned most state laws prohibiting abortion. In 2022, the supreme court reversed its decision in Roe v Wade, finding no constitutional basis for requiring states to permit abortion, effectively returning the authority to the states to decide.

Regents of the University of California v. Bakke

Regents of the University of California v. Bakke was a 1978 Supreme Court case that banned **quota systems** in the college admissions process but ruled that programs providing **advantages to minorities** are constitutionally sound. The case originated when Allan Bakke, a white male who was a strong student, applied to the University of California at Davis Medical School and was rejected. The school had a program that reserved admissions spots for minority applicants; the program had grown along with the overall size of the school since its opening in 1968. Bakke complained to the school but was still not admitted, and he finally brought his case before the Superior Court of California. The California court ruled in favor of Bakke, who claimed that he had been discriminated against because of his race, and the school appealed to the US Supreme Court. The Supreme Court ruled that race could be used as one factor by discriminatory boards such as college admissions boards; however, quotas were ruled to be **discriminatory**.

Americans with Disabilities Act (ADA)

The ADA was passed by Congress in 1990. This act outlines the rights of individuals with disabilities in society in all ways besides education. It states that they should receive **nondiscriminatory treatment** in jobs, **access** to businesses and other stores, and other services. Due to this law all businesses must be wheelchair accessible, having a ramp that fits the standards of the law, and all doors and bathrooms within those businesses must be able to be used and maneuvered through by someone in a wheelchair. If these rules are not followed, businesses can be subject to large fines until these modifications have been complied with. The ADA also ensures fair treatment when applying for jobs to make sure that there is no unfair discrimination for any person with a disability who is applying to the job.

The Civil Rights Act of 1991

The Civil Rights Act of 1991 is a statute that was passed as a result of a number of Supreme Court decisions that restricted the rights of individuals who had sued their employers on the basis of discrimination. The passing of the **Civil Rights Act of 1991** was the first time since the Civil Rights Act of 1964 was passed that modifications were made to the rights granted under federal laws to individuals in cases involving **employment discrimination**. Specifically, the Civil Rights Act of 1991 granted the right to a trial by jury to individuals involved in cases of employment discrimination, and it also addressed for the first time the potential for emotional distress damages and limited the amount awarded by a jury in such cases.

Planned Parenthood v. Casey

Planned Parenthood of Southeastern Pennsylvania v. Casey was a 1992 Supreme Court case that challenged the constitutionality of Pennsylvania abortion laws. The case was brought before the US District Court for the Eastern District of Pennsylvania by abortion clinics and physicians to challenge four clauses of the **Pennsylvania Abortion Control Act of 1982** as unconstitutional under Roe v. Wade. The district court ruled that all of the clauses of the Pennsylvania act were unconstitutional. The case was then appealed to the Third Circuit Court of Appeals, which ruled to uphold all of the clauses except for one requiring notification of a husband prior to abortion. The case was then appealed to the Supreme Court, which ruled to uphold the constitutional right to have an abortion, thereby upholding Roe v. Wade.

Adarand Constructors, Inc. v. Peña

Adarand Constructors, Inc. v. Peña was a 1995 United States Supreme Court case in which the court ruled that any **racial classifications** that are instituted by representatives of federal, state, or local governments have to be reviewed and analyzed by a court. The court that reviews such racial classifications must abide by a policy of **strict scrutiny**. Strict scrutiny represents the highest standard of Supreme Court review. Racial classifications are deemed constitutional solely under circumstances in which they are being used as specific measures to advance critical and important governmental interests. The ruling of the Supreme Court in this case requiring strict scrutiny as a standard of review for racial classifications overturned the case of **Metro Broadcasting, Inc. v. FCC**, in which the Supreme Court established a two-level method of reviewing and analyzing racial classifications.

The Employment Non-Discrimination Act (ENDA) and the Equality Act

The Employment Non-Discrimination Act was a proposed United States federal law that was introduced various times before Congress but was never passed by both the House and the Senate. The **Employment Non-Discrimination Act** would ban employers from discriminating against their employees based on their **sexual orientation**. A number of states have already passed laws that ban discrimination based on sexual orientation, including California, Connecticut, Hawaii, Maryland, Massachusetts, Minnesota, Nevada, New Hampshire, New Jersey, New Mexico, New York, Rhode Island, Vermont, and Wisconsin. The ENDA has largely been encompassed by a broader resolution known as the Equality Act, which is a bill that would amend the Civil Rights Act of 1964 to further add gender identity and sexual orientation to the list of prohibited categories of discrimination for employment, public accomodations, the jury system, and housing. It has been met with opposition and has not yet been passed by both bodies of Congress.

Public Policy

Public policy is the study of how the various levels of government formulate and implement policies. **Public policy** also refers to the set of policies that a government adopts and implements, including laws, plans, actions, and behaviors, for the purpose of governing society. Public policy is developed and adapted through the process of **policy analysis**. Public policy analysis is the systematic evaluation of alternative means of reaching social goals. Public policy is divided into various policy areas, including domestic policy, foreign policy, healthcare policy, education policy, criminal policy, national defense policy, and energy policy.

Grutter v. Bollinger

Grutter v. Bollinger was a 2003 Supreme Court case that upheld an **affirmative action policy** of the University of Michigan Law School admissions process. The case originated in 1996 when Barbara Grutter, a white in-state resident with a strong academic record, applied to the law school and was denied admission. In 1997, she filed a lawsuit claiming that her rejection was based on racial discrimination and violated her Fourteenth Amendment rights, as well as Title VI of the Civil Rights Act of 1964. The case was heard in 2001 in a US District Court, which ruled that the university's admissions policies were unconstitutional. In 2002, the case was appealed to the Sixth Circuit Court of Appeals, which overturned the lower court's decision. The case was then appealed to the US Supreme Court in 2003, which ruled that the school's affirmative action policy could remain in place, upholding the case of Regents of the University of California v. Bakke permitting race to be a factor in admissions but banning quotas.

Chapter Quiz

Ready to see how well you retained what you just read? Scan the QR code to go directly to the chapter quiz interface for this study guide. If you're using a computer, simply visit the bonus page at **mometrix.com/bonus948/fsot** and click the Chapter Quizzes link.

United States History, Society, Customs, and Culture

Transform passive reading into active learning! After immersing yourself in this chapter, put your comprehension to the test by taking a quiz. The insights you gained will stay with you longer this way. Scan the QR code to go directly to the chapter quiz interface for this study guide. If you're using a computer, simply visit the bonus page at **mometrix.com/bonus948/fsot** and click the Chapter Quizzes link.

American History Pre-Columbian to 1789

Well-Known Native Americans

The following are five well-known Native Americans and their roles in early US history:

1. **Squanto**, an Algonquian, helped early English settlers survive the hard winter by teaching them the native methods of planting corn, squash, and pumpkins.
2. **Pocahontas**, also Algonquian, became famous as a liaison with John Smith's Jamestown colony in 1607.
3. **Sacagawea**, a Shoshone, served a vital role in the Lewis and Clark expedition when the two explorers hired her as their guide in 1805.
4. **Crazy Horse** and **Sitting Bull** led Sioux and Cheyenne troops in the Battle of the Little Bighorn in 1876, soundly defeating George Armstrong Custer.
5. **Chief Joseph**, a leader of the Nez Perce who supported peaceful interaction with white settlers, attempted to relocate his tribe to Canada rather than move them to a reservation.

Major Regional Native American Groups

The major regional Native American groups and the major traits of each are as follows:

- The **Algonquians** in the eastern part of the United States lived in wigwams. The northern tribes subsisted on hunting and gathering, while those who were farther south grew crops such as corn.
- The **Iroquois**, also an east coast tribe, spoke a different language from the Algonquians and lived in rectangular longhouses.
- The **Plains tribes** lived between the Mississippi River and the Rocky Mountains. These nomadic tribes lived in teepees and followed the buffalo herds. Plains tribes included the Sioux, Cheyenne, Comanche, and Blackfoot.
- **Pueblo tribes** included the Zuni, Hopi, and Acoma. They lived in the Southwest deserts in homes made of stone or adobe. They domesticated animals and cultivated corn and beans.
- On the Pacific coast, tribes such as the **Tlingit**, **Chinook**, and **Salish** lived on fish,deer, native berries, and roots. Their rectangular homes housed large family groups, and they used totem poles.
- In the far north, the **Aleuts** and **Inuit** lived in skin tents or igloos. Talented fishermen, they built kayaks and umiaks and also hunted caribou, seals, whales, and walrus.

Review Video: Major Regional Native American Groups
Visit mometrix.com/academy and enter code: 550136

Age of Exploration

The Age of Exploration is also called the **Age of Discovery**. It is generally considered to have begun in the early 15th century and continued into the 17th century. Major developments of the **Age of Exploration** included technological advances in navigation, mapmaking, and shipbuilding. These advances led to expanded European exploration of the rest of the world. Explorers set out from several European countries, including Portugal, Spain, France, and England, seeking new routes to Asia. These efforts led to the discovery of new lands, as well as colonization in India, Asia, Africa, and North America.

> **Review Video: Age of Exploration**
> Visit mometrix.com/academy and enter code: 612972

Impact of Technological Advances in Navigation and Seafaring Exploration

For long ocean journeys, it was important for sailors to be able to find their way home even when their vessels sailed far out to sea. A variety of navigational tools enabled them to launch ambitious journeys over long distances. The **compass** and **astrolabe** were particularly important advancements. Chinese navigators used the magnetic compass in approximately 200 BC, and knowledge of the astrolabe came to Europe from Arab navigators and traders who had refined designs developed by the ancient Greeks. The Portuguese developed a ship called a **caravel** in the 1400s that incorporated navigational advancements with the ability to make long sea journeys. Equipped with this advanced vessel, the Portuguese achieved a major goal of the Age of Exploration by discovering a **sea route** from Europe to Asia in 1498.

Significance of Christopher Columbus's Voyage

In 1492, Columbus, a Genoan explorer, obtained financial backing from King Ferdinand and Queen Isabella of Spain to seek a sea route to Asia. He sought a trade route with the Asian Indies to the west. With three ships, the *Niña*, the *Pinta*, and the *Santa Maria*, he eventually landed in the **West Indies**. While Columbus failed in his effort to discover a western route to Asia, he is credited with the discovery of the **Americas**.

> **Review Video: Christopher Columbus**
> Visit mometrix.com/academy and enter code: 496598

French, Spanish, Dutch, and British Goals in Colonization of the Americas

France, Spain, the Netherlands, and England each had specific goals in the colonization of the Americas:

- Initial **French colonies** were focused on expanding the fur trade. Later, French colonization led to the growth of plantations in Louisiana, which brought numerous African slaves to the New World.
- **Spanish colonists** came to look for wealth and to convert the natives to Christianity. For some, the desire for gold led to mining in the New World, while others established large ranches.
- The **Dutch** were also involved in the fur trade and imported slaves as the need for laborers increased.
- **British colonists** arrived with various goals. Some were simply looking for additional income, while others were fleeing Britain to escape religious persecution.

> **Review Video: European Colonization of the Americas**
> Visit mometrix.com/academy and enter code: 438412

New England Colonies

The New England colonies were New Hampshire, Connecticut, Rhode Island and Massachusetts. These colonies were founded largely to escape **religious persecution** in England. The beliefs of the **Puritans**, who migrated to America in the 1600s, significantly influenced the development of these colonies. Situated in the northeast coastal areas of America, the New England colonies featured numerous harbors as well as dense forests. The soil, however, was rocky and had a very short growing season, so was not well suited for agriculture. The economy of New England during the colonial period centered around fishing, shipbuilding and trade along with some small farms and lumber mills. Although some groups congregated in small farms, life centered mainly in towns and cities where **merchants** largely controlled the trade economy. Coastal cities such as Boston grew and thrived.

Review Video: The Massachusetts Bay Colony
Visit mometrix.com/academy and enter code: 407058

Middle or Middle Atlantic Colonies

The Middle or Middle Atlantic Colonies were New York, New Jersey, Pennsylvania, and Delaware. Unlike the New England colonies, where most colonists were from England and Scotland, the Middle Colonies founders were from various countries, including the Netherlands and Sweden. Various factors led these colonists to America. More fertile than New England, the Middle Colonies became major producers of **crops**, including rye, oats, potatoes, wheat, and barley. Some particularly wealthy inhabitants owned large farms and/or businesses. Farmers, in general, were able to produce enough to have a surplus to sell. Tenant farmers also rented land from larger landowners.

Southern Colonies

The Southern Colonies were Maryland, Virginia, North Carolina, South Carolina, and Georgia. Of the Southern Colonies, Virginia was the first permanent English colony and Georgia the last. The warm climate and rich soil of the south encouraged **agriculture**, and the growing season was long. As a result, economy in the south was based largely on labor-intensive **plantations**. Crops included tobacco, rice, and indigo, all of which became valuable cash crops. Most land in the south was controlled by wealthy plantation owners and farmers. Labor on the farms came in the form of indentured servants and African slaves. The first of these **African slaves** arrived in Virginia in 1619.

Review Video: The Southern Colonies
Visit mometrix.com/academy and enter code: 703830

Review Video: The English Colony of Virginia
Visit mometrix.com/academy and enter code: 537399

Significance of the French and Indian Wars

The **British defeat of the Spanish Armada** in 1588 led to the decline of Spanish power in Europe. This, in turn, led the British and French into battle several times between 1689 and 1748. These wars were:

- King William's War, or the Nine Years War, 1689-1697. This war was fought largely in Flanders.
- The War of Spanish Succession, or Queen Anne's War, 1702-1713
- War of Austrian Succession, or King George's War, 1740-1748

The fourth and final war, the **French and Indian War** (1754-1763), was fought largely in the North American territory and resulted in the end of France's reign as a colonial power in North America. Although the French held many advantages, including more cooperative colonists and numerous Native American allies, the strong leadership of **William Pitt** eventually led the British to victory. Costs incurred during the wars eventually led to discontent in the colonies and helped spark the **American Revolution**.

Review Video: French and Indian Wars
Visit mometrix.com/academy and enter code: 502183

Navigation Acts

The Navigation Acts, enacted in 1651, were an attempt by Britain to dominate international trade. Aimed largely at the Dutch, the acts banned foreign ships from transporting goods to the British colonies and from transporting goods to Britain from elsewhere in Europe. While the restrictions on trade angered some colonists, these acts were helpful to other American colonists who, as members of the British Empire, were legally able to provide ships for Britain's growing trade interests and use the ships for their own trading ventures. By the time the French and Indian War had ended, one-third of British merchant ships were built in the American colonies. Many colonists amassed fortunes in the shipbuilding trade.

Acts of British Parliament that Occurred After the French and Indian Wars

After the French and Indian Wars, the British Parliament passed four major acts:

1. The **Sugar Act**, 1764—this act not only required taxes to be collected on molasses brought into the colonies but gave British officials the right to search the homes of anyone suspected of violating it.
2. The **Stamp Act**, 1765—this act taxed printed materials such as newspapers and legal documents. Protests led the Stamp Act to be repealed in 1766, but the repeal also included the Declaratory Act, which stated that Parliament had the right to govern the colonies.
3. The **Quartering Act**, 1765—this act required colonists to provide accommodations and supplies for British troops. In addition, colonists were prohibited from settling west of the Appalachians until given permission by Britain.
4. The **Townshend Acts**, 1767—these acts taxed paper, paint, lead, and tea that came into the colonies. Colonists led boycotts in protest, and in Massachusetts leaders like Samuel and John Adams began to organize resistance against British rule.

Britain's Taxation of the American Colonies After the French and Indian War

The French and Indian War created circumstances for which the British desperately needed more revenue. These needs included:

- Paying off the war debt
- Defending the expanding empire
- Governing Britain's 33 far-flung colonies, including the American colonies

To meet these needs, the British passed additional laws, increasing revenues from the colonies. Because they had spent so much money to defend the American colonies, the British felt it was appropriate to collect considerably higher **taxes** from them. The colonists felt this was unfair, and many were led to protest the increasing taxes. Eventually, protest led to violence.

Triangular Trade

Triangular trade began in the colonies with ships setting off for **Africa**, carrying rum. In Africa, the rum was traded for gold or slaves. Ships then went from Africa to the **West Indies**, trading slaves for sugar, molasses, or money. To complete the triangle, the ships returned to the **colonies** with sugar or molasses to make more rum, as well as stores of gold and silver. This trade triangle violated the Molasses Act of 1733, which required the colonists to pay high duties to Britain on molasses acquired from French, Dutch, and Spanish colonies. The colonists ignored these duties, and the British government adopted a policy of salutary neglect by not enforcing them.

Review Video: The Triangular Trade
Visit mometrix.com/academy and enter code: 415470

Effects of New Laws on British-Colonial Relations

While earlier revenue-generating acts such as the Navigation Acts brought money to the colonists, the new laws after 1763 required colonists to pay money back to **Britain**. The British felt this was fair since the colonists were British subjects and since they had incurred debt protecting the Colonies. The colonists felt it was not only unfair but illegal.

The development of **local government** in America had given the colonists a different view of the structure and role of government. This made it difficult for the British to understand the colonists' protests against what the British felt was a fair and reasonable solution to the mother country's financial problems.

Factors that Led to Increasing Discontent in the American Colonies

More and more colonists were born on American soil, decreasing any sense of kinship with the far-away British rulers. Their new environment had led to new ideas of government and a strong view of the colonies as a separate entity from Britain. Colonists were allowed to **self-govern** in domestic issues, but **Britain** controlled international issues. In fact, the American colonies were largely left to form their own local government bodies, giving them more freedom than any other colonial territory. This gave the colonists a sense of **independence**, which led them to resent control from Britain. Threats during the French and Indian War led the colonists to call for unification in order to protect themselves.

Colonial Government and British Government Differences that Led to "No Taxation Without Representation"

As new towns and other legislative districts developed in America, the colonists began to practice **representative government**. Colonial legislative bodies were made up of elected representatives chosen by male property owners in the districts. These individuals represented the interests of the districts from which they had been elected.

By contrast, in Britain, the **Parliament** represented the entire country. Parliament was not elected to represent individual districts. Instead, they represented specific classes. Because of this drastically different approach to government, the British did not understand the colonists' statement that they had no representation in the British Parliament.

Factors that Led to the Boston Massacre

With the passage of the **Stamp Act**, nine colonies met in New York to demand its repeal. Elsewhere, protest arose in New York City, Philadelphia, Boston, and other cities. These protests sometimes escalated into violence, often targeting ruling British officials. The passage of the **Townshend Acts** in 1767 led to additional tension in the colonies. The British sent troops to New York City and Boston. On March 5, 1770, protesters began to taunt the British troops, throwing snowballs. The soldiers responded by firing into the crowd. This clash between protesters and soldiers led to five deaths and eight injuries, and was christened the **Boston Massacre**. Shortly thereafter, Britain repealed the majority of the Townshend Acts.

Tea Act that Led to the Boston Tea Party

The majority of the **Townshend Acts** were repealed after the Boston Massacre in 1770, but Britain kept the tax on tea. In 1773, the **Tea Act** was passed. This allowed the East India Company to sell tea for much lower prices and also allowed them to bypass American distributors, selling directly to shopkeepers instead. Colonial tea merchants saw this as a direct assault on their business. In December of 1773, the **Sons of Liberty** boarded ships in Boston Harbor and dumped 342 chests of tea into the sea in protest of the new laws. This act of protest came to be known as the **Boston Tea Party**.

Coercive Acts Passed after the Boston Tea Party

The Coercive Acts passed by Britain in 1774 were meant to punish Massachusetts for defying British authority. These became collectively known as the **Intolerable Acts** in the colonies and mandated the following:

- Shut down ports in Boston until the city paid back the value of the tea destroyed during the Boston Tea Party
- Required that local government officials in Massachusetts be appointed by the governor rather than being elected by the people

- Allowed trials of British soldiers to be transferred to Britain rather than being held in Massachusetts
- Required locals to provide lodging for British soldiers any time there was a disturbance, even if lodging required them to stay in private homes

These acts led to the assembly of the First Continental Congress in Philadelphia on September 5, 1774. Fifty-five delegates met, representing 12 of the American colonies. They sought compromise with England over England's increasingly harsh efforts to control the colonies.

First Continental Congress

The goal of the First Continental Congress was to achieve a peaceful agreement with Britain. Made up of delegates from 12 of the 13 colonies, the Congress affirmed loyalty to Britain and the power of Parliament to dictate foreign affairs in the colonies. However, they demanded that the **Intolerable Acts** be repealed, and instituted a trade embargo with Britain until this came to pass.

In response, George III of England declared that the American colonies must submit or face military action. The British sought to end assemblies that opposed their policies. These assemblies gathered weapons and began to form militias. On April 19, 1775, the British military was ordered to disperse a meeting of the Massachusetts Assembly. A battle ensued on Lexington Common as the armed colonists resisted. The resulting battles became the **Battle of Lexington and Concord**—the first battles of the **American Revolution**.

Significance of the Second Continental Congress

The Second Continental Congress met in Philadelphia on May 10, 1775, a month after Lexington and Concord. Their discussions centered on the defense of the American colonies and how to conduct the growing war, as well as local government. The delegates also discussed declaring independence from Britain, with many members in favor of this drastic move. They established an army, and on June 15, named **George Washington** as its commander in chief. By 1776, it was obvious that there was no turning back from full-scale war with Britain. The colonial delegates of the Continental Congress signed the **Declaration of Independence** on July 4, 1776.

Review Video: The First and Second Continental Congress
Visit mometrix.com/academy and enter code: 835211

Origins and Basic Ideas of the Declaration of Independence

Penned by Thomas Jefferson and signed on July 4, 1776, the **Declaration of Independence** stated that King George III had violated the rights of the colonists and was establishing a tyrannical reign over them. Many of Jefferson's ideas of natural rights and property rights were shaped by 17th-century philosopher **John Locke**. Jefferson asserted all people's rights to "life, liberty and the pursuit of happiness." Locke's comparable idea asserted "life, liberty, and private property." Both felt that the purpose of government was to protect the rights of the people, and that individual rights were more important than individuals' obligations to the state.

Review Video: Declaration of Independence
Visit mometrix.com/academy and enter code: 256838

Battles of the Revolutionary War

The following are five major battles of the Revolutionary War and their significance:

- The **Battle of Lexington and Concord** (April 1775) is considered the first engagement of the Revolutionary War.
- The **Battle of Bunker Hill** (June 1775) was one of the bloodiest of the entire war. Although American troops withdrew, about half of the British army was lost. The colonists proved they could stand against professional British soldiers. In August, Britain declared that the American colonies were officially in a state of rebellion.

- The first colonial victory occurred in Trenton, New Jersey, when Washington and his troops **crossed the Delaware River** on Christmas Day, 1776, for a December 26 surprise attack on British and Hessian troops.
- The **Battle of Saratoga** effectively ended a plan to separate the New England colonies from their Southern counterparts. The surrender of British general John Burgoyne led to France joining the war as allies of the Americans and is generally considered a turning point of the war.
- On October 19, 1781, General Cornwallis surrendered after a defeat in the **Battle of Yorktown**, ending the Revolutionary War.

> **Review Video: The American Revolutionary War**
> Visit mometrix.com/academy and enter code: 935282

SIGNIFICANCE OF THE TREATY OF PARIS

The Treaty of Paris was signed on September 3, 1783, bringing an official end to the Revolutionary War. In this document, Britain officially recognized the United States of America as an **independent nation**. The treaty established the Mississippi River as the country's western border. The treaty also restored Florida to Spain, while France reclaimed African and Caribbean colonies seized by the British in 1763. On November 25, 1783, the last British troops departed from the newly born United States of America.

SIGNIFICANCE OF THE ARTICLES OF CONFEDERATION

A precursor to the Constitution, the **Articles of Confederation** represented the first attempt of the newly independent colonies to establish the basics of government. The Continental Congress approved the Articles on November 15, 1777. They went into effect on March 1, 1781, following ratification by the thirteen states. The articles prevented a central government from gaining too much power, instead giving power to a **congressional body** made up of **delegates** from all thirteen states. However, the individual states retained final authority.

Without a strong central **executive**, though, this weak alliance among the new states proved ineffective in settling disputes or enforcing laws. The idea of a weak central government needed to be revised. Recognition of these weaknesses eventually led to the drafting of a new document, the **Constitution**.

> **Review Video: Articles of Confederation**
> Visit mometrix.com/academy and enter code: 927401

INITIAL PROPOSITION AND DRAFT OF THE CONSTITUTION

Delegates from twelve of the thirteen states (Rhode Island was not represented) met in Philadelphia in May of 1787, initially intending to revise the Articles of Confederation. However, it quickly became apparent that a simple revision would not provide the workable governmental structure the newly formed country needed. After vowing to keep all the proceedings secret until the final document was completed, the delegates set out to draft what would eventually become the **Constitution of the United States of America**. By keeping the negotiations secret, the delegates were able to present a completed document to the country for ratification, rather than having every small detail hammered out by the general public.

GENERAL STRUCTURE OF GOVERNMENT PROPOSED BY THE DELEGATES

The delegates agreed that the new nation required a **strong central government** but that its overall power should be **limited**. The various branches of the government should have **balanced power**, so that no one group could control the others. Final power belonged to the **citizens** who voted officials into office based on who would provide the best representation.

Objections Against the Constitution

Once the Constitution was drafted, it was presented for approval by the states. Nine states needed to approve the document for it to become official. However, debate and discussion continued. Major **concerns** included:

- There was no bill of rights to protect individual freedoms.
- States felt too much power was being handed over to the central government.
- Voters wanted more control over their elected representatives.

Discussion about necessary changes to the Constitution was divided into two camps: Federalists and Anti-Federalists. **Federalists** wanted a strong central government. **Anti-Federalists** wanted to prevent a tyrannical government from developing if a central government held too much power

Major Players in the Federalist and Anti-Federalist Camps

Major Federalist leaders included Alexander Hamilton, John Jay, and James Madison. They wrote a series of letters, called the **Federalist Papers**, aimed at convincing the states to ratify the Constitution. These were published in New York papers. Anti-Federalists included Thomas Jefferson and Patrick Henry. They argued against the Constitution as it was originally drafted in a series of **Anti-Federalist Papers**.

The final compromise produced a strong central government controlled by checks and balances. A **Bill of Rights** was also added, becoming the first ten amendments to the Constitution. These amendments protected rights such as freedom of speech, freedom of religion, and other basic rights. Aside from various amendments added throughout the years, the United States Constitution has remained unchanged.

Individuals Who Formed the First Administration of the New Government

The individuals who formed the first administration of the new government were:

- **George Washington**—elected as the first President of the United States in 1789
- **John Adams**—finished second in the election and became the first Vice President
- **Thomas Jefferson**—appointed by Washington as Secretary of State
- **Alexander Hamilton**—appointed Secretary of the Treasury

Significance of the Virginia Plan, the New Jersey Plan, and the Great Compromise

Disagreement immediately occurred between delegates from large states and those from smaller states. James Madison and Edmund Randolph (the governor of Virginia) felt that representation in Congress should be based on state population. This was the **Virginia Plan**. The **New Jersey Plan**, presented by William Paterson from New Jersey, proposed that each state should have equal representation. Finally, Roger Sherman from Connecticut formulated the **Connecticut Compromise**, also called the Great Compromise. The result was the familiar structure we have today. Each state has the equal representation of two Senators in the Senate, with the number of representatives in the House of Representatives based on population. This is called a **bicameral congress**. Both houses may draft bills, but financial matters must originate in the House of Representatives.

Effects of the Three-fifths Compromise and the Number of Representatives for Each State

During debate on the US Constitution, a disagreement arose between the Northern and Southern states involving how **slaves** should be counted when determining a state's quota of representatives. In the South, large numbers of slaves were commonly used to run plantations. Delegates wanted slaves to be counted to determine the number of representatives but not counted to determine the amount of taxes the states would pay. The Northern states wanted exactly the opposite arrangement. The final decision was to count three-fifths of the slave population both for tax purposes and to determine representation. This was called the **Three-fifths Compromise**.

Provisions of the Commerce Compromise

The Commerce Compromise also resulted from a North/South disagreement. In the North, the economy was centered on **industry and trade**. The Southern economy was largely **agricultural**. The Northern states wanted to give the new government the ability to regulate exports as well as trade between the states. The South opposed this plan. Another compromise was in order. In the end, Congress received regulatory power over all trade, including the ability to collect **tariffs** on exported goods. In the South, this raised another red flag regarding the slave trade, as they were concerned about the effect on their economy if tariffs were levied on slaves. The final agreement allowed importing slaves to continue for twenty years without government intervention. Import taxes on slaves were limited, and after the year 1808, Congress could decide whether to allow continued imports of slaves.

American History 1790 to 1898

Alien and Sedition Acts

When **John Adams** became president, a war was raging between Britain and France. While Adams and the **Federalists** backed the British, Thomas Jefferson and the **Republican Party** supported the French. The United States nearly went to war with France during this time period, while France worked to spread its international standing and influence under the leadership of **Napoleon Bonaparte**. The **Alien and Sedition Acts** grew out of this conflict and made it illegal to speak in a hostile fashion against the existing government. They also allowed the president to deport anyone in the US who was not a citizen and who was suspected of treason or treasonous activity. When Jefferson became the third president in 1800, he repealed these four laws and pardoned anyone who had been convicted under them.

Development of Political Parties in Early US Government

Many in the US were against political parties after seeing the way parties, or factions, functioned in Britain. The factions in Britain were more interested in personal profit than the overall good of the country, and they did not want this to happen in the US.

However, the differences of opinion between Thomas Jefferson and Alexander Hamilton led to the formation of **political parties**. Hamilton favored a stronger central government, while Jefferson felt that more power should remain with the states. Jefferson was in favor of strict Constitutional interpretation, while Hamilton believed in a more flexible approach. As others joined the two camps, Hamilton backers began to call themselves **Federalists**, while those supporting Jefferson became identified as **Democratic-Republicans**.

Development of the Whig, the Democratic, and the Republican Parties

Thomas Jefferson was elected president in 1800 and again in 1804. The **Federalist Party** began to decline, and its major figure, Alexander Hamilton, died in a duel with Aaron Burr in 1804. By 1816, the Federalist Party had virtually disappeared.

New parties sprang up to take its place. After 1824, the **Democratic-Republican Party** suffered a split. The **Whigs** rose, backing John Quincy Adams and industrial growth. The new Democratic Party formed in opposition to the Whigs, and their candidate, Andrew Jackson, was elected as president in 1828.

By the 1850s, issues regarding slavery led to the formation of the **Republican Party**, which was anti-slavery, while the Democratic Party, with a larger interest in the South, favored slavery. This Republican/Democrat division formed the basis of today's **two-party system**.

Significance of Marbury v. Madison

The main duty of the Supreme Court today is **judicial review**. This power was largely established by **Marbury v. Madison**. When John Adams was voted out of office in 1800, he worked during his final days in office to appoint Federalist judges to Supreme Court positions, knowing Jefferson, his replacement, held opposing views. As late as March 3, the day before Jefferson was to take office, Adams made last-minute appointments referred to as "Midnight Judges." One of the late appointments was William Marbury. The next day, March 4, Jefferson ordered his Secretary of State, James Madison, not to deliver Marbury's commission. This decision was backed by Chief Justice Marshall, who determined that the **Judiciary Act of 1789**, which granted the power to deliver commissions, was illegal in that it gave the Judicial Branch powers not granted in the Constitution. This case set precedent for the Supreme Court to nullify laws it found to be **unconstitutional**.

Review Video: Marbury v Madison
Visit mometrix.com/academy and enter code: 573964

Political Motivations Behind France Selling the Louisiana Purchase

With tension still high between France and Britain, Napoleon was in need of money to support his continuing war efforts. To secure necessary funds, he decided to sell the **Louisiana Territory** to the US. President **Thomas Jefferson** wanted to buy New Orleans, feeling US trade was made vulnerable to both Spain and France at that port. Instead, Napoleon sold him the entire territory for the bargain price of $15 million. The Louisiana Territory was larger than all the rest of the United States put together, and it eventually became 15 additional states.

Federalists in Congress were opposed to the purchase. They feared that the Louisiana Purchase would extend slavery, and that further western growth would weaken the power of the northern states.

Lewis and Clark Expedition

The purchase of the **Louisiana Territory** from France in 1803 more than doubled the size of the United States. President Thomas Jefferson wanted to have the area mapped and explored, since much of the territory was wilderness. He chose Meriwether Lewis and William Clark to head an expedition into the Louisiana Territory. After two years, Lewis and Clark returned, having traveled all the way to the Pacific Ocean. They brought maps, detailed journals, and a multitude of information about the wide expanse of land they had traversed. The **Lewis and Clark Expedition** opened up the west in the Louisiana Territory and beyond for further exploration and settlement.

Review Video: Purpose of the Lewis and Clark Expedition
Visit mometrix.com/academy and enter code: 570657

Causes and Result of the War of 1812

The War of 1812 grew out of the continuing tension between France and Great Britain. Napoleon continued striving to conquer Britain, while the US continued trade with both countries but favored France and the French colonies. Because of what Britain saw as an alliance between America and France, they determined to bring an end to trade between the two nations.

With the British preventing US trade with the French and the French preventing trade with the British, James Madison's presidency introduced acts to **regulate international trade**. If either Britain or France removed their restrictions, America would not trade with the other country. Napoleon acted first, and Madison prohibited trade with England. England saw this as the US formally siding with the French, and war ensued in 1812.

The **War of 1812** has been called the **Second American Revolution**. It established the superiority of the US naval forces and reestablished US independence from Britain and Europe.

The British had two major objections to America's continued trade with France. First, they saw the US as helping France's war effort by providing supplies and goods. Second, the United States had grown into a competitor, taking trade and money away from British ships and tradesmen. In its attempts to end American trade with France, the British put into effect the **Orders in Council**, which made any and all French-owned ports off-limits to American ships. They also began to seize American ships and conscript their crews.

> **Review Video: Overview of the War of 1812**
> Visit mometrix.com/academy and enter code: 507716
>
> **Review Video: Opinions About the War of 1812**
> Visit mometrix.com/academy and enter code: 274558

Major Military Events of the War of 1812

Two major naval battles, at **Lake Erie** and **Lake Champlain**, kept the British from invading the US via Canada. American attempts to conquer Canadian lands were not successful.

In another memorable British attack, the British invaded Washington, DC and burned the White House on August 24, 1814. Legend has it that **Dolley Madison**, the First Lady, salvaged the portrait of George Washington from the fire. On Christmas Eve, 1814, the **Treaty of Ghent** officially ended the war. However, Andrew Jackson, unaware that the war was over, managed another victory at New Orleans on January 8, 1815. This victory improved American morale and led to a new wave of national pride and support known as the "**Era of Good Feelings**."

Influence of the American System on American Economics

Spurred by the trade conflicts of the War of 1812 and supported by Henry Clay among others, the **American System** set up tariffs to help protect American interests from competition with overseas products. Reducing competition led to growth in employment and an overall increase in American industry. The higher tariffs also provided funds for the government to pay for various improvements. Congress passed high tariffs in 1816 and also chartered a federal bank. The **Second Bank of the United States** was given the job of regulating America's money supply.

McCulloch v. Maryland

Judicial review was further exercised by the Supreme Court in **McCulloch v. Maryland**. When Congress chartered a national bank, the **Second Bank of the United States**, Maryland voted to tax any bank business dealing with banks chartered outside the state, including the federally chartered bank. Andrew McCulloch, an employee of the Second Bank of the US in Baltimore, refused to pay this tax. The resulting lawsuit from the State of Maryland went to the Supreme Court for judgment.

John Marshall, Chief Justice of the Supreme Court, stated that Congress was within its rights to charter a national bank. In addition, the State of Maryland did not have the power to levy a tax on the federal bank or on the federal government in general. In cases where state and federal government collided, precedent was set for the **federal government** to prevail.

Effects of the Missouri Compromise on the Tensions Between the North and South

By 1819, the United States had developed a tenuous balance between slave and free states, with exactly 22 senators in Congress from each faction. However, Missouri was ready to join the union. As a slave state, it would tip the balance in Congress. To prevent this imbalance, the **Missouri Compromise** brought the northern part of Massachusetts into the union as Maine, establishing it as a free state to balance the admission of Missouri as a slave state. In addition, the remaining portion of the Louisiana Purchase was to remain free north of **latitude 36°30'**. Since cotton did not grow well this far north, this limitation was acceptable to congressmen representing the slave states.

However, the proposed Missouri constitution presented a problem, as it outlawed immigration of free blacks into the state. Another compromise was in order, this time proposed by **Henry Clay**. According to this new compromise, Missouri would never pass a law that prevented anyone from entering the state. Through this and other work, Clay earned his title of the "**Great Compromiser**."

> **Review Video: The Missouri Compromise**
> Visit mometrix.com/academy and enter code: 848091

Monroe Doctrine

On December 2, 1823, President Monroe delivered a message to Congress in which he introduced the **Monroe Doctrine**. In this address, he stated that any attempts by European powers to establish new colonies on the North American continent would be considered interference in American politics. The US would stay out of European matters, and expected Europe to offer America the same courtesy. This approach to foreign policy stated in no uncertain terms that America would not tolerate any new European colonies in the New World, and that events occurring in Europe would no longer influence the policies and doctrines of the US.

Effect of the Treaty of Paris on Native Americans

After the Revolutionary War, the **Treaty of Paris**, which outlined the terms of surrender of the British to the Americans, granted large parcels of land to the US that were occupied by Native Americans. The new government attempted to claim the land, treating the natives as a conquered people. This approach proved unenforceable.

Next, the government tried purchasing the land from the Native Americans via a series of **treaties** as the country expanded westward. In practice, however, these treaties were not honored, and Native Americans were simply dislocated and forced to move farther and farther west, often with military action, as American expansion continued.

Indian Removal Act of 1830 and the Treaty of New Echota

The Indian Removal Act of 1830 gave the new American government power to form treaties with Native Americans. In theory, America would claim land east of the Mississippi in exchange for land west of the Mississippi, to which the natives would relocate voluntarily. In practice, many tribal leaders were forced into signing the treaties, and relocation at times occurred by force.

The **Treaty of New Echota** in 1835 was supposedly a treaty between the US government and Cherokee tribes in Georgia. However, the treaty was not signed by tribal leaders but rather by a small portion of the represented people. The leaders protested and refused to leave, but President Martin Van Buren enforced the treaty by sending soldiers. During their forced relocation, more than 4,000 Cherokees died on what became known as the **Trail of Tears**.

> **Review Video: Indian Removal Act**
> Visit mometrix.com/academy and enter code: 666738

Jacksonian Democracy vs. Preceding Political Climate

Jacksonian Democracy is largely seen as a shift from politics favoring the wealthy to politics favoring the common man. The right to vote was given to all free white males, not just property owners, as had been the case previously. Jackson's approach favored the patronage system, laissez-faire economics, and relocation of the Native American tribes from the Southeast portion of the country. Jackson opposed the formation of a federal bank and allowed the Second Bank of the United States to collapse by vetoing a bill to renew the charter. Jackson also faced the challenge of the **Nullification Crisis** when South Carolina claimed that it could ignore or nullify any federal law it considered unconstitutional. Jackson sent troops to the state to enforce the protested tariff laws, and a compromise engineered by Henry Clay in 1833 settled the matter for the time being.

Second Great Awakening

Led by Protestant evangelical leaders, the **Second Great Awakening** occurred between 1800 and 1830. Several missionary groups grew out of the movement, including the **American Home Missionary Society**, which formed in 1826. The ideas behind the Second Great Awakening focused on personal responsibility, both as an individual and in response to injustice and suffering. The **American Bible Society** and the **American Tract Society** provided literature, while various traveling preachers spread the word. New denominations arose, including the Latter-day Saints and Seventh-day Adventists.

Another movement associated with the Second Great Awakening was the **temperance movement**, focused on ending the production and use of alcohol. One major organization behind the temperance movement was the **Society for the Promotion of Temperance**, formed in 1826 in Boston.

Attitudes Toward Education in the Early 19th Century

Horace Mann, among others, felt that schools could help children become better citizens, keep them away from crime, prevent poverty, and help American society become more unified. His *Common School Journal* brought his ideas of the importance of education into the public consciousness and proposed his suggestions for an improved American education system. Increased literacy led to increased awareness of current events, Western expansion, and other major developments of the time period. Public interest and participation in the arts and literature also increased. By the end of the 19th century, all children had access to a **free public elementary education**.

Development of Economic Trends as the US Continued to Grow

In the Northeast, the economy mostly depended on **manufacturing, industry, and industrial development**. This led to a dichotomy between rich business owners and industrial leaders and the much poorer workers who supported their businesses. The South continued to depend on **agriculture**, especially on large-scale farms or plantations worked mostly by slaves and indentured servants. In the West, where new settlements had begun to develop, the land was largely wild. Growing communities were essentially **agricultural**, raising crops and livestock. The differences between regions led each to support different interests both politically and economically.

Industrial Activity Before and After 1800

During the 18th century, goods were often manufactured in houses or small shops. With increased technology allowing for the use of machines, **factories** began to develop. In factories, a large volume of salable goods could be produced in a much shorter amount of time. Many Americans, including increasing numbers of **immigrants**, found jobs in these factories, which were in constant need of labor. Another major invention was the **cotton gin**, which significantly decreased the processing time of cotton and was a major factor in the rapid expansion of cotton production in the South.

Development of Labor Movements in the 1800s

In 1751, a group of bakers held a protest in which they stopped baking bread. This was technically the first American **labor strike**. In the 1830s and 1840s, labor movements began in earnest. Boston's masons, carpenters, and stoneworkers protested the length of the workday, fighting to reduce it to ten hours. In 1844, a group of women in the textile industry also fought to reduce their workday to ten hours, forming the **Lowell Female Labor Reform Association**. Many other protests occurred and organizations developed through this time period with the same goal in mind.

Major Ideas Driving American Foreign Policy

The three major ideas driving American foreign policy during its early years were:

- **Isolationism**—the early US government did not intend to establish colonies, though they did plan to grow larger within the bounds of North America.
- **No entangling alliances**—both George Washington and Thomas Jefferson were opposed to forming any permanent alliances with other countries or becoming involved in other countries' internal issues.
- **Nationalism**—a positive patriotic feeling about the United States blossomed quickly among its citizens, particularly after the War of 1812, when the US once again defeated Britain. The Industrial Revolution also sparked increased nationalism by allowing even the most far-flung areas of the US to communicate with each other via telegraph and the expanding railroad.

Effects of Manifest Destiny on American Politics

In the 1800s, many believed America was destined by God to expand west, bringing as much of the North American continent as possible under the umbrella of the US government. With the Northwest Ordinance and the Louisiana Purchase, over half of the continent became American. However, the rapid and relentless expansion brought conflict with the Native Americans, Great Britain, Mexico, and Spain. One result of "**Manifest Destiny**" was the **Mexican-American War** from 1846 to 1848. By the end of the war, Texas, California, and a large portion of what is now the American Southwest joined the growing nation. Conflict also arose over the **Oregon Territory**, shared by the US and Britain. In 1846, President James Polk resolved this problem by compromising with Britain, establishing a US boundary south of the 49th parallel.

Review Video: Manifest Destiny
Visit mometrix.com/academy and enter code: 957409

Mexican-American War

Spain had held colonial interests in America since the 1540s—earlier even than Great Britain. In 1810, **Mexico** revolted against Spain, becoming a free nation in 1821. **Texas** followed suit, declaring its independence after an 1836 revolution. In 1844, the Democrats pressed President Tyler to annex Texas. Unlike his predecessor, Andrew Jackson, Tyler agreed to admit Texas into the Union, and in 1845, Texas became a state.

During Mexico's war for independence, the nation incurred $4.5 million in war debts to the US. Newly elected James K. Polk offered to forgive the debts in return for New Mexico and Upper California, but Mexico refused. In 1846, war was declared in response to a Mexican attack on American troops that President Polk had moved into a disputed zone between the Rio Grande and Nueces River. As US victory grew more certain, dispute arose over how to handle slavery in any newly acquired territory. The **Wilmot Proviso**, though it was never passed, was a large source of contention, as it aimed to prohibit slavery in any territory acquired from Mexico—sowing further seeds of tension between the North and the South. The Mexican-American War ended in 1848 with Mexico agreeing to sell California and its remaining territory north of the Rio Grande.

Review Video: The Mexican-American War
Visit mometrix.com/academy and enter code: 271216

Review Video: Sectional Crisis: The Wilmot Proviso
Visit mometrix.com/academy and enter code: 974842

Popular Sovereignty and the Compromise of 1850

In addition to the pro-slavery and anti-slavery factions, a third group rose, who felt that each individual state should decide whether to allow or permit slavery within its borders. The idea that a state could make its own choices was referred to as **popular sovereignty**.

When California applied to join the union in 1849, the balance of congressional power was again threatened. The **Compromise of 1850** introduced a group of laws meant to bring an end to the conflict:

- California's admittance as a free state
- The outlaw of the slave trade in Washington, DC
- An increase in efforts to capture escaped slaves
- The right of New Mexico and Utah territories to decide individually whether to allow slavery

In spite of these measures, debate raged each time a new state prepared to enter the union.

Gadsden Purchase and the 1853 Post-War Treaty with Mexico

After the Mexican-American war, a **second treaty** in 1853 determined hundreds of miles of America's southwest borders. In 1854, the **Gadsden Purchase** was finalized, providing even more territory to aid in the building of the transcontinental railroad. This purchase added what would eventually become the southernmost regions of Arizona and New Mexico to the growing nation. The modern outline of the United States was by this time nearly complete.

Kansas-Nebraska Act Trigger of Additional Conflict

With the creation of the Kansas and Nebraska territories in 1854, another debate began. Congress allowed popular sovereignty in these territories, but slavery opponents argued that the Missouri Compromise had already made slavery illegal in this region. In Kansas, two separate governments arose, one pro-slavery and one anti-slavery. Conflict between the two factions rose to violence, leading Kansas to gain the nickname of "**Bleeding Kansas**."

> **Review Video: Sectional Crisis: The Kansas-Nebraska Act**
> Visit mometrix.com/academy and enter code: 982119

Early Leaders in the Women's Rights Movement

The women's rights movement began in the 1840s, with leaders including Elizabeth Cady Stanton, Sojourner Truth, Ernestine Rose, and Lucretia Mott. In 1869, Elizabeth Cady Stanton and Susan B. Anthony formed the **National Woman Suffrage Association**, fighting for women's right to vote.

In 1848, in Seneca Falls, the first women's rights convention was held, with about 300 attendees. The two-day **Seneca Falls Convention** discussed the rights of women to vote (suffrage) as well as equal treatment in careers, legal proceedings, etc. The convention produced a "Declaration of Sentiments," which outlined a plan for women to attain the rights they deserved. **Frederick Douglass** supported the women's rights movement, as well as the abolition movement. In fact, women's rights and abolition movements often went hand-in-hand during this time period.

> **Review Video: The Women's Rights Movement in America**
> Visit mometrix.com/academy and enter code: 987734

Major Events and Developments that Brought the North and South into Conflict

The conflict between the North and South coalesced around the issue of **slavery**, but other elements contributed to the growing disagreement. Though most farmers in the South worked small farms with little or no slave labor, the huge plantations run by the South's rich depended on slaves or indentured servants to remain profitable. They had also become more dependent on **cotton**, with slave populations growing in concert with the rapid increase in cotton production. In the North, a more diverse agricultural economy and the growth of **industry** made slaves rarer. The **abolitionist movement** grew steadily, with Harriet Beecher Stowe's *Uncle Tom's Cabin* giving many an idea to rally around. A collection of anti-slavery organizations formed, with many actively working to free slaves in the South, often bringing them to the northern states or Canada.

DRED SCOTT DECISION

Abolitionist factions coalesced around the case of **Dred Scott**, using his case to test the country's laws regarding slavery. Scott, a slave, had been taken by his owner from Missouri, which was a slave state. He then traveled to Illinois, a free state, then on to the Minnesota Territory, also free based on the Missouri Compromise. After several years, he returned to Missouri, and his owner subsequently died. Abolitionists took Scott's case to court, stating that Scott was no longer a slave but free, since he had lived in free territory. The case went to the Supreme Court.

The Supreme Court stated that, because Scott, as a slave, was not a US citizen, his time in free states did not change his status. He also did not have the right to sue. In addition, the Court determined that the **Missouri Compromise** was unconstitutional, stating that Congress had overstepped its bounds by outlawing slavery in the territories.

ANTI-SLAVERY ORGANIZATIONS

Five anti-slavery organizations and their significance are:

- **American Colonization Society**—Protestant churches formed this group, aimed at returning black slaves to Africa. Former slaves subsequently formed Liberia, but the colony did not do well, as the region was not well-suited for agriculture.
- **American Anti-Slavery Society**—William Lloyd Garrison, a Quaker, was the major force behind this group and its newspaper, *The Liberator.*
- **Philadelphia Female Anti-Slavery Society**—this women-only group was formed by Margaretta Forten because women were not allowed to join the Anti-Slavery Society formed by her father.
- **Anti-Slavery Convention of American Women**—this group continued meeting even after pro-slavery factions burned down their original meeting place.
- **Female Vigilant Society**—this organization raised funds to help the Underground Railroad, as well as slave refugees.

INCIDENTS AT HARPER'S FERRY AND JOHN BROWN'S ROLE

John Brown, an abolitionist, had participated in several anti-slavery activities, including killing five pro-slavery men in retaliation, after the sacking of Lawrence, Kansas, an anti-slavery town. He and other abolitionists also banded together to pool their funds and build a runaway slave colony.

In 1859, Brown seized a federal arsenal in **Harper's Ferry**, located in what is now West Virginia. Brown intended to seize guns and ammunition and lead a slave rebellion. **Robert E. Lee** captured Brown and 21 followers, who were subsequently tried and hanged. While Northerners took the executions as an indication that the government supported slavery, Southerners were of the opinion that most of the North supported Brown and were, in general, anti-slavery.

PRESIDENTIAL CANDIDATES FOR THE 1860 ELECTION

The 1860 presidential candidates represented four different parties, each with a different opinion on slavery:

- **John Breckinridge**, representing the Southern Democrats, was pro-slavery but urged compromise to preserve the Union.
- **Abraham Lincoln**, of the Republican Party, was anti-slavery.
- **Stephen Douglas**, of the Northern Democrats, felt that the issue should be determined locally, on a state-by-state basis.
- **John Bell**, of the Constitutional Union Party, focused primarily on keeping the Union intact.

In the end, Abraham Lincoln won both the popular and electoral election. Southern states, who had sworn to secede from the Union if Lincoln was elected, did so, led by South Carolina. Shortly thereafter, the Civil War began when Confederate shots were fired on **Fort Sumter** in Charleston.

North vs. South in the Civil War

The Northern states had significant advantages, including:

- **Larger population**—the North consisted of 24 states, while the South had 11.
- **Better transportation and finances**—with railroads primarily in the North, supply chains were much more dependable, as was overseas trade.
- **Raw materials**—the North held the majority of America's gold, as well as iron, copper, and other minerals vital to wartime.

The South's advantages included the following:

- **Better-trained military officers**—many of the Southern officers were West Point trained and had commanded in the Mexican and Indian wars.
- **Familiarity with weapons**—the climate and lifestyle of the South meant most of the people were experienced with both guns and horses. The industrial North had less extensive experience.
- **Defensive position**—the South felt that victory was guaranteed, since they were protecting their own lands, while the North would be invading.
- **Well-defined goals**—the South fought an ideological war to be allowed to govern themselves and preserve their way of life. The North originally fought to preserve the Union and later to free the slaves.

Review Video: American Civil War: North vs. South Overview
Visit mometrix.com/academy and enter code: 370788

Benefit of the Emancipation Proclamation on the Union's Military Strategy

The Emancipation Proclamation, issued by President Lincoln on January 1, 1863, freed all slaves in **Confederate states** that were still in rebellion against the Union. While the original proclamation did not free any slaves in the states actually under Union control, it did set a precedent for the emancipation of slaves as the war progressed.

The **Emancipation Proclamation** worked in the Union's favor, as many freed slaves and other black troops joined the **Union Army**. Almost 200,000 blacks fought in the Union army, and over 10,000 served in the navy. By the end of the war, over 4 million slaves had been freed, and in 1865 slavery was abolished in the **13th amendment** to the Constitution.

Review Video: The Civil War: The Emancipation Proclamation
Visit mometrix.com/academy and enter code: 181778

Major Events of the Civil War

Six major events of the Civil War and their outcomes or significance are:

- The **First Battle of Bull Run** (July 21, 1861)—this was the first major land battle of the war. Observers, expecting to enjoy an entertaining skirmish, set up picnics nearby. Instead, they found themselves witness to a bloodbath. Union forces were defeated, and the battle set the course of the Civil War as long, bloody, and costly.
- The **Capture of Fort Henry** by Ulysses S. Grant—this battle in February of 1862 marked the Union's first major victory.
- The **Battle of Gettysburg** (July 1-3, 1863)—often seen as the turning point of the war, Gettysburg also saw the largest number of casualties of the war, with over 50,000 dead, wounded, or missing. Robert E. Lee was defeated, and the Confederate army, significantly crippled, withdrew.
- The **Overland Campaign** (May and June of 1864)—Grant, now in command of all the Union armies, led this high casualty campaign that eventually positioned the Union for victory.

- **Sherman's March to the Sea**—William Tecumseh Sherman, in May of 1864, conquered Atlanta. He then continued to Savannah, destroying vast amounts of property as he went.
- Following Lee's defeat at the Appomattox Courthouse, General Grant accepted **Lee's surrender** in the home of Wilmer McLean in Appomattox, Virginia on April 9, 1865.

Circumstances of Lincoln's Assassination

The Civil War ended with the surrender of the South on April 9, 1865. Five days later, Lincoln and his wife, Mary, went to the play *Our American Cousin* at the Ford Theater. John Wilkes Booth, who did not know that the war was over, did his part in a plot to help the Confederacy by shooting Lincoln. He was carried from the theater to a nearby house, where he died the next morning. Booth was tracked down and killed by Union soldiers twelve days later.

Review Video: Overview of the American Civil War
Visit mometrix.com/academy and enter code: 239557

Goals of Reconstruction and the Freedmen's Bureau

In the aftermath of the Civil War, the South was left in chaos. From 1865 to 1877, government on all levels worked to help restore order to the South, ensure civil rights to the freed slaves, and bring the Confederate states back into the Union. This became known as the **Reconstruction period**. In 1866, Congress passed the **Reconstruction Acts**, placing former Confederate states under military rule and stating the grounds for readmission into the Union.

The **Freedmen's Bureau** was formed to help freedmen both with basic necessities like food and clothing and also with employment and finding of family members who had been separated during the war. Many in the South felt the Freedmen's Bureau worked to set freed slaves against their former owners. The Bureau was intended to help former slaves become self-sufficient, and to keep them from falling prey to those who would take advantage of them. It eventually closed due to lack of funding and to violence from the **Ku Klux Klan**.

Policies of the Radical and Moderate Republicans

The **Radical Republicans** wished to treat the South quite harshly after the war. **Thaddeus Stevens**, the House Leader, suggested that the Confederate states be treated as if they were territories again, with ten years of military rule and territorial government before they would be readmitted. He also wanted to give all black men the right to vote. Former Confederate soldiers would be required to swear they had never supported the Confederacy (knows as the "Ironclad Oath") in order to be granted full rights as American citizens.

In contrast, the **moderate Republicans** wanted only black men who were literate or who had served as Union troops to be able to vote. All Confederate soldiers except troop leaders would also be able to vote. Before his death, **Lincoln** had favored a more moderate approach to Reconstruction, hoping this approach might bring some states back into the Union before the end of the war.

Phases of Reconstruction

The three phases of Reconstruction are:

- **Presidential Reconstruction**—largely driven by President Andrew Johnson's policies, the presidential phase of Reconstruction was lenient on the South and allowed continued discrimination against and control over blacks.
- **Congressional Reconstruction**—Congress, controlled largely by Radical Republicans, took a different stance, providing a wider range of civil rights for blacks and greater control over Southern government. Congressional Reconstruction is marked by military control of the former Confederate States.

- **Redemption**—gradually, the Confederate states were readmitted into the Union. During this time, white Democrats took over the government of most of the South. In 1877, President Rutherford Hayes withdrew the last federal troops from the South.

Carpetbaggers and Scalawags

The chaos in the South attracted a number of people seeking to fill the power vacuums and take advantage of the economic disruption. **Scalawags** were southern whites who aligned with freedmen to take over local governments. Many in the South who could have filled political offices refused to take the necessary oath required to grant them the right to vote, leaving many opportunities for Scalawags and others. **Carpetbaggers** were Northerners who traveled to the South for various reasons. Some provided assistance, while others sought to make money or to acquire political power during this chaotic period.

Black Codes and the Civil Rights Bill

The Black Codes were proposed to control freed slaves. They would not be allowed to bear arms, assemble, serve on juries, or testify against whites. Schools would be segregated, and unemployed blacks could be arrested and forced to work. The **Civil Rights Act** countered these codes, providing much wider rights for the freed slaves.

Andrew Johnson, who became president after Lincoln's death, supported the Black Codes and vetoed the Civil Rights Act in 1865 and again in 1866. The second time, Congress overrode his veto, and it became law.

Two years later, Congress voted to **impeach** Johnson, the culmination of tensions between Congress and the president. He was tried and came within a single vote of being convicted, but ultimately was acquitted and finished his term in office.

Purpose of the Thirteenth, Fourteenth, and Fifteenth Amendments

The Thirteenth, Fourteenth and Fifteenth Amendments were all passed shortly after the end of the Civil War:

- The **Thirteenth Amendment** was ratified by the states on December 6, 1865. This amendment prohibited slavery in the United States.
- The **Fourteenth Amendment** overturned the Dred Scott decision and was ratified July 9, 1868. American citizenship was redefined: a citizen was any person born or naturalized in the US, with all citizens guaranteed equal legal protection by all states. It also guaranteed citizens of any race the right to file a lawsuit or serve on a jury.
- The **Fifteenth Amendment** was ratified on February 3, 1870. It states that no citizen of the United States can be denied the right to vote based on race, color, or previous status as a slave.

Developments in Transportation

As America expanded its borders, it also developed new technology to travel the rapidly growing country. Roads and railroads traversed the nation, with the **Transcontinental Railroad** eventually allowing travel from one coast to the other. Canals and steamboats simplified water travel and made shipping easier and less expensive. The **Erie Canal** (1825) connected the Great Lakes to the Hudson River. Other canals connected other major waterways, further facilitating transportation and the shipment of goods.

Transcontinental Railroad

In 1869, the **Union Pacific Railroad** completed the first section of a planned **transcontinental railroad**. This section went from Omaha, Nebraska to Sacramento, California. Ninety percent of the workers were Chinese, working in very dangerous conditions for very low pay. With the rise of the railroad, products were much more easily transported across the country. While this was positive overall for industry throughout the country, it was often damaging to family farmers, who found themselves paying high shipping costs for smaller supply orders while larger companies received major discounts.

Measures to Limit Immigration in the 19th Century

In 1870, the **Naturalization Act** put limits on US citizenship, allowing full citizenship only to whites and those of African descent. The **Chinese Exclusion Act of 1882** put limits on Chinese immigration. The **Immigration Act of 1882** taxed immigrants, charging 50 cents per person. These funds helped pay administrative costs for regulating immigration. **Ellis Island** opened in 1892 as a processing center for those arriving in New York. The year 1921 saw the **Emergency Quota Act** passed, also known as the **Johnson Quota Act**, which severely limited the number of immigrants allowed into the country.

Agriculture in the 19th Century

Technological Advances in Agricultural Changes

During the mid-1800s, irrigation techniques improved significantly. Advances occurred in cultivation and breeding, as well as fertilizer use and crop rotation. In the Great Plains, also known as the Great American Desert, the dense soil was finally cultivated with steel plows. In 1892, gasoline-powered tractors arrived, and they were widely used by 1900. Other advancements in agriculture's toolset included barbed wire fences, combines, silos, deep-water wells, and the cream separator.

Major Actions That Helped Improve Agriculture

Four major government actions that helped improve US agriculture in the 19th century are:

- The **Department of Agriculture** came into being in 1862, working for the interests of farmers and ranchers across the country.
- The **Morrill Land-Grant Acts** were a series of acts passed between 1862 and 1890, allowing land-grant colleges.
- In conjunction with land-grant colleges, the **Hatch Act of 1887** brought agriculture experiment stations into the picture, helping discover new farming techniques.
- In 1914, the **Smith-Lever Act** provided cooperative programs to help educate people about food, home economics, community development, and agriculture. Related agriculture extension programs helped farmers increase crop production to feed the rapidly growing nation.

Inventors from the 1800s

Major inventors from the 1800s and their inventions include:

- Alexander Graham Bell—the telephone
- Orville and Wilbur Wright—the airplane
- Richard Gatling—the machine gun
- Walter Hunt, Elias Howe, and Isaac Singer—the sewing machine
- Nikola Tesla—alternating current motor
- George Eastman—the Kodak camera
- Thomas Edison—light bulbs, motion pictures, the phonograph
- Samuel Morse—the telegraph
- Charles Goodyear—vulcanized rubber
- Cyrus McCormick—the reaper
- George Westinghouse—the transformer, the air brake

This was an active period for invention, with about 700,000 patents registered between 1860 and 1900.

Gilded Age

The time period from the end of the Civil War to the beginning of the First World War is often referred to as the **Gilded Age**, or the **Second Industrial Revolution**. The US was changing from an agricultural-based economy to an **industrial economy**, with rapid growth accompanying the shift. In addition, the country itself was expanding, spreading into the seemingly unlimited west.

This time period saw the beginning of banks, department stores, chain stores, and trusts—all familiar features of the modern-day landscape. Cities also grew rapidly, and large numbers of immigrants arrived in the country, swelling the urban ranks.

Review Video: The Gilded Age: An Overview
Visit mometrix.com/academy and enter code: 684770

Review Video: The Gilded Age: Chinese Immigration
Visit mometrix.com/academy and enter code: 624166

Factors Leading to the Development of the Populist Party

A major **recession** struck the United States during the 1890s, with crop prices falling dramatically. **Drought** compounded the problems, leaving many American farmers in crippling debt. The **Farmers' Alliance** formed in 1875, drawing the rural poor into a single political entity.

Recession also affected the more industrial parts of the country. The **Knights of Labor**, formed in 1869 by **Uriah Stephens**, was able to unite workers into a union to protect their rights. Dissatisfied by views espoused by industrialists, the Farmers Alliance and the Knights of Labor, joined to form the **Populist Party**, also known as the People's Party, in 1892. Some of the elements of the party's platform included:

- National currency
- Graduated income tax
- Government ownership of railroads as well as telegraph and telephone systems
- Secret ballots for voting
- Immigration restriction
- Single-term limits for president and vice-president

The Populist Party was in favor of decreasing elitism and making the voice of the common man more easily heard in the political process.

Growth of the Labor Movement Through the Late 19th Century

One of the first large, well-organized strikes occurred in 1892. Called the **Homestead Strike**, it occurred when the Amalgamated Association of Iron and Steel Workers struck against the Carnegie Steel Company. Gunfire ensued, and Carnegie was able to eliminate the plant's union. In 1894, workers in the American Railway Union, led by Eugene Debs, initiated the **Pullman Strike** after the Pullman Palace Car Co. cut their wages by 28 percent. President Grover Cleveland called in troops to break up the strike on the grounds that it interfered with mail delivery. Mary Harris "Mother" Jones organized the **Children's Crusade** to protest child labor. A protest march proceeded to the home of President Theodore Roosevelt in 1903. Jones also worked with the United Mine Workers of America and helped found the **Industrial Workers of the World**.

Panic of 1893

Far from a US-centric event, the **Panic of 1893** was an economic crisis that affected most of the globe. As a response, President Grover Cleveland repealed the **Sherman Silver Purchase Act**, afraid it had caused the downturn rather than boosting the economy as intended. The Panic led to bankruptcies, with banks and railroads going under and factory unemployment rising as high as 25 percent. In the end, the **Republican Party** regained power due to the economic crisis.

Progressive Era

From the 1890s to the end of the First World War, **Progressives** set forth an ideology that drove many levels of society and politics. The Progressives were in favor of workers' rights and safety and wanted measures taken against waste and corruption. They felt science could help improve society and that the government could—and should—provide answers to a variety of social problems. Progressives came from a wide variety of backgrounds but were united in their desire to improve society.

Muckrakers and the Progressive Movement

"Muckrakers" was a term used to identify aggressive investigative journalists who exposed scandals, corruption, and many other wrongs in late 19th-century society. Among these intrepid writers were:

- **Ida Tarbell**—she exposed John D. Rockefeller's Standard Oil Trust.
- **Jacob Riis**—a photographer, he brought the living conditions of the poor in New York to the public's attention.
- **Lincoln Steffens**—he worked to expose political corruption in municipal government.
- **Upton Sinclair**—his book *The Jungle* led to reforms in the meat-packing industry.

Through the work of these journalists, many new policies came into being, including workmen's compensation, child labor laws, and trust-busting.

Government Dealings with Native Americans Through the End of the 19th Century

America's westward expansion led to conflict and violent confrontations with Native Americans such as the **Battle of Little Bighorn**. In 1876, the American government ordered all Native Americans to relocate to reservations. Lack of compliance led to the **Dawes Act** in 1887, which ordered assimilation rather than separation: Native Americans were offered American citizenship and a piece of their tribal land if they would accept the lot chosen by the government and live on it separately from the tribe. This act remained in effect until 1934. Reformers also forced Native American children to attend **boarding schools**, where they were not allowed to speak their native language and were immersed into a Euro-American culture and religion. Children were often abused in these schools and were indoctrinated to abandon their identity as Native Americans.

In 1890, the massacre at **Wounded Knee**, accompanied by Geronimo's surrender, led the Native Americans to work to preserve their culture rather than fight for their lands.

Review Video: Government Dealings with Native Americans Through 1900
Visit mometrix.com/academy and enter code: 635645

Role of Native Americans in Wartime Through the Beginning of the 20th Century

The **Spanish-American War** (1898) saw a number of Native Americans serving with Teddy Roosevelt in the Rough Riders. Apache scouts accompanied General John J. Pershing to Mexico, hoping to find **Pancho Villa**. More than 17,000 Native Americans were drafted into service for **World War I**, though at the time, they were not considered legal citizens. In 1924, Native Americans were finally granted official citizenship by the **Indian Citizenship Act**.

After decades of relocation, forced assimilation, and genocide, the number of Native Americans in the US has greatly declined. Though many Native Americans have chosen—or have been forced—to assimilate, about 300 reservations exist today, with most of their inhabitants living in abject poverty.

Review Video: Wartime Role of Native Americans
Visit mometrix.com/academy and enter code: 419128

Events Leading up to the Spanish-American War

Spain had controlled **Cuba** since the 15th century. Over the centuries, the Spanish had quashed a variety of revolts. In 1886, slavery ended in Cuba, and another revolt was rising.

In the meantime, the US had expressed interest in Cuba, offering Spain $130 million for the island in 1853, during Franklin Pierce's presidency. In 1898, the Cuban revolt was underway. In spite of various factions supporting the Cubans, the US President, William McKinley, refused to recognize the rebellion, preferring negotiation over involvement in war. Then, the *Maine*, a US battleship in Havana Harbor, was blown up, killing 266 crew members. The US declared war two months later, and the war ended with a **Spanish surrender** in less than four months.

American History 1899 to Present

Influence of Big Stick Diplomacy on American Foreign Policy in Latin America

Theodore Roosevelt's famous quote, "Speak softly and carry a big stick," is supposedly of African origins, at least according to Roosevelt. He used this proverb to justify expanded involvement in foreign affairs during his tenure as President. The US military was deployed to protect American interests in **Latin America**. Roosevelt also worked to maintain an equal or greater influence in Latin America than those held by European interests. As a result, the US Navy grew larger, and the US generally became more involved in foreign affairs. Roosevelt felt that if any country was left vulnerable to control by Europe due to economic issues or political instability, the US had not only a right to intervene but was **obligated** to do so. This led to US involvement in Cuba, Nicaragua, Haiti, and the Dominican Republic over several decades leading into the First and Second World Wars.

Importance of the Panama Canal

Initial work began on the **Panama Canal** in 1881, though the idea had been discussed since the 1500s. The canal greatly reduces the length and time needed to sail from one ocean to the other by connecting the Atlantic to the Pacific through the Isthmus of Panama, which joins South America to North America. Before the canal was built, travelers had to sail around the entire perimeter of South America to reach the West Coast of the US. The French began the work after successfully completing the **Suez Canal**, which connected the Mediterranean Sea to the Red Sea. However, due to disease and high expense, the work moved slowly, and after eight years, the company went bankrupt, suspending work. The US purchased the holdings, and the first ship sailed through the canal in 1914. The Panama Canal was constructed as a lock-and-lake canal, with ships lifted on locks to travel from one lake to another over the rugged, mountainous terrain. In order to maintain control of the Canal Zone, the US assisted Panama in its battle for independence from **Colombia**.

Taft's Dollar Diplomacy vs. Roosevelt's Diplomatic Theories

During William Howard Taft's presidency, Taft instituted "**Dollar Diplomacy**." This approach was America's effort to influence Latin America and East Asia through economic rather than military means. Taft saw past efforts in these areas to be political and warlike, while his efforts focused on peaceful economic goals. His justification of the policy was to protect the **Panama Canal**, which was vital to US trade interests.

In spite of Taft's assurance that Dollar Diplomacy was a peaceful approach, many interventions proved violent. During Latin American revolts, such as those in **Nicaragua**, the US sent troops to settle the revolutions. Afterward, bankers moved in to help support the new leaders through loans. Dollar Diplomacy continued until 1913, when Woodrow Wilson was elected president.

Growth of Civil Rights for African Americans

Marcus Garvey founded the **Universal Negro Improvement Association and African Communities League (UNIA-ACL)**, which became a large and active organization focused on building black nationalism. In 1909, the **National Association for the Advancement of Colored People (NAACP)** came into being, working to defeat Jim Crow laws. The NAACP also helped prevent racial segregation from becoming federal law, fought against lynchings, helped black soldiers in WWI become officers, and helped defend the Scottsboro Boys, who were unjustly accused of rape.

Wilson's Approach to International Diplomacy

Turning away from Taft's "Dollar Diplomacy," Wilson instituted a foreign policy he referred to as "**moral diplomacy**." This approach still influences American foreign policy today.

Wilson felt that **representative government and democracy** in all countries would lead to worldwide stability. Democratic governments, he felt, would be less likely to threaten American interests. He also saw the US and Great Britain as the great role models in this area, as well as champions of world peace and self-government. Free trade and international commerce would allow the US to speak out regarding world events.

Main elements of Wilson's policies included:

- Maintaining a strong military
- Promoting democracy throughout the world
- Expanding international trade to boost the American economy

Provisions of the Sixteenth, Seventeenth, Eighteenth, and Nineteenth Amendments

The early 20th century saw several amendments made to the US Constitution:

- The **Sixteenth Amendment** (1913) established a federal income tax.
- The **Seventeenth Amendment** (1913) allowed popular election of senators.
- The **Eighteenth Amendment** (1919) prohibited the sale, production, and transportation of alcohol. This amendment was later repealed by the Twenty-first Amendment.
- The **Nineteenth Amendment** (1920) gave women the right to vote.

These amendments largely grew out of the Progressive Era, as many citizens worked to improve American society.

Goals of the Anti-Defamation League

In 1913, the Anti-Defamation League was formed to prevent anti-Semitic behavior and practices. Its actions also worked to prevent all forms of racism and to prevent individuals from being discriminated against for any reason involving their race. They spoke against the Ku Klux Klan, as well as other racist or anti-Semitic organizations. This organization still works to fight discrimination against all minorities.

Role of the Federal Trade Commission in Eliminating Trusts

Muckrakers such as Ida Tarbell and Lincoln Steffens brought to light the damaging trend of trusts—huge corporations working to monopolize areas of commerce so they could control prices and distribution. The **Sherman Antitrust Act** and the **Clayton Antitrust Act** set out guidelines for competition among corporations and set out to eliminate these trusts. The **Federal Trade Commission** was formed in 1914 in order to enforce antitrust measures and ensure that companies were operated fairly and did not create controlling monopolies.

Major Events of World War I

World War I occurred from 1914 to 1918 and was fought largely in Europe. Triggered by the assassination of Austrian Archduke Franz Ferdinand, the war rapidly escalated. At the beginning of the conflict, Woodrow Wilson declared the US neutral. Major events influencing US involvement included:

- **Sinking of the *Lusitania***—the British passenger liner RMS *Lusitania* was sunk by a German U-boat in 1915. Among the 1,000 civilian victims were over 100 American citizens. Outraged by this act, many Americans began to push for US involvement in the war, using the *Lusitania* as a rallying cry.
- **German U-boat aggression**—Wilson continued to keep the US out of the war, using as his 1916 reelection slogan, "He kept us out of war." While he continued to work toward an end of the war, German U-boats began to indiscriminately attack American and Canadian merchant ships carrying supplies to Germany's enemies in Europe.

- **Zimmerman Telegram** —the final event that brought the US into World War I was the interception of the Zimmerman Telegram (also known as the Zimmerman Note). In this telegram, Germany proposed forming an alliance with Mexico if the US entered the war.

Efforts in the US During World War I Supporting the War Effort

American **railroads** came under government control in December 1917. The widespread system was consolidated into a single system, with each region assigned a director. This greatly increased the efficiency of the railroad system, allowing the railroads to supply both domestic and military needs. Control returned to private ownership in 1920. In 1918, **telegraph, telephone, and cable services** also came under Federal control, to be returned to private management the next year. The **American Red Cross** supported the war effort by knitting clothes for Army and Navy troops. They also helped supply hospital and refugee clothing and surgical dressings. Over 8 million people participated in this effort. To generate wartime funds, the US government sold **Liberty Bonds**. In four issues, they sold nearly $25 billion—more than one-fifth of Americans purchased them. After the war, a fifth bond drive was held but sold "**Victory Liberty Bonds**."

Review Video: WWI Overview
Visit mometrix.com/academy and enter code: 659767

Influence of Wilson's Fourteen Points on the Final Peace Treaties that Ended World War I

President Woodrow Wilson proposed **Fourteen Points** as the basis for a peace settlement to end the war. Presented to the US Congress in January 1918, the Fourteen Points included:

- Five points outlining **general ideals**
- Eight points to resolve **immediate problems** of political and territorial nature
- One point proposing an **organization of nations** (the League of Nations) with the intent of maintaining world peace

In November of that same year, Germany agreed to an **armistice**, assuming the final treaty would be based on the Fourteen Points. However, during the peace conference in Paris 1919, there was much disagreement, leading to a final agreement that punished Germany and the other Central Powers much more than originally intended. Henry Cabot Lodge, who had become the Foreign Relations Committee chairman in 1918, wanted an unconditional surrender from Germany and was concerned about the article in the **Treaty of Versailles** that gave the League of Nations power to declare war without a vote from the US Congress. A **League of Nations** was included in the Treaty of Versailles at Wilson's insistence. The Senate rejected the Treaty of Versailles, and in the end, Wilson refused to concede to Lodge's demands. As a result, the US did not join the League of Nations.

Origins of the Red Scare

World War I created many jobs, but after the war ended, these jobs disappeared, leaving many unemployed. In the wake of these employment changes, the **International Workers of the World** and the **Socialist Party**, headed by Eugene Debs, became more and more visible. Workers initiated strikes in an attempt to regain the favorable working conditions that had been put into place before the war. Unfortunately, many of these strikes became violent, and the actions were blamed on "Reds," or Communists, for trying to spread their views into America. With the recent Bolshevik Revolution in Russia, many Americans feared a similar revolution might occur in the US. The **Red Scare** ensued, with many individuals jailed for supposedly holding communist, anarchist, or socialist beliefs.

Major Changes and Events that Took Place in America During the 1920s

The post-war 1920s saw many Americans moving from the farm to the city, with growing prosperity in the US. The **Roaring Twenties**, or the **Jazz Age**, was driven largely by growth in the automobile and entertainment industries. Individuals like Charles Lindbergh, the first aviator to make a solo flight across the Atlantic Ocean, added to the American admiration of individual accomplishment. Telephone lines, distribution of electricity, highways, the radio, and other inventions brought great changes to everyday life.

Review Video: 1920's
Visit mometrix.com/academy and enter code: 124996

Major Cultural Movements of the 1920s Influenced by African Americans

The **Harlem Renaissance** saw a number of African-American artists settling in Harlem in New York. This community produced a number of well-known artists and writers, including Langston Hughes, Nella Larsen, Zora Neale Hurston, Claude McKay, Countee Cullen, and Jean Toomer. The growth of jazz, also largely driven by African Americans, defined the **Jazz Age**. Its unconventional, improvisational style matched the growing sense of optimism and exploration of the decade. Originating as an offshoot of the blues, jazz began in New Orleans. Some significant jazz musicians were Duke Ellington, Louis Armstrong, and Jelly Roll Morton. **Big Band** and **Swing Jazz** also developed in the 1920s. Well-known musicians of this movement included Bing Crosby, Frank Sinatra, Count Basie, Benny Goodman, Billie Holiday, Ella Fitzgerald, and The Dorsey Brothers.

American Civil Liberties Union

The American Civil Liberties Union (**ACLU**), founded in 1920, grew from the American Union Against Militarism. The ACLU helped conscientious objectors avoid going to war during WWI, and also helped those being prosecuted under the **Espionage Act** (1917) and the **Sedition Act** (1918), many of whom were immigrants. Their major goals were to protect immigrants and other citizens who were threatened with prosecution for their political beliefs, and to support labor unions, which were also under threat by the government during the Red Scare.

Provisions and Importance of the National Origins Act of 1924

The National Origins Act (Johnson-Reed Act) placed limitations on **immigration**. The number of immigrants allowed into the US was based on the population of each nationality of immigrants who were living in the country in 1890. Only two percent of each nationality's 1890 population numbers were allowed to immigrate. This led to great disparities between immigrants from various nations, and Asian immigration was not allowed at all. Some of the impetus behind the Johnson-Reed Act came as a result of paranoia following the **Russian Revolution**. Fear of communist influences in the US led to a general fear of immigrants.

Ku Klux Klan

In 1866, Confederate Army veterans came together to fight against Reconstruction in the South, forming a group called the **Ku Klux Klan (KKK)**. With white supremacist beliefs, including anti-Semitism, nativism, anti-Catholicism, and overt racism, this organization relied heavily on violence to get its message across. In 1915, they grew again in power, using a film called *The Birth of a Nation*, by D.W. Griffith, to spread their ideas. In the 1920s, the reach of the KKK spread far into the north and midwest, and members controlled a number of state governments. Its membership and power began to decline during the Great Depression but experienced a resurgence later.

Roosevelt's New Deal

The **Great Depression**, which began in 1929 with the stock market crash, grew out of several factors that had developed over the previous years, including:

- Growing economic disparity between the rich and middle classes, with the rich amassing wealth much more quickly than the lower classes
- Disparity in economic distribution in industries
- Growing use of credit, leading to an inflated demand for some goods
- Government support of new industries rather than agriculture
- Risky stock market investments, leading to the stock market crash

Additional factors contributing to the Depression also included the **Labor Day Hurricane** in the Florida Keys (1935) and the **Great Hurricane of 1938** in New England, along with the **Dust Bowl** in the Great Plains, which destroyed crops and resulted in the displacement of as many as 2.5 million people.

Review Video: Causes of the Great Depression
Visit mometrix.com/academy and enter code: 635912

Franklin D. Roosevelt was elected president in 1932 with his promise of a "**New Deal**" for Americans. His goals were to provide government work programs to provide jobs, wages, and relief to numerous workers throughout the beleaguered US. Congress gave Roosevelt almost free rein to produce relief legislation. The goals of this legislation were:

- **Relief**—creating jobs for the high numbers of unemployed
- **Recovery**—stimulating the economy through the National Recovery Administration
- **Reform**—passing legislation to prevent future, similar economic crashes

The Roosevelt Administration also passed legislation regarding ecological issues, including the Soil Conservation Service, aimed at preventing another Dust Bowl.

Roosevelt's Alphabet Organizations

So-called "alphabet organizations" set up during Roosevelt's administration included:

- **Civilian Conservation Corps** (CCC)—provided jobs in the forestry service
- **Agricultural Adjustment Administration** (AAA)—increased agricultural income by adjusting both production and prices
- **Tennessee Valley Authority** (TVA)—organized projects to build dams in the Tennessee River for flood control and production of electricity, resulting in increased productivity for industries in the area, and easier navigation of the Tennessee River
- **Public Works Administration** (PWA) and Civil Works Administration (CWA)—provided a multitude of jobs, initiating over 34,000 projects
- **Works Progress Administration** (WPA)—helped unemployed persons to secure employment on government work projects or elsewhere

Actions Taken During the Roosevelt Administration to Prevent Future Crashes

The Roosevelt administration passed several laws and established several institutions to initiate the "reform" portion of the New Deal, including:

- **Glass-Steagall Act**—separated investment from commercial banking
- **Securities Exchange Commission (SEC)**—helped regulate Wall Street investment practices, making them less dangerous to the overall economy
- **Wagner Act**—provided worker and union rights to improve relations between employees and employers
- **Social Security Act of 1935**—provided pensions as well as unemployment insurance

Other actions focused on insuring bank deposits and adjusting the value of American currency. Most of these regulatory agencies and government policies and programs still exist today.

Major Regulations Regarding Labor After the Great Depression

Three major regulations regarding labor that were passed after the Great Depression are:

- The **Wagner Act** (1935)—also known as the National Labor Relations Act, it established that unions were legal, protected members of unions, and required collective bargaining. This act was later amended by the Taft-Hartley Act of 1947 and the Landrum-Griffin Act of 1959, which further clarified certain elements.
- **Davis-Bacon Act** (1931)—provided fair compensation for contractors and subcontractors.
- **Walsh-Healey Act** (1936)—established a minimum wage, child labor laws, safety standards, and overtime pay.

Interventionist and Isolationist Approaches in World War II

When war broke out in Europe in 1939, President Roosevelt stated that the US would remain **neutral**. However, his overall approach was considered "**interventionist**," as he was willing to provide aid to the Allies without actually entering the conflict. Thus, the US supplied a wide variety of war materials to the Allied nations in the early years of the war.

Isolationists believed the US should not provide any aid to the Allies, including supplies. They felt Roosevelt, by assisting the Allies, was leading the US into a war for which it was not prepared. Led by Charles Lindbergh, the Isolationists believed that any involvement in the European conflict endangered the US by weakening its national defense.

Sequence of Events that Led the US to Declare War and Enter World War II

In 1937, Japan invaded China, prompting the US to eventually halt exports to Japan. Roosevelt also did not allow Japanese interests to withdraw money held in US banks. In 1941, **General Tojo** rose to power as the Japanese prime minister. Recognizing America's ability to bring a halt to Japan's expansion, he authorized the bombing of **Pearl Harbor** on December 7. The US responded by declaring war on Japan. Partially because of the **Tripartite Pact** among the Axis Powers, Germany and Italy then declared war on the US, later followed by Bulgaria, Hungary, and other Axis nations.

Review Video: World War II Overview
Visit mometrix.com/academy and enter code: 759402

Occurrences of World War II that Led to the Surrender of Germany

In 1941, **Hitler** violated the non-aggression pact he had signed with Stalin two years earlier by invading the USSR. **Stalin** then joined the **Allies**. Stalin, Roosevelt, and Winston Churchill planned to defeat Germany first, then Japan, bringing the war to an end.

In 1942-1943, the Allies drove **Axis** forces out of Africa. In addition, the Germans were soundly defeated at Stalingrad.

The **Italian Campaign** involved Allied operations in Italy between July 1943 and May 1945, including Italy's liberation. On June 6, 1944, known as **D-Day**, the Allies invaded France at Normandy. Soviet troops moved on the eastern front at the same time, driving German forces back. By April 25, 1945, Berlin was surrounded by Soviet troops. On May 7, Germany surrendered.

Major Events of World War II that Led to the Surrender of Japan

War continued with **Japan** after Germany's surrender. Japanese forces had taken a large portion of Southeast Asia and the Western Pacific, all the way to the Aleutian Islands in Alaska. **General Doolittle** bombed several Japanese cities while American troops scored a victory at Midway. Additional fighting in the Battle of the Coral Sea further weakened Japan's position. As a final blow, the US dropped two **atomic bombs** on Japan, one on Hiroshima and the other on Nagasaki. This was the first time atomic bombs had been used in warfare, and the devastation was horrific and demoralizing. Japan surrendered on September 2, 1945, which became **V-J Day** in the US.

Significance of the 442nd Regimental Combat Team, the Tuskegee Airmen, and the Navajo Code Talkers during World War II

The 442nd Regimental Combat Team consisted of Japanese-Americans fighting in Europe for the US. The most highly decorated unit per member in US history, they suffered a 93% casualty rate during the war. The **Tuskegee Airmen** were African American aviators, the first black Americans allowed to fly for the military. In spite of being ineligible to become official navy pilots, they flew over 15,000 missions and were highly decorated. The **Navajo Code Talkers** were native Navajo who used their traditional language to transmit information among Allied forces. Because Navajo is a language and not simply a code, the Axis powers were never able to translate it. The use of Navajo Code Talkers to transmit information was instrumental in the taking of Iwo Jima and other major victories of the war.

Circumstances and Opportunities for Women During World War II

Women served widely in the military during WWII, working in numerous positions, including the **Flight Nurses Corps**. Women also moved into the workforce while men were overseas, leading to over 19 million women in the US workforce by 1944. **Rosie the Riveter** stood as a symbol of these women and a means of recruiting others to take needed positions. Women, as well as their families left behind during wartime, also grew **Victory Gardens** to help provide food.

Importance of the Atomic Bomb During World War II

The atomic bomb, developed during WWII, was the most powerful bomb ever invented. A single bomb, carried by a single plane, held enough power to destroy an entire city. This devastating effect was demonstrated with the bombing of **Hiroshima** and **Nagasaki** in 1945 in what later became a controversial move, but ended the war. The bombings resulted in as many as 150,000 immediate deaths and many more as time passed after the bombings, mostly due to **radiation poisoning**.

Whatever the arguments against the use of "The Bomb," the post-WWII era saw many countries develop similar weapons to match the newly expanded military power of the US. The impact of those developments and use of nuclear weapons continues to haunt international relations today.

Importance of the Yalta Conference and the Potsdam Conference

In February 1945, Joseph Stalin, Franklin D. Roosevelt, and Winston Churchill met in Yalta to discuss the post-war treatment of the **Axis nations**, particularly Germany. Though Germany had not yet surrendered, its defeat was imminent. After Germany's official surrender, Joseph Stalin, Harry Truman (Roosevelt's successor), and Clement Attlee (replacing Churchill partway through the conference) met to formalize those plans. This meeting was called the **Potsdam Conference**. Basic provisions of these agreements included:

- Dividing Germany and Berlin into four zones of occupation
- Demilitarization of Germany
- Poland remaining under Soviet control
- Outlawing the Nazi Party
- Trials for Nazi leaders
- Relocation of numerous German citizens
- The USSR joining the United Nations, established in 1945
- Establishment of the United Nations Security Council, consisting of the US, the UK, the USSR, China, and France

Agreements Made with Post-War Japan

General Douglas MacArthur led the American **military occupation of Japan** after the country surrendered. The goals of the US occupation included removing Japan's military and making the country a democracy. A

1947 constitution removed power from the emperor and gave it to the people, as well as granting voting rights to women. Japan was no longer allowed to declare war, and a group of 28 government officials were tried for war crimes. In 1951, the US finally signed a peace treaty with Japan. This treaty allowed Japan to rearm itself for purposes of self-defense but stripped the country of the empire it had built overseas.

US Treatment of Immigrants During and After World War II

In 1940, the US passed the **Alien Registration Act**, which required all aliens older than fourteen to be fingerprinted and registered. They were also required to report changes of address within five days.

Tension between whites and Japanese immigrants in **California**, which had been building since the beginning of the century, came to a head with the bombing of **Pearl Harbor** in 1941. Believing that even those Japanese living in the US were likely to be loyal to their native country, the president ordered numerous Japanese to be arrested on suspicion of subversive action and isolated in exclusion zones known as **War Relocation Camps**. Approximately 120,000 Japanese-Americans, two-thirds of them US citizens, were sent to these camps during the war.

General State of the US After World War II

Following WWII, the US became the strongest political power in the world, becoming a major player in world affairs and foreign policies. The US determined to stop the spread of **communism**, having named itself the "**arsenal of democracy**" during the war. In addition, America emerged with a greater sense of itself as a single, integrated nation, with many regional and economic differences diminished. The government worked for greater equality, and the growth of communications increased contact among different areas of the country. Both the aftermath of the Great Depression and the necessities of WWII had given the government greater **control** over various institutions as well as the economy. This also meant that the American government took on greater responsibility for the well-being of its citizens, both in the domestic arena, such as providing basic needs, and in protecting them from foreign threats. This increased role of providing basic necessities for all Americans has been criticized by some as "**the welfare state**."

US Policy Toward Immigrants After World War II

Prior to WWII, the US had been limiting **immigration** for several decades. After WWII, policy shifted slightly to accommodate political refugees from Europe and elsewhere. So many people were displaced by the war that in 1946, the UN formed the **International Refugee Organization** to deal with the problem. In 1948, the US Congress passed the **Displaced Persons Act**, which allowed over 400,000 European refugees to enter the US, most of them concentration camp survivors and refugees from Eastern Europe.

In 1952, the **United States Escapee Program (USEP)** increased the quotas, allowing refugees from communist Europe to enter the US, as did the **Refugee Relief Act**, passed in 1953. At the same time, however, the **Internal Security Act of 1950** allowed deportation of declared communists, and Asians were subjected to a quota based on race, rather than country of origin. Later changes included:

- **Migration and Refugee Assistance Act** (1962)—provided aid for refugees in need
- **Immigration and Nationality Act** (1965)—ended quotas based on nation of origin
- **Immigration Reform and Control Act** (1986)—prohibited the hiring of illegal immigrants but also granted amnesty to about three million illegals already in the country

Accomplishments of Harry S. Truman

Harry S. Truman took over the presidency from Franklin D. Roosevelt near the end of WWII. He made the final decision to drop atomic bombs on Japan and played a major role in the final decisions regarding the treatment of post-war Germany. On the domestic front, Truman initiated a 21-point plan known as the **Fair Deal**. This plan expanded Social Security, provided public housing, and made the Fair Employment Practice Committee permanent. Truman helped support Greece and Turkey (which were under threat from the USSR), supported

South Korea against communist North Korea, and helped with recovery in Western Europe. He also participated in the formation of **NATO**, the North Atlantic Treaty Organization.

Events and Importance of the Korean War

The Korean War began in 1950 and ended in 1953. For the first time in history, a world organization—the **United Nations**—played a military role in a war. North Korea sent communist troops into South Korea, seeking to bring the entire country under communist control. The UN sent out a call to member nations, asking them to support South Korea. Truman sent troops, as did many other UN member nations. The war ended three years later with a **truce** rather than a peace treaty, and Korea remains divided at the **38th parallel north**, with communist rule remaining in the North and a democratic government ruling the South.

Effects of US Cold War Foreign Policy Acts on the International Relationships

The following are US Cold War foreign policy acts and how they affected international relationships, especially between the US and the Soviet Union:

- **Marshall Plan**—this sent aid to war-torn Europe after WWII, largely focusing on preventing the spread of communism.
- **Containment Policy**—proposed by George F. Kennan, the containment policy focused on containing the spread of Soviet communism.
- **Truman Doctrine**—Harry S. Truman stated that the US would provide both economic and military support to any country threatened by Soviet takeover.
- **National Security Act**—passed in 1947, this act reorganized the government's military departments into the Department of Defense and created the Central Intelligence Agency and the National Security Council.

The combination of these acts led to the **Cold War**, with Soviet communists attempting to spread their influence and the US and other countries trying to contain or stop this spread.

Accomplishments of Dwight D. Eisenhower

Eisenhower carried out a middle-of-the-road foreign policy and brought the US several steps forward in equal rights. He worked to minimize tensions during the Cold War and negotiated a peace treaty with Russia after the death of Stalin. He enforced desegregation by sending troops to Little Rock Central High School in Arkansas, as well as ordering the desegregation of the military. Organizations formed during his administration included the Department of Health, Education, and Welfare, and the National Aeronautics and Space Administration (NASA).

Effect of the Arms Race on Post WWII International Relations

After World War II, major nations, particularly the US and USSR, rushed to develop highly advanced weapons systems such as the **atomic bomb** and later the **hydrogen bomb**. These countries seemed determined to outpace each other with the development of numerous, deadly weapons. These weapons were expensive and extremely dangerous, and it is possible that the war between US and Soviet interests remained "cold" due to the fear that one side or the other would use these powerful weapons.

Technological Advances that Occurred Throughout the 1900s

Numerous technological advances throughout the 1900s led to more effective treatment of diseases, more efficient communication and transportation, and new means of generating power. Advances in **medicine** increased the human lifespan in developed countries, and near-instantaneous **communication** opened up a myriad of possibilities. Some of these advances include:

- Discovery of penicillin (1928)
- Supersonic air travel (1947)
- Nuclear power plants (1951)

- Orbital satellite leading to manned space flight (Sputnik, 1957)
- First man on the moon (1969)

NATO, Warsaw Pact, and the Berlin Wall

NATO, the **North Atlantic Treaty Organization**, came into being in 1949. It essentially amounted to an agreement among the US and Western European countries that an attack on any one of these countries was to be considered an attack against the entire group. Under the influence of the Soviet Union, the Eastern European countries of the USSR, Bulgaria, East Germany, Poland, Romania, Albania, Hungary, and Czechoslovakia responded with the **Warsaw Pact**, which created a similar agreement among those nations. In 1961, a wall was built to separate communist East Berlin from democratic West Berlin. This was a literal representation of the "**Iron Curtain**" that separated the democratic and communist countries throughout the world.

Presidency of John F. Kennedy

Although his term was cut short by his assassination, **JFK** instituted economic programs that led to a period of continuous expansion in the US unmatched since before WWII. He formed the Alliance for Progress and the Peace Corps, organizations intended to help developing nations. He also oversaw the passage of new civil rights legislation and drafted plans to attack poverty and its causes, along with support of the arts. Kennedy's presidency ended when he was assassinated by **Lee Harvey Oswald** in 1963.

Events of the Cuban Missile Crisis

The Cuban Missile Crisis occurred in 1962, during John F. Kennedy's presidency. Russian Premier **Nikita Khrushchev** decided to place nuclear missiles in **Cuba** to protect the island from invasion by the US. An American U-2 plane flying over the island photographed the missile bases as they were being built. Tensions rose, with the US concerned about nuclear missiles so close to its shores, and the USSR concerned about American missiles that had been placed in **Turkey**. Eventually, the missile sites were removed, and a US naval blockade turned back Soviet ships carrying missiles to Cuba. During negotiations, the US agreed to remove their missiles from Turkey and agreed to sell surplus wheat to the USSR. A telephone hotline between Moscow and Washington was set up to allow instant communication between the two heads of state to prevent similar incidents in the future.

Accomplishments of the Lyndon B. Johnson Presidency

Kennedy's vice president, **Lyndon Johnson**, assumed the presidency after Kennedy's **assassination**. He supported civil rights bills, tax cuts, and other wide-reaching legislation that Kennedy had also supported. Johnson saw America as a "**Great Society**," and enacted legislation to fight disease and poverty, renew urban areas, and support education and environmental conservation. Medicare and Medicaid were instituted under his administration. He continued Kennedy's support of space exploration, and he is also known, although less positively, for his handling of the **Vietnam War**.

Factors that Led to the Growth of the Civil Rights Movement

In the 1950s, post-war America was experiencing a rapid growth in prosperity. However, African-Americans found themselves left behind. Following the lead of **Mahatma Gandhi**, who led similar class struggles in India, African-Americans began to demand equal rights. Major figures in this struggle included:

- **Rosa Parks**—often called the "mother of the Civil Rights Movement," her refusal to give up her seat on the bus to a white man served as a seed from which the movement grew.
- **Martin Luther King, Jr.**—the best-known leader of the movement, King drew on Gandhi's beliefs and encouraged non-violent opposition. He led a march on Washington in 1963, received the Nobel Peace Prize in 1964, and was assassinated in 1968.
- **Malcolm X**—espousing less peaceful means of change, Malcolm X became a Black Muslim and supported black nationalism.

Policies and Legislation Enacted Expanding Minority Rights

Several major acts have been passed, particularly since WWII, to protect the rights of minorities in America. These include:

- Civil Rights Act (1964)
- Voting Rights Act (1965)
- Age Discrimination Act (1967)
- Americans with Disabilities Act (1990)

Other important movements for civil rights included a prisoner's rights movement, movements for immigrant rights, and the women's rights movement. The National Organization for Women (NOW) was established in 1966 and worked to pass the Equal Rights Amendment. The amendment was passed, but not enough states ratified it for it to become part of the US Constitution.

Impact of Stokely Carmichael, Adam Clayton Powell, and Jesse Jackson on the Civil Rights Movement

- **Stokely Carmichael**—Carmichael originated the term "Black Power" and served as head of the Student Nonviolent Coordinating Committee. He believed in black pride and black culture and felt separate political and social institutions should be developed for blacks.
- **Adam Clayton Powell**—chairman of the Coordinating Committee for Employment, he led rent strikes and other actions, as well as a bus boycott, to increase the hiring of blacks.
- **Jesse Jackson**—Jackson was selected to head the Chicago Operation Breadbasket in 1966, and went on to organize boycotts and other actions. He also had an unsuccessful run for president.

Events of the Civil Rights Movement

Three major events of the Civil Rights Movement are:

- **Montgomery Bus Boycott**—in 1955, Rosa Parks refused to give her seat on the bus to a white man. As a result, she was tried and convicted of disorderly conduct and of violating local ordinances. A 381-day bus boycott ensued, protesting segregation on public buses.
- **Desegregation of Little Rock**—in 1957, after the Supreme Court decision on Brown v. Board of Education, which declared "separate but equal" unconstitutional, the Arkansas school board voted to desegregate their schools. Even though Arkansas was considered progressive, its governor brought in the Arkansas National Guard to prevent nine black students from entering Central High School in Little Rock. President Eisenhower responded by federalizing the National Guard and ordering them to stand down.
- **Birmingham Campaign**—protestors organized a variety of actions such as sit-ins and an organized march to launch a voting campaign. When the City of Birmingham declared the protests illegal, the protestors, including Martin Luther King, Jr., persisted and were arrested and jailed.

Pieces of Legislation Passed as a Result of the Civil Rights Movement

Three major pieces of legislation passed as a result of the Civil Rights movement are:

- **Brown v. Board of Education** (1954)—the Supreme Court declared that "separate but equal" accommodations and services were unconstitutional.
- **Civil Rights Act of 1964**—this declared discrimination illegal in employment, education, or public accommodation.
- **Voting Rights Act of 1965**—this act ended various activities practiced, mostly in the South, to bar blacks from exercising their voting rights. These included poll taxes and literacy tests.

EVENTS OF THE RICHARD NIXON PRESIDENCY

Richard Nixon is best known for the **Watergate scandal** during his presidency, but other important events marked his tenure as president, including:

- End of the Vietnam War
- Improved diplomatic relations between the US and China, and the US and the USSR
- National Environmental Policy Act passed, providing for environmental protection
- Compulsory draft ended
- Supreme Court legalized abortion in Roe v. Wade (subsequently overturned in 2022)
- Watergate

The Watergate scandal of 1972 ended Nixon's presidency. Rather than face impeachment and removal from office, he **resigned** in 1974.

US PERSPECTIVE ON THE PROGRESSION OF THE VIETNAM WAR

After World War II, the US pledged, as part of its foreign policy, to come to the assistance of any country threatened by **communism**. When Vietnam was divided into a communist North and democratic South, much like Korea before it, the eventual attempts by the North to unify the country under Communist rule led to intervention by the US. On the home front, the **Vietnam War** became more and more unpopular politically, with Americans growing increasingly discontent with the inability of the US to achieve the goals it had set for the Asian country. When President **Richard Nixon** took office in 1969, his escalation of the war led to protests at Kent State in Ohio, during which several students were killed by National Guard troops. Protests continued, eventually resulting in the end of the compulsory draft in 1973. In that same year, the US departed Vietnam. In 1975, the South surrendered, and Vietnam became a unified country under communist rule.

EVENTS OF THE GERALD FORD PRESIDENCY

Gerald Ford was appointed to the vice presidency after Nixon's vice president **Spiro Agnew** resigned in 1973 under charges of tax evasion. With Nixon's resignation, Ford became president.

Ford's presidency saw negotiations with Russia to limit nuclear arms, as well as struggles to deal with inflation, economic downturn, and energy shortages. Ford's policies sought to reduce governmental control of various businesses and reduce the role of government overall. He also worked to prevent escalation of conflicts in the Middle East.

END OF THE COLD WAR AND THE DISSOLUTION OF THE SOVIET UNION

In the late 1980s, **Mikhail Gorbachev** led the Soviet Union. He introduced a series of reform programs. **Ronald Reagan** famously urged Gorbachev to tear down the **Berlin Wall** as a gesture of growing freedom in the Eastern Bloc, and in 1989 it was demolished, ending the separation of East and West Germany. The Soviet Union relinquished its power over the various republics in Eastern Europe, and they became independent nations with their own individual governments. In 1991, the **USSR** was dissolved and the Cold War also came to an end.

Review Video: The End of the Cold War
Visit mometrix.com/academy and enter code: 278032

EVENTS OF THE JIMMY CARTER PRESIDENCY

Jimmy Carter was elected as president in 1976. Faced with a budget deficit, high unemployment, and continued inflation, Carter also dealt with numerous matters of international diplomacy, including:

- **Torrijos-Carter Treaties**—the US gave control of the Panama Canal to Panama.
- **Camp David Accords**—negotiations between Anwar el-Sadat, the president of Egypt, and Menachem Begin, the Israeli Prime Minister, led to a peace treaty between Egypt and Israel.

- **Strategic Arms Limitation Talks (SALT)**—these led to agreements and treaties between the US and the Soviet Union.
- **Iran Hostage Crisis**—after the Shah of Iran was deposed, an Islamic cleric, Ayatollah Khomeini, came to power. The shah came to the US for medical treatment, and Iran demanded his return so he could stand trial. In retaliation, a group of Iranian students stormed the US Embassy in Iran. Fifty-two American hostages were held for 444 days.

Jimmy Carter was awarded the **Nobel Peace Prize** in 2002.

Events of the Ronald Reagan Presidency

Ronald Reagan, at 69, became the oldest American president. The two terms of his administration included notable events such as:

- Reaganomics, also known as supply-side, trickle-down, or free-market economics, involving major tax cuts
- Economic Recovery Tax Act of 1981
- First female justice appointed to the Supreme Court—Sandra Day O'Connor
- Massive increase in the national debt—from $1 trillion to $3 trillion
- Reduction of nuclear weapons via negotiations with Mikhail Gorbachev
- Iran-Contra scandal—cover-up of US involvement in revolutions in El Salvador and Nicaragua
- Deregulation of savings and loan industry
- Loss of the space shuttle *Challenger*

Events of the George H. W. Bush Presidency

Reagan's presidency was followed by a term under his former vice president, **George H. W. Bush**. Bush's run for president included the famous "**thousand points of light**" speech, which was instrumental in increasing his standing in the election polls. During Bush's presidency, numerous international events took place, including:

- Fall of the Berlin wall and Germany's unification
- Panamanian dictator Manuel Noriega captured and tried on drug and racketeering charges
- Dissolution of the Soviet Union
- Gulf War, or Operation Desert Storm, triggered by Iraq's invasion of Kuwait
- Tiananmen Square Massacre in Beijing, China
- Ruby Ridge
- The arrival of the World Wide Web

Events of the William Clinton Presidency

William Jefferson "Bill" Clinton was the second president in US history to be impeached, but he was not convicted, and maintained high approval ratings in spite of the impeachment. Major events during his presidency included:

- Family and Medical Leave Act
- "Don't Ask, Don't Tell," a compromise position regarding homosexuals serving in the military
- North American Free Trade Agreement, or NAFTA
- Defense of Marriage Act
- Oslo Accords
- Siege at Waco, Texas, involving the Branch Davidians led by David Koresh
- Bombing of the Murrah Federal Building in Oklahoma City, Oklahoma
- Troops sent to Haiti, Bosnia, and Somalia to assist with domestic problems in those areas

Events of the George W. Bush Presidency

George W. Bush, son of George H. W. Bush, became president after Clinton. Major events during his presidency included:

- September 11, 2001, al-Qaeda terrorists hijack commercial airliners and fly into the World Trade Center towers and the Pentagon, killing nearly 3,000 Americans
- US troops sent to Afghanistan to hunt down al-Qaeda leaders, including the head of the organization, Osama Bin Laden; beginning of the War on Terror
- US troops sent to Iraq, along with a multinational coalition, to depose Saddam Hussein and prevent his deployment of suspected weapons of mass destruction
- Subprime mortgage crisis and near collapse of the financial industry, leading to the Great Recession; first of multiple government bailouts of the financial industry

Barack Obama

In 2008, Barack Obama, a senator from Illinois, became the first African American US president. His administration focused on improving the lot of a country suffering from a major recession. His major initiatives included:

- Economic bailout packages
- Improvements in women's rights
- Moves to broaden LGBT rights
- Health care reform legislation
- Reinforcement of the war in Afghanistan

Donald Trump

In 2016, Donald Trump, previously a real estate developer and television personality, was elected 45th president after a tumultuous election in which he won the electoral college but lost the popular vote. Marked by tension between the administration and domestic media, Trump's initiatives included:

- Appointing three Supreme Court Justices: Neil Gorsuch, Brett Kavanaugh, and Amy Coney Barrett
- Passing a major tax reform bill
- Enacting travel and emigration restrictions on eight nations: Iran, Libya, Syria, Yemen, Somalia, Chad, North Korea, and Venezuela
- Recognizing Jerusalem, rather than Tel Aviv, as the capital of Israel
- Responding to the novel coronavirus (SARS-CoV-2) outbreak

Almost completely along party lines, Donald Trump was impeached by the House on charges of abuse of power and obstruction of Congress; he was acquitted by the Senate.

Chapter Quiz

Ready to see how well you retained what you just read? Scan the QR code to go directly to the chapter quiz interface for this study guide. If you're using a computer, simply visit the bonus page at **mometrix.com/bonus948/fsot** and click the Chapter Quizzes link.

World History and Geography

Transform passive reading into active learning! After immersing yourself in this chapter, put your comprehension to the test by taking a quiz. The insights you gained will stay with you longer this way. Scan the QR code to go directly to the chapter quiz interface for this study guide. If you're using a computer, simply visit the bonus page at **mometrix.com/bonus948/fsot** and click the Chapter Quizzes link.

World History Pre-1400

Different Periods of Prehistory

Prehistory is the period of human history before writing was developed. The three major periods of prehistory are:

- **Lower Paleolithic**—Humans used crude tools.
- **Upper Paleolithic**—Humans began to develop a wider variety of tools. These tools were better made and more specialized. They also began to wear clothes, organize in groups with definite social structures, and practice art. Most lived in caves during this time period.
- **Neolithic**—Social structures became even more complex, including the growth of a sense of family and the ideas of religion and government. Humans learned to domesticate animals and produce crops, build houses, start fires with friction tools, and to knit, spin and weave.

Anthropology

Anthropology is the study of human culture. Anthropologists study groups of humans, how they relate to each other, and the similarities and differences between these different groups and cultures. Anthropological research takes two approaches: **cross-cultural research** and **comparative research**. Most anthropologists work by living among different cultures and participating in those cultures in order to learn about them.

There are four major **divisions** within anthropology:

- Biological anthropology
- Cultural anthropology
- Linguistic anthropology
- Archaeology

Science of Archaeology

Archaeology is the study of past human cultures by evaluating what they leave behind. This can include bones, buildings, art, tools, pottery, graves, and even trash. Archaeologists maintain detailed notes and records of their findings and use special tools to evaluate what they find. Photographs, notes, maps, artifacts, and surveys of the area can all contribute to the evaluation of an archaeological site. By studying all these elements of numerous archeological sites, scientists have been able to theorize that humans or near-humans have existed for about 600,000 years. Before that, more primitive humans are believed to have appeared about one million years ago. These humans eventually developed into **Cro-Magnon man**, and then **Homo sapiens**, or modern man.

Human Development from the Lower Paleolithic to the Iron Age

Human development has been divided into several phases:

- **Lower Paleolithic or Early Stone Age**, beginning two to three million years ago—early humans used tools like needles, hatchets, awls, and cutting tools.
- **Middle Paleolithic or Middle Stone Age**, beginning approximately 300,000 BC—sophisticated stone tools were developed, along with hunting, gathering, and ritual practices.
- **Upper Paleolithic or Late Stone Age**, beginning approximately 40,000 BC—including the Mesolithic and Neolithic eras, textiles and pottery were developed. Humans of this era discovered the wheel, began to practice agriculture, made polished tools, and had some domesticated animals.
- **Bronze Age**, beginning approximately 3000 BC—metals are discovered and the first civilizations emerge as humans become more technologically advanced.
- **Iron Age**, beginning 1200 to 1000 BC—metal tools replace stone tools as humans develop knowledge of smelting.

Requirements for Civilization and State Where the Earliest Civilizations Developed

Civilizations are defined as having the following characteristics:

- Use of metal to make weapons and tools
- Written language
- A defined territorial state
- A calendar

The **earliest civilizations** developed in river valleys where reliable, fertile land was easily found, including:

- The Nile River Valley in Egypt
- Mesopotamia
- The Indus Valley
- Hwang Ho in China

The very earliest civilizations developed in the **Tigris-Euphrates valley** in Mesopotamia, which is now part of Iraq, and in Egypt's **Nile valley**. These civilizations arose between 5000 and 3000 BC. The area where these civilizations grew is known as the Fertile Crescent. Geography and the availability of water made large-scale human habitation possible.

Importance of Rivers and Water to the Growth of Early Civilizations

The earliest civilizations are also referred to as **fluvial civilizations** because they were founded near rivers. Rivers and the water they provide were vital to these early groupings, offering:

- Water for drinking, cultivating crops, and caring for domesticated animals
- A gathering place for wild animals that could be hunted
- Rich soil deposits as a result of regular flooding

Irrigation techniques helped direct water where it was most needed, to sustain herds of domestic animals and to nourish crops of increasing size and quality.

Fertile Crescent

James Breasted, an archaeologist from the University of Chicago, popularized the term "**Fertile Crescent**" to describe the area in Southwest Asia and the Mediterranean basin where the earliest civilizations arose. The region includes modern-day Iraq, Syria, Lebanon, Israel, Palestine, and Jordan. It is bordered on the south by the Syrian and Arabian Deserts, the west by the Mediterranean Sea, and to the north and east by the Taurus and Zagros Mountains, respectively. This area not only provided the raw materials for the development of increasingly advanced civilizations but also saw waves of migration and invasion, leading to the earliest wars and genocides as groups conquered and absorbed each other's cultures and inhabitants.

Accomplishments of the Egyptian, Sumerian, Babylonian, and Assyrian Cultures

The **Egyptians** were one of the most advanced ancient cultures, having developed construction methods to build the great pyramids, as well as a form of writing known as hieroglyphics. Their religion was highly developed and complex and included advanced techniques for the preservation of bodies after death. They also made paper by processing papyrus, a plant commonly found along the Nile, invented the decimal system, devised a solar calendar, and advanced overall knowledge of mathematics.

The **Sumerians** were the first to invent the wheel, and also brought irrigation systems into use. Their cuneiform writing was simpler than Egyptian hieroglyphs, and they developed the timekeeping system we still use today.

The **Babylonians** are best known for the Code of Hammurabi, an advanced law code.

The **Assyrians** developed horse-drawn chariots and an organized military.

Accomplishments of the Hebrew, Persian, Minoan, and Mycenaean Cultures

The **Hebrew** or ancient Israelite culture developed the monotheistic religion that eventually developed into modern Judaism and Christianity.

The **Persians** were conquerors, but those they conquered were allowed to keep their own laws, customs, and religious traditions rather than being forced to accept those of their conquerors. They also developed an alphabet and practiced Zoroastrianism and Mithraism, religions that have influenced modern religious practice.

The **Minoans** used a syllabic writing system and built large, colorful palaces. These ornate buildings included sewage systems, running water, bathtubs, and even flushing toilets. Their script, known as Linear A, has yet to be deciphered.

The **Mycenaeans** practiced a religion that grew into the Greek pantheon, worshipping Zeus and other Olympian gods. They developed Linear B, a writing system used to write the earliest known form of Greek.

Phoenicians and Early Culture in India and Ancient China

Skilled seafarers and navigators, the Phoenicians used the stars to navigate their ships at night. They developed a purple dye that was in great demand in the ancient world, and worked with glass and metals. They also devised a phonetic alphabet, using symbols to represent individual sounds rather than whole words or syllables.

The Indus Valley Civilization (IVC) was an urban civilization arose in the Indus Valley, located in between the modern countries of Iran, India, and Pakistan. These ancient humans developed the concept of zero in mathematics, practiced an early form of the Hindu religion, and developed the caste system which is still prevalent in India today. Archeologists are still uncovering information about this highly developed ancient civilization.

In ancient **China**, human civilization developed along the **Yangtze River**. These people produced silk, grew millet, and made pottery, including Longshan black pottery.

Civilizations of Mesopotamia

The major civilizations of Mesopotamia, in what is now called the **Middle East**, were:

- Sumerians
- Amorites
- Hittites
- Assyrians
- Chaldeans
- Persians

These cultures controlled different areas of Mesopotamia during various time periods but were similar in that they were **autocratic**: a single ruler served as the head of the government and often was the main religious ruler as well. These rulers were often tyrannical, militaristic leaders who controlled all aspects of life, including law, trade, and religious activity. Portions of the legacies of these civilizations remain in cultures today. These include mythologies, religious systems, mathematical innovations, and even elements of various languages.

Sumerians

Sumer, located in the southern part of Mesopotamia, consisted of a dozen **city-states**. Each city-state had its own gods, and the leader of each city-state also served as the high priest. Cultural legacies of Sumer include:

- The invention of writing
- The invention of the wheel
- The first library—established in Assyria by Ashurbanipal
- The Hanging Gardens of Babylon—one of the Seven Wonders of the Ancient World
- First written laws—Ur-Nammu's Codes and the Codes of Hammurabi
- The *Epic of Gilgamesh*—the first recorded epic story

Review Video: Early Mesopotamia: The Sumerians
Visit mometrix.com/academy and enter code: 939880

Kushites

Kush, or Cush, was located in Nubia, south of ancient Egypt, and the earliest existing records of this civilization were found in Egyptian texts. At one time, Kush was the largest empire on the Nile River, ruling not only Nubia but Upper and Lower Egypt as well.

In Neolithic times, Kushites lived in villages, with buildings made of mud bricks. They were settled rather than nomadic and practiced hunting and fishing, cultivated grain, and also herded cattle. **Kerma**, the capital, was a major center of trade.

Kush determined leadership through **matrilineal descent** of their kings, as did Egypt. Their heads of state, the Kandake or Kentake, were female. Their polytheistic religion included the primary Egyptian gods as well as regional gods, including a lion-headed god, which is commonly found in African cultures.

Kush was conquered by the **Aksumite Empire** in the 4th century AD.

Minoans

The Minoans lived on the island of Crete, just off the coast of Greece. This civilization reigned from approximately 4000 to 1400 BC and is considered to be the first advanced civilization in Europe. The Minoans developed writing systems known to linguists as **Linear A** and **Linear B**. Linear A has not yet been translated; Linear B evolved into classical Greek script. "Minoans" is not the name they used for themselves but is instead a variation on the name of King Minos, a king in Greek mythology believed by some to have been a denizen of Crete. The Minoan civilization subsisted on trade, and their way of life was often disrupted by earthquakes and volcanoes. Much is still unknown about the Minoans, and archaeologists continue to study their architecture and archaeological remains. The Minoan culture eventually fell to Greek invaders and was supplanted by the **Mycenaean civilization**.

Ancient India

The civilizations of ancient India gave rise to both **Hinduism** and **Buddhism**, major world religions that have influenced countries far from their place of origin. Practices such as yoga, increasingly popular in the West, can trace their roots to these earliest Indian civilizations, and the poses are still formally referred to by Sanskrit names. Literature from ancient India includes the *Mahabharata* containing the *Bhagavad Gita*, the *Ramayana*, *Arthashastra*, and the *Vedas*, a collection of sacred texts. Indo-European languages, including English, find their beginnings in these ancient cultures. Ancient Indo-Aryan languages such as Sanskrit are still used in some formal Hindu practices.

Earliest Civilizations in China

Many historians believe **Chinese civilization** is the oldest uninterrupted civilization in the world. The **Neolithic age** in China goes back to 10,000 BC, with agriculture in China beginning as early as 5000 BC. Their system of writing dates to 1500 BC. The Yellow River served as the center for the earliest Chinese settlements. In Ningxia, in northwest China, there are carvings on cliffs that date back to the Paleolithic Period, indicating the extreme antiquity of Chinese culture. Literature from ancient China includes Confucius' *Analects*, the *Tao Te Ching*, and a variety of poetry.

Ancient Cultures in the Americas

Less is known of ancient American civilizations since less was left behind. Some of the more well-known cultures include:

- The **Norte Chico civilization** in Peru, an agricultural society of up to 30 individual communities, existed over 5,000 years ago. This culture is also known as the Caral-Supe civilization, and is the oldest known civilization in the Americas.
- The **Anasazi**, or Ancestral Pueblo People, lived in what is now the southwestern United States. Emerging about 1200 BC, the Anasazi built complex adobe dwellings and were the forerunners of later Pueblo Indian cultures.
- The **Maya** emerged in southern Mexico and northern Central America as early as 2600 BC. They developed a written language and a complex calendar.

Mycenaeans

In contrast to the Minoans, whom they displaced, the **Mycenaeans** relied more on conquest than on trade. Mycenaean states included Sparta, Athens, and Corinth. The history of this civilization, including the **Trojan War**, was recorded by the Greek poet **Homer**. His work was largely considered mythical until archaeologists discovered evidence of the city of **Troy** in Hisarlik, Turkey. Archaeologists continue to add to the body of information about this ancient culture, translating documents written in Linear B, a script derived from the Minoan Linear A. It is theorized that the Mycenaean civilization was eventually destroyed in either a Dorian invasion or an attack by Greek invaders from the north.

Dorian Invasion

A Dorian invasion does not refer to an invasion by a particular group of people, but rather is a hypothetical theory to explain the end of the **Mycenaean civilization** and the growth of **classical Greece**. Ancient tradition refers to these events as "the return of the Heracleidae," or the sons (descendants) of Hercules. Archaeologists and historians still do not know exactly who conquered the Mycenaeans, but it is believed to have occurred around 1200 BC, contemporaneous with the destruction of the **Hittite civilization** in what is now modern Turkey. The Hittites speak of an attack by people of the Aegean Sea, or the "Sea People." Only Athens was left intact.

Spartans vs. Athenians

Both powerful city-states, Sparta and Athens fought each other in the **Peloponnesian War** (431-404 BC). Despite their proximity, the Spartans and the Athenians nurtured contrasting cultures:

- The **Spartans**, located in Peloponnesus, were ruled by an oligarchic military state. They practiced farming, disallowed trade for Spartan citizens, and valued military arts and strict discipline. They emerged as the strongest military force in the area and maintained this status for many years. In one memorable encounter, a small group of Spartans held off a huge army of Persians at Thermopylae.
- The **Athenians** were centered in Attica, where the land was rocky and unsuitable for farming. Like the Spartans, they descended from invaders who spoke Greek. Their government was very different from Sparta's; it was in Athens that democracy was created by Cleisthenes of Athens in 508 BC. Athenians excelled in art, theater, architecture, and philosophy.

Contributions of Ancient Greece that Still Exist Today

Ancient Greece made numerous major contributions to cultural development, including:

- **Theater**—Aristophanes and other Greek playwrights laid the groundwork for modern theatrical performance.
- **Alphabet**—the Greek alphabet, derived from the Phoenician alphabet, developed into the Roman alphabet, and then into our modern-day alphabet.
- **Geometry**—Pythagoras and Euclid pioneered much of the system of geometry still taught today. Archimedes made various mathematical discoveries, including calculating a very accurate value of pi.
- **Historical writing**—much of ancient history doubles as mythology or religious texts. Herodotus and Thucydides made use of research and interpretation to record historical events.
- **Philosophy**—Socrates, Plato, and Aristotle served as the fathers of Western philosophy. Their work is still required reading for philosophy students.

Review Video: Ancient Greece Timeline
Visit mometrix.com/academy and enter code: 800829

Alexander the Great

Born to Philip II of Macedon and tutored by Aristotle, **Alexander the Great** is considered one of the greatest conquerors in history. He conquered Egypt and the Achaemenid/Persian Empire, a powerful empire founded by Cyrus the Great that spanned three continents, and he traveled as far as India and the Iberian Peninsula. Though Alexander died from malaria at age 32, his conquering efforts spread **Greek culture** into the east. This cultural diffusion left a greater mark on history than did his empire, which fell apart due to internal conflict not long after his death. Trade between the East and West increased, as did an exchange of ideas and beliefs that influenced both regions greatly. The **Hellenistic traditions** his conquest spread were prevalent in Byzantine culture until as late as the 15th century.

Hittites

The Hittites were centered in what is now Turkey, but their empire extended into Palestine and Syria. They conquered the Babylonian civilization, but adopted their religion, laws, and literature. Overall, the Hittites tended to tolerate other religions, unlike many other contemporary cultures, and absorbed foreign gods into their own belief systems rather than forcing their religion onto peoples they conquered. The **Hittite Empire** reached its peak in 1600-1200 BC. After a war with Egypt, which weakened them severely, they were eventually conquered by the **Assyrians**.

Persian Wars

The Persian Empire, ruled by **Cyrus the Great**, encompassed an area from the Black Sea to Afghanistan and beyond into Central Asia. After the death of Cyrus, **Darius I** became king in 522 BC. The empire reached its zenith during his reign, and Darius attempted to conquer Greece as well. From 499 to 449 BC, the Greeks and Persians fought in the **Persian Wars**. The **Peace of Callias** brought an end to the fighting, after the Greeks were able to repel the invasion.

Battles of the Persian Wars included:

- The **Battle of Marathon**—heavily outnumbered Greek forces managed to achieve victory.
- The **Battle of Thermopylae**—a small band of Spartans held off a throng of Persian troops for several days before Persia defeated the Greeks and captured an evacuated Athens.
- The **Battle of Salamis**—this was a naval battle that again saw outnumbered Greeks achieving victory.
- The **Battle of Plataea**—this was another Greek victory, but one in which they outnumbered the Persians. This ended the invasion of Greece.

Maurya Empire

The Maurya Empire was a large, powerful empire established in India. It was one of the largest ever to rule in the Indian subcontinent and existed from 322 to 185 BC, ruled by **Chandragupta Maurya** after the withdrawal from India of Alexander the Great. The Maurya Empire was highly developed, including a standardized economic system, waterways, and private corporations. Trade to the Greeks and others became common, with goods including silk, exotic foods, and spices. Religious development included the rise of Buddhism and Jainism. The laws of the Maurya Empire protected not only civil and social rights of the citizens, but they also protected animals, establishing protected zones for economically important creatures such as elephants, lions, and tigers. This period of time in Indian history was largely peaceful, perhaps due to the strong Buddhist beliefs of many of its leaders. The empire finally fell after a succession of weak leaders and was taken over by **Demetrius**, a Greco-Bactrian king who took advantage of this lapse in leadership to conquer southern Afghanistan and Pakistan around 180 BC, forming the **Indo-Greek Kingdom**.

Development and Growth of the Chinese Empires

In China, history was divided into a series of **dynasties**. The most famous of these, the **Han dynasty**, existed from 206 BC to AD 220. Accomplishments of the Chinese empires included:

- Building the Great Wall of China
- Numerous inventions, including paper, paper money, printing, and gunpowder
- High level of artistic development
- Silk production

The Chinese dynasties were comparable to Rome as far as their artistic and intellectual accomplishments, as well as the size and scope of their influence.

Roman Empire and Republic

Rome began humbly, in a single town that grew out of Etruscan settlements and traditions, founded, according to legend, by twin brothers Romulus and Remus, who were raised by wolves. Romulus killed Remus, and from his legacy grew Rome. A thousand years later, the **Roman Empire** covered a significant portion of the known world, from what is now Scotland, across Europe, and into the Middle East. **Hellenization**, or the spread of Greek culture throughout the world, served as an inspiration and a model for the spread of Roman culture. Rome brought in belief systems of conquered peoples as well as their technological and scientific accomplishments, melding the disparate parts into a Roman core. Rome began as a **republic** ruled by consuls, but after the assassination of **Julius Caesar**, it became an **empire** led by emperors. Rome's overall government was autocratic, but local officials came from the provinces where they lived. This limited administrative system was probably a major factor in the long life of the empire.

Review Video: Roman Republic Part One
Visit mometrix.com/academy and enter code: 360192

Review Video: Roman Republic Part Two
Visit mometrix.com/academy and enter code: 881514

Development of the Byzantine Empire from the Roman Empire

In the early 4th century, the Roman Empire split, with the eastern portion becoming the Eastern Empire, or the **Byzantine Empire**. In AD 330, **Constantine** founded the city of **Constantinople**, which became the center of the Byzantine Empire. Its major influences came from Mesopotamia and Persia, in contrast to the Western Empire, which maintained traditions more closely linked to Greece and Carthage. Byzantium's position gave it an advantage over invaders from the West and the East, as well as control over trade from both regions. It protected the Western empire from invasion from the Persians and the Ottomans, and practiced a more centralized rule than in the West. The Byzantines were famous for lavish art and architecture, as well as the Code of Justinian, which collected Roman law into a clear system. The Byzantine Empire finally fell to the **Ottomans** in 1453.

Significance of the Nicene Creed

The **Byzantine Empire** was Christian-based but incorporated Greek language, philosophy, and literature and drew its law and government policies from Rome. However, there was as yet no unified doctrine of Christianity, as it was a relatively new religion that had spread rapidly and without a great deal of organization. In 325, the **First Council of Nicaea** addressed this issue. From this conference came the **Nicene Creed**, addressing the Trinity and other basic Christian beliefs. The **Council of Chalcedon** in 451 further defined the view of the Trinity.

Factors that Led to the Fall of the Western Roman Empire

Germanic tribes, including the Visigoths, Ostrogoths, Vandals, Saxons, and Franks, controlled most of Europe. The Roman Empire faced major opposition on that front. The increasing size of the empire also made it harder to manage, leading to dissatisfaction throughout the empire as Roman government became less efficient. Germanic tribes refused to adhere to the Nicene Creed, instead following **Arianism**, which led the Roman Catholic Church to declare them heretics. The **Franks** proved a powerful military force in their defeat of the Muslims in 732. In 768, **Charlemagne** became king of the Franks. These tribes waged several wars against Rome, including the invasion of Britannia by the Angles and Saxons. Far-flung Rome lost control over this area of its empire, and eventually, Rome itself was **invaded**.

Iconoclasm and the Conflict Between the Roman Catholic and Eastern Orthodox Churches

Emperor Leo III ordered the destruction of all icons throughout the Byzantine Empire. Images of Jesus were replaced with crosses, and images of Jesus, Mary, or other religious figures were considered blasphemy on the grounds of idolatry. **Pope Gregory II** called a synod to discuss the issue. The synod declared that the images were not heretical and that strong disciplinary measures would result for anyone who destroyed them. Leo's response was an attempt to kill Pope Gregory, but this plan ended in failure.

Effect of the Viking Invasions on the Culture of England and Europe

Vikings invaded Northern France in the 10th century, eventually becoming the **Normans**. Originating in Scandinavia, the **Vikings** were accomplished seafarers with advanced knowledge of trade routes. With overpopulation plaguing their native lands, they began to travel. From the 8th to the 11th centuries, they spread throughout Europe, conquering and colonizing. Vikings invaded and colonized England in several waves, including the **Anglo-Saxon invasions** that displaced Roman control. Their influence remained significant in England, affecting everything from the language of the country to place names and even the government and social structure. By 900, Vikings had settled in **Iceland**. They proceeded then to **Greenland** and eventually to **North America**, arriving in the New World even before the Spanish and British who claimed the lands several centuries later. They also traded with the Byzantine Empire until the 11th century, when their significant level of activity came to an end.

West vs. East 10th-Century Events

In **Europe**, the years AD 500-1000 are largely known as the **Dark Ages**. In the 10th century, numerous Viking invasions disrupted societies that had been more settled under Roman rule. Vikings settled in Northern France, eventually becoming the Normans. By the 11th century, Europe would rise again into the **High Middle Ages** with the beginning of the **Crusades**.

In **China**, wars also raged. This led the Chinese to make use of gunpowder for the first time in warfare.

In the **Americas**, the **Mayan Empire** was winding down while the **Toltec** became more prominent. **Pueblo** Indian culture was also at its zenith.

In the **East**, the **Muslims** and the **Byzantine Empire** were experiencing a significant period of growth and development.

World History 1400 to 1914

Feudalism in Europe in the Middle Ages

A major element of the social and economic life of Europe, **feudalism** developed as a way to ensure European rulers would have the wherewithal to quickly raise an army when necessary. **Vassals** swore loyalty and promised to provide military service for lords, who in return offered a **fief**, or a parcel of land, for them to use to generate their livelihood. Vassals could work the land themselves, have it worked by **peasants** or **serfs**—workers who had few rights and were little more than slaves—or grant the fief to someone else. The king legally owned all the land, but in return, promised to protect the vassals from invasion and war. Vassals returned a certain percentage of their income to the lords, who in turn, passed a portion of their income on to the king. A similar practice was **manorialism**, in which the feudal system was applied to a self-contained manor. These manors were often owned by the lords who ran them but were usually included in the same system of loyalty and promises of protection that drove feudalism.

Review Video: The Middle Ages: Feudalism
Visit mometrix.com/academy and enter code: 165907

Effect of Black Death on Medieval Politics and Economic Conditions

The Black Death, believed to be **bubonic plague**, most likely came to Europe on fleas carried by rats on sailing vessels. The plague killed more than a third of the entire population of Europe and effectively ended **feudalism** as a political system. Many who had formerly served as peasants or serfs found different work, as a demand for skilled labor grew. Nation-states grew in power, and in the face of the pandemic, many began to turn away from faith in God and toward the ideals of ancient Greece and Rome for government and other beliefs.

Review Video: Black Death (An Overview)
Visit mometrix.com/academy and enter code: 431857

Influence of the Roman Catholic Church Over Medieval Society

The Roman Catholic Church extended significant influence both politically and economically throughout medieval society. The church supplied **education**, as there were no established schools or universities. To a large extent, the church had filled a power void left by various invasions throughout the former Roman Empire, leading it to exercise a role that was far more **political** than religious. Kings were heavily influenced by the pope and other church officials, and churches controlled large amounts of land throughout Europe.

Progression of the Crusades and Major Figures Involved

The Crusades began in the 11th century and continued into the 15th. The major goal of these various military ventures was to slow the progression of Muslim forces into Europe and to expel them from the **Holy Land**, where they had taken control of Jerusalem and Palestine. Alexius I, the Byzantine emperor, called for help from **Pope Urban** II when Palestine was taken. In 1095, the pope, hoping to reunite Eastern and Western Christianity, encouraged all Christians to help the cause. Amidst great bloodshed, this crusade recaptured **Jerusalem**, but over the next centuries, Jerusalem and other areas of the Holy Land changed hands numerous times. The **Second Crusade** (1147-1149) consisted of an unsuccessful attempt to retake Damascus. The **Third Crusade**, under Pope Gregory VIII, attempted to recapture Jerusalem but failed. The **Fourth Crusade**, under Pope Innocent III, attempted to come into the Holy Land via Egypt. The Crusades led to greater power for the pope and the Catholic Church in general and also opened numerous trading and cultural routes between Europe and the East.

Political Developments in India Through the 11th Century

After the Mauryan dynasty, the **Guptas** ruled India, maintaining a long period of peace and prosperity in the area. During this time, the Indian people invented the decimal system and the concept of zero. They produced cotton and calico, as well as other products in high demand in Europe and Asia, and developed a complex system of medicine. The Gupta Dynasty ended in the 6th century. First, the **Huns** invaded, and then the **Hephthalites** (an Asian nomadic tribe) destroyed the weakened empire. In the 14th century, **Tamerlane**, a Muslim who envisioned restoring Genghis Khan's empire, expanded India's borders and founded the **Mogul Empire**. His grandson Akbar promoted freedom of religion and built a widespread number of mosques, forts, and other buildings throughout the country.

Development of Chinese and Japanese Governments Through the 11th Century

After the Mongols, led by Genghis Khan and his grandson Kublai Khan, unified the Mongol Empire, **China** was led by the **Ming Dynasty** (1368-1644) and the **Manchu (also known as Qing) Dynasty** (1644-1912). Both dynasties were isolationist, ending China's interaction with other countries until the 18th century. The Ming Dynasty was known for its porcelain, while the Manchus focused on farming and road construction as the population grew.

Japan developed independently of China but borrowed the Buddhist religion, the Chinese writing system, and other elements of Chinese society. Ruled by the divine emperor, Japan basically functioned on a feudal system led by **daimyo**, or warlords, and soldiers known as **samurai**. Japan remained isolationist, not interacting significantly with the rest of the world until the 1800s.

Ming Dynasty

The Ming dynasty lasted in China from AD 1368 to 1644. This dynasty was established by a Buddhist monk, **Zhu Yuanzhang**, who quickly became obsessed with consolidating power in the central government and was known for the brutality with which he achieved his ends. It was during the **Ming dynasty** that China developed and introduced its famous civil service examinations, rigorous tests on the **Confucian classics**. The future of an ambitious Chinese youth depended on his performance on this exam. The capital was transferred from Nanjing to Beijing during this period, and the **Forbidden City** was constructed inside the new capital. The Ming period, despite its constant expansionary wars, also continued China's artistic resurgence; the porcelain of this period is especially admired.

Developments in Africa Through the 11th Century

Much of Africa was difficult to traverse early on, due to the large amount of desert and other inhospitable terrain. **Egypt** remained important, though most of the northern coast became Muslim as their armies spread through the area. **Ghana** rose as a trade center in the 9th century, lasting into the 12th century, primarily trading in gold, which it exchanged for Saharan salt. **Mali** rose somewhat later, with the trade center Timbuktu becoming an important exporter of goods such as iron, leather, and tin. Mali also dealt in agricultural trade, becoming one of the most significant trading centers in West Africa. The Muslim religion dominated, and technological advancement was sparse.

African culture was largely defined through migration, as Arab merchants and others settled on the continent, particularly along the east coast. Scholars from the Muslim nations gravitated to Timbuktu, which in addition to its importance in trade, had also become a magnet for those seeking Islamic knowledge and education.

History of Islam and Its Role in Bringing Unity to the Middle East

Born in AD 570, **Muhammad** began preaching around 613, leading his followers in a new religion called **Islam**, which means "submission to God's will." Before this time, the Arabian Peninsula was inhabited largely by Bedouins, nomads who battled amongst each other and lived in tribal organizations. But by the time Muhammad died in 632, most of Arabia had become Muslim to some extent.

Muhammad conquered **Mecca**, where a temple called the **Kaaba** had long served as a center of the nomadic religions. He declared this temple the most sacred of Islam, and Mecca as the holy city. His writings became the **Koran**, or **Qur'an**, divine revelations he said had been delivered to him by the angel Gabriel.

Muhammad's teachings gave the formerly tribal Arabian people a sense of unity that had not existed in the area before. After his death, the converted Muslims of Arabia conquered a vast territory, creating an empire and bringing advances in literature, technology, science, and art as Europe was declining under the scourge of the Black Death. Literature from this period includes the *Arabian Nights* and the *Rubaiyat* of Omar Khayyam.

Later in its development, Islam split into two factions; the **Shiite** and the **Sunni** Muslims. Conflict continues today between these groups.

Ottoman Empire

By 1400, the Ottomans had grown in power in Anatolia and had begun attempts to take Constantinople. In 1453, they finally conquered the Byzantine capital and renamed it **Istanbul**. The **Ottoman Empire's** major strength, much like Rome before it, lay in its ability to unite widely disparate people through religious tolerance. This tolerance, which stemmed from the idea that Muslims, Christians, and Jews were fundamentally related and could coexist, enabled the Ottomans to develop a widely varied culture. They also believed in just laws and just government, with government centered in a monarch, known as the **sultan**.

Renaissance

Renaissance literally means "rebirth." After the darkness of the Dark Ages and the Black Plague, interest rose again in the beliefs and politics of ancient Greece and Rome. Art, literature, music, science, and philosophy all burgeoned during the Renaissance.

Many of the ideas of the Renaissance began in **Florence, Italy** in the 14th century, spurred by the **Medici** family. Education for the upper classes expanded to include law, math, reading, writing, and classical Greek and Roman works. As the Renaissance progressed, the world was presented through art and literature in a realistic way that had never been explored before. This **realism** drove culture to new heights.

Review Video: The Renaissance
Visit mometrix.com/academy and enter code: 123100

Renaissance Artists, Authors, and Scientists

Artists of the Renaissance included Leonardo da Vinci, also an inventor; Michelangelo, also an architect; and others who focused on realism in their work. In **literature**, major contributions came from humanist authors like Petrarch, Erasmus, Sir Thomas More, and Boccaccio, who believed man should focus on reality rather than on the ethereal. Shakespeare, Cervantes, and Dante followed in their footsteps, and their works found a wide audience thanks to Gutenberg's development of the printing press.

Scientific developments of the Renaissance included the work of Copernicus, Galileo, and Kepler, who challenged the geocentric philosophies of the day by proving that the earth was not the center of the solar system.

Two Phases of the Reformation Period

The Reformation consisted of both the Protestant and the Catholic Reformation. The **Protestant Reformation** rose in Germany when **Martin Luther** protested abuses of the Catholic Church. **John Calvin** led the movement in Switzerland, while in England, King Henry VIII made use of the Reformation's ideas to further his own political goals. The **Catholic Reformation**, or **Counter-Reformation**, occurred in response to the Protestant movement, leading to various changes in the Catholic Church. Some provided wider tolerance of different religious viewpoints, but others actually increased the persecution of those deemed to be heretics.

From a **religious** standpoint, the Reformation occurred due to abuses by the Catholic Church such as indulgences and dispensations, religious offices being offered up for sale, and an increasingly dissolute clergy. **Politically**, the Reformation was driven by increased power of various ruling monarchs, who wished to take all power to themselves rather than allowing power to remain with the church. They also had begun to chafe at papal taxes and the church's increasing wealth. The ideas of the Protestant Revolution removed power from the Catholic Church and the Pope himself, playing nicely into the hands of those monarchs, such as Henry VIII, who wanted out from under the church's control.

Review Video: Martin Luther and the Reformation
Visit mometrix.com/academy and enter code: 691828

Review Video: The Counter-Reformation
Visit mometrix.com/academy and enter code: 950498

Review Video: The Protestants
Visit mometrix.com/academy and enter code: 583582

Developments of the Scientific Revolution

In addition to holding power in the political realm, church doctrine also governed scientific belief. During the **Scientific Revolution**, astronomers and other scientists began to amass evidence that challenged the church's scientific doctrines. Major figures of the Scientific Revolution included:

- **Nicolaus Copernicus**—wrote *On the Revolutions of the Celestial Spheres*, arguing that the earth revolved around the sun
- **Tycho Brahe**—cataloged astronomical observations
- **Johannes Kepler**—developed laws of planetary motion
- **Galileo Galilei**—defended the heliocentric theories of Copernicus and Kepler, discovered four moons of Jupiter, and died under house arrest by the church, charged with heresy
- **Isaac Newton**—discovered gravity; studied optics, calculus, and physics; and believed the workings of nature could be studied and proven through observation

Review Video: The Scientific Revolution
Visit mometrix.com/academy and enter code: 974600

MAJOR IDEAS OF THE ENLIGHTENMENT

During the Enlightenment, philosophers and scientists began to rely more and more on **observation** to support their ideas rather than building on past beliefs, particularly those held by the church. A focus on **ethics and logic** drove their work. Major philosophers of the **Enlightenment** included:

- **Rene Descartes**—he famously wrote, "I think, therefore I am." He believed strongly in logic and rules of observation.
- **David Hume**—he pioneered empiricism and skepticism, believing that truth could only be found through direct experience and that what others said to be true was always suspect.
- **Immanuel Kant**—he believed in self-examination and observation and that the root of morality lay within human beings.
- **Jean-Jacques Rousseau**—he developed the idea of the social contract, that government existed by the agreement of the people, and that the government was obligated to protect the people and their basic rights. His ideas heavily influenced the founding fathers.

Review Video: Age of Enlightenment
Visit mometrix.com/academy and enter code: 143022

AMERICAN REVOLUTION VS. FRENCH REVOLUTION

Both the American and French Revolution came about as a protest against the excesses and overly controlling nature of their respective monarchs. In **America**, the British colonies had been left mostly to self-govern until the British monarchs began to increase control, spurring the colonies to revolt. In **France**, the nobility's excesses had led to increasingly difficult economic conditions, with inflation, heavy taxation, and food shortages creating great burdens on the lower classes. Both revolutions led to the development of republics to replace the monarchies that were displaced. However, the French Revolution eventually led to the rise of the dictator **Napoleon Bonaparte**, while the American Revolution produced a working **republic** from the beginning.

EVENTS AND FIGURES OF THE FRENCH REVOLUTION

In 1789, **King Louis XVI**, faced with a huge national debt, convened parliament. The **Third Estate**, or Commons, a division of the French parliament, then claimed power, and the king's resistance led to the storming of the **Bastille**, the royal prison. The people established a constitutional monarchy. When King Louis XVI and Marie Antoinette attempted to leave the country, they were executed on the guillotine. From 1793 to 1794, **Robespierre** and extreme radicals, the **Jacobins**, instituted a **Reign of Terror**, executing tens of thousands of nobles as well as anyone considered an enemy of the Revolution. Robespierre was then executed as well, and the **Directory** came into power, leading to a temporary return to bourgeois values. This governing body proved incompetent and corrupt, allowing **Napoleon Bonaparte** to come to power in 1799, first as a dictator, then as emperor. While the French Revolution threw off the power of a corrupt monarchy, its immediate results were likely not what the original perpetrators of the revolt had intended.

Review Video: The French Revolution: Napoleon Bonaparte
Visit mometrix.com/academy and enter code: 876330

INDUSTRIAL REVOLUTION

EFFECTS OF THE INDUSTRIAL REVOLUTION ON SOCIETY

The Industrial Revolution began in Great Britain in the 18th century, bringing coal- and steam-powered machinery into widespread use. Industry began a period of rapid growth with these developments. Goods that had previously been produced in small workshops or even in homes were produced more efficiently and in much larger quantities in **factories**. Where society had been largely agrarian-based, the focus swiftly shifted to an **industrial** outlook. As electricity and internal combustion engines replaced coal and steam as energy sources, even more drastic and rapid changes occurred. Western European countries, in particular, turned to colonialism, taking control of portions of Africa and Asia to ensure access to the raw materials needed to produce factory goods. Specialized labor became very much in demand, and businesses grew rapidly, creating monopolies, increasing world trade, and developing large urban centers. Even agriculture changed fundamentally as the Industrial Revolution led to a second **Agricultural Revolution** with the addition of new technology to advance agricultural production.

Review Video: Industrialization
Visit mometrix.com/academy and enter code: 893924

FIRST AND SECOND PHASES OF THE INDUSTRIAL REVOLUTION

The **first phase** of the Industrial Revolution took place from roughly 1750 to 1830. The textile industry experienced major changes as more and more elements of the process became mechanized. Mining benefited from the steam engine. Transportation became easier and more widely available as waterways were improved and the railroad came into prominence. In the **second phase**, from 1830 to 1910, industries further improved in efficiency, and new industries were introduced as photography, various chemical processes, and electricity became more widely available to produce new goods or new, improved versions of old goods. Petroleum and hydroelectricity became major sources of power. During this time, the Industrial Revolution spread out of Western Europe and into the US and Japan.

POLITICAL, SOCIAL AND ECONOMIC SIDE EFFECTS OF THE INDUSTRIAL REVOLUTION

The Industrial Revolution led to widespread education, a wider franchise, and the development of mass communication in the political arena. **Economically**, conflicts arose between companies and their employees, as struggles for fair treatment and fair wages increased. Unions gained power and became more active. Government regulation over industries increased, but at the same time, growing businesses fought for the right to free enterprise. In the **social** sphere, populations increased and began to concentrate around centers of industry. Cities became larger and more densely populated. Scientific advancements led to more efficient agriculture, greater supply of goods, and increased knowledge of medicine and sanitation, leading to better overall health.

Review Video: The Industrial Revolution
Visit mometrix.com/academy and enter code: 372796

CAUSES AND PROGRESSION OF THE RUSSIAN REVOLUTION OF 1905

In Russia, rule lay in the hands of the **czars**, and the overall structure was **feudalistic**. Beneath the czars was a group of rich nobles, landowners whose lands were worked by peasants and serfs. The **Russo-Japanese War** (1904-1905) made conditions much worse for the lower classes. When peasants demonstrated outside the czar's Winter Palace, the palace guard fired upon the crowd. The demonstration had been organized by a trade union leader, and after the violent response, many unions and political parties blossomed and began to lead numerous strikes. When the economy ground to a halt, Czar Nicholas II signed a document known as the **October Manifesto**, which established a constitutional monarchy and gave legislative power to parliament. However, he violated the manifesto shortly thereafter, disbanding parliament and ignoring the civil liberties granted by the manifesto. This eventually led to the **Bolshevik Revolution**.

World History 1914 to Present

NATIONALISM AND ITS EFFECT ON SOCIETY THROUGH THE 18TH AND 19TH CENTURIES

Nationalism, put simply, is a strong belief in, identification with, and allegiance to a particular nation and people. **Nationalistic belief** unified various areas that had previously seen themselves as fragmented, which led to **patriotism** and, in some cases, **imperialism**. As nationalism grew, individual nations sought to grow, bringing in other, smaller states that shared similar characteristics such as language and cultural beliefs. Unfortunately, a major side effect of these growing nationalistic beliefs was often conflict and outright **war**.

In Europe, imperialism led countries to spread their influence into Africa and Asia. **Africa** was eventually divided among several European countries that wanted certain raw materials. **Asia** also came under European control, with the exception of China, Japan, and Siam (now Thailand). In the US, **Manifest Destiny** became the rallying cry as the country expanded west. Italy and Germany formed larger nations from a variety of smaller states.

Review Video: Historical Nationalism
Visit mometrix.com/academy and enter code: 510185

Review Video: Nationalism
Visit mometrix.com/academy and enter code: 865693

Events of World War I in the European Theater

WWI began in 1914 with the assassination of **Archduke Franz Ferdinand**, heir to the throne of Austria-Hungary, by a Serbian national. This led to a conflict between Austria-Hungary and Serbia that quickly escalated into the First World War. Europe split into the **Allies**—Britain, France, and Russia, and later Italy, Japan, and the US, against the **Central Powers**—Austria-Hungary, Germany, the Ottoman Empire, and Bulgaria. As the war spread, countries beyond Europe became involved. The war left Europe deeply in debt, and particularly devastated the German economy. The ensuing **Great Depression** made matters worse, and economic devastation opened the door for communist, fascist, and socialist governments to gain power.

Trench Warfare and Its Use in World War I

Fighting during WWI largely took place in a series of **trenches** built along the Eastern and Western Fronts. These trenches added up to more than 24,000 miles. This produced fronts that stretched over 400 miles, from the coast of Belgium to the border of Switzerland. The Allies made use of straightforward open-air trenches with a front line, supporting lines, and communications lines. By contrast, the German trenches sometimes included well-equipped underground living quarters.

Bolshevik Revolution

Factors Leading to the Bolshevik Revolution of 1917

Throughout its modern history, Russia had lagged behind other countries in development. The continued existence of a feudal system, combined with harsh conditions and the overall size of the country, led to massive food shortages and increasingly harsh conditions for the majority of the population. The tyrannical rule of the czars only made this worse, as did repeated losses in various military conflicts. Increasing poverty, decreasing supplies, and the czar's violation of the **October Manifesto,** which had given some political power and civil rights to the people, finally came to a head with the **Bolshevik Revolution**.

Events of the Bolshevik Revolution

A **workers' strike in Petrograd** in 1917 set the revolutionary wheels in motion when the army sided with the workers. While parliament set up a provisional government made up of nobles, the workers and military joined to form their own governmental system known as **soviets**, which consisted of local councils elected by the people. The ensuing chaos opened the doors for formerly exiled leaders Vladimir Lenin, Joseph Stalin, and Leon Trotsky to move in and gain popular support as well as the support of the Red Guard. Overthrowing parliament, they took power, creating a **communist** state in Russia. This development led to the spread of communism throughout Eastern Europe and elsewhere, greatly affecting diplomatic policies throughout the world for several decades.

Communism vs. Socialism

At their roots, socialism and communism both focus on public ownership and distribution of goods and services. However, **communism** works toward revolution by drawing on what it sees to be inevitable class antagonism, eventually overthrowing the upper classes and the systems of capitalism. **Socialism** makes use of democratic procedures, building on the existing order. This was particularly true of the utopian socialists, who saw industrial capitalism as oppressive, not allowing workers to prosper. While socialism struggled between the World Wars, communism took hold, especially in Eastern Europe. After WWII, **democratic socialism** became more common. Later, **capitalism** took a stronger hold again, and today most industrialized countries in the western world function under an economy that mixes elements of capitalism and socialism.

Review Video: Communism vs. Socialism
Visit mometrix.com/academy and enter code: 917677

Conditions That Led to the Rise of the Nazi Party in Germany

The **Great Depression** had a particularly devastating effect on Germany's economy, especially after the US was no longer able to supply reconstruction loans to help the country regain its footing. With unemployment rising rapidly, dissatisfaction with the government grew. Fascist and Communist parties rose, promising change and improvement.

Led by **Adolf Hitler**, the fascist **Nazi Party** eventually gained power in Parliament based on these promises and the votes of desperate German workers. When Hitler became chancellor, he launched numerous expansionist policies, violating the peace treaties that had ended WWI. His military buildup and conquering of neighboring countries sparked the aggression that soon led to WWII.

Importance of the German Blitzkrieg to the Progression of World War II

The blitzkrieg, or "lightning war," consisted of fast, powerful surprise attacks that disrupted communications, made it difficult if not impossible for the victims to retaliate, and demoralized Germany's foes. The "blitz," or the aerial bombing of England in 1940, was one example, with bombings occurring in London and other cities 57 nights in a row. The **Battle of Britain** in 1940 also brought intense raids by Germany's air force, the **Luftwaffe**, mostly targeting ports and British air force bases. Eventually, Britain's Royal Air Force blocked the Luftwaffe, ending Germany's hopes for conquering Britain.

Battle of the Bulge

Following the **D-Day Invasion**, Allied forces gained considerable ground and began a major campaign to push through Europe. In December of 1944, Hitler launched a counteroffensive, attempting to retake Antwerp, an important port. The ensuing battle became the largest land battle on the war's Western Front and was known as the Battle of the Ardennes, or the **Battle of the Bulge**. The battle lasted from December 16, 1944, to January 25, 1945. The Germans pushed forward, making inroads into Allied lines, but in the end, the Allies brought the advance to a halt. The Germans were pushed back, with massive losses on both sides. However, those losses proved crippling to the German army.

Holocaust

As Germany sank deeper and deeper into dire economic straits, the tendency was to look for a person or group of people to blame for the problems of the country. With distrust of the Jewish people already ingrained, it was easy for German authorities to set up the **Jews** as scapegoats for Germany's problems. Under the rule of Hitler and the Nazi party, the "Final Solution" for the supposed Jewish problem was devised. Millions of Jews, as well as Gypsies, homosexuals, communists, Catholics, the mentally ill, and others, simply named as criminals, were transported to concentration camps during the course of the war. At least six million were slaughtered in death camps such as **Auschwitz**, where horrible conditions and torture of prisoners were commonplace. The Allies were aware of rumors of mass slaughter throughout the war, but many discounted the reports. Only when troops went in to liberate the prisoners was the true horror of the concentration camps brought to light. The **Holocaust** resulted in massive loss of human life, but also in the loss and destruction of cultures. Because the genocide focused on specific ethnic groups, many traditions, histories, knowledge, and other cultural elements were lost, particularly among the Jewish and Gypsy populations. After World War II, the United Nations recognized **genocide** as a "crime against humanity." The UN passed the **Universal Declaration of Human Rights** in 1948 in order to further specify what rights the organization protected. Nazi war criminals faced justice during the **Nuremberg Trials**. There, individuals, rather than their governments, were held accountable for war crimes.

Review Video: The Holocaust
Visit mometrix.com/academy and enter code: 350695

World War II and the Ensuing Diplomatic Climate that Led to the Cold War

With millions of military and civilian deaths and over 12 million persons displaced, **WWII** left large regions of Europe and Asia in disarray. **Communist** governments moved in with promises of renewed prosperity and economic stability. The **Soviet Union** backed communist regimes in much of Eastern Europe. In China, **Mao Zedong** led communist forces in the overthrow of the Chinese Nationalist Party and instituted a communist government in 1949. While the new communist governments restored a measure of stability to much of Eastern Europe, it brought its own problems, with dictatorial governments and an oppressive police force. The spread of communism also led to several years of tension between communist countries and the democratic West, as the West fought to slow the spread of oppressive regimes throughout the world. With both sides in possession of nuclear weapons, tensions rose. Each side feared the other would resort to nuclear attack. This standoff lasted until 1989, when the **Berlin Wall** fell. The Soviet Union was dissolved two years later.

Origins of the United Nations

The United Nations (**UN**) came into being toward the end of World War II. A successor to the less-than-successful League of Nations formed after World War I, the UN built and improved on those ideas. Since its inception, the UN has worked to bring the countries of the world together for **diplomatic solutions** to international problems, including sanctions and other restrictions. It has also initiated military action, calling for peacekeeping troops from member countries to move against countries violating UN policies. The **Korean War** was the first example of UN involvement in an international conflict.

Effects of Decolonization on the Post-War Period

A rise of nationalism among European colonies led to many of them declaring independence. **India** and **Pakistan** became independent of Britain in 1947, and numerous African and Asian colonies declared independence as well. This period of **decolonization** lasted into the 1960s. Some colonies moved successfully into independence, but many, especially in Africa and Asia, struggled to create stable governments and economies and suffered from ethnic and religious conflicts, some of which continue today.

Factors and Shifts in Power that Led to the Korean War

In 1910, Japan annexed Korea and maintained this control until 1945. After WWII, Soviet and US troops occupied Korea, with the **Soviet Union** controlling North Korea and the **US** controlling South Korea. In 1947, the UN ordered elections in Korea to unify the country, but the Soviet Union refused to allow them to take place in North Korea, instead setting up a communist government. In 1950, the US withdrew troops, and the North Korean troops moved to invade South Korea. The **Korean War** was the first war in which the UN—or any international organization—played a major role. The US, Australia, Canada, France, Netherlands, Great Britain, Turkey, China, the USSR, and other countries sent troops at various times, for both sides, throughout the war. In 1953, the war ended in a truce, but no peace agreement was ever achieved, and Korea remains divided.

Events that Led to the Vietnam War

Vietnam had previously been part of a French colony called French Indochina. The **Vietnam War** began with the **First Indochina War** from 1946 to 1954, in which France battled with the Democratic Republic of Vietnam, ruled by Ho Chi Minh.

In 1954, a siege at Dien Bien Phu ended in a Vietnamese victory. Vietnam was then divided into North and South, much like Korea. Communist forces controlled the North, and the South was controlled by South Vietnamese forces, supported by the US. Conflict ensued, leading to another war. US troops eventually led the fight, in support of South Vietnam. The war became a major political issue in the US, with many citizens protesting American involvement. In 1975, South Vietnam surrendered, and Vietnam became the **Socialist Republic of Vietnam**.

Globalism

In the modern era, globalism has emerged as a popular political ideology. **Globalism** is based on the idea that all people and all nations are **interdependent**. Each nation is dependent on one or more other nations for production of and markets for goods, and for income generation. Today's ease of international travel and communication, including technological advances such as the airplane, has heightened this sense of interdependence. The global economy and the general idea of globalism have shaped many economic and political choices since the beginning of the 20th century. Many of today's issues, including environmental awareness, economic struggles, and continued warfare, often require the cooperation of many countries if they are to be dealt with effectively.

Effect of Globalization on the Way Countries Interact With Each Other

Countries worldwide often seek the same resources, leading to high demand, particularly for **nonrenewable resources**. This can result in heavy fluctuations in price. One major example is the demand for petroleum products such as oil and natural gas. Increased travel and communication make it possible to deal with diseases in remote locations; however, this also allows diseases to be spread via travelers.

A major factor contributing to increased globalization over the past few decades has been the **internet**. By allowing instantaneous communication with anyone nearly anywhere on the globe, the internet has led to interaction between far-flung individuals and countries, and an ever-increasing awareness of events all over the world.

Review Video: Globalization
Visit mometrix.com/academy and enter code: 551962

Role of the Middle East in International Relations and Economics

The location on the globe, with ease of access to Europe and Asia, and its preponderance of oil deposits, makes the **Middle Eastern countries** crucial in many international issues, both diplomatic and economic. Because of its central location, the Middle East has been a hotbed for violence since before the beginning of recorded history. Conflicts over land, resources, and religious and political power continue in the area today, spurred by conflict over control of the area's vast oil fields as well as over territories that have been disputed for thousands of years.

Major Occurrences of Genocide in Modern History

Five major occurrences of genocide in modern history other than the Holocaust are:

- **Armenian genocide**—from 1914 to 1918, the Young Turks, heirs to the Ottoman Empire, slaughtered between 800,000 and 1.5 million Armenians. This constituted approximately half of the Armenian population at the time.
- **Holodomor**—from 1932 to 1933, the people of Ukraine suffered the effects of a famine created by Joseph Stalin's collectivization of agriculture. Millions of Ukranians starved to death due to a lack of access to food.
- **Cambodian genocide**—from 1975 to 1979, the Khmer Rouge, a communist group, inflicted violence on the people of Cambodia. Between 1.5 million and 3 million Cambodians were killed. The Khmer Rouge were removed from power when the Vietnamese military took the capital of Cambodia.
- **Rwandan genocide**—in 1994, hundreds of thousands of Tutsis and Hutu sympathizers were slaughtered during the Rwandan Civil War. The UN did not act or authorize intervention during these atrocities.

- **Darfur genocide**—In 2003, militias tasked with combating rebel activity in Darfur kept the people of Darfur from accessing food and resources. This resulted in the death of hundreds of thousands of people in Darfur.

Geography

Geography is the study of Earth. Geographers study **physical characteristics** of Earth as well as man-made borders and boundaries. They also study the **distribution of life** on the planet, such as where certain species of animals can be found or how different forms of life interact. Major elements of the study of geography include:

- Locations
- Regional characteristics
- Spatial relations
- Natural and man-made forces that change elements of Earth

These elements are studied from regional, topical, physical, and human perspectives. Geography also focuses on the origins of Earth, as well as the history and backgrounds of different human populations.

Physical vs. Cultural Geography

Physical geography is the study of the physical characteristics of Earth: how they relate to each other, how they were formed, and how they develop. These characteristics include climate, land, and water, and also how they affect human population in various areas. Different landforms, in combination with various climates and other conditions, determine the characteristics of various cultures.

Cultural geography is the study of how the various aspects of physical geography affect individual cultures. Cultural geography also compares various cultures: how their lifestyles and customs are affected by their geographical location, climate, and other factors, as well as how they interact with their environment.

Review Video: Regional Geography
Visit mometrix.com/academy and enter code: 350378

Divisions of Geographical Study and Tools Used

The four divisions of geographical study and tools used are:

- **Topical**—the study of a single feature of Earth or one specific human activity that occurs worldwide.
- **Physical**—the various physical features of Earth, how they are created, the forces that change them, and how they are related to each other and to various human activities.
- **Regional**—specific characteristics of individual places and regions.
- **Human**—how human activity affects the environment. This includes the study of political, historical, social, and cultural activities.

Tools used in geographical study include special research methods like mapping, field studies, statistics, interviews, mathematics, and the use of various scientific instruments.

Important Ancient Geographers

The following are three important ancient geographers and their contributions to the study of geography:

- **Eratosthenes** lived in ancient Greek times and mathematically calculated the circumference of Earth and the tilt of Earth's axis. He also created the first map of the world.

- **Strabo** wrote a description of the ancient world called *Geographica* in seventeen volumes.
- **Ptolemy**, primarily an astronomer, was an experienced mapmaker. He wrote a treatise entitled *Geography*, which was used by Christopher Columbus in his travels.

Ways Geographers Analyze Areas of Human Population

In cities, towns, or other areas where many people have settled, geographers focus on the **distribution** of populations, neighborhoods, industrial areas, transportation, and other elements important to the society in question. For example, they would map out the locations of hospitals, airports, factories, police stations, schools, and housing groups. They would also make note of how these facilities are distributed in relation to the areas of habitation, such as the number of schools in a certain neighborhood or how many grocery stores are located in a specific suburban area. Another area of study and discussion is the distribution of **towns** themselves, from widely spaced rural towns to large cities that merge into each other to form a megalopolis.

Role of a Cartographer

A cartographer is a mapmaker. Mapmakers produce detailed illustrations of geographic areas to record where various features are located within that area. These illustrations can be compiled into maps, charts, graphs, and even globes. When constructing maps, **cartographers** must take into account the problem of **distortion**. Because Earth is round, a flat map does not accurately represent the correct proportions, especially if a very large geographical area is being depicted. Maps must be designed in such a way as to minimize this distortion and maximize accuracy. Accurately representing Earth's features on a flat surface is achieved through **projection**.

Types of Projection Used in Creating World Maps

The three major types of projection used in creating world maps are:

- **Cylindrical projection**—this is created by wrapping the globe of Earth in a cylindrical piece of paper, then using a light to project the globe onto the paper. The largest distortion occurs at the outermost edges.
- **Conical projection**—the paper is shaped like a cone and contacts the globe only at the cone's base. This type of projection is most useful for middle latitudes.
- **Flat-Plane projections**—also known as a gnomonic projection, this type of map is projected onto a flat piece of paper that only touches the globe at a single point. Flat-plane projections make it possible to map out Great-Circle routes, or the shortest route between one point and another on the globe, as a straight line.

Specific Types of Map Projections

Four specific types of map projections that are commonly used today are:

- **Winkel tripel projection**—this is the most common projection used for world maps since it was accepted in 1998 by the National Geographic Society as a standard. The Winkel tripel projection balances size and shape, greatly reducing distortion.
- **Robinson projection**—east and west sections of the map are less distorted, but continental shapes are somewhat inaccurate.
- **Goode homolosine projection**—sizes and shapes are accurate, but distances are not. This projection basically represents a globe that has been cut into connected sections so that it can lie flat.
- **Mercator projection**—though distortion is high, particularly in areas farther from the equator, this cylindrical projection is commonly used by seafarers.

Major Elements of Any Map

The five major elements of any map are:

- **Title**—this tells basic information about the map, such as the area represented.
- **Legend**—also known as the key, the legend explains what symbols used on a particular map represent, such as symbols for major landmarks.
- **Grid**—this most commonly represents the geographic grid system, or latitude and longitude marks used to precisely locate specific locations.
- **Directions**—a compass rose or other symbol is used to indicate the cardinal directions.
- **Scale**—this shows the relation between a certain distance on the map and the actual distance. For example, one inch might represent one mile, or ten miles, or even more, depending on the size of the map.

Review Video: Elements of a Map
Visit mometrix.com/academy and enter code: 437727

Equal-Area Maps vs. Conformal Maps

An equal-area map is designed such that the proportional sizes of various areas are accurate. For example, if one landmass is one-fifth the size of another, the lines on the map will be shifted to accommodate for distortion so that the proportional size is accurate. In many maps, areas farther from the equator are greatly distorted; this type of map compensates for this phenomenon. A **conformal map** focuses on representing the correct shape of geographical areas, with less concern for comparative size.

Consistent Scale Maps and Thematic Maps

With a consistent scale map, the same scale, such as one inch being equal to ten miles, is used throughout the entire map. This is most often used for maps of smaller areas, as maps that cover larger areas, such as the full globe, must make allowances for distortion. Maps of very large areas often make use of more than one scale, with scales closer to the center representing a larger area than those at the edges.

A **thematic map** is constructed to show very specific information about a chosen theme. For example, a thematic map might represent political information, such as how votes were distributed in an election, or could show population distribution or climatic features.

Relief Maps

A relief map is constructed to show details of various **elevations** across the area of the map. Higher elevations are represented by different colors than lower elevations. **Relief maps** often also show additional details, such as the overall ruggedness or smoothness of an area. Mountains would be represented as ridged and rugged, while deserts would be shown as smooth.

Elevation in relief maps can also be represented by contour lines, or lines that connect points of the same elevation. Some relief maps even feature textures, reconstructing details in a sort of miniature model.

Geographical Features

- **Mountains** are elevated areas that measure 2,000 feet or more above sea level. Often steep and rugged, they usually occur in groups called chains or ranges. Six of the seven continents on Earth contain at least one range.
- **Hills** are of lower elevation than mountains, at about 500-2,000 feet. Hills are usually more rounded and are found throughout every continent.
- **Plains** are large, flat areas and are usually very fertile. The majority of Earth's population is supported by crops grown on vast plains.

- **Valleys** lie between hills and mountains. Depending on their location, their specific features can vary greatly, from fertile and habitable to rugged and inhospitable.
- **Plateaus** are elevated, but flat on top. Some plateaus are extremely dry, such as the Kenya Plateau, because surrounding mountains prevent them from receiving moisture.
- **Deserts** receive less than ten inches of rain per year. They are usually large areas, such as the Sahara Desert in Africa or the Australian Outback.
- **Deltas** occur at river mouths. Because the rivers carry sediment to the deltas, these areas are often very fertile.
- **Mesas** are flat, steep-sided mountains or hills. The term is sometimes used to refer to plateaus.
- **Basins** are areas of low elevation where rivers drain.
- **Foothills** are the transitional area between plains and mountains, usually consisting of hills that gradually increase in size as they approach a mountain range.
- **Marshes** and **swamps** are also lowlands, but they are very wet and largely covered in vegetation such as reeds and rushes.

Geographical Terms Referring to Bodies of Water

- The **ocean** refers to the salt water that covers about two-thirds of Earth's surface.
- **Ocean basins** are named portions of the ocean. The five major ocean basins are the Atlantic, Pacific, Indian, Southern, and Arctic.
- **Seas** are generally also salt water, but are smaller than ocean basins and surrounded by land. Examples include the Mediterranean Sea, the Caribbean Sea, and the Caspian Sea.
- **Lakes** are bodies of fresh water found inland. Sixty percent of all lakes are located in Canada.
- **Rivers** are moving bodies of water that flow from higher elevations to lower. They usually start as rivulets or streams and grow until they finally empty into a sea or the ocean.
- **Canals**, such as the Panama Canal and the Suez Canal, are man-made waterways connecting two large bodies of water.

How Communities Develop

Communities, or groups of people who settle together in a specific area, typically gather where certain conditions exist. These conditions include:

- Easy access to resources such as food, water, and raw materials
- Ability to easily transport raw materials and goods, such as access to a waterway
- Room to house a sufficient workforce

People also tend to form groups with others who are similar to them. In a typical **community**, people can be found who share values, a common language, and common or similar cultural characteristics and religious beliefs. These factors will determine the overall composition of a community as it develops.

Differences Between Cities in Various Areas of the World

Cities develop and grow as an area develops. Modern statistics show that over half of the world's people live in **cities**. That percentage is even higher in developed areas of the globe. Cities are currently growing more quickly in developing regions, and even established cities continue to experience growth throughout the world. In developing or developed areas, cities often are surrounded by a metropolitan area made up of both urban and suburban sections. In some places, cities have merged into each other and become a **megalopolis**—a single, huge city.

Cities develop differently in different areas of the world. The area available for cities to grow, as well as cultural and economic forces, drives how cities develop. For example, North American cities tend to cover wider areas. European cities tend to have better-developed transportation systems. In Latin America, the richest inhabitants can be found in the city centers, while in North America, wealthier inhabitants tend to live in suburban areas.

In other parts of the world, transportation and communication between cities are less developed. Technological innovations such as the cell phone have increased communication even in these areas. Urban areas must also maintain communication with rural areas in order to procure food, resources, and raw materials that cannot be produced within the city limits.

Weather vs. Climate

Weather and climate are physical systems that affect geography. Though they deal with similar information, the way this information is measured and compiled is different.

Weather involves daily conditions in the atmosphere that affect temperature, precipitation (rain, snow, hail, or sleet), wind speed, air pressure, and other factors. Weather focuses on the short-term—what the conditions will be today, tomorrow, or over the next few days.

In contrast, **climate** aggregates information about daily and seasonal weather conditions in a region over a long period of time. The climate takes into account average monthly and yearly temperatures, average precipitation over long periods of time, and the growing season of an area. Climates are classified according to latitude, or how close they lie to Earth's equator. The three major divisions are:

- **Low Latitudes**, lying from 0 to approximately 23.5 degrees
- **Middle Latitudes**, found from approximately 23.5 to 66.5 degrees
- **High Latitudes**, found from approximately 66.5 degrees to the poles

Review Video: Climates
Visit mometrix.com/academy and enter code: 991320

Climates Found in the Low Latitudes

Rainforests, savannas, and deserts occur in low latitudes:

- **Rainforest** climates, near the equator, experience high average temperatures and humidity, as well as relatively high rainfall.
- **Savannas** are found on either side of the rainforest region. Mostly grasslands, they typically experience dry winters and wet summers.
- Beyond the savannas lie the **desert** regions, with hot, dry climates, sparse rainfall, and temperature fluctuations of up to fifty degrees from day to night.

Climate Regions Found in the Middle Latitudes

The climate regions found in the middle latitudes are:

- **Mediterranean**—the Mediterranean climate occurs between 30- and 40-degrees latitude, both north and south, on the western coasts of continents. Characteristics include a year-long growing season; hot, dry summers followed by mild winters; and sparse rainfall that occurs mostly during the winter months.
- **Humid-subtropical**—humid-subtropical regions are located in southeastern coastal areas. Winds that blow in over warm ocean currents produce long summers, mild winters, and a long growing season. These areas are highly productive and support a larger part of Earth's population than any other climate.
- **Humid-continental**—the humid continental climate produces the familiar four seasons typical of a good portion of the US. Some of the most productive farmlands in the world lie in these climates. Winters are cold, and summers are hot and humid.

Marine, Steppe, and Desert Climates

The climate regions found in the middle latitudes are:

- **Marine**—marine climates are found near water or on islands. Ocean winds help make these areas mild and rainy. Summers are cooler than humid-subtropical summers, but winters also bring milder temperatures due to the warmth of the ocean winds.
- **Steppe**—steppe climates, or prairie climates, are found far inland on large continents. Summers are hot and winters are cold, but rainfall is sparser than in continental climates.
- **Desert**—desert climates occur where steppe climates receive even less rainfall. Examples include the Gobi Desert in Asia as well as desert areas of Australia and the southwestern US.

Climates Found in the High Latitudes

The high latitudes consist of two major climate areas, the tundra and taiga:

- **Tundra** means "marshy plain." The ground is frozen throughout long, cold winters, but there is little snowfall. During the short summers, it becomes wet and marshy. Tundras are not amenable to crops, but many plants and animals have adapted to the conditions.
- **Taigas** lie south of tundra regions and include the largest forest areas in the world, as well as swamps and marshes. Large mineral deposits exist here, as well as many animals valued for their fur. In the winter, taiga regions are colder than the tundra, and summers are hotter. The growing season is short.

A **vertical climate** exists in high mountain ranges. Increasing elevation leads to varying temperatures, growing conditions, types of vegetation and animals, and occurrence of human habitation, often encompassing elements of various other climate regions.

Factors Affecting Climate

Because Earth is tilted, its **rotation** brings about changes in **seasons**. Regions closer to the equator, and those nearest the poles, experience very little change in seasonal temperatures. Mid-range latitudes are most likely to experience distinct seasons. Large bodies of water also affect climate. Ocean currents and wind patterns can change the climate for an area that lies in a typically cold latitude, such as England, to a much more temperate climate. Mountains can affect both short-term weather and long-term climates. Some deserts occur because precipitation is stopped by the wall of a mountain range.

Over time, established **climate patterns** can shift and change. While the issue is hotly debated, it has been theorized that human activity has also led to climate change.

Effect of Human Systems

Human Systems that Geographers Incorporate into the Study of Earth

Human systems affect geography in the way in which they settle, form groups that grow into large-scale habitations, and even create permanent changes in the landscape. **Geographers** study movements of people, how they distribute goods among each other and to other settlements or cultures, and how ideas grow and spread. Migrations, wars, forced relocations, and trade can all spread cultural ideas, language, goods, and other practices to widespread areas. Throughout history, cultures have been changed due to a wide range of events, including major migrations and the conquering of one people by another. In addition, **human systems** can lead to various conflicts or alliances to control access to and the use of natural resources.

Human Systems that Form the Basis of Cultures in North America

North America consists of 23 countries, including (in decreasing population order) the United States of America, Mexico, Canada, Guatemala, Cuba, Haiti, and the Dominican Republic. The US and Canada support similarly diverse cultures, as both were formed from groups of native races and large numbers of immigrants. Many **North American cultures** come from a mixture of indigenous and colonial European influences. Agriculture is important to North American countries, while service industries and technology also play a large part in the economy. On average, North America supports a high standard of living and a high level of development and supports trade with countries throughout the world.

Human Systems that Shape South America

Home to twelve sovereign states, including Brazil (largest in area and population), Colombia, Argentina, Venezuela, and Peru; two independent territories; and one internal territory, **South America** is largely defined by its prevailing languages. The majority of countries in South America speak Spanish or Portuguese. Most of South America has experienced a similar history, having been originally dominated by Native cultures and then conquered by European nations. The countries of South America have since gained independence, but there is a wide disparity between various countries' economic and political factors. Most South American countries rely on only one or two exports, usually agricultural, with suitable lands often controlled by rich families. Most societies in South America feature major separations between classes, both economically and socially. Challenges faced by developing South American countries include geographical limitations, economic issues, and sustainable development, including the need to preserve the existing rainforests.

Human Systems Influencing Europe

Europe contains a wide variety of cultures, ethnic groups, physical geographical features, climates, and resources, all of which have influenced the distribution of its varied population. **Europe**, in general, is industrialized and developed, with cultural differences giving each individual country its own unique characteristics. Greek and Roman influences played a major role in European culture, as did Christianity. European countries spread their beliefs and cultural elements throughout the world by means of migration and colonization. They have had a significant influence on nearly every other continent in the world. While Western Europe has been largely democratic, Eastern Europe functioned under communist rule for many years. The formation of the European Union (EU) in 1993 has increased stability and positive diplomatic relations among European nations. Like other industrialized regions, Europe is now focusing on various environmental issues.

Human Systems that Have Shaped Russia

After numerous conflicts, Russia became a Communist state, known as the **USSR**. With the collapse of the USSR in 1991, the country has struggled in its transition to a market-driven economy. Attempts to build a workable system have led to the destruction of natural resources as well as problems with nuclear power, including accidents such as Chernobyl. To complete the transition to a market economy, Russia would need to improve its transportation and communication systems and find a way to more efficiently use its natural resources.

The population of Russia is not distributed evenly, with three-quarters of the population living west of the Ural Mountains. The people of Russia encompass over a hundred different ethnic groups. Over eighty percent of the population is ethnically Russian, and Russian is the official language of the country.

Human Systems that Have Shaped North Africa and Southwest and Central Asia

The largely desert climate of these areas has led most population centers to rise around sources of **water**, such as the Nile River. This area is the home of the **earliest known civilizations** and the origin of Christianity, Judaism, and Islam. After serving as the site of huge, independent civilizations in ancient times, North Africa and Southwest and Central Asia were largely parceled out as **European colonies** during the 18th and 19th centuries. The beginning of the 20th century saw many of these countries gain their independence. **Islam** has served as a unifying force for large portions of these areas, and many of the inhabitants speak Arabic. In spite of the arid climate, agriculture is a large business, but the most valuable resource is **oil**. Centuries of conflict throughout this area have led to ongoing political problems. These political problems have also contributed to environmental issues.

Human Systems that Shape and Influence the Culture of Sub-Saharan Africa

South of the Sahara Desert, **Africa** is divided into a number of culturally diverse nations. The inhabitants are unevenly distributed due to geographical limitations that prevent settlement in vast areas. **AIDS** has become a major plague throughout this part of Africa, killing millions, largely due to restrictive beliefs that prevent education about the disease, as well as abject poverty and unsettled political situations that make it impossible to manage the pandemic. The population of this area of Africa is widely diverse due to extensive **migration**. Many of the people still rely on **subsistence farming** for their welfare. Starvation and poverty are rampant due to drought and political instability. Some areas are far more stable than others due to the greater availability of resources. These areas have been able to begin the process of **industrialization**.

HUMAN SYSTEMS THAT DETERMINE THE CULTURAL MAKEUP OF SOUTH ASIA

South Asia is home to one of the first human civilizations, which grew up in the **Indus River Valley**. With a great deal of disparity between rural and urban life, South Asia has much to do to improve the quality of life for its lower classes. Two major religions, **Hinduism** and **Buddhism**, have their origins in this region. Parts of South Asia, most notably India, were subject to **British rule** for several decades and are still working to improve independent governments and social systems. Overall, South Asia is very culturally diverse, with a wide mix of religions and languages throughout. Many individuals are **farmers**, but a growing number have found prosperity in the spread of **high-tech industries**. Industrialization is growing in South Asia but continues to face environmental, social, religious, and economic challenges.

HUMAN SYSTEMS SHAPING THE CULTURE OF EAST ASIA

Governments in East Asia are varied, ranging from communist to democratic governments, with some governments that mix both approaches. **Isolationism** throughout the area limited the countries' contact with other nations until the early 20th century. The unevenly distributed population of East Asia consists of over one and a half billion people with widely diverse ethnic backgrounds, religions, and languages. More residents live in **urban** areas than in **rural** areas, creating shortages of farmworkers at times. Japan, Taiwan, and South Korea are overall more urban, while China and Mongolia are more rural. Japan stands as the most industrial country in East Asia. Some areas of East Asia are suffering from major environmental issues. Japan has dealt with many of these problems and now has some of the strictest environmental laws in the world.

HUMAN SYSTEMS THAT HAVE INFLUENCED SOUTHEAST ASIA

Much of Southeast Asia was **colonized** by European countries during the 18th and 19th centuries, with the exception of Siam, now known as Thailand. All Southeast Asian countries are now independent, but the 20th century saw numerous conflicts between **communist** and **democratic** forces.

Southeast Asia has been heavily influenced by both Buddhist and Muslim religions. Industrialization is growing, with the population moving in large numbers from rural to urban areas. Some have moved to avoid conflict, oppression, and poverty.

Natural disasters, including volcanoes, typhoons, and flash flooding, are fairly common in Southeast Asia, creating extensive economic damage and societal disruption.

HUMAN SYSTEMS THAT AFFECT THE DEVELOPMENT AND CULTURE OF AUSTRALIA, OCEANA, AND ANTARCTICA

South Pacific cultures originally migrated from Southeast Asia, creating hunter-gatherer or sometimes settled agricultural communities. **European** countries moved in during later centuries, seeking the plentiful natural resources of the area. Today, some South Pacific islands remain under the control of foreign governments, and culture in these areas mixes modern, industrialized society with indigenous culture. Population is unevenly distributed, largely due to the inhabitability of many parts of the South Pacific, such as the extremely hot desert areas of Australia. **Agriculture** still drives much of the economy, with **tourism** growing. **Antarctica** remains the only continent that has not been claimed by any country. There are no permanent human habitations in Antarctica, but scientists and explorers visit the area on a temporary basis.

Human-Environment Interaction

Geography also studies the ways people interact with, use, and change their **environment**. The effects, reasons, and consequences of these changes are studied, as are the ways the environment limits or influences human behavior. This kind of study can help determine the best course of action when a nation or group of people is considering making changes to the environment, such as building a dam or removing natural landscape to build or expand roads. Study of the **consequences** can help determine if these actions are manageable and how long-term, detrimental results can be mitigated.

Physical Geography and Climates

Physical Geography and Climate of North America

Together, the US and Canada make up the majority of North America and both have a similar distribution of geographical features: mountain ranges in both the east and the west, stretches of fertile plains through the center, and lakes and waterways. Both areas were shaped by **glaciers**, which also deposited highly fertile soil. Because they are so large, Canada and the US experience several varieties of **climate**, including continental climates with four seasons in median areas, tropical climates in the southern part of the US, and arctic climes in the far north. The remaining area of North America includes Mexico, Central America, the Caribbean Isles, and Greenland.

Physical Geography and Climate of South America

South America contains a wide variety of geographical features, including high **mountains** such as the Andes, wide **plains**, and high-altitude **plateaus**. The region contains numerous natural resources, but many of them have remained unused due to various obstacles, including political issues, geographic barriers, and lack of sufficient economic power. Climate zones in South America are largely **tropical**, with rainforests and savannas, but vertical climate zones and grasslands also exist in some places.

Physical Geography and Climate of Europe

Europe spans a wide area with a variety of climate zones. In the east and south are **mountain** ranges, while the north is dominated by a **plains** region. The long coastline and the island nature of some countries, such as Britain, mean the climate is often warmer than other lands at similar latitudes, as the area is warmed by **ocean currents**. Many areas of western Europe have a moderate climate, while areas of the south are dominated by the classic Mediterranean climate. Europe carries a high level of natural resources. Numerous waterways help connect the inner regions with the coastal areas. Much of Europe is **industrialized**, and **agriculture** has been developed for thousands of years.

Physical Geography and Climate of Russia

Russia's area encompasses part of Asia and Europe. From the standpoint of square footage alone, **Russia** is the largest country in the world. Due to its size, Russia encompasses a wide variety of climatic regions, including **plains**, **plateaus**, **mountains**, and **tundra**.

Russia's **climate** can be quite harsh, with rivers that are frozen most of the year, making transportation of the country's rich natural resources more difficult. Siberia, in northern Russia, is dominated by **permafrost**. Native peoples in this area still follow a hunting and gathering lifestyle, living in portable yurts and subsisting largely on herds of reindeer or caribou. Other areas include taiga with extensive, dense woods in north-central Russia and more temperate steppes and grasslands in the southwest.

Physical Geography and Climate of North Africa, Southwest, and Central Asia

This area of the world is complex in its geographical structure and climate, incorporating seas, peninsulas, rivers, mountains, and numerous other features. **Earthquakes** are common, with tectonic plates in the area remaining active. Much of the world's **oil** lies in this area. The tendency of the large rivers of North Africa, especially the Nile, to follow a set pattern of **drought** and extreme **fertility**, led people to settle there from prehistoric times. As technology has advanced, people have tamed this river, making its activity more predictable and the land around it more productive. The extremely arid nature of many other parts of this area has also led to **human intervention** such as irrigation to increase agricultural production.

Physical Geography and Climate of the Southern Portion of Africa

South of the Sahara Desert, the high elevations and other geographical characteristics have made it very difficult for human travel or settlement to occur. The geography of the area is dominated by a series of **plateaus**. There are also mountain ranges and a large rift valley in the eastern part of the country. Contrasting the wide desert areas, sub-Saharan Africa contains numerous lakes, rivers, and world-famous waterfalls. The area has **tropical** climates, including rainforests, savannas, steppes, and desert areas. The main natural resources are minerals, including gems and water.

Physical Geography and Climate of South Asia

The longest **alluvial plain**, a plain caused by shifting floodplains of major rivers and river systems over time, exists in South Asia. South Asia boasts three major **river systems** in the Ganges, Indus, and Brahmaputra. It also has large deposits of **minerals**, including iron ore that is in great demand internationally. South Asia holds mountains, plains, plateaus, and numerous islands. The climates range from tropical to highlands and desert areas. South Asia also experiences monsoon winds that cause a long rainy season. Variations in climate, elevation, and human activity influence agricultural production.

Geography and Climate of East Asia

East Asia includes North and South Korea, Mongolia, China, Japan, and Taiwan. Mineral resources are plentiful but not evenly distributed throughout. The coastlines are long, and while the population is large, farmlands are sparse. As a result, the surrounding ocean has become a major source of sustenance. East Asia is large enough to encompass several climate regions. **Ocean currents** provide milder climates to coastal areas, while **monsoons** provide the majority of the rainfall for the region. **Typhoons** are somewhat common, as are **earthquakes**, **volcanoes**, and **tsunamis**. The latter occur because of the tectonic plates that meet beneath the continent and remain somewhat active.

Geography and Climate of Southeast Asia

Southeast Asia lies largely on the **equator**, and roughly half of the countries of the region are island nations. These countries include Indonesia, the Philippines, Vietnam, Thailand, Myanmar, and Malaysia (which is partially on the mainland and partially an island country). The island nations of Southeast Asia feature mountains that are considered part of the **Ring of Fire**, an area where tectonic plates remain active, leading to extensive volcanic activity as well as earthquakes and tsunamis. Southeast Asia boasts many rivers and abundant natural resources, including gems, fossil fuels, and minerals. There are basically two seasons: wet and dry. The wet season arrives with the **monsoons**. In general, Southeast Asia consists of **tropical rainforest climates**, but there are some mountain areas and tropical savannas.

Geography and Climate of Australia, Oceania, and Antarctica

In the far southern hemisphere of the globe, Australia and Oceania present their own climatic combinations. **Australia**, the only island on Earth that is also a continent, has extensive deserts as well as mountains and lowlands. The economy is driven by agriculture, including ranches and farms, and minerals. While the steppes bordering extremely arid inland areas are suitable for livestock, only the coastal areas receive sufficient rainfall for crops without using irrigation. **Oceania** refers to over 10,000 Pacific islands created by volcanic activity. Most of these have tropical climates with wet and dry seasons. **New Zealand**, Australia's nearest neighbor, boasts rich forests, mountain ranges, and relatively moderate temperatures, including rainfall throughout the year. **Antarctica** is covered with ice. Its major resource consists of scientific information. It supports some wildlife, such as penguins, and little vegetation, primarily mosses or lichens.

Theory of Plate Tectonics

According to the geological theory of plate tectonics, Earth's crust is made up of ten major and several minor **tectonic plates**. These plates are the solid areas of the crust. They float on top of Earth's mantle, which is made up of molten rock. Because the plates float on this liquid component of Earth's crust, they move, creating major changes in Earth's surface. These changes can happen very slowly over a long time period, such as in continental drift, or rapidly, such as when earthquakes occur. **Interaction** between the different continental plates can create mountain ranges, volcanic activity, major earthquakes, and deep rifts.

Types of Plate Boundaries

Plate tectonics defines three types of plate boundaries, determined by how the edges of the plates interact. These **plate boundaries** are:

- **Convergent boundaries**—the bordering plates move toward one another. When they collide directly, this is known as continental collision, which can create very large, high mountain ranges such as the Himalayas and the Andes. If one plate slides under the other, this is called subduction. Subduction can lead to intense volcanic activity. One example is the Ring of Fire that lies along the northern Pacific coastlines.
- **Divergent boundaries**—plates move away from each other. This movement leads to rifts such as the Mid-Atlantic Ridge and East Africa's Great Rift Valley.
- **Transform boundaries**—plate boundaries slide in opposite directions against each other. Intense pressure builds up along transform boundaries as the plates grind along each other's edges, leading to earthquakes. Many major fault lines, including the San Andreas Fault, lie along transform boundaries.

Erosion, Weathering, Transportation, and Deposition

Erosion involves movement of any loose material on Earth's surface. This can include soil, sand, or rock fragments. These loose fragments can be displaced by natural forces such as wind, water, ice, plant cover, and human factors. **Mechanical erosion** occurs due to natural forces. **Chemical erosion** occurs as a result of human intervention and activities. **Weathering** occurs when atmospheric elements affect Earth's surface. Water, heat, ice, and pressure all lead to weathering. **Transportation** refers to loose material being moved by wind, water, or ice. Glacial movement, for example, carries everything from pebbles to boulders, sometimes over long distances. **Deposition** is the result of transportation. When material is transported, it is eventually deposited, and builds up to create formations like moraines and sand dunes.

Effects of Human Interaction and Conflict on Geographical Boundaries

Human societies and their interaction have led to divisions of territories into **countries** and various other subdivisions. While these divisions are at their root artificial, they are important to geographers in discussing various populations' interactions.

Geographical divisions often occur through conflict between different human populations. The reasons behind these divisions include:

- Control of resources
- Control of important trade routes
- Control of populations

Conflict often occurs due to religious, political, language, or race differences. Natural resources are finite and so often lead to conflict over how they are distributed among populations.

State Sovereignty

State sovereignty recognizes the division of geographical areas into areas controlled by various governments or groups of people. These groups control not only the territory but also all its natural resources and the inhabitants of the area. The entire planet Earth is divided into **political** or **administratively sovereign areas** recognized to be controlled by a particular government, with the exception of the continent of Antarctica.

ALLIANCES

Alliances form between different countries based on similar interests, political goals, cultural values, or military issues. Six existing **international alliances** include:

- North Atlantic Treaty Organization (NATO)
- Common Market
- European Union (EU)
- United Nations (UN)
- Caribbean Community
- Council of Arab Economic Unity

In addition, very large **companies** and **multi-national corporations** can create alliances and various kinds of competition based on the need to control resources, production, and the overall marketplace.

WAYS AGRICULTURAL REVOLUTION CHANGED SOCIETY

The agricultural revolution began approximately 6,000 years ago when the **plow** was invented in **Mesopotamia**. Using a plow drawn by animals, people were able to cultivate crops in large quantities rather than gathering available seeds and grains and planting them by hand. Because large-scale agriculture was labor-intensive, this led to the development of stable communities where people gathered to make farming possible. As **stable farming communities** replaced groups of nomadic hunter-gatherers, human society underwent profound changes. Societies became dependent on limited numbers of crops as well as subject to the vagaries of weather. Trading livestock and surplus agricultural output led to the growth of large-scale **commerce** and **trade routes**.

WAYS HUMAN POPULATIONS MODIFY THEIR SURROUNDING ENVIRONMENT

The agricultural revolution led human societies to begin changing their surroundings to accommodate their needs for shelter and room to cultivate food and to provide for domestic animals. Clearing ground for crops, redirecting waterways for irrigation purposes, and building permanent settlements all create major changes in the **environment**. Large-scale agriculture can lead to loose topsoil and damaging erosion. Building large cities leads to degraded air quality, water pollution from energy consumption, and many other side effects that can severely damage the environment. Recently, many countries have taken action by passing laws to **reduce human impact** on the environment and reduce the potentially damaging side effects. This is called **environmental policy**.

ECOLOGY

Ecology is the study of the way living creatures interact with their environment. **Biogeography** explores the way physical features of Earth affect living creatures.

Ecology bases its studies on three different levels of the environment:

- **Ecosystem**—this is a specific physical environment and all the organisms that live there.
- **Biome**—this is a group of ecosystems, usually consisting of a large area with similar flora and fauna as well as similar climate and soil. Examples of biomes include deserts, tropical rain forests, taigas, and tundra.
- **Habitat**—this is an area in which a specific species usually lives. The habitat includes the necessary soil, water, and resources for that particular species, as well as predators and other species that compete for the same resources.

Types of Interactions Occurring Between Species in an Individual Habitat

Different interactions occur among species and members of single species within a habitat. These **interactions** fall into three categories:

- **Competition** — competition occurs when different animals, either of the same species or of different species, compete for the same resources. Robins can compete with other robins for available food, but other insectivores also compete for these same resources.
- **Predation**— predation occurs when one species depends on the other species for food, such as a fox who subsists on small mammals.
- **Symbiosis** — symbiosis occurs when two different species exist in the same environment without negatively affecting each other. Some symbiotic relationships are beneficial to one or both organisms without harm occurring to either.

Importance of an Organism's Ability to Adapt

If a species is relocated from one habitat to another, it must **adapt** in order to survive. Some species are more capable of adapting than others. Those that cannot adapt will not survive. There are different ways a creature can adapt, including behavior modification and structural or physiological changes. Adaptation is also vital if an organism's environment changes around it. Although the creature has not been relocated, it finds itself in a new environment that requires changes in order to survive. The more readily an organism can adapt, the more likely it is to survive. The almost infinite ability of **humans** to adapt is a major reason why they are able to survive in almost any habitat in any area of the world.

Biodiversity

Biodiversity refers to the variety of habitats that exist on the planet, as well as the variety of organisms that can exist within these habitats. A greater level of **biodiversity** makes it more likely that an individual habitat will flourish along with the species that depend upon it. Changes in habitat, including climate change, human intervention, or other factors, can reduce biodiversity by causing the extinction of certain species.

Chapter Quiz

Ready to see how well you retained what you just read? Scan the QR code to go directly to the chapter quiz interface for this study guide. If you're using a computer, simply visit the bonus page at **mometrix.com/bonus948/fsot** and click the Chapter Quizzes link.

Economics

Transform passive reading into active learning! After immersing yourself in this chapter, put your comprehension to the test by taking a quiz. The insights you gained will stay with you longer this way. Scan the QR code to go directly to the chapter quiz interface for this study guide. If you're using a computer, simply visit the bonus page at **mometrix.com/bonus948/fsot** and click the Chapter Quizzes link.

Economics

Economics is the study of the ways specific societies **allocate** resources to individuals and groups within that society. Also important are the choices society makes regarding what efforts or initiatives are funded and which are not. Since resources in any society are finite, allocation becomes a vivid reflection of that society's values. In general, the economic system that drives an individual society is based on:

- What goods are produced
- How those goods are produced
- Who acquires the goods or benefits from them

Economics consists of two main categories: **macroeconomics**, which studies larger systems, and **microeconomics**, which studies smaller systems.

Market Economy

A market economy is based on supply and demand. **Demand** has to do with what customers want and need, as well as what quantity those consumers are able to purchase based on other economic factors. **Supply** refers to how much can be produced to meet demand, or how much suppliers are willing and able to sell. Where the needs of consumers meet the needs of suppliers is referred to as a market equilibrium price. This price varies depending on many factors, including the overall health of a society's economy and the overall beliefs and considerations of individuals in society. The following is a list of terms defined in the context of a market economy:

- **Elasticity**—this is based on how the quantity of a particular product responds to the price demanded for that product. If quantity responds quickly to changes in price, the supply/demand for that product is said to be elastic. If it does not respond quickly, then the supply/demand is inelastic.
- **Market efficiency**—this occurs when a market is capable of producing output high enough to meet consumer demand.
- **Comparative advantage**—in the field of international trade, this refers to a country focusing on a specific product that it can produce more efficiently and more cheaply, or at a lower opportunity cost, than another country, thus giving it a comparative advantage in production.

Review Video: Basics of Market Economy
Visit mometrix.com/academy and enter code: 791556

Planned Economy vs. Market Economy

In a **market economy**, supply and demand are determined by consumers. In a **planned economy**, a public entity or planning authority makes the decisions about what resources will be produced, how they will be produced, and who will be able to benefit from them. The means of production, such as factories, are also owned by a public entity rather than by private interests. In **market socialism**, the economic structure falls somewhere between the market economy and the planned economy. Planning authorities determine the allocation of resources at higher economic levels, while consumer goods are driven by a market economy.

Microeconomics

While economics generally studies how resources are allocated, **microeconomics** focuses on economic factors such as the way consumers behave, how income is distributed, and output and input markets. Studies are limited to the industry or firm level rather than an entire country or society. Among the elements studied in microeconomics are factors of production, costs of production, and factor income. These factors determine production decisions of individual firms, based on resources and costs.

Classification of Various Markets by Economists

The conditions prevailing in a given market are used to **classify** markets. Conditions considered include:

- Existence of competition
- Number and size of suppliers
- Influence of suppliers over price
- Variety of available products
- Ease of entering the market

Once these questions are answered, an economist can classify a certain market according to its structure and the nature of competition within the market.

Market Failure

When any of the elements for a successfully competitive market are missing, this can lead to a **market failure**. Certain elements are necessary to create what economists call "**perfect competition**." If one of these factors is weak or lacking, the market is classified as having "**imperfect competition**." Worse than imperfect competition, though, is a market failure. There are five major types of market failure:

- Inadequate competition
- Inadequate information
- Immobile resources
- Negative externalities, or side effects
- Failure to provide public goods

Externalities are side effects of a market that affect third parties. These effects can be either negative or positive.

Factors of Production and Costs of Production

Every good and service requires certain resources, or **inputs**. These inputs are referred to as **factors of production**. Every good and service requires four factors of production:

- Labor
- Capital
- Land
- Entrepreneurship

These factors can be fixed or variable and can produce fixed or variable costs. Examples of **fixed costs** include land and equipment. **Variable costs** include labor. The total of fixed and variable costs makes up the cost of production.

FACTOR INCOME

Factors of production each have an associated **factor income**. Factors that earn income include:

- **Labor**—earns wages
- **Capital**—earns interest
- **Land**—earns rent
- **Entrepreneurship**—earns profit

Each factor's income is determined by its **contribution**. In a market economy, this income is not guaranteed to be equal. How scarce the factor is and the weight of its contribution to the overall production process determines the final factor income.

KINDS OF MARKET STRUCTURES IN AN OUTPUT MARKET.

The four kinds of market structures in an output market are:

- **Perfect competition**—all existing firms sell an identical product. The firms are not able to control the final price. In addition, there is nothing that makes it difficult to become involved in or leave the industry. Anything that would prevent entering or leaving an industry is called a barrier to entry. An example of this market structure is agriculture.
- **Monopoly**—a single seller controls the product and its price. Barriers to entry, such as prohibitively high fixed cost structures, prevent other sellers from entering the market.
- **Monopolistic competition**—a number of firms sell similar products, but they are not identical, such as different brands of clothes or food. Barriers to entry are low.
- **Oligopoly**—only a few firms control the production and distribution of products, such as automobiles. Barriers to entry are high, preventing large numbers of firms from entering the market.

TYPES OF MONOPOLIES

Four types of monopolies are:

- **Natural monopoly**—a single supplier has a distinct advantage over the others.
- **Geographic monopoly**—only one business offers the product in a certain area.
- **Technological monopoly**—a single company controls the technology necessary to supply the product.
- **Government monopoly**—a government agency is the only provider of a specific good or service.

ACTIONS TAKEN BY THE US GOVERNMENT TO CONTROL MONOPOLIES

The US government has passed several acts to regulate businesses, including:

- **Sherman Antitrust Act (1890)**—this prohibited trusts, monopolies, and any other situations that eliminated competition.
- **Clayton Antitrust Act (1914)**—this prohibited price discrimination.
- **Robinson-Patman Act (1936)**—this strengthened provisions of the Clayton Antitrust Act, requiring businesses to offer the same pricing on products to any customer.

The government has also taken other actions to ensure competition, including requirements for public disclosure. The **Securities and Exchange Commission (SEC)** requires companies that provide public stock to provide financial reports on a regular basis. Because of the nature of their business, banks are further regulated and required to provide various information to the government.

Marketing and Utility

Marketing consists of all of the activity necessary to convince consumers to acquire goods. One major way to move products into the hands of consumers is to convince them that any single product will satisfy a need. The ability of a product or service to satisfy the need of a consumer is called **utility**. There are four types of utility:

- **Form utility**—a product's desirability lies in its physical characteristics.
- **Place utility**—a product's desirability is connected to its location and convenience.
- **Time utility**—a product's desirability is determined by its availability at a certain time.
- **Ownership utility**—a product's desirability is increased because ownership of the product passes to the consumer.

Marketing behavior will stress any or all of these types of utility when marketing to the consumer.

Producers Determining What Customers Desire for Their Products

Successful marketing depends not only on convincing customers they need the product but also on focusing the marketing towards those who already have a need or desire for the product. Before releasing a product into the general marketplace, many producers will **test** markets to determine which will be the most receptive to the product. There are three steps usually taken to evaluate a product's market:

- **Market research**—this involves researching a market to determine if it will be receptive to the product.
- **Market surveys**—a part of market research, market surveys ask consumers specific questions to help determine the marketability of a product to a specific group.
- **Test marketing**—this includes releasing the product into a small geographical area to see how it sells. Often test marketing is followed by wider marketing if the product does well.

Major Elements of a Marketing Plan

The four major elements of a marketing plan are:

- **Product**—this includes any elements pertaining directly to the product, such as packaging, presentation, or services to include along with it.
- **Price**—this calculates the cost of production, distribution, advertising, etc., as well as the desired profit to determine the final price.
- **Place**—this determines which outlets will be used to sell the product, whether traditional outlets such as brick and mortar stores or through direct mail or internet marketing.
- **Promotion**—this involves ways to let consumers know the product is available, through advertising and other means.

Once these elements have all been determined, the producer can proceed with production and distribution of his product.

Distribution Channels

Distribution channels determine the route a product takes on its journey from producer to consumer, and can also influence the final price and availability of the product. There are two major forms of distributions: wholesale and retail. A **wholesale distributor** buys in large quantities and then resells smaller amounts to other businesses. **Retailers** sell directly to the consumers rather than to businesses. In the modern marketplace, additional distribution channels have grown up with the rise of markets such as club warehouse stores as well as purchasing through catalogs or over the internet. Most of these newer distribution channels bring products more directly to the consumer, eliminating the need for middlemen.

Distribution of Income in a Society

Distribution of income in any society ranges from poorest to richest. In most societies, income is not distributed evenly. To determine **income distribution**, family incomes are ranked from lowest to highest. These rankings are divided into five sections called **quintiles**, which are compared to each other. The uneven distribution of income is often linked to higher levels of education and ability in the upper classes but can also be due to other factors such as discrimination and existing monopolies. The **income gap** in America continues to grow, largely due to growth in the service industry, changes in the American family unit, and reduced influence of labor unions. **Poverty** is defined by comparing incomes to poverty guidelines. Poverty guidelines determine the level of income necessary for a family to function. Those below the poverty line are often eligible for assistance from government agencies.

Macroeconomics

Macroeconomics examines economies on a much larger level than microeconomics. While **microeconomics** studies economics on a firm or industry level, **macroeconomics** looks at economic trends and structures on a national level. Variables studied in macroeconomics include:

- Output
- Consumption
- Investment
- Government spending
- Net exports

The overall economic condition of a nation is defined as the **Gross Domestic Product**, or GDP. GDP measures a nation's economic output over a limited time period, such as a year.

Review Video: Microeconomics and Macroeconomics
Visit mometrix.com/academy and enter code: 538837

Review Video: Gross Domestic Product
Visit mometrix.com/academy and enter code: 409020

Types of Consumer Behavior

The two major types of consumer behavior as defined in macroeconomics are:

- **Marginal propensity to consume (MPC)** defines the tendency of consumers to increase spending in conjunction with increases in income. In general, individuals with greater income will buy more. As individuals increase their income through job changes or growth of experience, they will also increase spending.
- **Utility** is a term that describes the satisfaction experienced by a consumer in relation to acquiring and using a good or service. Providers of goods and services will stress utility to convince consumers they want the products being presented.

Ways to Measure the Gross Domestic Product of a Country

The two major ways to measure the Gross Domestic Product of a country are:

- The **expenditures approach** calculates the GDP based on how much money is spent in each individual sector.
- The **income approach** calculates the GDP based on how much money is earned in each sector.

Both methods yield the same results, and both of these calculation methods are based on four **economic sectors** that make up a country's macro-economy:

- Consumers
- Business
- Government
- Foreign sector

Types of Earnings Generated by an Economy Considered to Calculate GDP

Several factors must be considered in order to accurately calculate the GDP using the incomes approach. **Income factors** are:

- Wages paid to laborers, or compensation of employees (CE)
- Rental income derived from land
- Interest income derived from invested capital
- Entrepreneurial income

Entrepreneurial income consists of two forms. **Proprietor's income** is income that comes back to the entrepreneur himself. **Corporate profit** is income that goes back into the corporation as a whole. Corporate profit is divided by the corporation into corporate profits taxes, dividends, and retained earnings. Two other figures must be subtracted in the incomes approach. These are **indirect business taxes**, including property and sales taxes, and **depreciation**.

Effects of Population of a Country on the Gross Domestic Product

Changes in population can affect the calculation of a nation's **GDP**, particularly since GDP and GNP (Gross National Product) are generally measured per capita. If a country's economic production is low but the population is high, the income per individual will be lower than if the income is high and the population is lower. Also, if the population grows quickly and the income grows slowly, individual income will remain low or even drop drastically.

Population growth can also affect overall **economic growth**. Economic growth requires both that consumers purchase goods and workers produce them. A population that does not grow quickly enough will not supply enough workers to support rapid economic growth.

Ideal Balance to be Obtained in an Economy

Ideally, an economy functions efficiently, with the **aggregate supply**, or the amount of national output, equal to the **aggregate demand**, or the amount of the output that is purchased. In these cases, the economy is stable and prosperous. However, economies more typically go through **phases**. These phases are:

- **Boom**—GDP is high and the economy prospers
- **Recession**—GDP falls and unemployment rises
- **Trough**—the recession reaches its lowest point
- **Recovery**—unemployment lessens, prices rise, and the economy begins to stabilize again

These phases tend to repeat in cycles that are not necessarily predictable or regular.

Unemployment and Inflation

When demand outstrips supply, prices are driven artificially high, or are **inflated**. This occurs when too much spending causes an imbalance in the economy. In general, inflation occurs because an economy is growing too quickly. When there is too little spending, and supply has moved far beyond demand, a **surplus** of product results. Companies cut back on production and reduce the number of employees, and **unemployment** rises as people lose their jobs. This imbalance occurs when an economy becomes sluggish. In general, both these economic instability situations are caused by an imbalance between supply and demand. Government intervention may be necessary to stabilize an economy when either inflation or unemployment becomes too serious.

Different Forms of Unemployment

- **Frictional**—when workers change jobs and are unemployed while waiting for new jobs
- **Structural**—when economic shifts reduce the need for workers
- **Cyclical**—when natural business cycles bring about loss of jobs
- **Seasonal**—when seasonal cycles reduce the need for certain jobs
- **Technological**—when advances in technology result in the elimination of certain jobs

Any of these factors can increase unemployment in certain sectors.

Inflation is classified by the overall rate at which it occurs:

- **Creeping inflation**—this is an inflation rate of about 1%-3% annually.
- **Walking inflation**—this is an inflation rate of 3%-10% annually.
- **Galloping inflation**— a severe inflation rate above 10 percent (to upwards of 100 percent and beyond) annually. Highly detrimental to the economy, this deeply impacts the lower and middle class populus.
- **Hyperinflation**— an inflation rate over 50% monthly or 500+ percent annually. Hyperinflation usually leads to complete monetary collapse in a society. Individuals are unable to have enough income to purchase their needed goods.

Government Intervention Policies that Can Help Mitigate Inflation and Unemployment

When an economy becomes too imbalanced, either due to excessive spending or not enough spending, **government intervention** often becomes necessary to put the economy back on track. Government fiscal policy can take several forms, including:

- Contractionary policy
- Expansionary policy
- Monetary policy

Contractionary policies help counteract inflation. These include increasing taxes and decreasing government spending to slow spending in the overall economy. **Expansionary policies** increase government spending and lower taxes in order to reduce unemployment and increase the level of spending in the economy overall. **Monetary policy** can take several forms and affects the amount of funds available to banks for making loans.

Study and Quantification of Populations and Population Growth

Populations are studied by **size**, rates of **growth** due to immigration, the overall **fertility rate**, and **life expectancy**. For example, though the population of the United States is considerably larger than it was two hundred years ago, the rate of population growth has decreased greatly, from about three percent per year to less than one percent per year.

In the US, the fertility rate is fairly low, with most choosing not to have large families, and life expectancy is high, creating a projected imbalance between older and younger people in the near future. In addition, immigration and the mixing of racially diverse cultures are projected to increase the percentages of Asians, Hispanics, and African Americans.

Functions and Types of Money

Money is used in three major ways:

- As an accounting unit
- As a store of value
- As an exchange medium

In general, money must be acceptable throughout a society in exchange for debts or to purchase goods and services. Money should be relatively scarce, its value should remain stable, and it should be easily carried, durable, and easy to divide up. There are three basic types of money: commodity, representative, and fiat. **Commodity money** includes gems or precious metals. **Representative money** can be exchanged for items such as gold or silver that have inherent value. **Fiat money**, or legal tender, has no inherent value but has been declared to function as money by the government. It is often backed by gold or silver but not necessarily on a one-to-one ratio.

Types of Money Available in the US and Economists' Measure of It

Money in the US is not just currency. When economists calculate the amount of money available, they must take into account other factors, such as deposits that have been placed in checking accounts, debit cards, and "near moneys," such as savings accounts, that can be quickly converted into cash. Currency, checkable deposits and traveler's checks, referred to as **M1**, are added up, and then **M2** is calculated by adding savings deposits, CDs, and various other monetary deposits. The final result is the total quantity of available money.

Aspects of Monetary Policy and the Role of the Federal Reserve System

The Federal Reserve System, also known as the **Fed**, implements all monetary policy in the US. Monetary policy regulates the amount of money available in the American banking system. The Fed can decrease or increase the amount of available money for loans, thus helping regulate the national economy. Monetary policies implemented by the Fed are part of expansionary or contractionary monetary policies that help counteract inflation or unemployment. The **discount rate** is an interest rate charged by the Fed when banks borrow money from them. A lower discount rate leads banks to borrow more money, leading to increased spending. A higher discount rate has the opposite effect.

How Banks Function

Banks earn their income by **loaning** out money and charging **interest** on those loans. If less money is available, fewer loans can be made, which affects the amount of spending in the overall economy. While banks function by making loans, they are not allowed to loan out all the money they hold in deposit. The amount of money they must maintain in reserve is known as the **reserve ratio**. If the reserve ratio is raised, less money is available for loans and spending decreases. A lower reserve ratio increases available funds and increases spending. This ratio is determined by the Federal Reserve System.

Open Market Operations

The Federal Reserve System can also expand or contract the overall money supply through **open market operations**. In this case, the Fed can buy or sell **bonds** it has purchased from banks or individuals. When the Fed buys bonds, more money is put into circulation, creating an expansionary situation to stimulate the economy. When the Fed sells bonds, money is withdrawn from the system, creating a **contractionary** situation to slow an economy suffering from inflation. Because of international financial markets, however, American banks often borrow and lend money in markets outside the US. By shifting their attention to international markets, domestic banks and other businesses can circumvent whatever contractionary policies the Fed may have put into place.

Major Characteristics of International Trade

International trade can take advantage of broader markets, bringing a wider variety of products within easy reach. By contrast, it can also allow individual countries to specialize in particular products that they can produce easily, such as those for which they have easy access to raw materials. Other products, more difficult to make domestically, can be acquired through trade with other nations. **International trade** requires efficient use of **native resources** as well as sufficient **disposable income** to purchase native and imported products. Many countries in the world engage extensively in international trade, but others still face major economic challenges.

Major Characteristics of a Developing Nation

The five major characteristics of a developing nation are:

- Low GDP
- Rapid growth of population
- Economy that depends on subsistence agriculture
- Poor conditions, including high infant mortality rates, high disease rates, poor sanitation, and insufficient housing
- Low literacy rate

Developing nations often function under oppressive governments that do not provide private property rights and withhold education and other rights from women. They also often feature an extreme disparity between upper and lower classes, with little opportunity for the lower classes to improve their position.

Stages of Economic Development

Economic development occurs in three stages that are defined by the activities that drive the economy:

- Agricultural stage
- Manufacturing stage
- Service sector stage

In developing countries, it is often difficult to acquire the necessary funding to provide equipment and training to move into the advanced stages of economic development. Some can receive help from developed countries via foreign aid and investment or international organizations such as the **International Monetary Fund** or the **World Bank**. Having developed countries provide monetary, technical, or military assistance can help developing countries move forward to the next stage in their development.

Obstacles Developing Nations Face Regarding Economic Growth

Developing nations typically struggle to overcome obstacles that prevent or slow economic development. Major **obstacles** can include:

- Rapid, uncontrolled population growth
- Trade restrictions
- Misused resources, often perpetrated by the government
- Traditional beliefs that can slow or reject change

Corrupt, oppressive governments often hamper the economic growth of developing nations, creating huge **economic disparities** and making it impossible for individuals to advance, in turn preventing overall growth. Governments sometimes export currency, called **capital flight**, which is detrimental to a country's economic development. In general, countries are more likely to experience economic growth if their governments encourage entrepreneurship and provide private property rights.

Problems When Industrialization Occurs Too Quickly

Rapid growth throughout the world leaves some nations behind and sometimes spurs their governments to move forward too quickly into **industrialization** and **artificially rapid economic growth**. While slow or nonexistent economic growth causes problems in a country, overly rapid industrialization carries its own issues. Four major problems encountered due to rapid industrialization are:

- Use of technology not suited to the products or services being supplied
- Poor investment of capital
- Lack of time for the population to adapt to new paradigms
- Lack of time to experience all stages of development and adjust to each stage

Economic failures in Indonesia were largely due to rapid growth that was poorly handled.

Importance of E-Commerce in Today's Marketplace

The growth of the internet has brought many changes to our society, not the least of which is the modern way of business. Where supply channels used to move in certain necessary ways, many of these channels are now bypassed as **e-commerce** makes it possible for nearly any individual to set up a direct market to consumers, as well as direct interaction with suppliers. Competition is fierce. In many instances, e-commerce can provide nearly instantaneous gratification, with a wide variety of products. Whoever provides the best product most quickly often rises to the top of a marketplace. How this added element to the marketplace will affect the economy in the future remains to be seen. Many industries are still struggling with the best ways to adapt to the rapid, continuous changes.

Knowledge Economy and Possible Effect on Future Economic Growth

The knowledge economy is a growing sector in the economy of developed countries, and includes the trade and development of:

- Data
- Intellectual property
- Technology, especially in the area of communications

Knowledge as a resource is steadily becoming more and more important. What is now being called the **Information Age** may prove to bring about changes in life and culture as significant as those brought on by the Agricultural and Industrial Revolutions.

Cybernomics

Related to the knowledge economy is what has been dubbed "**cybernomics**," or economics driven by e-commerce and other computer-based markets and products. Marketing has changed drastically with the growth of cyber communication, allowing suppliers to connect one-on-one with their customers. Other issues coming to the fore regarding cybernomics include:

- Secure online trade
- Intellectual property rights
- Rights to privacy
- Bringing developing nations into the fold

As these issues are debated and new laws and policies developed, the face of many industries continues to undergo drastic change. Many of the old ways of doing business no longer work, leaving industries scrambling to function profitably within the new system.

Chapter Quiz

Ready to see how well you retained what you just read? Scan the QR code to go directly to the chapter quiz interface for this study guide. If you're using a computer, simply visit the bonus page at **mometrix.com/bonus948/fsot** and click the Chapter Quizzes link.

Mathematics and Statistics

Fundamental Math Skills

NUMBER BASICS

CLASSIFICATIONS OF NUMBERS

Numbers are the basic building blocks of mathematics. Specific features of numbers are identified by the following terms:

Integer – any positive or negative whole number, including zero. Integers do not include fractions $\left(\frac{1}{3}\right)$, decimals (0.56), or mixed numbers $\left(7\frac{3}{4}\right)$.

Prime number – any whole number greater than 1 that has only two factors, itself and 1; that is, a number that can be divided evenly only by 1 and itself.

Composite number – any whole number greater than 1 that has more than two different factors; in other words, any whole number that is not a prime number. For example: The composite number 8 has the factors of 1, 2, 4, and 8.

Even number – any integer that can be divided by 2 without leaving a remainder. For example: 2, 4, 6, 8, and so on.

Odd number – any integer that cannot be divided evenly by 2. For example: 3, 5, 7, 9, and so on.

Decimal number – any number that uses a decimal point to show the part of the number that is less than one. Example: 1.234.

Decimal point – a symbol used to separate the ones place from the tenths place in decimals or dollars from cents in currency.

Decimal place – the position of a number to the right of the decimal point. In the decimal 0.123, the 1 is in the first place to the right of the decimal point, indicating tenths; the 2 is in the second place, indicating hundredths; and the 3 is in the third place, indicating thousandths.

The **decimal**, or base 10, system is a number system that uses ten different digits (0, 1, 2, 3, 4, 5, 6, 7, 8, 9). An example of a number system that uses something other than ten digits is the **binary**, or base 2, number system, used by computers, which uses only the numbers 0 and 1. It is thought that the decimal system originated because people had only their 10 fingers for counting.

Rational numbers include all integers, decimals, and fractions. Any terminating or repeating decimal number is a rational number.

Irrational numbers cannot be written as fractions or decimals because the number of decimal places is infinite and there is no recurring pattern of digits within the number. For example, pi (π) begins with 3.141592 and continues without terminating or repeating, so pi is an irrational number.

Real numbers are the set of all rational and irrational numbers.

Review Video: Classification of Numbers
Visit mometrix.com/academy and enter code: 461071

Review Video: Prime and Composite Numbers
Visit mometrix.com/academy and enter code: 565581

Numbers in Word Form and Place Value

When writing numbers out in word form or translating word form to numbers, it is essential to understand how a place value system works. In the decimal or base-10 system, each digit of a number represents how many of the corresponding place value—a specific factor of 10—are contained in the number being represented. To make reading numbers easier, every three digits to the left of the decimal place is preceded by a comma. The following table demonstrates some of the place values:

Power of 10	10^3	10^2	10^1	10^0	10^{-1}	10^{-2}	10^{-3}
Value	1,000	100	10	1	0.1	0.01	0.001
Place	thousands	hundreds	tens	ones	tenths	hundredths	thousandths

For example, consider the number 4,546.09, which can be separated into each place value like this:

4: thousands
5: hundreds
4: tens
6: ones
0: tenths
9: hundredths

This number in word form would be *four thousand five hundred forty-six and nine hundredths.*

Review Video: Place Value
Visit mometrix.com/academy and enter code: 205433

Rational Numbers

The term **rational** means that the number can be expressed as a ratio or fraction. That is, a number, r, is rational if and only if it can be represented by a fraction $\frac{a}{b}$ where a and b are integers and b does not equal 0. The set of rational numbers includes integers and decimals. If there is no finite way to represent a value with a fraction of integers, then the number is **irrational**. Common examples of irrational numbers include: $\sqrt{5}$, $\left(1+\sqrt{2}\right)$, and π.

Review Video: Rational and Irrational Numbers
Visit mometrix.com/academy and enter code: 280645

Review Video: Ordering Rational Numbers
Visit mometrix.com/academy and enter code: 419578

Number Lines

A number line is a graph to see the distance between numbers. Basically, this graph shows the relationship between numbers. So a number line may have a point for zero and may show negative numbers on the left side

Mathematics and Statistics

of the line. Any positive numbers are placed on the right side of the line. For example, consider the points labeled on the following number line:

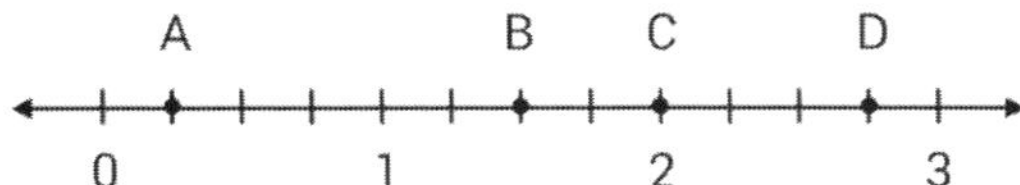

We can use the dashed lines on the number line to identify each point. Each dashed line between two whole numbers is $\frac{1}{4}$. The line halfway between two numbers is $\frac{1}{2}$.

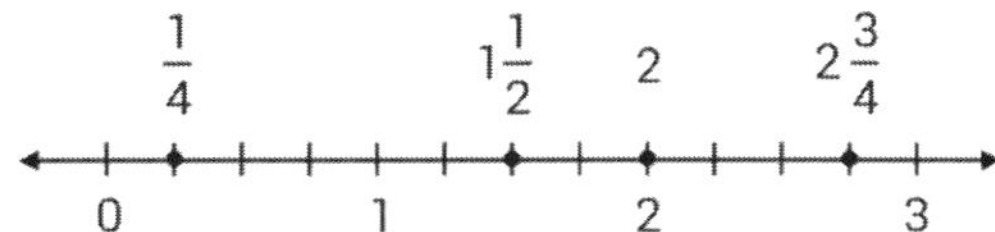

Review Video: The Number Line
Visit mometrix.com/academy and enter code: 816439

Rounding and Estimation

Rounding is reducing the digits in a number while still trying to keep the value similar. The result will be less accurate but in a simpler form and easier to use. Whole numbers can be rounded to the nearest ten, hundred, or thousand.

When you are asked to estimate the solution to a problem, you will need to provide only an approximate figure or **estimation** for your answer. In this situation, you will need to round each number in the calculation to the level indicated (nearest hundred, nearest thousand, etc.) or to a level that makes sense for the numbers involved. When estimating a sum **all numbers must be rounded to the same level**. You cannot round one number to the nearest thousand while rounding another to the nearest hundred.

Review Video: Rounding and Estimation
Visit mometrix.com/academy and enter code: 126243

Absolute Value

A precursor to working with negative numbers is understanding what **absolute values** are. A number's absolute value is simply the distance away from zero a number is on the number line. The absolute value of a number is always positive and is written $|x|$. For example, the absolute value of 3, written as $|3|$, is 3 because the distance between 0 and 3 on a number line is three units. Likewise, the absolute value of –3, written as $|-3|$, is 3 because the distance between 0 and –3 on a number line is three units. So $|3| = |-3|$.

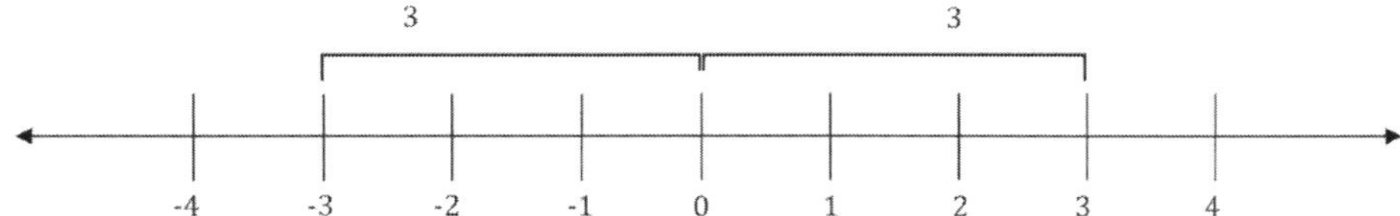

Review Video: Absolute Value
Visit mometrix.com/academy and enter code: 314669

Operations

An **operation** is simply a mathematical process that takes some value(s) as input(s) and produces an output. Elementary operations are often written in the following form: *value operation value*. For instance, in the expression $1 + 2$ the values are 1 and 2 and the operation is addition. Performing the operation gives the output of 3. In this way we can say that $1 + 2$ and 3 are equal, or $1 + 2 = 3$.

Addition

Addition increases the value of one quantity by the value of another quantity (both called **addends**). Example: $2 + 4 = 6$ or $8 + 9 = 17$. The result is called the **sum**. With addition, the order does not matter, $4 + 2 = 2 + 4$.

When adding signed numbers, if the signs are the same simply add the absolute values of the addends and apply the original sign to the sum. For example, $(+4) + (+8) = +12$ and $(-4) + (-8) = -12$. When the original signs are different, take the absolute values of the addends and subtract the smaller value from the larger value, then apply the original sign of the larger value to the difference. Example: $(+4) + (-8) = -4$ and $(-4) + (+8) = +4$.

Subtraction

Subtraction is the opposite operation to addition; it decreases the value of one quantity (the **minuend**) by the value of another quantity (the **subtrahend**). For example, $6 - 4 = 2$ or $17 - 8 = 9$. The result is called the **difference**. Note that with subtraction, the order does matter, $6 - 4 \neq 4 - 6$.

For subtracting signed numbers, change the sign of the subtrahend and then follow the same rules used for addition. Example: $(+4) - (+8) = (+4) + (-8) = -4$

Multiplication

Multiplication can be thought of as repeated addition. One number (the **multiplier**) indicates how many times to add the other number (the **multiplicand**) to itself. Example: $3 \times 2 = 2 + 2 + 2 = 6$. With multiplication, the order does not matter, $2 \times 3 = 3 \times 2$ or $3 + 3 = 2 + 2 + 2$, either way the result (the **product**) is the same.

If the signs are the same, the product is positive when multiplying signed numbers. Example: $(+4) \times (+8) = +32$ and $(-4) \times (-8) = +32$. If the signs are opposite, the product is negative. Example: $(+4) \times (-8) = -32$ and $(-4) \times (+8) = -32$. When more than two factors are multiplied together, the sign of the product is determined by how many negative factors are present. If there are an odd number of negative factors then the product is negative, whereas an even number of negative factors indicates a positive product. Example: $(+4) \times (-8) \times (-2) = +64$ and $(-4) \times (-8) \times (-2) = -64$.

Division

Division is the opposite operation to multiplication; one number (the **divisor**) tells us how many parts to divide the other number (the **dividend**) into. The result of division is called the **quotient**. Example: $20 \div 4 = 5$. If 20 is split into 4 equal parts, each part is 5. With division, the order of the numbers does matter, $20 \div 4 \neq 4 \div 20$.

The rules for dividing signed numbers are similar to multiplying signed numbers. If the dividend and divisor have the same sign, the quotient is positive. If the dividend and divisor have opposite signs, the quotient is negative. Example: $(-4) \div (+8) = -0.5$.

Review Video: Mathematical Operations
Visit mometrix.com/academy and enter code: 208095

Parentheses

Parentheses are used to designate which operations should be done first when there are multiple operations. Example: $4 - (2 + 1) = 1$; the parentheses tell us that we must add 2 and 1, and then subtract the sum from 4, rather than subtracting 2 from 4 and then adding 1 (this would give us an answer of 3).

Review Video: Mathematical Parentheses
Visit mometrix.com/academy and enter code: 978600

Exponents

An **exponent** is a superscript number placed next to another number at the top right. It indicates how many times the base number is to be multiplied by itself. Exponents provide a shorthand way to write what would be a longer mathematical expression, Example: $2^4 = 2 \times 2 \times 2 \times 2$. A number with an exponent of 2 is said to be "squared," while a number with an exponent of 3 is said to be "cubed." The value of a number raised to an exponent is called its power. So 8^4 is read as "8 to the 4th power," or "8 raised to the power of 4."

Review Video: Exponents
Visit mometrix.com/academy and enter code: 600998

Roots

A **root**, such as a square root, is another way of writing a fractional exponent. Instead of using a superscript, roots use the radical symbol ($\sqrt{\square}$) to indicate the operation. A radical will have a number underneath the bar, and may sometimes have a number in the upper left: $\sqrt[n]{a}$, read as "the nth root of a." The relationship between radical notation and exponent notation can be described by this equation:

$$\sqrt[n]{a} = a^{\frac{1}{n}}$$

The two special cases of $n = 2$ and $n = 3$ are called square roots and cube roots. If there is no number to the upper left, the radical is understood to be a square root ($n = 2$). Nearly all of the roots you encounter will be square roots. A square root is the same as a number raised to the one-half power. When we say that a is the square root of b ($a = \sqrt{b}$), we mean that a multiplied by itself equals b: ($a \times a = b$).

A **perfect square** is a number that has an integer for its square root. There are 10 perfect squares from 1 to 100: 1, 4, 9, 16, 25, 36, 49, 64, 81, 100 (the squares of integers 1 through 10).

Review Video: Roots
Visit mometrix.com/academy and enter code: 795655

Review Video: Perfect Squares and Square Roots
Visit mometrix.com/academy and enter code: 648063

Word Problems and Mathematical Symbols

When working on word problems, you must be able to translate verbal expressions or "math words" into math symbols. This chart contains several "math words" and their appropriate symbols:

Phrase	Symbol
equal, is, was, will be, has, costs, gets to, is the same as, becomes	$=$
times, of, multiplied by, product of, twice, doubles, halves, triples	$\times$
divided by, per, ratio of/to, out of	$\div$
plus, added to, sum, combined, and, more than, totals of	$+$
subtracted from, less than, decreased by, minus, difference between	$-$
what, how much, original value, how many, a number, a variable	x, n, etc.

Examples of Translated Mathematical Phrases

- The phrase four more than twice a number can be written algebraically as $2x + 4$.
- The phrase half a number decreased by six can be written algebraically as $\frac{1}{2}x - 6$.
- The phrase the sum of a number and the product of five and that number can be written algebraically as $x + 5x$.
- You may see a test question that says, "Olivia is constructing a bookcase from seven boards. Two of them are for vertical supports and five are for shelves. The height of the bookcase is twice the width of the bookcase. If the seven boards total 36 feet in length, what will be the height of Olivia's bookcase?" You would need to make a sketch and then create the equation to determine the width of the shelves. The height can be represented as double the width. (If x represents the width of the shelves in feet, then the height of the bookcase is $2x$. Since the seven boards total 36 feet, $2x + 2x + x + x + x + x + x = 36$ or $9x = 36$; $x = 4$. The height is twice the width, or 8 feet.)

Subtraction with Regrouping

A great way to make use of some of the features built into the decimal system would be regrouping when attempting longform subtraction operations. When subtracting within a place value, sometimes the minuend is smaller than the subtrahend, **regrouping** enables you to 'borrow' a unit from a place value to the left in order to get a positive difference. For example, consider subtracting 189 from 525 with regrouping.

First, set up the subtraction problem in vertical form:

$$\begin{array}{r} 525 \\ -\ 189 \\ \hline \end{array}$$

Notice that the numbers in the ones and tens columns of 525 are smaller than the numbers in the ones and tens columns of 189. This means you will need to use regrouping to perform subtraction:

$$\begin{array}{cccc} & 5 & 2 & 5 \\ - & 1 & 8 & 9 \\ \hline \end{array}$$

To subtract 9 from 5 in the ones column you will need to borrow from the 2 in the tens columns:

$$\begin{array}{cccc} & 5 & 1 & 15 \\ - & 1 & 8 & 9 \\ \hline & & & 6 \end{array}$$

Next, to subtract 8 from 1 in the tens column you will need to borrow from the 5 in the hundreds column:

$$\begin{array}{cccc} & 4 & 11 & 15 \\ - & 1 & 8 & 9 \\ \hline & & 3 & 6 \end{array}$$

Last, subtract the 1 from the 4 in the hundreds column:

$$\begin{array}{cccc} & 4 & 11 & 15 \\ - & 1 & 8 & 9 \\ \hline & 3 & 3 & 6 \end{array}$$

Review Video: Subtracting Large Numbers
Visit mometrix.com/academy and enter code: 603350

Mathematics and Statistics

Order of Operations

The **order of operations** is a set of rules that dictates the order in which we must perform each operation in an expression so that we will evaluate it accurately. If we have an expression that includes multiple different operations, the order of operations tells us which operations to do first. The most common mnemonic for the order of operations is **PEMDAS**, or "Please Excuse My Dear Aunt Sally." PEMDAS stands for parentheses, exponents, multiplication, division, addition, and subtraction. It is important to understand that multiplication and division have equal precedence, as do addition and subtraction, so those pairs of operations are simply worked from left to right in order.

For example, evaluating the expression $5 + 20 \div 4 \times (2 + 3)^2 - 6$ using the correct order of operations would be done like this:

- **P:** Perform the operations inside the parentheses: $(2 + 3) = 5$
- **E:** Simplify the exponents: $(5)^2 = 5 \times 5 = 25$
  - The expression now looks like this: $5 + 20 \div 4 \times 25 - 6$
- **MD:** Perform multiplication and division from left to right: $20 \div 4 = 5$; then $5 \times 25 = 125$
  - The expression now looks like this: $5 + 125 - 6$
- **AS:** Perform addition and subtraction from left to right: $5 + 125 = 130$; then $130 - 6 = 124$

Review Video: Order of Operations
Visit mometrix.com/academy and enter code: 259675

Properties of Exponents

The properties of exponents are as follows:

Property	Description
$a^1 = a$	Any number to the power of 1 is equal to itself
$1^n = 1$	The number 1 raised to any power is equal to 1
$a^0 = 1$	Any number raised to the power of 0 is equal to 1
$a^n \times a^m = a^{n+m}$	Add exponents to multiply powers of the same base number
$a^n \div a^m = a^{n-m}$	Subtract exponents to divide powers of the same base number
$(a^n)^m = a^{n \times m}$	When a power is raised to a power, the exponents are multiplied
$(a \times b)^n = a^n \times b^n$ $(a \div b)^n = a^n \div b^n$	Multiplication and division operations inside parentheses can be raised to a power. This is the same as each term being raised to that power.
$a^{-n} = \frac{1}{a^n}$	A negative exponent is the same as the reciprocal of a positive exponent

Note that exponents do not have to be integers. Fractional or decimal exponents follow all the rules above as well. Example: $5^{\frac{1}{4}} \times 5^{\frac{3}{4}} = 5^{\frac{1}{4}+\frac{3}{4}} = 5^1 = 5$.

Review Video: Properties of Exponents
Visit mometrix.com/academy and enter code: 532558

Scientific Notation

Scientific notation is a way of writing large numbers in a shorter form. The form $a \times 10^n$ is used in scientific notation, where a is greater than or equal to 1 but less than 10, and n is the number of places the decimal must move to get from the original number to a. Example: The number 230,400,000 is cumbersome to write. To write the value in scientific notation, place a decimal point between the first and second numbers, and include all digits through the last non-zero digit ($a = 2.304$). To find the appropriate power of 10, count the number of places the decimal point had to move ($n = 8$). The number is positive if the decimal moved to the left, and negative if it moved to the right. We can then write 230,400,000 as 2.304×10^8. If we look instead at the number 0.00002304, we have the same value for a, but this time the decimal moved 5 places to the right ($n = -5$). Thus, 0.00002304 can be written as 2.304×10^{-5}. Using this notation makes it simple to compare very large or very small numbers. By comparing exponents, it is easy to see that 3.28×10^4 is smaller than 1.51×10^5, because 4 is less than 5.

Review Video: Scientific Notation
Visit mometrix.com/academy and enter code: 976454

FACTORS AND MULTIPLES

FACTORS AND GREATEST COMMON FACTOR

Factors are numbers that are multiplied together to obtain a **product**. For example, in the equation $2 \times 3 = 6$, the numbers 2 and 3 are factors. A **prime number** has only two factors (1 and itself), but other numbers can have many factors.

A **common factor** is a number that divides exactly into two or more other numbers. For example, the factors of 12 are 1, 2, 3, 4, 6, and 12, while the factors of 15 are 1, 3, 5, and 15. The common factors of 12 and 15 are 1 and 3.

A **prime factor** is also a prime number. Therefore, the prime factors of 12 are 2 and 3. For 15, the prime factors are 3 and 5.

The **greatest common factor** (**GCF**) is the largest number that is a factor of two or more numbers. For example, the factors of 15 are 1, 3, 5, and 15; the factors of 35 are 1, 5, 7, and 35. Therefore, the greatest common factor of 15 and 35 is 5.

Review Video: Factors
Visit mometrix.com/academy and enter code: 920086

Review Video: Prime Numbers and Factorization
Visit mometrix.com/academy and enter code: 760669

Review Video: Greatest Common Factor and Least Common Multiple
Visit mometrix.com/academy and enter code: 838699

MULTIPLES AND LEAST COMMON MULTIPLE

Often listed out in multiplication tables, **multiples** are integer increments of a given factor. In other words, dividing a multiple by the factor will result in an integer. For example, the multiples of 7 include: $1 \times 7 = 7$, $2 \times 7 = 14$, $3 \times 7 = 21$, $4 \times 7 = 28$, $5 \times 7 = 35$. Dividing 7, 14, 21, 28, or 35 by 7 will result in the integers 1, 2, 3, 4, and 5, respectively.

The least common multiple (**LCM**) is the smallest number that is a multiple of two or more numbers. For example, the multiples of 3 include 3, 6, 9, 12, 15, etc.; the multiples of 5 include 5, 10, 15, 20, etc. Therefore, the least common multiple of 3 and 5 is 15.

Review Video: Multiples
Visit mometrix.com/academy and enter code: 626738

Fractions, Decimals, and Percentages

Fractions

A **fraction** is a number that is expressed as one integer written above another integer, with a dividing line between them $\left(\frac{x}{y}\right)$. It represents the **quotient** of the two numbers "x divided by y." It can also be thought of as x out of y equal parts.

The top number of a fraction is called the **numerator**, and it represents the number of parts under consideration. The 1 in $\frac{1}{4}$ means that 1 part out of the whole is being considered in the calculation. The bottom number of a fraction is called the **denominator**, and it represents the total number of equal parts. The 4 in $\frac{1}{4}$ means that the whole consists of 4 equal parts. A fraction cannot have a denominator of zero; this is referred to as "*undefined.*"

Fractions can be manipulated, without changing the value of the fraction, by multiplying or dividing (but not adding or subtracting) both the numerator and denominator by the same number. If you divide both numbers by a common factor, you are **reducing** or simplifying the fraction. Two fractions that have the same value but are expressed differently are known as **equivalent fractions**. For example, $\frac{2}{10}, \frac{3}{15}, \frac{4}{20}$, and $\frac{5}{25}$ are all equivalent fractions. They can also all be reduced or simplified to $\frac{1}{5}$.

When two fractions are manipulated so that they have the same denominator, this is known as finding a **common denominator**. The number chosen to be that common denominator should be the least common multiple of the two original denominators. Example: $\frac{3}{4}$ and $\frac{5}{6}$; the least common multiple of 4 and 6 is 12. Manipulating to achieve the common denominator: $\frac{3}{4} = \frac{9}{12}; \frac{5}{6} = \frac{10}{12}$.

Review Video: Overview of Fractions
Visit mometrix.com/academy and enter code: 262335

Proper Fractions and Mixed Numbers

A fraction whose denominator is greater than its numerator is known as a **proper fraction**, while a fraction whose numerator is greater than its denominator is known as an **improper fraction**. Proper fractions have values *less than one* and improper fractions have values *greater than one*.

A **mixed number** is a number that contains both an integer and a fraction. Any improper fraction can be rewritten as a mixed number. Example: $\frac{8}{3} = \frac{6}{3} + \frac{2}{3} = 2 + \frac{2}{3} = 2\frac{2}{3}$. Similarly, any mixed number can be rewritten as an improper fraction. Example: $1\frac{3}{5} = 1 + \frac{3}{5} = \frac{5}{5} + \frac{3}{5} = \frac{8}{5}$.

Review Video: Proper and Improper Fractions and Mixed Numbers
Visit mometrix.com/academy and enter code: 211077

Adding and Subtracting Fractions

If two fractions have a common denominator, they can be added or subtracted simply by adding or subtracting the two numerators and retaining the same denominator. If the two fractions do not already have the same denominator, one or both of them must be manipulated to achieve a common denominator before they can be added or subtracted. Example: $\frac{1}{2}+\frac{1}{4}=\frac{2}{4}+\frac{1}{4}=\frac{3}{4}$.

Review Video: Adding and Subtracting Fractions
Visit mometrix.com/academy and enter code: 378080

Multiplying Fractions

Two fractions can be multiplied by multiplying the two numerators to find the new numerator and the two denominators to find the new denominator. Example: $\frac{1}{3}\times\frac{2}{3}=\frac{1\times 2}{3\times 3}=\frac{2}{9}$.

Dividing Fractions

Two fractions can be divided by flipping the numerator and denominator of the second fraction and then proceeding as though it were a multiplication problem. Example: $\frac{2}{3}\div\frac{3}{4}=\frac{2}{3}\times\frac{4}{3}=\frac{8}{9}$.

Review Video: Multiplying and Dividing Fractions
Visit mometrix.com/academy and enter code: 473632

Multiplying a Mixed Number by a Whole Number or a Decimal

When multiplying a mixed number by something, it is usually best to convert it to an improper fraction first. Additionally, if the multiplicand is a decimal, it is most often simplest to convert it to a fraction. For instance, to multiply $4\frac{3}{8}$ by 3.5, begin by rewriting each quantity as a whole number plus a proper fraction. Remember, a mixed number is a fraction added to a whole number and a decimal is a representation of the sum of fractions, specifically tenths, hundredths, thousandths, and so on:

$$4\frac{3}{8}\times 3.5=\left(4+\frac{3}{8}\right)\times\left(3+\frac{1}{2}\right)$$

Next, the quantities being added need to be expressed with the same denominator. This is achieved by multiplying and dividing the whole number by the denominator of the fraction. Recall that a whole number is equivalent to that number divided by 1:

$$=\left(\frac{4}{1}\times\frac{8}{8}+\frac{3}{8}\right)\times\left(\frac{3}{1}\times\frac{2}{2}+\frac{1}{2}\right)$$

When multiplying fractions, remember to multiply the numerators and denominators separately:

$$=\left(\frac{4\times 8}{1\times 8}+\frac{3}{8}\right)\times\left(\frac{3\times 2}{1\times 2}+\frac{1}{2}\right)$$
$$=\left(\frac{32}{8}+\frac{3}{8}\right)\times\left(\frac{6}{2}+\frac{1}{2}\right)$$

Now that the fractions have the same denominators, they can be added:

$$=\frac{35}{8}\times\frac{7}{2}$$

Finally, perform the last multiplication and then simplify:

$$=\frac{35\times 7}{8\times 2}=\frac{245}{16}=\frac{240}{16}+\frac{5}{16}=15\frac{5}{16}$$

Mathematics and Statistics

Comparing Fractions

It is important to master the ability to compare and order fractions. This skill is relevant to many real-world scenarios. For example, carpenters often compare fractional construction nail lengths when preparing for a project, and bakers often compare fractional measurements to have the correct ratio of ingredients. There are three commonly used strategies when comparing fractions. These strategies are referred to as the common denominator approach, the decimal approach, and the cross-multiplication approach.

Using a Common Denominator to Compare Fractions

The fractions $\frac{2}{3}$ and $\frac{4}{7}$ have different denominators. $\frac{2}{3}$ has a denominator of 3, and $\frac{4}{7}$ has a denominator of 7. In order to precisely compare these two fractions, it is necessary to use a common denominator. A common denominator is a common multiple that is shared by both denominators. In this case, the denominators 3 and 7 share a multiple of 21. In general, it is most efficient to select the least common multiple for the two denominators.

Rewrite each fraction with the common denominator of 21. Then, calculate the new numerators as illustrated below.

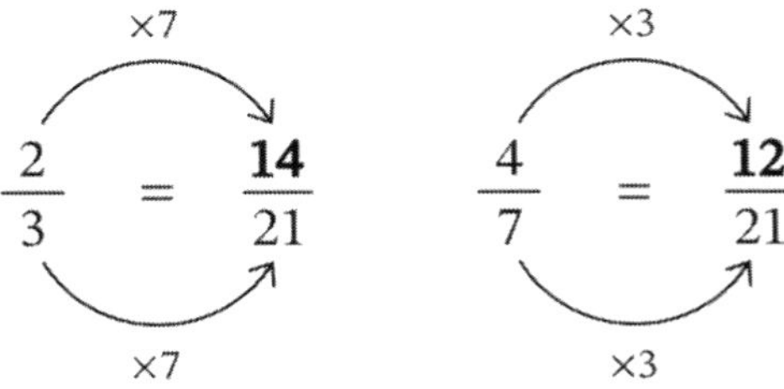

For $\frac{2}{3}$, multiply the numerator and denominator by 7. The result is $\frac{14}{21}$.

For $\frac{4}{7}$, multiply the numerator and denominator by 3. The result is $\frac{12}{21}$.

Now that both fractions have a denominator of 21, the fractions can accurately be compared by comparing the numerators. Since 14 is greater than 12, the fraction $\frac{14}{21}$ is greater than $\frac{12}{21}$. This means that $\frac{2}{3}$ is greater than $\frac{4}{7}$.

Using Decimals to Compare Fractions

Sometimes decimal values are easier to compare than fraction values. For example, $\frac{5}{8}$ is equivalent to 0.625 and $\frac{3}{5}$ is equivalent to 0.6. This means that the comparison of $\frac{5}{8}$ and $\frac{3}{5}$ can be determined by comparing the decimals 0.625 and 0.6. When both decimal values are extended to the thousandths place, they become 0.625 and 0.600, respectively. It becomes clear that 0.625 is greater than 0.600 because 625 thousandths is greater than 600 thousandths. In other words, $\frac{5}{8}$ is greater than $\frac{3}{5}$ because 0.625 is greater than 0.6.

Using Cross-Multiplication to Compare Fractions

Cross-multiplication is an efficient strategy for comparing fractions. This is a shortcut for the common denominator strategy. Start by writing each fraction next to one another. Multiply the numerator of the fraction on the left by the denominator of the fraction on the right. Write down the result next to the fraction on the left. Now multiply the numerator of the fraction on the right by the denominator of the fraction on the left. Write down the result next to the fraction on the right. Compare both products. The fraction with the larger result is the larger fraction.

Consider the fractions $\frac{4}{7}$ and $\frac{5}{9}$.

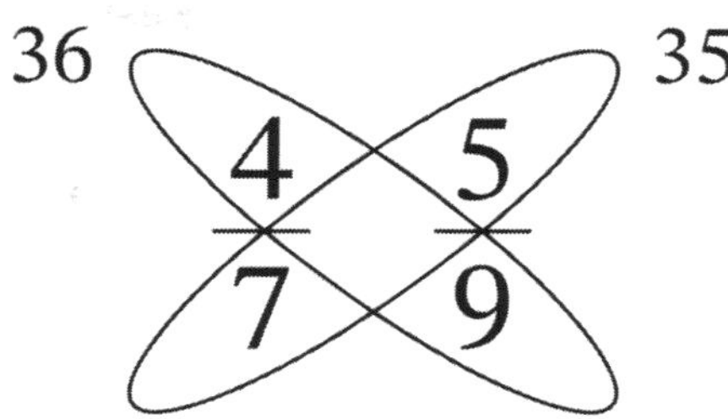

36 is greater than 35. Therefore, $\frac{4}{7}$ is greater than $\frac{5}{9}$.

DECIMALS

Decimals are one way to represent parts of a whole. Using the place value system, each digit to the right of a decimal point denotes the number of units of a corresponding *negative* power of ten. For example, consider the decimal 0.24. We can use a model to represent the decimal. Since a dime is worth one-tenth of a dollar and a penny is worth one-hundredth of a dollar, one possible model to represent this fraction is to have 2 dimes representing the 2 in the tenths place and 4 pennies representing the 4 in the hundredths place:

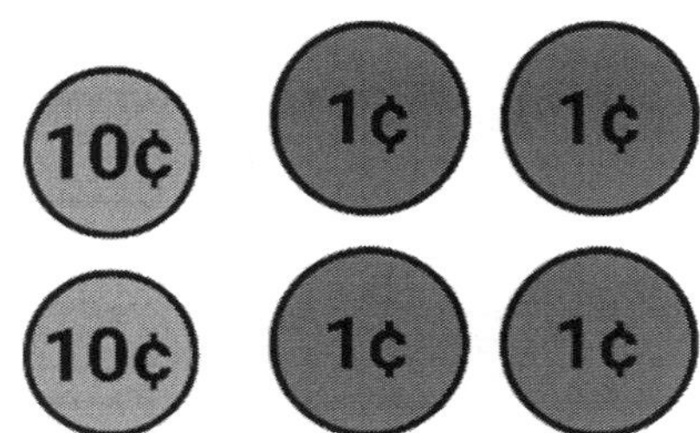

To write the decimal as a fraction, put the decimal in the numerator with 1 in the denominator. Multiply the numerator and denominator by tens until there are no more decimal places. Then simplify the fraction to lowest terms. For example, converting 0.24 to a fraction:

$$0.24 = \frac{0.24}{1} = \frac{0.24 \times 100}{1 \times 100} = \frac{24}{100} = \frac{6}{25}$$

Review Video: Decimals
Visit mometrix.com/academy and enter code: 837268

OPERATIONS WITH DECIMALS

ADDING AND SUBTRACTING DECIMALS

When adding and subtracting decimals, the decimal points must always be aligned. Adding decimals is just like adding regular whole numbers. Example: $4.5 + 2.0 = 6.5$.

If the problem-solver does not properly align the decimal points, an incorrect answer of 4.7 may result. An easy way to add decimals is to align all of the decimal points in a vertical column visually. This will allow you to see exactly where the decimal should be placed in the final answer. Begin adding from right to left. Add each column in turn, making sure to carry the number to the left if a column adds up to more than 9. The same rules apply to the subtraction of decimals.

Review Video: Adding and Subtracting Decimals
Visit mometrix.com/academy and enter code: 381101

MULTIPLYING DECIMALS

A simple multiplication problem has two components: a **multiplicand** and a **multiplier**. When multiplying decimals, work as though the numbers were whole rather than decimals. Once the final product is calculated,

Mathematics and Statistics

count the number of places to the right of the decimal in both the multiplicand and the multiplier. Then, count that number of places from the right of the product and place the decimal in that position.

For example, 12.3×2.56 has a total of three places to the right of the respective decimals. Multiply 123×256 to get 31,488. Now, beginning on the right, count three places to the left and insert the decimal. The final product will be 31.488.

Review Video: How to Multiply Decimals
Visit mometrix.com/academy and enter code: 731574

Dividing Decimals

Every division problem has a **divisor** and a **dividend**. The dividend is the number that is being divided. In the problem $14 \div 7$, 14 is the dividend and 7 is the divisor. In a division problem with decimals, the divisor must be converted into a whole number. Begin by moving the decimal in the divisor to the right until a whole number is created. Next, move the decimal in the dividend the same number of spaces to the right. For example, 4.9 into 24.5 would become 49 into 245. The decimal was moved one space to the right to create a whole number in the divisor, and then the same was done for the dividend. Once the whole numbers are created, the problem is carried out normally: $245 \div 49 = 5$.

Review Video: Dividing Decimals
Visit mometrix.com/academy and enter code: 560690

Review Video: Dividing Decimals by Whole Numbers
Visit mometrix.com/academy and enter code: 535669

Percentages

Percentages can be thought of as fractions that are based on a whole of 100; that is, one whole is equal to 100%. The word **percent** means "per hundred." Percentage problems are often presented in three main ways:

- Find what percentage of some number another number is.
  - Example: What percentage of 40 is 8?
- Find what number is some percentage of a given number.
  - Example: What number is 20% of 40?
- Find what number another number is a given percentage of.
  - Example: What number is 8 20% of?

There are three components in each of these cases: a **whole** (W), a **part** (P), and a **percentage** (%). These are related by the equation: $P = W \times \%$. This can easily be rearranged into other forms that may suit different questions better: $\% = \frac{P}{W}$ and $W = \frac{P}{\%}$. Percentage problems are often also word problems. As such, a large part of solving them is figuring out which quantities are what. For example, consider the following word problem:

In a school cafeteria, 7 students choose pizza, 9 choose hamburgers, and 4 choose tacos. What percentage of student choose tacos?

To find the whole, you must first add all of the parts: $7 + 9 + 4 = 20$. The percentage can then be found by dividing the part by the whole $\left(\% = \frac{P}{W}\right)$: $\frac{4}{20} = \frac{20}{100} = 20\%$.

Review Video: Computation with Percentages
Visit mometrix.com/academy and enter code: 693099

Converting Between Percentages, Fractions, and Decimals

Converting decimals to percentages and percentages to decimals is as simple as moving the decimal point. To *convert from a decimal to a percentage*, move the decimal point **two places to the right**. To *convert from a percentage to a decimal*, move it **two places to the left**. It may be helpful to remember that the percentage number will always be larger than the equivalent decimal number. Example:

$$0.23 = 23\% \quad 5.34 = 534\% \quad 0.007 = 0.7\%$$
$$700\% = 7.00 \quad 86\% = 0.86 \quad 0.15\% = 0.0015$$

To convert a fraction to a decimal, simply divide the numerator by the denominator in the fraction. To convert a decimal to a fraction, put the decimal in the numerator with 1 in the denominator. Multiply the numerator and denominator by tens until there are no more decimal places. Then simplify the fraction to lowest terms. For example, converting 0.24 to a fraction:

$$0.24 = \frac{0.24}{1} = \frac{0.24 \times 100}{1 \times 100} = \frac{24}{100} = \frac{6}{25}$$

Fractions can be converted to a percentage by finding equivalent fractions with a denominator of 100. Example:

$$\frac{7}{10} = \frac{70}{100} = 70\% \quad \frac{1}{4} = \frac{25}{100} = 25\%$$

To convert a percentage to a fraction, divide the percentage number by 100 and reduce the fraction to its simplest possible terms. Example:

$$60\% = \frac{60}{100} = \frac{3}{5} \quad 96\% = \frac{96}{100} = \frac{24}{25}$$

Review Video: Converting Fractions to Percentages and Decimals
Visit mometrix.com/academy and enter code: 306233

Review Video: Converting Percentages to Decimals and Fractions
Visit mometrix.com/academy and enter code: 287297

Review Video: Converting Decimals to Fractions and Percentages
Visit mometrix.com/academy and enter code: 986765

Review Video: Converting Decimals, Improper Fractions, and Mixed Numbers
Visit mometrix.com/academy and enter code: 696924

Proportions and Ratios

Proportions

A proportion is a relationship between two quantities that dictates how one changes when the other changes. A **direct proportion** describes a relationship in which a quantity increases by a set amount for every increase in the other quantity, or decreases by that same amount for every decrease in the other quantity. Example:

Mathematics and Statistics

Assuming a constant driving speed, the time required for a car trip increases as the distance of the trip increases. The distance to be traveled and the time required to travel are directly proportional.

An **inverse proportion** is a relationship in which an increase in one quantity is accompanied by a decrease in the other, or vice versa. Example: the time required for a car trip decreases as the speed increases and increases as the speed decreases, so the time required is inversely proportional to the speed of the car.

> **Review Video: Proportions**
> Visit mometrix.com/academy and enter code: 505355

Ratios

A **ratio** is a comparison of two quantities in a particular order. Example: If there are 14 computers in a lab, and the class has 20 students, there is a student to computer ratio of 20 to 14, commonly written as $20:14$. Ratios are normally reduced to their smallest whole number representation, so $20:14$ would be reduced to $10:7$ by dividing both sides by 2.

> **Review Video: Ratios**
> Visit mometrix.com/academy and enter code: 996914

Constant of Proportionality

When two quantities have a proportional relationship, there exists a **constant of proportionality** between the quantities. The product of this constant and one of the quantities is equal to the other quantity. For example, if one lemon costs \$0.25, two lemons cost \$0.50, and three lemons cost \$0.75, there is a proportional relationship between the total cost of lemons and the number of lemons purchased. The constant of proportionality is the **unit price**, namely \$0.25/lemon. Notice that the total price of lemons, t, can be found by multiplying the unit price of lemons, p, and the number of lemons, n: $t = pn$.

Work/Unit Rate

Unit rate expresses a quantity of one thing in terms of one unit of another. For example, if you travel 30 miles every two hours, a unit rate expresses this comparison in terms of one hour: in one hour you travel 15 miles, so your unit rate is 15 miles per hour. Other examples are how much one ounce of food costs (price per ounce) or figuring out how much one egg costs out of the dozen (price per 1 egg, instead of price per 12 eggs). The denominator of a unit rate is always 1. Unit rates are used to compare different situations to solve problems. For example, to make sure you get the best deal when deciding which kind of soda to buy, you can find the unit rate of each. If soda #1 costs \$1.50 for a 1-liter bottle, and soda #2 costs \$2.75 for a 2-liter bottle, it would be a better deal to buy soda #2, because its unit rate is only \$1.375 per 1-liter, which is cheaper than soda #1. Unit rates can also help determine the length of time a given event will take. For example, if you can paint 2 rooms in 4.5 hours, you can determine how long it will take you to paint 5 rooms by solving for the unit rate per room and then multiplying that by 5.

> **Review Video: Rates and Unit Rates**
> Visit mometrix.com/academy and enter code: 185363

Data and Statistics

Introduction to Statistics

Statistics is the branch of mathematics that deals with collecting, recording, interpreting, illustrating, and analyzing large amounts of **data**. The following terms are often used in the discussion of data and **statistics**:

- **Data** – the collective name for pieces of information (singular is datum)
- **Quantitative data** – measurements (such as length, mass, and speed) that provide information about quantities in numbers
- **Qualitative data** – information (such as colors, scents, tastes, and shapes) that cannot be measured using numbers
- **Discrete data** – information that can be expressed only by a specific value, such as whole or half numbers. (e.g., since people can be counted only in whole numbers, a population count would be discrete data.)
- **Continuous data** – information (such as time and temperature) that can be expressed by any value within a given range
- **Primary data** – information that has been collected directly from a survey, investigation, or experiment, such as a questionnaire or the recording of daily temperatures. (Primary data that has not yet been organized or analyzed is called **raw data**.)
- **Secondary data** – information that has been collected, sorted, and processed by the researcher
- **Ordinal data** – information that can be placed in numerical order, such as age or weight
- **Nominal data** – information that *cannot* be placed in numerical order, such as names or places

Data Collection

Population

In statistics, the **population** is the entire collection of people, plants, etc., that data can be collected from. For example, a study to determine how well students in local schools perform on a standardized test would have a population of all the students enrolled in those schools, although a study may include just a small sample of students from each school. A **parameter** is a numerical value that gives information about the population, such as the mean, median, mode, or standard deviation. Remember that the symbol for the mean of a population is μ and the symbol for the standard deviation of a population is σ.

Sample

A **sample** is a portion of the entire population. Whereas a parameter helped describe the population, a **statistic** is a numerical value that gives information about the sample, such as mean, median, mode, or standard deviation. Keep in mind that the symbols for mean and standard deviation are different when they are referring to a sample rather than the entire population. For a sample, the symbol for mean is $\bar{x}$ and the symbol for standard deviation is s. The mean and standard deviation of a sample may or may not be identical to that of the entire population due to a sample only being a subset of the population. However, if the sample is random and large enough, statistically significant values can be attained. Samples are generally used when the population is too large to justify including every element or when acquiring data for the entire population is impossible.

Inferential Statistics

Inferential statistics is the branch of statistics that uses samples to make predictions about an entire population. This type of statistic is often seen in political polls, where a sample of the population is questioned about a particular topic or politician to gain an understanding of the attitudes of the entire population of the country. Often, exit polls are conducted on election days using this method. Inferential statistics can have a large margin of error if you do not have a valid sample.

Sampling Distribution

Statistical values calculated from various samples of the same size make up the **sampling distribution**. For example, if several samples of identical size are randomly selected from a large population and then the mean of each sample is calculated, the distribution of values of the means would be a sampling distribution.

The **sampling distribution of the mean** is the distribution of the sample mean, $\bar{x}$, derived from random samples of a given size. It has three important characteristics. First, the mean of the sampling distribution of the mean is equal to the mean of the population that was sampled. Second, assuming the standard deviation is non-zero, the standard deviation of the sampling distribution of the mean equals the standard deviation of the sampled population divided by the square root of the sample size. This is sometimes called the standard error. Finally, as the sample size gets larger, the sampling distribution of the mean gets closer to a normal distribution via the central limit theorem.

Survey Study

A **survey study** is a method of gathering information from a small group in an attempt to gain enough information to make accurate general assumptions about the population. Once a survey study is completed, the results are then put into a summary report.

Survey studies are generally in the format of surveys, interviews, or questionnaires as part of an effort to find opinions of a particular group or to find facts about a group.

It is important to note that the findings from a survey study are only as accurate as the sample chosen from the population.

Correlational Studies

Correlational studies seek to determine how much one variable is affected by changes in a second variable. For example, correlational studies may look for a relationship between the amount of time a student spends studying for a test and the grade that student earned on the test or between student scores on college admissions tests and student grades in college.

It is important to note that correlational studies cannot show a cause and effect, but rather can show only that two variables are or are not potentially correlated.

Experimental Studies

Experimental studies take correlational studies one step farther, in that they attempt to prove or disprove a cause-and-effect relationship. These studies are performed by conducting a series of experiments to test the hypothesis. For a study to be scientifically accurate, it must have both an experimental group that receives the specified treatment and a control group that does not get the treatment. This is the type of study pharmaceutical companies do as part of drug trials for new medications. Experimental studies are only valid when the proper scientific method has been followed. In other words, the experiment must be well-planned and executed without bias in the testing process, all subjects must be selected at random, and the process of determining which subject is in which of the two groups must also be completely random.

Observational Studies

Observational studies are the opposite of experimental studies. In observational studies, the tester cannot change or in any way control all of the variables in the test. For example, a study to determine which gender does better in math classes in school is strictly observational. You cannot change a person's gender, and you cannot change the subject being studied. The big downfall of observational studies is that you have no way of proving a cause-and-effect relationship because you cannot control outside influences. Events outside of school can influence a student's performance in school, and observational studies cannot take that into consideration.

Random Samples

For most studies, a **random sample** is necessary to produce valid results. Random samples should not have any particular influence to cause sampled subjects to behave one way or another. The goal is for the random sample to be a **representative sample**, or a sample whose characteristics give an accurate picture of the characteristics of the entire population. To accomplish this, you must make sure you have a proper **sample size**, or an appropriate number of elements in the sample.

Biases

In statistical studies, biases must be avoided. **Bias** is an error that causes the study to favor one set of results over another. For example, if a survey to determine how the country views the president's job performance only speaks to registered voters in the president's party, the results will be skewed because a disproportionately large number of responders would tend to show approval, while a disproportionately large number of people in the opposite party would tend to express disapproval. **Extraneous variables** are, as the name implies, outside influences that can affect the outcome of a study. They are not always avoidable but could trigger bias in the result.

Data Analysis

Dispersion

A **measure of dispersion** is a single value that helps to "interpret" the measure of central tendency by providing more information about how the data values in the set are distributed about the measure of central tendency. The measure of dispersion helps to eliminate or reduce the disadvantages of using the mean, median, or mode as a single measure of central tendency, and give a more accurate picture of the dataset as a whole. To have a measure of dispersion, you must know or calculate the range, standard deviation, or variance of the data set.

Range

The **range** of a set of data is the difference between the greatest and lowest values of the data in the set. To calculate the range, you must first make sure the units for all data values are the same, and then identify the greatest and lowest values. If there are multiple data values that are equal for the highest or lowest, just use one of the values in the formula. Write the answer with the same units as the data values you used to do the calculations.

Review Video: Statistical Range
Visit mometrix.com/academy and enter code: 778541

Sample Standard Deviation

Standard deviation is a measure of dispersion that compares all the data values in the set to the mean of the set to give a more accurate picture. To find the **standard deviation of a sample**, use the formula

$$s = \sqrt{\frac{\sum_{i=1}^{n}(x_i - \bar{x})^2}{n-1}}$$

Note that s is the standard deviation of a sample, x_i represents the individual values in the data set, $\bar{x}$ is the mean of the data values in the set, and n is the number of data values in the set. The higher the value of the standard deviation is, the greater the variance of the data values from the mean. The units associated with the standard deviation are the same as the units of the data values.

Review Video: Standard Deviation
Visit mometrix.com/academy and enter code: 419469

Sample Variance

The **variance of a sample** is the square of the sample standard deviation (denoted s^2). While the mean of a set of data gives the average of the set and gives information about where a specific data value lies in relation to the average, the variance of the sample gives information about the degree to which the data values are spread out and tells you how close an individual value is to the average compared to the other values. The units associated with variance are the same as the units of the data values squared.

Percentile

Percentiles and quartiles are other methods of describing data within a set. **Percentiles** tell what percentage of the data in the set fall below a specific point. For example, achievement test scores are often given in percentiles. A score at the 80th percentile is one which is equal to or higher than 80 percent of the scores in the set. In other words, 80 percent of the scores were lower than that score.

Quartiles are percentile groups that make up quarter sections of the data set. The first quartile is the 25th percentile. The second quartile is the 50th percentile; this is also the median of the dataset. The third quartile is the 75th percentile.

Skewness

Skewness is a way to describe the symmetry or asymmetry of the distribution of values in a dataset. If the distribution of values is symmetrical, there is no skew. In general the closer the mean of a data set is to the median of the data set, the less skew there is. Generally, if the mean is to the right of the median, the data set is *positively skewed*, or right-skewed, and if the mean is to the left of the median, the data set is *negatively skewed*, or left-skewed. However, this rule of thumb is not infallible. When the data values are graphed on a curve, a set with no skew will be a perfect bell curve.

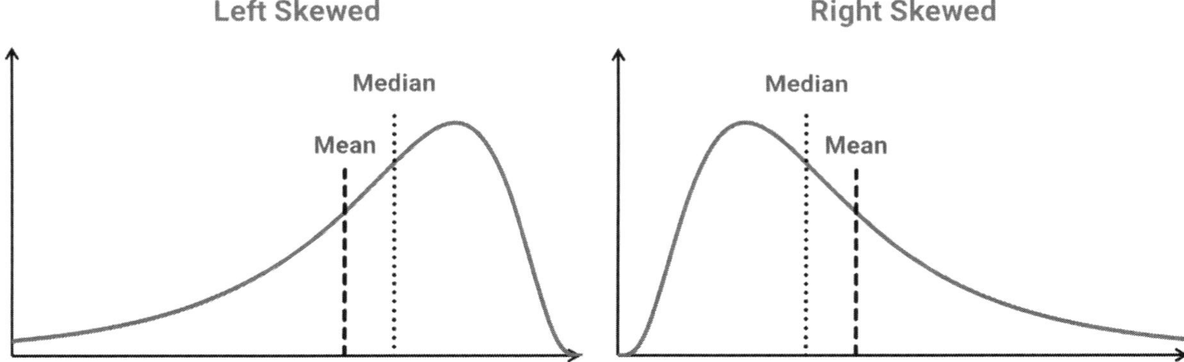

To estimate skew, use the formula:

$$\text{skew} = \frac{\sqrt{n(n-1)}}{n-2}\left(\frac{\frac{1}{n}\sum_{i=1}^{n}(x_i - \bar{x})^3}{\left(\frac{1}{n}\sum_{i=1}^{n}(x_i - \bar{x})^2\right)^{\frac{3}{2}}}\right)$$

Note that n is the datapoints in the set, x_i is the ith value in the set, and $\bar{x}$ is the mean of the set.

Review Video: Skew
Visit mometrix.com/academy and enter code: 661486

UNIMODAL VS. BIMODAL

If a distribution has a single peak, it would be considered **unimodal**. If it has two discernible peaks it would be considered **bimodal**. Bimodal distributions may be an indication that the set of data being considered is actually the combination of two sets of data with significant differences. A **uniform distribution** is a distribution in which there is *no distinct peak or variation* in the data. No values or ranges are particularly more common than any other values or ranges.

OUTLIER

An outlier is an extremely high or extremely low value in the data set. It may be the result of measurement error, in which case, the outlier is not a valid member of the data set. However, it may also be a valid member of the distribution. Unless a measurement error is identified, the experimenter cannot know for certain if an outlier is or is not a member of the distribution. There are arbitrary methods that can be employed to designate an extreme value as an outlier. One method designates an outlier (or possible outlier) to be any value less than $Q_1 - 1.5(IQR)$ or any value greater than $Q_3 + 1.5(IQR)$.

DATA ANALYSIS

SIMPLE REGRESSION

In statistics, **simple regression** is using an equation to represent a relation between independent and dependent variables. The independent variable is also referred to as the explanatory variable or the predictor and is generally represented by the variable x in the equation. The dependent variable, usually represented by the variable y, is also referred to as the response variable. The equation may be any type of function – linear, quadratic, exponential, etc. The best way to handle this task is to use the regression feature of your graphing calculator. This will easily give you the curve of best fit and provide you with the coefficients and other information you need to derive an equation.

LINE OF BEST FIT

In a scatter plot, the **line of best fit** is the line that best shows the trends of the data. The line of best fit is given by the equation $\hat{y} = ax + b$, where a and b are the regression coefficients. The regression coefficient a is also the slope of the line of best fit, and b is also the y-coordinate of the point at which the line of best fit crosses the y-axis. Not every point on the scatter plot will be on the line of best fit. The differences between the y-values of the points in the scatter plot and the corresponding y-values according to the equation of the line of best fit are the residuals. The line of best fit is also called the least-squares regression line because it is also the line that has the lowest sum of the squares of the residuals.

CORRELATION COEFFICIENT

The **correlation coefficient** is the numerical value that indicates how strong the relationship is between the two variables of a linear regression equation. A correlation coefficient of –1 is a perfect negative correlation. A correlation coefficient of +1 is a perfect positive correlation. Correlation coefficients close to –1 or +1 are very strong correlations. A correlation coefficient equal to zero indicates there is no correlation between the two variables. This test is a good indicator of whether or not the equation for the line of best fit is accurate. The formula for the correlation coefficient is

$$r = \frac{\sum_{i=1}^{n}(x_i - \bar{x})(y_i - \bar{y})}{\sqrt{\sum_{i=1}^{n}(x_i - \bar{x})^2}\sqrt{\sum_{i=1}^{n}(y_i - \bar{y})^2}}$$

where r is the correlation coefficient, n is the number of data values in the set, (x_i, y_i) is a point in the set, and $\bar{x}$ and $\bar{y}$ are the means.

Mathematics and Statistics

Z-Score

A **z-score** is an indication of how many standard deviations a given value falls from the sample mean. To calculate a z-score, use the formula:

$$\frac{x - \bar{x}}{\sigma}$$

In this formula x is the data value, $\bar{x}$ is the mean of the sample data, and σ is the standard deviation of the population. If the z-score is positive, the data value lies above the mean. If the z-score is negative, the data value falls below the mean. These scores are useful in interpreting data such as standardized test scores, where every piece of data in the set has been counted, rather than just a small random sample. In cases where standard deviations are calculated from a random sample of the set, the z-scores will not be as accurate.

Central Limit Theorem

According to the **central limit theorem**, regardless of what the original distribution of a sample is, the distribution of the means tends to get closer and closer to a normal distribution as the sample size gets larger and larger (this is necessary because the sample is becoming more all-encompassing of the elements of the population). As the sample size gets larger, the distribution of the sample mean will approach a normal distribution with a mean of the population mean and a variance of the population variance divided by the sample size.

Measures of Central Tendency

A **measure of central tendency** is a statistical value that gives a reasonable estimate for the center of a group of data. There are several different ways of describing the measure of central tendency. Each one has a unique way it is calculated, and each one gives a slightly different perspective on the data set. Whenever you give a measure of central tendency, always make sure the units are the same. If the data has different units, such as hours, minutes, and seconds, convert all the data to the same unit, and use the same unit in the measure of central tendency. If no units are given in the data, do not give units for the measure of central tendency.

Mean

The **statistical mean** of a group of data is the same as the arithmetic average of that group. To find the mean of a set of data, first convert each value to the same units, if necessary. Then find the sum of all the values, and count the total number of data values, making sure you take into consideration each individual value. If a value appears more than once, count it more than once. Divide the sum of the values by the total number of values and apply the units, if any. Note that the mean does not have to be one of the data values in the set, and may not divide evenly.

$$\text{mean} = \frac{\text{sum of the data values}}{\text{quantity of data values}}$$

For instance, the mean of the data set {88, 72, 61, 90, 97, 68, 88, 79, 86, 93, 97, 71, 80, 84, 89} would be the sum of the fifteen numbers divided by 15:

$$\frac{88 + 72 + 61 + 90 + 97 + 68 + 88 + 79 + 86 + 93 + 97 + 71 + 80 + 84 + 89}{15} = \frac{1242}{15} = 82.8$$

While the mean is relatively easy to calculate and averages are understood by most people, the mean can be very misleading if it is used as the sole measure of central tendency. If the data set has outliers (data values that are unusually high or unusually low compared to the rest of the data values), the mean can be very distorted, especially if the data set has a small number of values. If unusually high values are countered with unusually low values, the mean is not affected as much. For example, if five of twenty students in a class get a 100 on a test, but the other 15 students have an average of 60 on the same test, the class average would appear as 70. Whenever the mean is skewed by outliers, it is always a good idea to include the median as an alternate measure of central tendency.

A **weighted mean**, or weighted average, is a mean that uses "weighted" values. The formula is weighted mean $= \frac{w_1x_1+w_2x_2+w_3x_3...+w_nx_n}{w_1+w_2+w_3+\cdots+w_n}$. Weighted values, such as $w_1, w_2, w_3, ... w_n$ are assigned to each member of the set $x_1, x_2, x_3, ... x_n$. When calculating the weighted mean, make sure a weight value for each member of the set is used.

Review Video: All About Averages
Visit mometrix.com/academy and enter code: 176521

Median

The **statistical median** is the value in the middle of the set of data. To find the median, list all data values in order from smallest to largest or from largest to smallest. Any value that is repeated in the set must be listed the number of times it appears. If there are an odd number of data values, the median is the value in the middle of the list. If there is an even number of data values, the median is the arithmetic mean of the two middle values.

For example, the median of the data set {88, 72, 61, 90, 97, 68, 88, 79, 86, 93, 97, 71, 80, 84, 88} is 86 since the ordered set is {61, 68, 71, 72, 79, 80, 84, **86**, 88, 88, 88, 90, 93, 97, 97}.

The big disadvantage of using the median as a measure of central tendency is that is relies solely on a value's relative size as compared to the other values in the set. When the individual values in a set of data are evenly dispersed, the median can be an accurate tool. However, if there is a group of rather large values or a group of rather small values that are not offset by a different group of values, the information that can be inferred from the median may not be accurate because the distribution of values is skewed.

Mode

The **statistical mode** is the data value that occurs the greatest number of times in the data set. It is possible to have exactly one mode, more than one mode, or no mode. To find the mode of a set of data, arrange the data like you do to find the median (all values in order, listing all multiples of data values). Count the number of times each value appears in the data set. If all values appear an equal number of times, there is no mode. If one value appears more than any other value, that value is the mode. If two or more values appear the same number of times, but there are other values that appear fewer times and no values that appear more times, all of those values are the modes.

For example, the mode of the data set {**88**, 72, 61, 90, 97, 68, **88**, 79, 86, 93, 97, 71, 80, 84, **88**} is 88.

The main disadvantage of the mode is that the values of the other data in the set have no bearing on the mode. The mode may be the largest value, the smallest value, or a value anywhere in between in the set. The mode only tells which value or values, if any, occurred the greatest number of times. It does not give any suggestions about the remaining values in the set.

Review Video: Mean, Median, and Mode
Visit mometrix.com/academy and enter code: 286207

Standard Deviation

The **standard deviation** (σ) of a data set measures variation, or how spread out the values are. To calculate it, first find the mean of the data set. Then find the difference of each value and the mean and square the differences. Find the **variance** (σ^2)by adding each of these squared differences together and dividing by one less than the number of values. Finally, take the root of the variance and you have the standard deviation.

Review Video: Standard Deviation
Visit mometrix.com/academy and enter code: 419469

EXAMPLE

For the following data set (4, 8, 2, 7, 11, 13, 6, 5, 7), we first find the mean:

$$\frac{4+8+2+7+11+13+6+5+7}{9} = 7$$

Then we find the difference of each value and the mean, square and add them, and divide by one less than the number of data points:

$$\begin{aligned}\sigma^2 &= \frac{(7-4)^2+(7-8)^2+(7-2)^2+(7-7)^2+(7-11)^2+(7-13)^2+(7-6)^2+(7-5)^2+(7-7)^2}{9-1}\\ &= \frac{9+1+25+0+16+36+1+4+0}{8}\\ &= \frac{92}{8}\\ &= 11.5\end{aligned}$$

So the variance is 11.5, and we take the root to find the standard deviation: $\sigma = \sqrt{11.5} \approx 3.39$.

DISTRIBUTIONS

NORMAL DISTRIBUTIONS

If a distribution is **normal**, this means that the variables are mostly symmetrical about the mean. Approximately half of the values are below the mean and half are above. Most values are clustered closely about the mean, with approximately 68% within one standard deviation, 95% within two standard deviations, and 99.7% within three standard deviations. Anything beyond this is an **outlier**.

EXAMPLE

If the height of freshman women at a university is normally distributed with a mean of 66" and a standard deviation of 1.5", we can calculate the percentage of women in various height brackets. Since the standard deviation is 1.5" and 68% of values in a normal distribution fall within one distribution, we can say that approximately 68% of the freshman women are between 64.5" and 67.5", 95% are between 63" and 69", and 99.7% within 61.5" and 70.5". Anyone shorter than 61.5" or taller than 70.5" is an outlier.

UNIFORM DISTRIBUTIONS

In a **uniform distribution**, every outcome is equally likely. For instance, in flipping a fair coin or rolling a die, each outcome is as likely as any of the others. A random generator is another example, since each number within the parameters has an equal chance of being selected.

EXAMPLE

Suppose a collection of songs has a range of anywhere from 4 to 11 notes, inclusive, and they are distributed uniformly. We could find the probability that a given song has six or fewer notes. There are eight possibilities (from 4 to 11) and three of them have six or fewer notes (4, 5, 6). So the probability is $\frac{3}{8}$ or 0.375.

BINOMIAL DISTRIBUTIONS

A binomial distribution has two possible outcomes, like flipping a coin or a true/false quiz. It is typically used on a series of trials (like flipping a coin 50 times). None of the trials impact the others, so the probability of success or failure is the same on each, but the number of trials can affect overall probability. For example, flipping a coin 20 times gives a much higher probability of getting at least one heads than flipping it once, even though the probability for each individual flip is the same. The formula for **binomial distribution** is $P_x = \binom{n}{x} p^x q^{n-x}$, where P is the probability, n is the number of trials, x is the number of times of the desired outcome, p is the probability of success on any trial, and q is the probability of failure on any trial.

EXAMPLE

Suppose a jar has 20 marbles, 10 red and 10 blue. If Lea draws a marble 10 times, replacing it after each draw, there is a 50% chance on each draw of getting red, and a 50% chance of getting blue, so this is a binomial distribution. The probability of getting three reds can be calculated:

$$P_3 = \binom{10}{3}\left(\frac{1}{2}\right)^3\left(\frac{1}{2}\right)^7 = \frac{10!}{3!\,7!}(0.5)^3(0.5)^7 = \frac{10 \times 9 \times 8 \times 7 \times 6 \times 5 \times 4 \times 3 \times 2 \times 1}{7 \times 6 \times 5 \times 4 \times 3 \times 2 \times 1 \times 3 \times 2 \times 1}\left(\frac{1}{2}\right)^{10} = \frac{15}{128}$$

STATISTICS

SAMPLE MEAN

A **sample mean** is the mean (average) of a specific set of data taken as a sample from a much larger population. It is often the most manageable way to assess central tendency and other measures for groups that would be impractical or impossible to survey completely. It is calculated like a normal mean: adding all values from the sample and dividing by the total number of values in the sample.

EXAMPLE

Suppose a scientist has 15 different experimental results. He decides to take a sample of five to calculate a sample mean of the weights by taking every 3rd value. If his individual results weigh 1.2, 0.9, 1.1, 0.8, 1.3, 1.0, 0.6, 1.2, 0.7, 0.8, 0.9, 0.9, 1.3, 0.8, and 0.6 grams, we select every third value, add them together, and divide by 5:

$$\frac{1.1 + 1.0 + 0.7 + 0.9 + 0.6}{5} = \frac{4.3}{5} = 0.86$$

SAMPLE PROPORTION

The sample proportion is a proportion calculated from a specific sample of a population. For many occasions the full population may be difficult or impossible to calculate, so a sample is taken to provide a more manageable amount of data but still give a good representation of the whole population. The sample proportion is calculated by dividing the number of desired or measured outcomes by the total sample size.

EXAMPLE

At an ice cream stand, 100 customers purchase ice cream between 1:00pm and 2:00pm. Out of these, 32 choose chocolate ice cream. Our sample size is 100, because it is a sample of the total ice cream purchases for the day, and the sample proportion of those who chose chocolate is $\frac{32}{100} = 0.32$, or 32%.

CONFIDENCE INTERVALS FOR A SINGLE POPULATION MEAN

A **confidence interval** is calculated to measure how a sample compares to the full population. An upper and lower value are calculated to state that the population mean can be assumed to be within these values with a certain level of confidence (often 95%, but other percentages can also be used). The first step is to find the mean and standard deviation (also called the **error bound**) of the sample. The error bound is both added and subtracted from the mean to find the confidence interval.

EXAMPLE

If a sample has a mean of 0.72 and an error bound of 0.03, we can calculate the confidence interval by simply subtracting and then adding the error bound from the sample mean. Since $0.72 - 0.03 = 0.69$ and $0.72 +$

Mathematics and Statistics

$0.03 = 0.75$, the confidence interval is $[0.69, 0.75]$. In other words, there is a 95% probability that the true mean of the population lies between 0.69 and 0.75.

Confidence Interval for Proportions

Confidence intervals for proportions are used in instances with two possible outcomes. For instance, if a store took a sample of 100 customers and found that 72 of them made a purchase before leaving, we could find that the sample proportion of customers who make a purchase is $\frac{72}{100}$ or 0.72. This can then be used to calculate the confidence interval by both adding and subtracting the margin of error. There are multiple levels that can be found, but the standard is 95%.

Example

Val sells 150 donuts and notes that 45 of them were chocolate glazed. Given that the margin of error is 0.073, we can calculate the confidence interval. First, we find that the sample proportion is: $\frac{45}{150} = \frac{3}{10} = 0.3$. So the confidence level is: 0.3 ± 0.073. So we both add to and subtract the margin of error from the sample proportion to find the bounds of the confidence interval: $[0.227, 0.373]$, or $[22.7\%, 37.3\%]$. In other words, Val can say with 95% confidence that, based on the sample, between 22.7% and 37.3% of her customers purchase chocolate glazed donuts. Note that the confidence interval will become smaller as the sample size grows, because it becomes more and more likely to be true to the whole population.

Hypothesis Tests for Single Population Means

A **hypothesis test** can be conducted on a random sample of a population, using a smaller amount of data to test a hypothesis about the entire population. For example, if a company claims that each bag of candy it produces contains, on average, 25 pieces, we could test this hypothesis by taking a sample of the total bags of candy produced and seeing how the mean of this sample compares to the hypothesis. To find whether the difference in a sample mean and the purported population mean is within reason, we run a ***t*-test**. The value of t is a way of comparing two means to see how different they are. This could be a sample mean compared to the supposed population mean. From this t-value, we can find the p-value in a table to find the exact probability, but we can often get an idea of it simply from the t-value.

Example

A store claims that it averages 520 sales per day. Jon obtains records from the past 50 days and finds that the average number of sales is 505, with a standard deviation of 15. To see if the store's claim is likely true, he runs a t-test and discovers that $t = -7.07$. This means that the sample data is 7 standard deviations below the claimed value. It is highly unlikely that the claim is true if the sample is this far off.

Hypothesis Tests for Proportion Claims

A hypothesis test can also be conducted to test a proportion claim. For example, if someone wanted to test the claim that a flipped coin lands on heads exactly half the time, he or she could create a sample, flipping a coin a number of times and calculating the proportion. From this, one can calculate the ***p*-value**. This is the probability that the sample results differ from the claim by mere chance. A small p-value means that it is more unlikely that the original claim is true, since the sample is significantly different. A large p-value means it is difficult to disprove or reject the original claim, which is more likely to be true. The p-value is compared to the level of significance (α), which is the probability that the original claim could be true but still rejected due to a faulty sample. This is typically set at 5%, or 0.05, but can be other percentages as well. If the p-value is less than the level of significance, this means it is statistically significant: the original claim (also called the null hypothesis) can be rejected. A p-value greater than or equal to the level of significance means that the null hypothesis cannot be rejected: the sample data is not significantly different.

Example

Suppose a store claimed that 75% of its clientele were women (so the null hypothesis is that the proportion of female clients is 0.75). To test that claim, a sample of 2,000 customers is taken, and a sample proportion is calculated, along with the p-value. If the level of significance is 5% and $p = 0.039$, we can conclude that the sample data is statistically significant and reject the null hypothesis. In other words, we can say with 95% certainty that women do NOT make up 75% of the store's clientele.

Displaying Information

Frequency Tables

Frequency tables show how frequently each unique value appears in a set. A **relative frequency table** is one that shows the proportions of each unique value compared to the entire set. Relative frequencies are given as percentages; however, the total percent for a relative frequency table will not necessarily equal 100 percent due to rounding. An example of a frequency table with relative frequencies is below.

Favorite Color	Frequency	Relative Frequency
Blue	4	13%
Red	7	22%
Green	3	9%
Purple	6	19%
Cyan	12	38%

Review Video: Data Interpretation of Graphs
Visit mometrix.com/academy and enter code: 200439

Circle Graphs

Circle graphs, also known as *pie charts*, provide a visual depiction of the relationship of each type of data compared to the whole set of data. The circle graph is divided into sections by drawing radii to create central angles whose percentage of the circle is equal to the individual data's percentage of the whole set. Each 1% of data is equal to 3.6° in the circle graph. Therefore, data represented by a 90° section of the circle graph makes up 25% of the whole. When complete, a circle graph often looks like a pie cut into uneven wedges. The pie chart below shows the data from the frequency table referenced earlier where people were asked their favorite color.

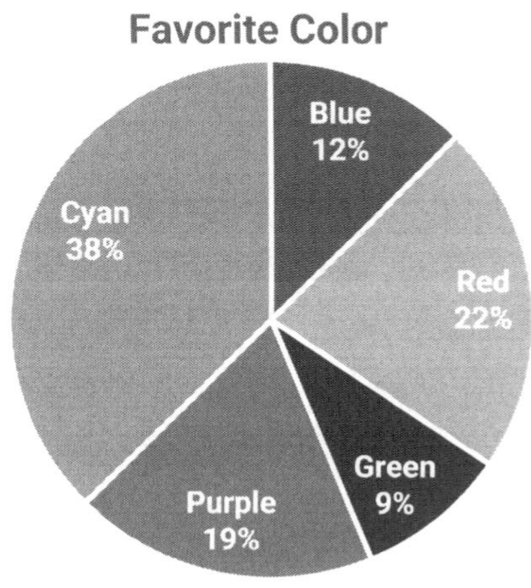

PICTOGRAPHS

A **pictograph** is a graph, generally in the horizontal orientation, that uses pictures or symbols to represent the data. Each pictograph must have a key that defines the picture or symbol and gives the quantity each picture or symbol represents. Pictures or symbols on a pictograph are not always shown as whole elements. In this case, the fraction of the picture or symbol shown represents the same fraction of the quantity a whole picture or symbol stands for. For example, a row with $3\frac{1}{2}$ ears of corn, where each ear of corn represents 100 stalks of corn in a field, would equal $3\frac{1}{2} \times 100 = 350$ stalks of corn in the field.

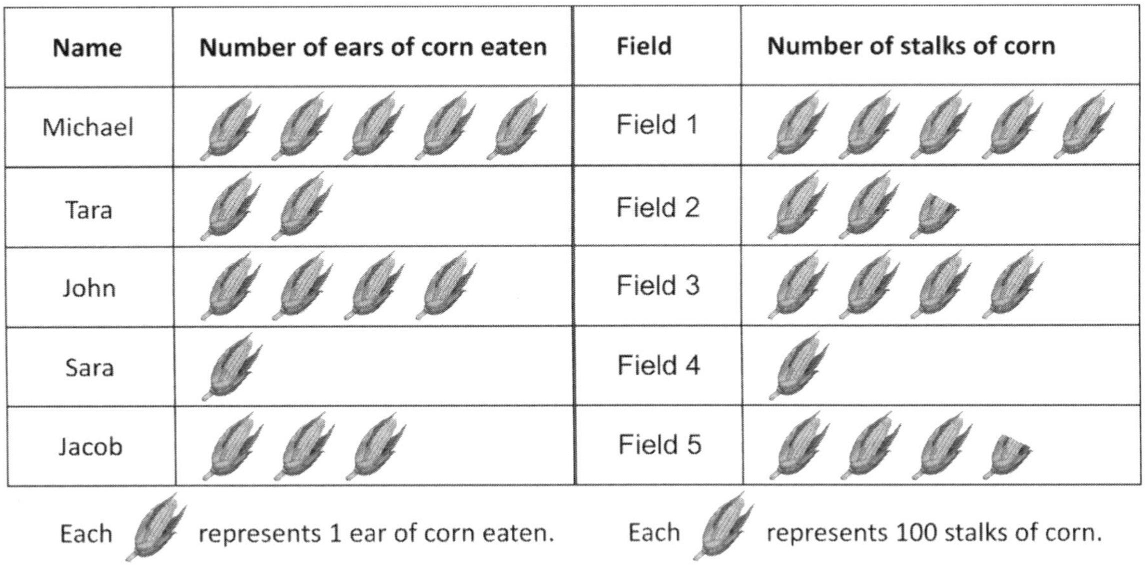

Name	Number of ears of corn eaten	Field	Number of stalks of corn
Michael		Field 1	
Tara		Field 2	
John		Field 3	
Sara		Field 4	
Jacob		Field 5	

Each represents 1 ear of corn eaten. Each represents 100 stalks of corn.

Review Video: Pictographs
Visit mometrix.com/academy and enter code: 147860

LINE GRAPHS

Line graphs have one or more lines of varying styles (solid or broken) to show the different values for a set of data. The individual data are represented as ordered pairs, much like on a Cartesian plane. In this case, the x- and y-axes are defined in terms of their units, such as dollars or time. The individual plotted points are joined by line segments to show whether the value of the data is increasing (line sloping upward), decreasing (line sloping downward), or staying the same (horizontal line). Multiple sets of data can be graphed on the same line graph to give an easy visual comparison. An example of this would be graphing achievement test scores for different groups of students over the same time period to see which group had the greatest increase or decrease in performance from year to year (as shown below).

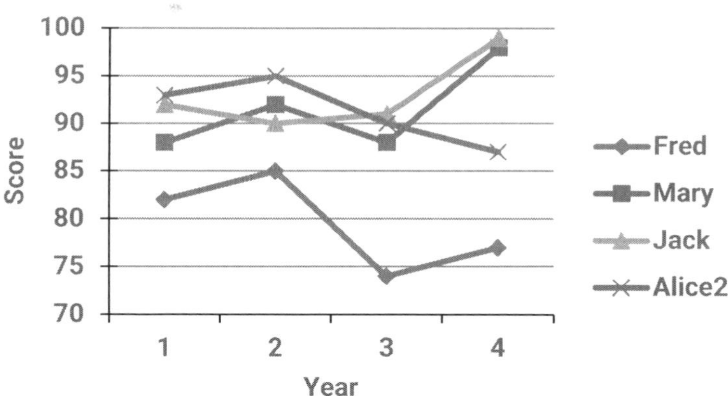

Review Video: How to Create a Line Graph
Visit mometrix.com/academy and enter code: 480147

Line Plots

A **line plot**, also known as a *dot plot*, has plotted points that are not connected by line segments. In this graph, the horizontal axis lists the different possible values for the data, and the vertical axis lists the number of times the individual value occurs. A single dot is graphed for each value to show the number of times it occurs. This graph is more closely related to a bar graph than a line graph. Do not connect the dots in a line plot or it will misrepresent the data.

Review Video: Line Plot
Visit mometrix.com/academy and enter code: 754610

Stem and Leaf Plots

A **stem and leaf plot** is useful for depicting groups of data that fall into a range of values. Each piece of data is separated into two parts: the first, or left, part is called the stem; the second, or right, part is called the leaf. Each stem is listed in a column from smallest to largest. Each leaf that has the common stem is listed in that stem's row from smallest to largest. For example, in a set of two-digit numbers, the digit in the tens place is the stem, and the digit in the ones place is the leaf. With a stem and leaf plot, you can easily see which subset of numbers (10s, 20s, 30s, etc.) is the largest. This information is also readily available by looking at a histogram, but a stem and leaf plot also allows you to look closer and see exactly which values fall in that range. Using a sample set of test scores (82, 88, 92, 93, 85, 90, 92, 95, 74, 88, 90, 91, 78, 87, 98, 99), we can assemble a stem and leaf plot like the one below.

Test Scores

7	4	8							
8	2	5	7	8	8				
9	0	0	1	2	2	3	5	8	9

Review Video: Stem and Leaf Plots
Visit mometrix.com/academy and enter code: 302339

Mathematics and Statistics

Bar Graphs

A **bar graph** is one of the few graphs that can be drawn correctly in two different configurations – both horizontally and vertically. A bar graph is similar to a line plot in the way the data is organized on the graph. Both axes must have their categories defined for the graph to be useful. Rather than placing a single dot to mark the point of the data's value, a bar, or thick line, is drawn from zero to the exact value of the data, whether it is a number, percentage, or other numerical value. Longer bar lengths correspond to greater data values. To read a bar graph, read the labels for the axes to find the units being reported. Then, look where the bars end in relation to the scale given on the corresponding axis and determine the associated value.

The bar chart below represents the responses from our favorite-color survey.

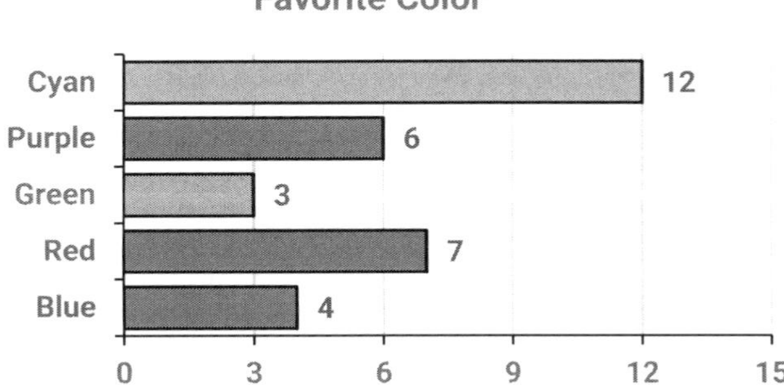

Histograms

At first glance, a **histogram** looks like a vertical bar graph. The difference is that a bar graph has a separate bar for each piece of data and a histogram has one continuous bar for each *range* of data. For example, a histogram may have one bar for the range 0–9, one bar for 10–19, etc. While a bar graph has numerical values on one axis, a histogram has numerical values on both axes. Each range is of equal size, and they are ordered left to right from lowest to highest. The height of each column on a histogram represents the number of data values within that range. Like a stem and leaf plot, a histogram makes it easy to glance at the graph and quickly determine which range has the greatest quantity of values. A simple example of a histogram is below.

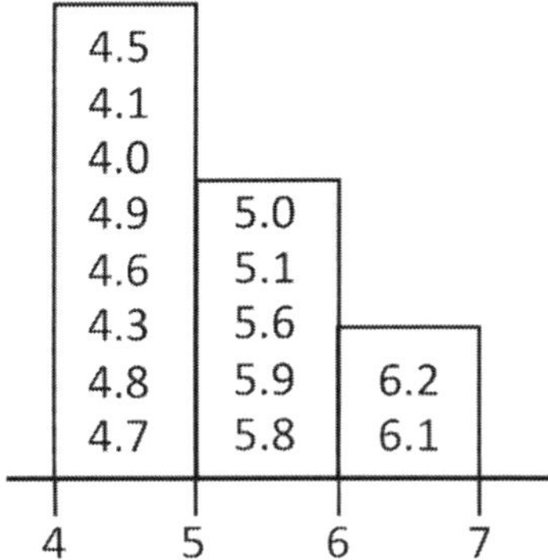

5-Number Summary

The **5-number summary** of a set of data gives a very informative picture of the set. The five numbers in the summary include the minimum value, maximum value, and the three quartiles. This information gives the reader the range and median of the set, as well as an indication of how the data is spread about the median.

Box and Whisker Plots

A **box-and-whiskers plot** is a graphical representation of the 5-number summary. To draw a box-and-whiskers plot, plot the points of the 5-number summary on a number line. Draw a box whose ends are through the points for the first and third quartiles. Draw a vertical line in the box through the median to divide the box in half. Draw a line segment from the first quartile point to the minimum value, and from the third quartile point to the maximum value.

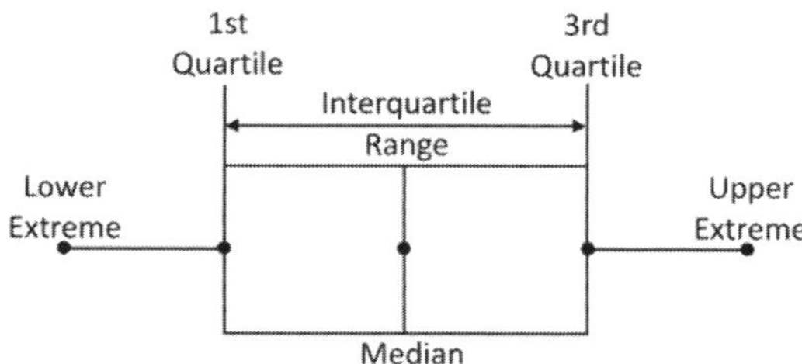

Review Video: Box and Whisker Plots
Visit mometrix.com/academy and enter code: 810817

Example

Given the following data (32, 28, 29, 26, 35, 27, 30, 31, 27, 32), we first sort it into numerical order: 26, 27, 27, 28, 29, 30, 31, 32, 32, 35. We can then find the median. Since there are ten values, we take the average of the 5th and 6th values to get 29.5. We find the lower quartile by taking the median of the data smaller than the median. Since there are five values, we take the 3rd value, which is 27. We find the upper quartile by taking the median of the data larger than the overall median, which is 32. Finally, we note our minimum and maximum, which are simply the smallest and largest values in the set: 26 and 35, respectively. Now we can create our box plot:

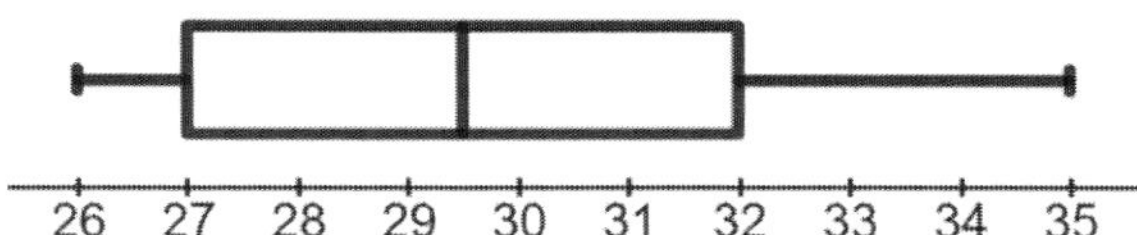

This plot is fairly "long" on the right whisker, showing one or more unusually high values (but not quite outliers). The other quartiles are similar in length, showing a fairly even distribution of data.

Interquartile Range

The **interquartile range, or IQR**, is the difference between the upper and lower quartiles. It measures how the data is dispersed: a high IQR means that the data is more spread out, while a low IQR means that the data is clustered more tightly around the median. To find the IQR, subtract the lower quartile value (Q_1) from the upper quartile value (Q_3).

Example

To find the upper and lower quartiles, we first find the median and then take the median of all values above it and all values below it. In the following data set (16, 18, 13, 24, 16, 51, 32, 21, 27, 39), we first rearrange the values in numerical order: 13, 16, 16, 18, 21, 24, 27, 32, 39, 51. There are 10 values, so the median is the average of the 5th and 6th: $\frac{21+24}{2} = \frac{45}{2} = 22.5$. We do not actually need this value to find the upper and lower quartiles. We look at the set of numbers below the median: 13, 16, 16, 18, 21. There are five values, so the 3rd is the median (16), or the value of the lower quartile (Q_1). Then we look at the numbers above the median: 24, 27, 32, 39, 51. Again there are five values, so the 3rd is the median (32), or the value of the upper quartile (Q_3). We find the IQR by subtracting Q_1 from Q_3: $32 - 16 = 16$.

68-95-99.7 RULE

The **68–95–99.7 rule** describes how a normal distribution of data should appear when compared to the mean. This is also a description of a normal bell curve. According to this rule, 68 percent of the data values in a normally distributed set should fall within one standard deviation of the mean (34 percent above and 34 percent below the mean), 95 percent of the data values should fall within two standard deviations of the mean (47.5 percent above and 47.5 percent below the mean), and 99.7 percent of the data values should fall within three standard deviations of the mean, again, equally distributed on either side of the mean. This means that only 0.3 percent of all data values should fall more than three standard deviations from the mean. On the graph below, the normal curve is centered on the y-axis. The x-axis labels are how many standard deviations away from the center you are. Therefore, it is easy to see how the 68-95-99.7 rule can apply.

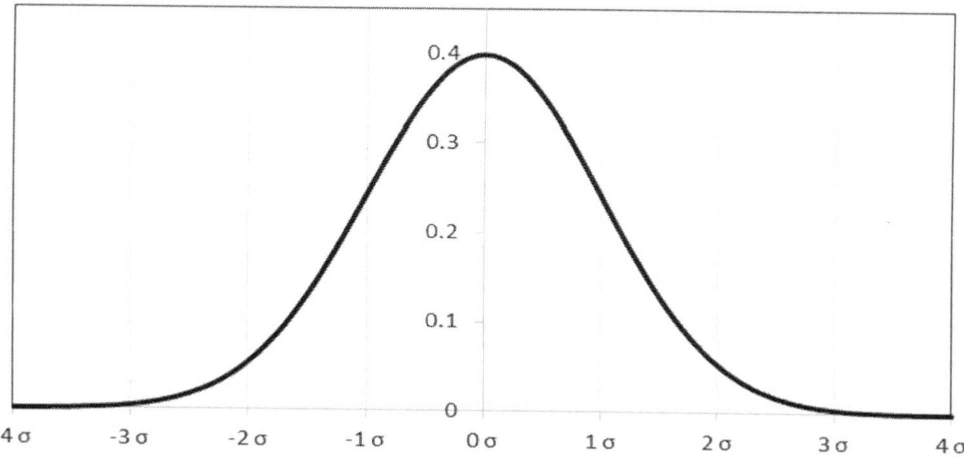

FREQUENCY DISTRIBUTIONS

A **frequency distribution** sorts data to give a clear visual representation of the distribution. Numbers are grouped with like numbers (for instance, all numbers in their twenties may be grouped together) to measure the frequency.

EXAMPLE

We can sort the following set of numbers into a frequency distribution based on the value of the tens place: 20, 12, 37, 18, 21, 19, 32, 21, 16, and 14. To do this, we group them into sets by first digit and create a table. This can include just category and frequency, but can also include relative frequency or percentage:

Category	Frequency	Relative Frequency	Percentage
Tens	5	0.5	50%
Twenties	3	0.3	30%
Thirties	2	0.2	20%

We can see that there is a higher concentration of numbers in the tens than any other group. This means that the data will likely be skewed right, with the mean greater than the median.

CUMULATIVE FREQUENCY DISTRIBUTIONS

A **cumulative frequency distribution**, rather than showing the amount in each category, shows the *cumulative* amount. In other words, the amount for each new category is added to each of the previous amounts to show the cumulative sum. This is helpful when the goal is to compare not single groups against each other, but to look at several groups as a sample. For instance, in a cumulative frequency distribution based on employees' salaries, a person could immediately see how many employees make at or below a certain amount per year.

EXAMPLE

A teacher could create a cumulative frequency distribution out of the following test grades: 89, 76, 74, 92, 83, 86, 90, 87, 85, 82, 95, 68, 97, 94, 86, 82, 89, 81, 78, 82. The grades could be divided into groups and placed in a table, adding on each new group to the previous to find the cumulative frequency:

Limits	Frequency	Cumulative frequency
0–75	2	2
76–80	2	4
81–85	6	10
86–90	6	16
91–95	3	19
96–100	1	20

Now the teacher can easily see, for instance, that 10 of the 20 students are scoring at 85 or below.

CORRELATION COEFFICIENTS

A **correlation coefficient** describes the relationship between data. The value can be anywhere between –1 and 1, where –1 is a strong negative correlation (meaning that as one value increases, the other decreases proportionally), 1 is a strong positive correlation (both values increase proportionally), and 0 means no relationship between the values.

EXAMPLE

Zac calculated the correlation coefficient between the number of rainy days in a month and the number of times he had to mow. If he found a correlation coefficient of 0.89, this shows a strong positive correlation between the rainy days and the number of times Zac had to mow. In other words, the rain and growth of the grass appear to be closely linked in a positive way: as one value increases, the other increases proportionally.

SCATTER PLOTS

BIVARIATE DATA

Bivariate data is simply data from two different variables. (The prefix *bi-* means *two*.) In a *scatter plot*, each value in the set of data is plotted on a grid similar to a Cartesian plane, where each axis represents one of the two variables. By looking at the pattern formed by the points on the grid, you can often determine whether or not there is a relationship between the two variables, and what that relationship is, if it exists. The variables may be directly proportionate, inversely proportionate, or show no proportion at all. It may also be possible to determine if the data is linear, and if so, to find an equation to relate the two variables. The following scatter plot shows the relationship between preference for brand "A" and the age of the consumers surveyed.

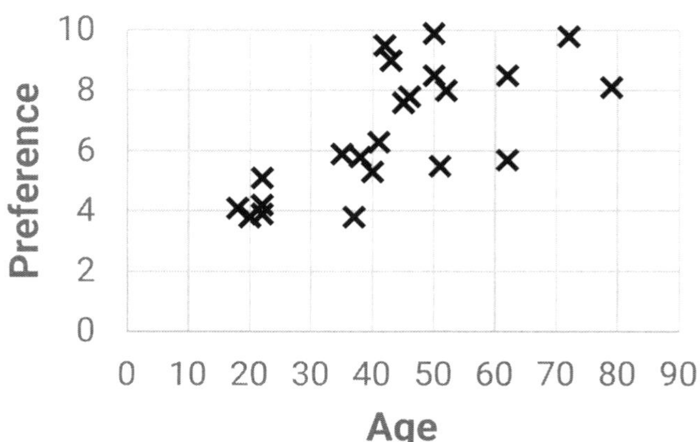

Scatter Plots

Scatter plots are also useful in determining the type of function represented by the data and finding the simple regression. Linear scatter plots may be positive or negative. Nonlinear scatter plots are generally exponential or quadratic. Below are some common types of scatter plots:

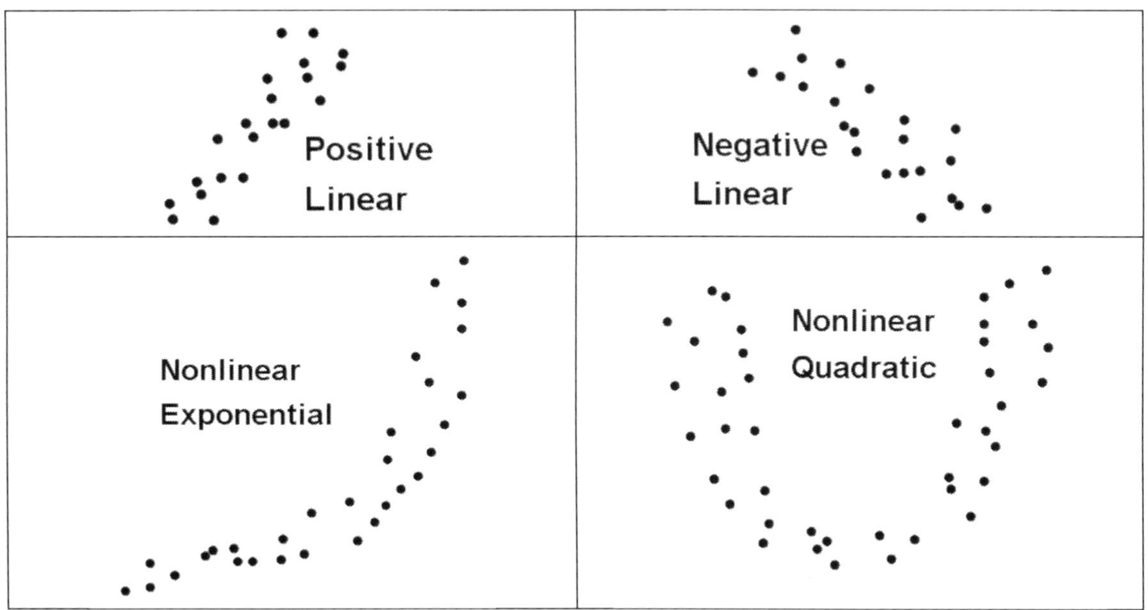

Review Video: Scatter Plot
Visit mometrix.com/academy and enter code: 596526

Management Principles, Psychology, and Human Behavior

Transform passive reading into active learning! After immersing yourself in this chapter, put your comprehension to the test by taking a quiz. The insights you gained will stay with you longer this way. Scan the QR code to go directly to the chapter quiz interface for this study guide. If you're using a computer, simply visit the bonus page at **mometrix.com/bonus948/fsot** and click the Chapter Quizzes link.

Human Resource Management

Staffing Process

Planning Stage

It is important for human resource personnel to properly plan the staffing process. First, they need to perform **human resources audits**. This is the process in which all the functions, policies, and characteristics of a company's human resources department are examined to look for problems, find best practices, and increase efficacy and efficiency. It is also done to make sure practices properly protect the company legally and effectively. The company will then perform a job analysis to look at a job to understand all of its functions and attributes as well as those needed of the employee who will perform the job. Next, human resource employees can create a job description with specifications on what needs to be done and who could do it. They can then start to look for the employee. Sometimes they look inwards. **Succession planning** is the process of looking at existing employees and planning and preparing them to move up in the company to leadership positions. It can make things move more smoothly when the company grows or a key person leaves.

Staffing Procedures

There are a number of **staffing procedures** companies must perform. First, they must recruit potential employees. This can be done in a number of ways. They may send out job advertisements or contact a recruiting agency. They can go to job fairs. Once they have an employee, the company must train him (or her). They must have a good training program that prepares him to do his job satisfactorily. The company must also evaluate its employees. Many companies formally evaluate employees on an annual basis, but in reality, employees are constantly evaluated for performance. The company can help employees to improve themselves. Evaluations can be used as a basis for raises. At times, employees need to be terminated. This can be because of a company situation, or due to the fault of the employee. Procedures should be put in place so this is as smooth as possible for both the employee and the company. With the right procedures in place, the company will run more efficiently.

Addressing Diversity in the Workplace

It is important for businesses to embrace and promote **diversity**. People from different backgrounds have different ideas and can contribute in many positive ways. Companies should make sure that there is diversity at their office and no unfair hiring practices. Many companies make a concerted effort to hire people from all different backgrounds. In the office, it is vital to promote an atmosphere of acceptance and tolerance. There should be a zero-tolerance policy for discrimination of any type. This should be communicated to employees regularly. Avenues should be provided to report any problems. With diligence, every workplace can celebrate and enjoy the benefits of diversity.

Cross-Training

Cross-training is when employees are trained to perform functions outside of the typical functions of their job. For instance, someone who works in the copywriting department of a firm might spend a little time in the graphic design department. There are various advantages to cross-training. First, if an employee is absent, someone else may be able to take over without a problem, which ensures that the job functions are completed even when someone is absent. It can also help a person better do his or her job. For instance, the copywriter who learns about graphic design might get a better idea of how her copy is going to look as a whole. Employees might also be able to communicate better with other departments when they understand more of what they are doing. Additionally, it can promote teamwork and help motivate employees because it helps them to better understand the company. Employees who are cross-trained are easier to promote because they already understand multiple parts of the company and the organization as a whole, which is an advantage for both the company and employee.

Maslow's Hierarchy of Needs

In his work on human motivation, Abraham Maslow created **Maslow's hierarchy of needs**, a five-tiered approach to needs and motivation. The pyramid-shaped hierarchy places basic needs at the bottom, which must be attained before higher levels are reached. The desire for these needs will increase the longer they are denied. This level of the pyramid encompasses **physiological needs**. These are what a human needs to survive such as food, water, air, and sleep. The need for **security** comes next. These include important needs such as the desire for a safe home, medical care, and a secure job. Once these are achieved, a person moves on to **social needs**. People want love, affection, and belonging though friends, social involvement, and romance. The next tier is **esteem needs**. These make a person feel like they are worthwhile. People look for a sense of accomplishment and recognition from others. Once a person has achieved these four basic needs, they can progress to the **growth need**, the top tier of self-actualization. This is where people have enjoyed personal growth and are reaching their potential. They do not worry as much about others' opinions and instead focus on their own growth.

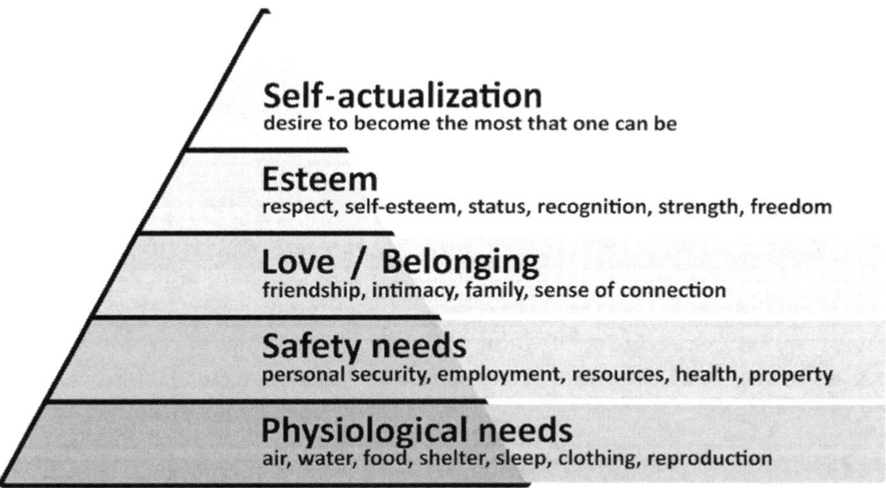

Collective Bargaining

Collective bargaining occurs when a company's management engages in talks with representatives of a workforce (often a trade union). They discuss numerous aspects of the business and its labor including working conditions, pay, hours, benefits, and more. It is advantageous to employees because they can have more bargaining power and more of a say when they band together. It is advantageous for the company because they just negotiate with one group and can get everything arranged and set without needing to go through the same process with every single employee. It avoids many future problems and arguments. Collective bargaining is commonly seen in many different industries and fields.

Conflict Resolution Strategies

When **conflict** occurs in the workplace, efficiency and efficacy can be impacted, thus it is important to employ conflict resolution strategies. There are numerous strategies a company can utilize. First, the company should address the situation right away. Small conflicts can grow into large ones with time. The manager should talk to the parties separately to get their side of the story. Sometimes the conflict is more of a misunderstanding than anything, and it can be simply solved by understanding the two points of view. The manager should understand what each person wants and see if there is a way to compromise and make everyone happy. They can try to mediate between the two people, allowing each party to speak. This meeting should be civil, calm, and constructive. Managers should try to come up with a solution that is beneficial for everyone. If necessary, a follow-up meeting should occur.

Effects of Group Dynamics on Individual Behavior

People can behave differently when in a group, and how groups act is an area of study called **group dynamics**. It is important for managers to understand these forces so they can promote positive behavior. **Groupthink** is a negative behavior that occurs when the people in a group want harmony so much that they minimize opposing viewpoints. They make a decision without considering all of the alternatives because the people do not want conflict. People will typically feel loyalty to certain others that they identify with or respect. Also, they may have the mistaken impression that others agree it can't be wrong, even if many are harboring their own doubts. It is important to avoid this. Sometimes there can be conflict in a group and this can prevent the group from making decisions. Groups can also be good, especially if there is **group cohesion**, where people like and respect each other. If people are encouraged to speak their minds, then new opinions can emerge and the group can make the best decision possible.

Organizational Culture and Subculture Within the Workplace

Corporate culture encompasses many facets, including values, traditions, and customs. For instance, there may be a **formal culture** in which people dress formally and address each other in a formal manner. There might be a very **polite culture** in which people try to be very kind to each other. Management plays a big part in making the culture, which can have a large effect on the work that gets done. Within each culture, there are **subcultures** that may be very unique. For instance, the computer department in a firm may have a different subculture than the rest of the company, formed by their shared values, interests, etc. The various subcultures can affect the organization's culture as a whole. A positive culture can have a positive effect on the company.

Strategies to Promote Teamwork

Employees must work together even with differing and (at times) conflicting personalities. There are different measures employers can take to promote teamwork. One method is to incorporate **team-building exercising**. These might involve games or fun activities. There are companies that perform team-building sessions for companies. They can help employees get to know each other better and learn how to work together. There should be rules for teams to promote respect. For instance, employees should never insult others at the office. Employers should make sure employees adhere to the rules. If there is one person who is a problem, then management should talk to that person to address the situation. **Recognition** of teams is another way to promote teamwork. A company can recognize groups that work well together and accomplish their goals. The team members should have clear roles. This can help stop disagreements from a misunderstanding of roles and responsibilities. With strong teamwork comes better efficiency and productivity.

Influences on Employees' Morale and Motivation

First, employees should be fairly compensated. Employees who are underpaid may feel cheated and not motivated. Likewise, if a person is overworked, he or she will feel less motivated at the job. Jobs that allow the workers some flexibility can promote motivation. Also, workers who feel appreciated and valued have higher morale and motivation. Companies can accomplish this by praising employees or having recognition programs such as an **employee-of-the-month program**. Workers also like to have some say or responsibility in their work rather than just being told what to do. Workers will feel more motivated and have higher morale in a positive culture where people are respectful of each other. Working conditions affect employee motivation; employees will not feel very motivated if they are in a hot room crowded with 10 other people. The ability of the boss to lead well and create a good atmosphere also affects employee attitudes. Companies should work hard to control these factors to promote high morale and motivation.

Promoting Job Satisfaction Among Employees

If possible, employers can increase satisfaction by being flexible in employee schedules. When workers do not feel overworked, they are happier. Also, workers like to feel satisfied at their job—delegating some responsibility and letting them contribute instead of dictating every move can promote job satisfaction. Employers should be respectful of employees and provide a professional culture. Employees do not want to be talked down to or treated as if they are inferior. Employers can show that they care about employees with something as simple as a manager recognizing when an employee is going through a difficult time, or offering a reward for a success. Employees like to be recognized for their hard work. Allowing employees to grow and feel like they are contributing is important. People will also be more satisfied if there is a place they can go with their complaints. It is worthwhile for a company to spend the time, effort, and money to promote job satisfaction. With higher satisfaction comes increased productivity.

Pertinent Factors When Determining Compensation

First, the company should consider the **experience** the employee possesses. An individual with 10 years of experience is generally more valuable than an employee directly out of college; he or she will expect and deserve higher compensation. The years the employee has been with the company also affects compensation. Many companies give a raise every year to reflect cost of living, merit, or both. **Skills** should also be considered. An employee with better or rarer skills should be compensated for them. The **education** of the employee matters as well. Generally, the higher the degree, the greater the compensation. Companies may have a salary range for the position based upon the wages paid for similar people in similar companies. This will depend on location and cost of living. Some companies pay a little more to attract higher quality employees or a little less to save money. Also, the company's **financial state** might affect pay. A company that is doing well will have more cash to spread around while one that is having difficulty might be more frugal. The other types of **benefits** offered will also affect pay.

Common Benefits Employees Receive

Employees receive many benefits in addition to financial compensation. Most full-time employees receive some type of paid time off. This may include sick, vacation, and personal days. Often, this number increases depending on the length of time the employee has been with the company. Companies also typically offer time off for holidays such as Thanksgiving and Christmas. The company may offer health insurance plans and even contribute to the premiums. Some employers also offer vision benefits, dental plans, and life insurance plans. Companies also often offer retirement benefits. It might be in the form of a pension, 401(k) plan, or an employee stock plan. The company may contribute to these as well. These benefits can be worth a great deal to an employee.

Retirement Plans

There are different types of retirement plans for which an employee may be eligible. A **pension** provides a fixed sum on a regular basis to an employee after retirement. This is often given to people who worked in public office or military service. Some employees are also eligible for an **employee stock ownership plan (ESOP)**. In this type of retirement plan, the company puts stock or money for stock into an account on behalf of the employee. This may have to vest over time. The employee does not control the stock directly until he or she leaves the firm, and then it is distributed. Many companies offer **401(k) plans**. These are tax-advantageous plans that allow people to defer their income taxes, both in earnings and contributions. A lot of employers will match a percentage of the contributions of the employee. A person can also get an individual retirement account that provides tax advantages.

Managing Employee Paid Time Off

Employers give employees paid time off in the form of vacation, sick time, and holidays. Companies may manage these by giving a certain amount of leave for each year of service, an amount that may increase when the person reaches a milestone such as five years. They will often do it as an accrual process, with each pay period showing how much the employee has accrued in time. Companies decide which holidays to give off to employees. Most offer New Years, Thanksgiving Day, Christmas, Independence Day, Labor Day, and Memorial Day, but others also offer days like Veteran's Day and Martin Luther King, Jr. Day. Some companies have decided to combine sick, personal, and vacation time so people can use the time as they wish. People will typically ask for the time off from their managers or the human resources department. Some companies have a computerized system for this, which makes it easier to manage.

Workers' Compensation

Workers' compensation is insurance that companies pay for to protect themselves and their employees. It covers medical expenses and partial salary losses to employees who are hurt while on the job. It does not matter if the person is at fault (i.e., if the person tripped over his own feet), he would still be eligible (although not necessarily if it is intentional or due to drugs or alcohol). The injury must occur while the person is working. Employers pay all costs of the program. There may also be payment for economic loss. In the case of an employee killed while on the job, money may be paid to dependents.

Unemployment Insurance

Unemployment insurance provides benefits for workers who lose their jobs without fault of their own. These programs are usually run by the state and are typically funded by employers through taxes. It does not typically cover the entire salary, but instead a portion of it for a specific amount of time. This limit can be extended at times, especially when the economy is particularly bad. A number of factors determine eligibility into the program. The person must not have done something to lose his job. For example, a person will not get unemployment if he is fired for showing up late to work repeatedly. Also, many states require that the individual search for a job while receiving benefits. He might not be eligible if he is receiving other income. The employee must have been at the job for a certain amount of time before being laid off. It does not count for temporary employees or those who voluntarily quit. The amount is based on what the employee was earning.

Laws and Acts Preventing Discrimination

A number of laws have been created to prevent and punish discrimination. The **Americans with Disabilities Act (ADA)** protects those with physical and mental disabilities from discrimination, as well as provides many other protections. Those with disabilities must be reasonably accommodated in a number of areas. For instance, someone can't be fired for having a disability. **The Equal Employment Opportunity Commission (EEOC)** forbids discrimination against an employee or job applicant due to color, race, gender, religion, age, disability, national origin, or genetic information. Companies must adhere to this in all practices, including hiring, training, pay, termination, benefits, promotions, and harassment. The **Age Discrimination in Employment Act (ADEA)** is similar, but forbids discrimination based on a person's age. Strict penalties could be enforced for any parties violating the above laws and acts.

FMLA

The **Family and Medical Leave Act (FMLA)** allows employees who are eligible to take up to 12 weeks of unpaid leave while having their job and group health insurance protected for one of the following reasons:

1. To care for a newborn or child under one year of age.
2. To care for an adopted or foster child with the employee for one year or less.
3. To provide support to a spouse, parent, or child with a serious medical issue.
4. To deal with the employee's own health condition that does not allow him or her to work.
5. To deal with an eligible exigency due to a parent's, child's, or spouse's position as a covered military member on covered active duty.

If the employee is taking time off to care for an injured or ill covered military member (parent, child, spouse, next of kin) then the eligible leave is extended to 26 weeks.

FICA

The **Federal Insurance Contributions Act (FICA)** is a law in the United States that requires money be deducted from income to fund Medicare and social security. The social security portion has a maximum while the Medicare part does not. How much is deducted is dependent on the person's income. It is 12.4 percent for social security and 2.9 percent for Medicare. Those who work for someone else will only have to pay for half the FICA amount while their employer will pay the other half. Self-employed individuals pay it all, but can deduct half from their taxes as an expense of the business. There is an additional 0.9 percent Medicare tax for those making over $200,000 annually.

COBRA

The **Consolidated Omnibus Budget Reconciliation Act (COBRA)** is an act that allows employees and their spouses, ex-spouses, and dependent children to continue with group health coverage when it would have been otherwise terminated. Various events can trigger this continuing coverage, including the employee losing his job (without major misconduct), a reduction in hours that would result in losing the benefits, the employee's death, divorce or legal separation, a child becoming no longer dependent, and new eligibility for Medicare. The covered individuals may have to pay for the insurance in its entirety, including an additional two percent for administrative fees. State and local governments must adhere to COBRA, as do companies with 20 or more employees. Some states have laws that cover smaller companies. Coverage may be extended for a maximum of 18 to 36 months depending on the qualifying event.

HIPAA

The **Health Insurance Portability and Accountability Act (HIPAA)** provides broad protection for American workers concerning the privacy of health insurance. It gives patients and other individuals broad protections for their identifiable health information and limits who can see the information without permission. In addition, those who hold the information, such as doctor's offices, must put in safeguards so it is not accidently seen by unauthorized individuals. It includes medical records, patient/provider conversations, billing information, and other health information. Parties that must adhere to the rules include health plans, the majority of health care providers and health care clearinghouses, as well as their business associates.

Safety in the Workplace

The government plays a large role in promoting safety in the workplace. The Occupational Safety and Health Act of 1970 was implemented to prevent accidents at work by requiring safe working conditions. The **Occupational Safety and Health Administration (OSHA)** was formed by this act and gives and enforces rules and regulations about workplace safety. It conducts investigations, takes complaints, and issues fines. It requires employers to clearly label any hazards, create records of injuries and illnesses related to work, do OSHA-required tests such as air sampling and medical tests (depending on the industry), and tell OSHA if a fatality occurs or three workers go to the hospital. There are various requirements by OSHA, including providing employees with protective equipment, preventing exposure to toxic chemicals, adhering to noise restrictions and more. Also, employees can't be discriminated against for making a complaint.

Review Video: Intro to OSHA
Visit mometrix.com/academy and enter code: 913559

Business Law and Ethics

Ethical Issues

Conflicts of Interest

A conflict of interest occurs when a person has two adversary interests, one of which might not be best for his or her business. An example is an employee of a general contractor who is making a decision on which of five bidding subcontractors to choose. If one of the subcontractors is his brother, he will have a conflict of interest because he might want to choose his brother, who might not be the best choice. He might choose his brother over someone better qualified. There are many instances of conflicts of interest in business. Oftentimes they are related to money. A person may accept gifts in exchange for a contract, for example. It is unethical to do something bad for the company because of personal interests. The employee should try to avoid this if possible. For instance, the person who works for the general contractor may ask someone else to make the decision so he doesn't have to choose between his brother and the company.

Privacy of Employees

There are a variety of ethical issues regarding the privacy of employees. Some of it stems from the monitoring of communications. Businesses can monitor employees' business calls, such as when a customer service agent is providing service to a customer, but it is murkier if employees are on personal calls. If employees are not supposed to be making personal calls at work, then employers may have the right to listen. Some people feel that it is not ethical, but then it is also not ethical for employees to spend time on personal matters when they should be working. Most companies monitor internet usage. Again, some people may worry about the ethical issues with privacy, but if it is on company time with company resources, the business could be liable for the employee's actions. A lot of companies perform background checks and drug testing, which is allowed, although there are guidelines in place that must be followed. They must be reasonable. Most companies fulfill ethical duties by getting consent before performing the checks. It is very important for employers to keep records about the employees confidential.

Compensation

Wages should be fair. It is important that one employee not make more or less for the wrong reasons. For instance, it is ethical for a company to pay more to an employee with more experience, but it is not ethical to pay more to a man than a woman solely because of gender. Still, this often happens, as does pay disparity among races, religions, and other categories. Sometimes advocates call out companies in which the top people make an exorbitant amount of money and the lower employees do very poorly. Ethical issues arise when people do not make a living wage. It is important to ensure pay disparity among workers is not occurring for the wrong reasons.

Insider Trading

Illegal insider trading occurs when someone makes a trade while having "insider" information that makes it unfair to other investors. This can occur when a corporate officer discovers something significant about a company and makes a trade because of that information. For instance, an employee may learn of a big problem about to occur and get rid of the stock before the price plummets. Insider trading can also be committed by employee friends, family, and acquaintances; government employees; law or banking employees who deal with a company; or just anyone who manages to obtain the illegal information. It is unethical because it makes it unfair to investors who have to trade without this information. Insider trading is taken very seriously by the US Securities and Exchange Commission and has serious consequences.

Business' Social Responsibility

Businesses have a social responsibility to their customers, employees, investors, and society in general. To their employees they should have fair labor practices. Employees should be treated fairly and without discrimination. Those companies that deal with international business have a responsibility to make sure laborers involved in their business are also treated fairly. They also have a responsibility to investors to try to build their money (in socially acceptable ways). To customers they should be fair, putting out quality products without deception. Business practices and tactics should be fair and not deceptive—they should not badmouth a competitor, for instance. There are different ways to be socially responsible to society as a whole. Businesses should have practices that do not harm the environment or animals or create unsafe waste. Many companies also give to charity. Some use fair trade products or sustainably grown and processed products. When companies show socially responsible practices, people take notice and may give them more business. Corporate social responsibility is the business' responsibility to both make money and act in a socially responsible way. This can include economic responsibility, legal responsibility, ethical responsibility and philanthropic responsibility.

Criminal and Civil Law

Criminal law involves someone accused of a crime. The individual broke a law and did something detrimental to society. Although it might involve a victim, that victim does not have to be the one to bring the case to life; the government (in the form of prosecution) will. There doesn't have to be a victim such as if someone was caught driving under the influence but did not hurt anyone. If the person is found guilty, he may have to pay money, could be sentenced to prison, or (in rare cases) executed. A civil case is a dispute between two parties. They are brought by one party against another because of a failure of a legal duty. The plaintiff may ask for compensation or for the party to fulfill the duty, but the defendant cannot be sentenced to prison or death. They both can occur in local or federal courts. Lawyers can be used for both, but are guaranteed for criminal defendants. Because of the seriousness of criminal law, defendants are presumed innocent and the state must prove the charges beyond a reasonable doubt. It is less difficult to prove guilt in civil cases.

Case, Administrative, Statutory, Constitutional, and Tort Law

Criminal law deals with crimes that are committed. **Case law** refers to the verdicts of courts that can now be used in new court cases to help plead cases and define the law. **Statutory law** refers to codes and statutes the legislative bodies have enacted. **Administrative law** refers to the procedures that administrative agencies create. It is very technical. Different agencies have different procedures and these must be fulfilled before a lawsuit can be brought. **Constitutional law** refers to how the United States Constitution is interpreted and implemented. **Tort law** refers to civil claims that one party brings against another. A plaintiff claims that a defendant harmed him in a way that constitutes a legal liability. Some attorneys specialize in one type of law while others practice a broader range.

Lawsuits

A **lawsuit** occurs when one party brings a case against another party in a court of law. This is also known as a civil action. The plaintiff makes the complaint that the other party (defendant) did something for which they are legally liable. Unlike criminal cases, a person's freedom is not in jeopardy—there is no prison sentence. The person may not have broken a law to have a lawsuit brought against him (or her). It can also involve negligence. The plaintiff may ask for compensatory damages, which compensate the plaintiff for the money he may have lost, as well as pain and suffering. There might also be punitive damages, which is like a punishment for being malicious, reckless, or grossly negligent. One person files the suit, followed by discovery, any pre-trial motions, and oftentimes discussions of settlement. If it doesn't get settled, then it will go to a trial and the judgment. Finally, one party can appeal. Sometimes, parties will come together to make a lawsuit as a group, which can appear much stronger because of the amount of people. This is called a class action lawsuit.

Court Systems

There are many different court systems in the United States, including a federal court system and state courts. State court systems consist of many different tiers. State trial courts may consist of county courts, circuit courts, and city or municipal courts, among others. Trial courts may have limited jurisdiction, hearing lower criminal charges, cases involving juveniles, traffic issues, and some civil cases. More serious cases, such as those with more serious crimes or higher stakes civil cases, may go to a court of general jurisdiction. These may include circuit courts, superior courts, or courts of common pleas. There are specialized courts in many states. These include courts such as family courts and juvenile courts. States usually also have a supreme court where cases that have worked their way up the lower courts can be heard. Federal courts are generally divided into circuits and districts, with at least one per state. Many federal lawsuits are heard in those. The highest court is the US Supreme Court, which shapes many laws. It hears a small number of very important cases.

Due Process, Liability, Damages, Burden of Proof, and Negligence

Due process refers to a person's right to have the state respect his legal rights. It is about providing fairness to those involved in legal matters such as by providing a notice of rights. Liability refers to a party's legal responsibility for behaviors, actions, or inactions. If someone does not meet his (or her) duty, he could have a lawsuit brought against him. Damages refer to the money that may be given to the plaintiff from the defendant during a lawsuit. The plaintiff with a civil lawsuit has the responsibility of providing the burden of proof, which means he must bring a "preponderance of evidence" or a "weight of evidence" to show that he has enough facts to win the case. In criminal cases, the burden of proof refers to a prosecutor needing to show that the defendant is guilty "beyond a reasonable doubt." Negligence is when a party does not show a reasonable amount of care. Though negligence can be accidental, a reasonable person would have acted differently. One can be liable for this.

Laws and Regulations That Affect Business

There are a wide variety of laws and regulations that affect businesses. Business or **corporate law** refers to the laws surrounding how corporations are formed, dissolved, and run. **Labor laws** deal with many aspects of the relationship between employer and employee such as working conditions, wages, and discrimination. **Tax law** deals with the taxes that businesses owe. **Contract laws** govern the contracts that many businesses enter into on a regular basis. **Property law** governs how property is owned, commonly seen in business. **Antitrust law** strives to keep a competitive marketplace by not allowing mergers that would form monopolies and other antitrust activities. The **Uniform Commercial Code (UCC)** helps make transactions easier between states by helping make uniformity in commercial laws. Companies are also subject to accounting and financial management laws, as well as laws regarding their insurance and credit.

FTC

Formed in 1914, the **Federal Trade Commission (FTC)** protects consumers by stopping businesses from performing deceptive, unfair, and anticompetitive practices. It strives to stop fraud and other types of deception and keep competition fair by stopping anticompetitive mergers. It is a federal agency that has competition jurisdiction and consumer protection jurisdiction. It helps make policies and shares information with the legislature and government agencies. When wrongdoing is suspected, the FTC will investigate and, at times, sue to stop it. They accept complaints about businesses regarding many matters including identity theft, deceptive advertising, and data security. They pass the information along to law enforcement agencies when appropriate. They also work to prevent mergers that would create anticompetitive organizations such as monopolies. They have had a large impact on the marketplace.

SEC

The United States **Securities and Exchange Commission (SEC)** plays a large role in protecting investors, maintaining the integrity of the market, and aiding in the forming of capital. It works to keep a fair market without unfair practices that would be detrimental to investors. It makes, investigates, and enforces requirements of fair disclosure of information so that one party does not have insider information that would compromise the market's fairness. Companies are required to disclose information on a regular basis so that investors can make informed decisions. It also investigates evidence of fraud. If the SEC finds a violation such as insider trading, a company purposely providing false information, or accounting fraud, it will bring a civil enforcement action against the party. It is led by five commissioners who are appointed by the president. Its main functions include making sure that federal securities laws are enforced; making rules; making sure brokers, securities firms, ratings agencies and investment advisors are inspected; watching private regulatory organizations; and working with authorities to coordinate United States securities regulations.

SARBANES-OXLEY ACT AND BANKRUPTCY REFORM ACT OF 2005

Two acts that played a large part in business were the Sarbanes-Oxley Act and the Bankruptcy Reform Act of 2005. The **Sarbanes-Oxley Act** was signed by President George W. Bush in 2002 and increased corporate responsibility and financial disclosure while fighting accounting and corporate fraud. It included new or improved standards for management firms, public accounting firms, and United States public company boards. It also led to the creation of the **Public Company Accounting Oversight Board (PCAOB)**, which oversees auditing professionals. It was created in an effort to prevent corporate scandals at a time when such scandals were becoming common. It also made some types of misconduct crimes. The **Bankruptcy Reform Act of 2005** was created to lower Bankruptcy Code filings. Parties filing for bankruptcy would now need to get financial counseling first. In addition, they would have to undergo a "means test" to see if they qualified. Filers had to wait eight years before using Chapter 7 bankruptcy again. In addition, it created a limit of $125,000 for homestead exemptions if the property was acquired within three years and a weakened automatic stay for multiple filers. This made it more difficult for people to file for Chapter 7 bankruptcy.

CONSUMER PROTECTION LAWS

There are a number of consumer protection laws that safeguard individuals from unscrupulous business practices. Many of these laws are related to food safety and sanitation. Food must be handled, stored, and prepared in certain ways to prevent health hazards. For instance, meat must be stored at certain temperatures and can only stay out for a certain amount of time. The Food and Drug Administration (FDA), Department of Agriculture (USDA) and Food Safety and Inspection Service (FSIS) all play a part in administering these laws. There are also laws about credit and warranties. For instance, the Federal Warranty Law covers written and implied warranties. There are a number of laws about credit that the Federal Trade Commission enforces such as the Truth in Lending Act (TILA), Fair Credit Reporting Act (FCRA), and Fair Debt Collection Practices Act (FDCPA). Additionally, unfair trade practices, such as misrepresentation and fraud, are banned. Many states have enacted laws against these, and consumers can complain to the appropriate consumer protection agency.

AGENCIES RELATED TO CONSUMER PROTECTION

The Federal Trade Commission is a national agency that protects consumers by taking complaints about unfair practices and stopping forbidden acts such as anticompetitive mergers. There are a wide variety of state, regional, and local agencies that provide the same services on a more local basis. These are often in the attorney general's office. They accept complaints, investigate claims, and take action as necessary. Another agency that provides consumer services is the **Better Business Bureau (BBB)**. The BBB keeps records on companies and list complaints. When people make a complaint, the BBB will contact the company and try to get it resolved. Businesses that have a good record with the BBB can use it to their advantage. Many consumers look up companies on the BBB website before doing business, thus many companies strive to keep good records. Sometimes consumers have a choice of several agencies from which to choose when making complaints.

PRODUCT TESTING AND SAFETY

LAWS

The Consumer Product Safety Act (1972) and the subsequent Consumer Product Safety Improvement Act address safety in toys, chemicals in products, and more. The government tests products, makes safety standards, and bans products it deems unsafe. There are numerous product labeling laws as well. The Fair Packaging and Labeling Act (FPLA) requires commodity producers to label the name of the product, the identity and source of the manufacturer, the distributor or packer, and the net quantity. It strives to help consumers understand what they are getting. There are laws that specifically regard food standards, like federal grading of meat products. As a result of the Federal Food, Drug, and Cosmetic Act, the US Food and Drug Administration (FDA) requires testing on drugs to ensure their safety and efficacy. They also monitor food and food additives for safety. Many agencies and laws help ensure product safety.

FEDERAL AGENCIES

Part of the US Department of Health and Human Services, the Food and Drug Administration plays a large part in protecting consumers by overseeing the safety of food, drugs, and medical devices. They require extensive testing on drugs to ensure both efficacy and safety. They regulate food and labeling and give guidelines for the conditions in which food is prepared. They inform the public on related issues. The US Department of Agriculture (USDA) creates and executes policies in the fields of agriculture, farming, food, and forestry. They help rural communities, assist with conservation efforts, make rules regarding food and nutrition, make rules and standards for products labeled organic, and play many other roles. They have had a large impact throughout the years.

GOVERNMENT AGENCIES AND LAWS CONCERNING ENVIRONMENTAL PROTECTION

The **Environmental Protection Agency (EPA)** strives to safeguard the environment. Its roles include reducing the environmental impact of business practices; providing information; creating regulations and national standards based on laws from Congress; giving grants to non-profit organizations, state environmental programs, and schools; and performing research into environmental concerns. The EPA was formed in 1970, and its main headquarters is in Washington, D.C. It has many programs based on specific issues such as fuel economy, air quality, and oil pollution, among others. There are a wide variety of laws to protect the environment in the United States such as the Clean Air Act, Clean Water Act, and Endangered Species Act. The EPA administers these and many more. Many of these also relate to business. The laws in other countries vary greatly, and many countries do not have the same environmental protections. Many international business agreements address these concerns.

Business Communication

GOALS OF BUSINESS CORRESPONDENCE

There are a number of goals commonly seen on business correspondence, and at times they overlap. One of the major goals of business correspondence is to give information. One employee may be providing information to another employee, or the company may be sharing business happenings to customers. Another common goal is to sell the company's goods and services. Many companies create advertisements, blogs, social media posts, and other promotional materials to convince consumers to purchase their offerings. Business correspondence may also be used to convince an audience of something. A person may send a letter to a client to convince him that his product is better. An employee may try to convince another employee to try a new policy. Business professionals often correspond as a response to a question. If a consumer emails a question, customer service will respond with the answer. Businesses will often send out confirmation emails. This may be in response to a purchase or a question. Another form of correspondence may be sent out if an adjustment needs to be made. Correspondence may be through paper, email, the Internet, or other methods.

COMMUNICATION MODALITIES

There are many different communication modalities used within a business, including emails, phone calls, and in-person meetings, each with its own uses. **Face-to-face communication** is very important in business, especially when delivering important or serious information. For instance, if there is a serious conflict with an employee, the supervisor is going to want to sit down and talk to him. If a business is going after a big client, a face-to-face meeting can show a lot of effort. Meetings can impart a lot of information to many people very quickly, engage people, and allow everyone to interact. **Email** is used very often for a wide variety of business matters because of its ease, speed, and convenience. This is often used in customer service because many customers prefer it. Also, it allows customers and customer service to interact even when the customer is not available during service business hours. The **telephone** is also commonly used, especially when it is a quick question that needs immediate attention. If there is a lot of back and forth required, a phone call can be quicker than an exchange of emails. Companies generally use many of these forms of communication.

Effective Communication Skills

Effective communication skills are important in business. First, it is important for people to practice active listening. This means perceiving everything about the communication by using all senses. Not only should a person listen, but they should also watch for body language and try to evaluate how the speaker feels. People want to feel like others are really listening to them and processing what they are saying. Eye contact is important. The person shouldn't interrupt or make it seem like he's making judgments. He should display interest. This can be done by nodding or making small comments. Nonverbal communication is also important. The person should appear engaged, relaxed, and open. He should not be fidgeting. He should use open body language. A person should be aware of what he says and how it comes across, choosing his words carefully. One can easily insult someone, even accidently. He should not argue, but try to work together to communicate effectively. In business, people should think logically and try to keep stress and emotion from influencing decisions. With practice, people can improve their communication skills.

Nonverbal Communication

Nonverbal communication can be just as important as verbal communication in business, thus it is important to know the best strategies to make it effective. First, eye contact is important because it shows that a person is interested, engaged, and actively listening. A person's facial expression can express a lot. When one smiles, she is showing friendliness, encouragement and/or satisfaction with the work. When one frowns or displays an angry face, she is showing displeasure. It is important to show the expression that matches the feelings a person wants to convey when communicating in business, because otherwise the recipient may get the wrong idea. Gestures can show a lot. Someone clenching his fists may show anger. Hand movements can also help convey information. A person's posture tells a lot. Someone who crosses her arms may show resistance. A business professional who is standing or sitting tall may show off confidence. If someone is fidgeting, he may show discomfort or nervousness, which is not good for business. Business professionals should evaluate their nonverbal communication to make sure it enhances what they want to portray.

Proper Etiquette in Personal and Business Communication

Individuals should always practice proper courtesy. Business professionals should ordinarily address each other in a formal way and conduct appropriate cultural moves such as shaking hands. It is important to practice cultural sensitivity and know the rules and traditions of the person being greeted. For instance, in some cultures people may bow, while in another they may hug. People should make every effort not to show any bias or stereotypes as this can be very insulting to business contacts. Sometimes a person can come across as insulting or rude if she is ignorant of cultural customs. It is important to study the culture before interaction to make sure this does not happen. Otherwise, business communication should be formal and free of insults. It should be professional and without errors as well.

Communication Types Commonly Seen in Business

Business letters are sent for a wide variety of reasons and can be very formal. These may contain confidential and important information. Memoranda, also known as memos, are a less formal method of communication and may be used for announcements, information dissemination, and directions. They may be sent to a lot of people at once and are generally short and to the point. Emails are now commonly used in business communications because of their ease of use and speed. These may be less formal than written out business letters, or they can be just as formal. Publicity materials, such as press releases, are used to publicize an event or garner support. Recruitment communications are used in the process of hiring employees. For instance, a classified ad may be made when the company is hiring. Companies also make a lot of advertisements to draw consumers. These may be flashy advertisements or more subdued forms of communication and may appear in places such as newspapers and magazines.

Terminology Commonly Used in Business Communication

A memorandum is a short, informal form of business communication used to disseminate information. When a company writes "Enclosures," it means there is/are one or more enclosures. In email, an attached file is known as an attachment. The return address is the address of the person sending the letter. The inside address, or letter mailing address, is the recipient's address. The salutation is the greeting used, very commonly "Dear." The body is the main content of the letter. The complementary close is the closing at the bottom of the letter. There may also be reference initials at the end of the letter, which refer to the person who actually typed it, if different than the writer. Knowing these terms can help an individual write a professional business letter.

Writing Business Letters

A business letter should follow conventional professional practices. It starts with the sender's address (but not the name). Sometimes the address will be on the letterhead; otherwise it should be the first part. Next should be the date the letter was finished, written as month, day, and year. It should be two inches below the top and flush left (although some formats allow it to go in the center). Underneath that will be the inside address, or the recipient's address, including the specific name and title of the addressee, always left justified. The salutation is under that and should include the personal title unless it is someone usually referred to by the first name. The body is next. Block format is common and is single spaced and flushed left. There is a line between each paragraph. The content should be succinct, to the point, and logical. It might start with an opening and the main idea of the letter, followed with information supporting or explaining the main point. The final paragraph may reiterate the point and ask for action. Below that is the closing. If there are enclosures, this should be stated under that.

Business Memorandum Format

A business **memorandum** is a relatively informal form of communication used in businesses to spread information, give announcements, explain company happenings, and provide similar functions. It is often sent out to a lot of people at once and does not generally contain confidential information. At the top it should state "Memorandum." Underneath that, flush left will be the word "TO:" along with the addressee(s). Underneath that and still flush left will be "FROM:" with the sender's name. If there are any CCs, this will be under that. Below that will be "DATE:" with the date. "SUBJECT:" is under that. Finally, the body of the memo will be underneath that, written in block format. A properly formatted memo is professional and succinct.

Presentations

Goals

Presentations can have one or more goals, and it is important for presenters to be aware of the specific objectives so they can tailor the presentation for maximum efficacy. One major goal of presentations is to give information to the audience. It might be to employees, the stockholders, the public, or another group, but the company may be presenting information about itself, its products, current news, or more. Reporting data is another common goal of presentations. For instance, a company may be reporting sales numbers to its stockholders. Sometimes presentations are made to convince an audience of something. For example, a company may give a presentation to a potential client in an effort to broker a deal. Inspiring is another common goal. This is often done in employee meetings. For instance, a company may have a meeting to motivate its employees to work harder to reach certain goals. It is vital for the presentation to match its goals and audience for the best chance of success.

Features of Successful Presentations

Presentations play a big part in business, so it is important to know the features of successful ones. First, the audience should be able to understand the presentation. It needs to be tailored to the audience so they can relate to it. It should be concise. The presenter should not carry on too long about the same thing because he or she could lose the audience. A good opening hook is important. It engages the audience from the start. Some people start with a story or quote. The presentation should also look good visually. Visual aids that can enhance a business presentation include graphs, charts, photographs, and videos. If the presentation contains a call to action, then it should be strong. The audience should be moved to do it. The presenter should be skilled. He should speak loud enough that everyone can hear, keep eye contact, and engage in good body language. He should appear confident. The presentation should flow well and keep the audience's attention. Many business presentations are participative because this can keep people's interest. All of these measures go a long way in making a business presentation successful.

Characteristics of Various Audiences

It is important for presenters to understand the characteristics of the audience for a business presentation because that can greatly influence the best presentation. The size of an audience matters. The presentation will be different for a small room of 10 people compared to a large audience of 500. The cultural composition will matter. People of different cultures have different beliefs and may perceive a presentation differently. The other personal characteristics of the group, such as age, gender, and religion, can also affect how presentations are viewed. The level of knowledge matters. A health presentation on the same subject will be very different if given to a group of doctors as compared to a group of patients. Presenters should evaluate the audience to formulate the best presentation.

Preparation Steps

First, the presenter must understand his or her goals. What does he want to accomplish with the presentation? Once he knows this, he can select the exact topic, narrowing it down to fit the size and timing of the presentation. He will then need to evaluate the audience. The presentation of the same subject will be very different if given to customers as compared to employees or stockholders. The audience should be able to understand the topic, terminology, and references. The presenter should understand what is important to the audience and what they are thinking. Next, he should come up with the main points he wants to cover and make sure they are well illustrated in the presentation. He should find material to support these points such as graphs, charts, tables, photographs, data, and other visual items. This can give the presentation more substance and validity. Finally, the presenter should practice, ideally in front of someone who can evaluate the performance. By taking the time to carefully perfect the presentation, he will be more likely to reach his goals.

Adjusting Based on Needs and Concerns of Audience

To make the most impact, a presenter should adjust his presentation based on the needs and concerns of the audience. First, he or she needs to understand the audience and how they will likely feel about the presentation. He or she should do as much research as possible into the characteristics of the audience, including whether they will accept the presentation with acceptance or hostility and should plan to address their concerns. For instance, if he or she thinks the audience might be potentially hostile, the presenter should right away include things that will help to alleviate their concerns or ease the news to them. He or she should explain things so that they understand and will hopefully accept the content. It is important for the presenter to show empathy to the audience so they feel like the presenter is on their side. Oftentimes, the presenter allows the audience to ask questions and participate so that he or she can address their concerns directly. If they are worried about something that will not happen, then the presenter should be reassuring, personable, and friendly. The more the presenter comes off as a caring and competent individual, the better the presentation will proceed.

Delivery Strategies

Different strategies can make presentation delivery more effective. One decision is whether to use an extemporaneous (unscripted) speech or a scripted one. If the person is knowledgeable enough and wants to engage the audience without looking at a paper or prompter, he or she might choose the unscripted version. If he thinks he would be too nervous or forgetful without it, he might choose to use a script. Anyone might need it for a very technical speech with a lot of statistics. No matter what, it is important for the presenter to display only positive body language. He should make eye contact with members of the audience and not just look down. He should use positive gestures, facial expressions, and enthusiasm. He should watch his words to make sure nothing can be interpreted as biased or inappropriate. It is important for the presenter to be aware of the audience at all times and respond as necessary. If he senses that they do not understand something, for instance, he should go into more detail. If they are upset about something, he should try to address their concerns. With the right strategies, the presentation has a greater chance of success.

Visual Aids

Visual aids can enhance a business presentation. Graphs and charts can give a visual representation of the subject. For instance, if a person is talking about how sales numbers have changed, a line graph can make this very clear by showing how sales have changed over time or in response to certain variables. Diagrams can give a visual explanation of a concept. They can make a technical subject easier to understand. For instance, if someone is explaining a new product to investors, a diagram can help explain how it works. Slideshows are commonly used in business presentations. They can reinforce what the presenter is saying and draw interest. If a company is talking about its charity work, a picture of a smiling child the company helped would be more compelling than just talking about it. Videos can also show people a great deal. For instance, a company can make a video showing its factories or a new design. Computer projections are used as well. Most presentations use one or more visual aids.

Whiteboards, Presentation Software, and Multimedia Equipment

Whiteboards are often used in presentations. These are dry erase boards that the presenter can write on as he is speaking. This is also useful for a participative presentation in which the presenter asks the audience a question and writes down the answers as they are given. He can show step-by-step how something is done. Presentation software is also very commonly used. PowerPoint is one of the most commonly used presentation software programs and allows presenters to create detailed slides of photographs, charts, graphs, and more to enhance the presentation. They can make it easier to understand numbers and statistics. There are also various types of multimedia equipment a presenter might use. They might use a projector or a television. All of these can catch the audience's attention and bring the presentation to life.

Telecommunication Modalities Used in Business

The telephone is one form of telecommunication modalities. Individuals can get immediate access to someone to ask a question or have a discussion. A disadvantage is that there is no record of it (unless the call is recorded) and someone may not be available for a phone call. Another common form is a fax machine. This allows someone else to see a document. It is almost immediate. Both locations must have faxing ability, and it creates a physical document instead of a digital record, which many businesses prefer. Videoconferencing is commonly used. Individuals can discuss matters in real time. They can also share charts, graphs, and other visual aids. It has lowered the need for many business trips. Network email is also commonly used in business. It is delivered almost immediately and leaves a record. It can take longer to explain something than a simple phone conversation, however. An advantage is that it can be less intrusive and sometimes quicker.

Internet Modalities Used in Business

Email can be used to communicate with other businesses and with customers. Many customers prefer to email a company and it can be less time consuming for the company than a phone call. People like the convenience of being able to do it at any time. Message boards are also used. This is advantageous because customers can look up threads with topics similar to their issues and might get the answer to the problem without needing to contact customer service themselves. Mailing lists allow businesses to send out emails to many people at once. It is a great way for a company to disseminate information. Many companies also have instant messaging, both between its employees and for customers. This can be a great way to give customer service because customers like getting answers right away. One employee can be on several chats at once, which lowers the number of employees needed as compared to phone support. Chat rooms are also convenient because multiple people can see the answers. Many businesses use a combination of these.

Communication Technologies Used in Business

Many businesses have switched to solely wireless technology use, such as tablets and phones that use wireless internet. Cell phones are advantageous because people can take them while they're on the go and be reachable even when not sitting at a desk in the office. Of course, they do not always get service everywhere. Fax machines are used to communicate a document over long distances. They are almost instantaneous, inexpensive, and create a hard copy. Bluetooth is a wireless technology that provides convenience by letting data travel over short distances. It has lowered the need for wires. Streaming technology has allowed multimedia to be constantly delivered and received from one party to another. For instance, a person can watch a live newscast on a phone. Voice over Internet Protocol (VoIP) allows voice and multimedia to go over the Internet and other Internet Protocol Networks (IP). An example is Skype. It is advantageous for businesses because it is inexpensive and offers high bandwidth efficiency. Because voice and data communications can use one network, infrastructure costs are lower. In addition, it can be run on inexpensive standard interfaces like personal computers. It can be less reliable, however.

Etiquette in Electronic Communications

It is important to use professionalism in electronic communications, especially if it is a business letter. Just because a message is sent via email does not mean it should be sloppy. Of course, how professional it is will depend on the recipient, but if it is to a professional contact, it should be formed professionally. The sender should make a proper introduction and closing and avoid emoticons, writing in all capitals, and using excessive exclamation marks. It is very important to make sure it is free of typos and grammatical errors. Senders should proofread it just as they would proofread a regular letter. It is also important to not bombard people with unnecessary emails. Senders should be careful about including someone in a chain of unnecessary emails. They should make use of BCC and not share people's addresses with others. They should write an appropriate subject line so people know what it is. Senders should be careful about confidential information because users can easily forward them. By following these rules, the email will be more professional.

Anthropology, Sociology, and Psychology

Importance of Socialization to Individuals within a Specific Culture

Individuals learn how to function within a specific culture, group, or society via a process called **socialization**. Social contact with other human beings is vitally important to early development so that children can grow up to function in society as expected.

During the early years, children receive socialization from their families, siblings, peers, and schoolmates, as well as from exposure to mass media when applicable. Observing the behavior of others and adapting it to their own use helps children learn to interact with others. This process continues throughout life as individuals learn to adapt to various situations and interact with new groups.

Processes Bringing About Cultural Change and Traits that Appear in all Cultures

Three major processes bring about the majority of changes in a culture:

1. **Discovery**—finding things that already exist, such as fire, a major cultural transformer
2. **Invention**—creating new equipment, machinery, etc., that changes the way tasks are accomplished
3. **Diffusion**—borrowing elements from other cultures

Over 70 **traits** have been identified that are found in nearly every culture to some level. These traits can be divided into four categories that determine the basic structure, mores, norms, and other characteristics of a culture:

- Language and cognition
- Society
- Myth, ritual, and aesthetics
- Technology

CULTURE

Culture refers to all learned human behaviors and behavioral patterns and is made up of:

- **Cultural universals**—traits shared by all human beings, such as language
- **Culture**—all traditions that define a society
- **Subculture**—groups within a culture that share specific traits

While culture serves as a survival mechanism by bringing people together in groups and helping individuals identify with each other, it also undergoes frequent and sometimes profound **change** as groups respond to new technologies, knowledge, or contact with other cultures.

CHARACTERISTICS AND IMPORTANCE OF RELIGION IN AN ANTHROPOLOGICAL SENSE

Strictly defined, **religion** consists of a belief system and usually a set of rituals involving worship of a supernatural force or forces that have some effect on both everyday life and the overall structure and functioning of the world around us. Religion provides meaning and explanation for various life events and profoundly affects a culture's **worldviews**. Religion provides emotional support for individuals and a sense of **community** within a group that has shared religious views. Religious organization also provides structured sets of **moral norms** and motivation to abide by these norms and rules.

Increased **secularization**, particularly in developed countries, has reduced the role of religion in everyday life, leading individuals to find other systems to fill these basic human needs.

BEHAVIORISM

John B. Watson, an American, developed the idea of **behaviorism**. In his theory, growth, learning, and training would always win out over any possible inborn tendencies. He believed that any person, regardless of origin, could learn to perform any type of art, craft, or enterprise with sufficient training and experience.

SCIENCE OF SOCIOLOGY

Sociology is a scientific discipline that focuses on the study of societies. Human societies are made up of institutions, groups, and individuals. How all these levels of organization **interact** is the major interest of sociologists. The way individuals organize themselves, how they interact with each other, and the attitudes and beliefs different groups develop all define those groups' cultural backgrounds. Groups of people in the same geographical area often develop similar organizational structures, beliefs, and attitudes.

MAJOR STUDY AREAS COVERED BY SOCIOLOGY

The five major study areas covered by sociology are:

1. **Population studies**—these studies involve observing social patterns of groups of people who live in the same area.
2. **Social behaviors**—sociologists study how general behaviors change over time, as well as attitudes such as morale, need for conformity, and other elements of social interaction.
3. **Cultural influences**—the influences of culture on social groups include art, religion, language, and overall knowledge and learning.
4. **Social change**—this involves the ways societies change over time, including major events such as wars and revolutions, or the way technology changes how people interact.
5. **Social institutions**—large groups of people are organized to fit specific niches in society, such as churches, hospitals, government, businesses, and schools. These organizations change over time and according to the overall needs and beliefs of an individual society.

How Sociologists Gather and Test Data

The three major methods of gathering data for sociological studies are:

1. **Surveys**—gathering information via direct questioning of members of the social group being studied
2. **Controlled experiments**—performing experiments that change an element of society
3. **Field observations**—living among members of a particular group or culture and observing how they interact and live their everyday lives

Major Classifications of Social Groups

Social groups are defined based on how they come into being, how they develop, and how they interact with wider society. The five major classifications are:

1. **Primary groups**—focused on members' need for support, such as a family or friend grouping
2. **Secondary groups**—form around the need to complete a task
3. **Reference groups**—help form an individual's identity
4. **In-groups and out-groups**—oppose each other or exclude members of other groups
5. **Social networks**—provide multiple links to an often large number of other individuals

Major Types of Social Interaction

Five main forms of social interaction help define social groups:

1. Cooperation
2. Coercion
3. Conflict
4. Conformity
5. Social exchange

All of these elements can bring a group into existence, break it apart, or transform it.

Major Social Institutions that Characterize and Meet the Needs of Any Society

Six major social institutions that characterize and meet the needs of any society are:

1. **Family**—this is the basic unit of any society and the most important social institution in all sociological study.
2. **Education**—in many societies, the values and norms of culture are communicated through institutionalized education as well as via the family.
3. **Political institutions**—political institutions in a society determine the distribution of power.
4. **Economic institutions**—these institutions determine the distribution of wealth.
5. **Religion**—this provides mores and beliefs that help unify a culture. Unfortunately, many religions also function in an in-group/out-group capacity.
6. **Sport**—this reflects values of society, promotes unity, and provides an outlet for aggression.

Various Patterns Used by Sociologists to Define Relationships Involving Race and Ethnicity

In general, relationships within cultures involving race and ethnicity are defined by either assimilation or conflict. **Assimilation** in the US can involve:

- **Anglo-conformity**—immigrants and racial minorities conform to the expectations of Anglo-American society, whether by choice, necessity, or force.
- **Cultural pluralism**—this involves the acceptance of varieties of racial and ethnic groups.
- **Accommodation**—this is mutual adaptation between majority and minority groups.
- **Melting pot**—the mixing together of various ethnic groups will bring about a new cultural group.

Patterns of **conflict** include:

- **Population transfer**—one group is required or forced to leave by another group.
- **Subjugation**—one group exercises control over the other.
- **Genocide**—one group slaughters another.

Ways Gender and Age Lead to Discrimination

In spite of legislation, education, and other attempts to bring about a higher level of equality, **discrimination** still exists against women and the elderly, particularly as it involves law, politics, and economic standing. Discrimination against **women** is particularly profound in most developing countries. It is believed that increasing the standing of women in a society is a major element in increasing the overall livelihood of that society.

While some societies value the **elderly** for their knowledge and experience, others discriminate against older people because of their decreased physical ability and ability to contribute economically. In the US, the poverty level for the elderly still stands at about ten percent. As lifespan increases, all societies must find a way to accommodate the needs of the elderly population.

Importance of Auguste Comte

Auguste Comte, a French philosopher, first used the term *sociology* to describe the study of human organizations and culture. His major theory was **positivism**. Positivism relies entirely on physical and sensory data to describe and evaluate human experience, completely discounting anything metaphysical. **Social behavior**, according to Comte, could be measured scientifically, as could major events that occurred in different populations. Comte is considered to be the first sociologist in the Western world.

Influence of Émile Durkheim on Sociology and Sociological Study

Through Durkheim's efforts, sociology eventually came to be considered a discipline in major universities. Heavily influenced by Comte's views of positivism, Durkheim felt the larger world was influenced by group beliefs, attitudes, and cultural aspects rather than by individuals. He performed in-depth studies on the cause of higher suicide rates among certain social groups. In the course of this study, he discussed **anomie**, a condition when people are affected by larger changes in society, such as unemployment or alienation of social groups, and receive little moral guidance from society.

Philosophy of Karl Marx and Friedrich Engels

According to Marx and Engels, society worldwide could be boiled down to a constant struggle between **classes**. This socioeconomic battle, as explained in *The Communist Manifesto*, would eventually lead to a revolution by the working class, since work itself is a social organization that involves large groups of people.

Herbert Spencer

Herbert Spencer is credited with the idea known as **Social Darwinism**. Though he and Darwin were technically rivals, Spencer applied Darwin's idea of "**survival of the fittest**" (a term actually coined by Spencer) to the way society develops. According to Spencer, **competition** is the major driving force behind the development and changes inherent in human society.

Max Weber

Weber's major thesis stated that the differing **religions** of the East and West led to differences in societal development. Weber believed **Protestantism** as a religion influenced the development of **capitalism** in the West. He also stated that the organization of the state felt **violence** was a legitimate means of protecting citizenry or enforcing rule. Police action, military action, and violence of individuals against each other in order to protect themselves or property demonstrate the state's propensity to solve problems through violence.

Science of Anthropology

While archaeology studies the physical remains of populations, **anthropology,** in contrast, is the study of human culture, its development, and how various cultural groups are similar or different. Anthropologists often engage in direct study of cultures by living among them, observing and participating in everyday activities. This is referred to as "**participant observation**." Anthropologists also perform cross-cultural and comparative research.

Anthropology can be divided into four major areas of study. Each one addresses a slightly different approach to culture and how it affects human beings, as well as how culture develops over time:

- **Archaeology**—this is the study of materials and physical items left behind by human settlements
- **Social-cultural anthropology**—focuses on cultural standards, beliefs, values, and norms
- **Biological anthropology**—this is the study of specific genetic characteristics of different populations
- **Linguistics**— this is the study of the development of languages over time

Subsistence Patterns and Its Major Classifications

The term *subsistence pattern* refers to ways in which societies obtain the necessities of life, such as food and shelter. The **subsistence pattern** of a society often directly correlates to its economy, population size, political systems, and overall technological development. Certain subsistence patterns can only support lower levels of societal development, while others can support a much more developed culture. The four major subsistence patterns are:

1. **Foraging**—the hunter-gatherer lifestyle
2. Pastoralism—herding
3. **Horticulture**—small-scale farming
4. Intensive agriculture—large-scale farming

Hunter-gatherer societies by nature are nomadic and do not tend to support highly developed cultures. Intensive agriculture, in contrast, can support a large population to a high subsistence level, allowing for the development of a sophisticated, modern culture.

Margaret Mead

Margaret Mead studied sexual beliefs and norms among **South Pacific** and **Southeast Asian** cultures. She acquired a PhD from Columbia University, and her work popularized sociology. She also studied how children were treated and brought up in different cultures and how breastfeeding was viewed in different population groups. Among other works, she wrote a book called *Coming of Age in Samoa* about the culture of these Pacific Islanders.

Mary and Louis Leakey and Discoveries at Olduvai Gorge

The Leakeys made major discoveries regarding the **origin of the human species** during their excavations in Olduvai Gorge in Tanzania, Africa, excavating wide varieties of stone tools and other artifacts dating back as far as two million years. Mary Leakey discovered footprints belonging to early humans at **Laetoli**, a palaeontological site in Tanzania, and developed a system to classify early human tools. The Leakeys also discovered prehistoric remains of humans, including early humans dating to nearly four million years ago, fifteen new species, and one new genus of early human ancestors. They also discovered the first fossil ape skull, and only three similar specimens exist to this day. Their findings fundamentally changed theories regarding the development and evolution of ancient humans.

Psychology

Psychology is the study of **human behavior** and how the **mind** works. Some psychologists pursue scientific psychology, while others focus on applied psychology. Psychologists correlate human behavior and can make use of this data to predict behavior or determine why a particular behavior has occurred. Psychologists also help work with people who have specific problems with relationships or with how they perceive the world. By observing patterns and recording them in detail, psychologists can apply these patterns to predictions about human behavior in individuals, groups, cultures, and even countries.

Techniques Used by Psychologists in Research

Psychological researchers study their discipline in various ways. Based on what they are studying, they generally use one of the following methods:

- **Naturalistic observation**—much as with sociological study, psychologists observe people and their natural behavior without interfering.
- **Survey method**—surveys are distributed among a wide range of people, and the answers are correlated.
- **Case studies**—specific individuals or groups are studied in depth over a period of time, sometimes for many years.
- **Experimental method**—this involves experimental and control groups and the use of specific experiments to prove or disprove a theory.
- **Correlational design**—this is concerned with relationships between variables, such as whether one factor causes or influences another.

Importance of Aristotle to the Science of Psychology

Aristotle is often cited as founding the science of **psychology** through his overall interest in the working of the human mind. His beliefs stated that the mind was part of the body, while the psyche functioned as a receiver of knowledge. He felt psychology's major focus was to uncover the soul. Later philosophers and scientists built on these ideas to eventually develop the modern science of psychology.

Nativism

Nativism is a theory that states that there is a certain **body of knowledge** all people are born with. This knowledge requires no learning or experience on the part of the individual. **René Descartes**, a French philosopher, developed this concept. He believed the body and mind affected each other profoundly, largely because they are separate from each other. The physical site of this interaction took place in the **pineal gland** (a small gland in the brain), according to his theory. Descartes developed several theories in the fields of philosophy and psychology that are still studied in modern universities.

Empiricism

Empiricism is in direct opposition to Descartes' theory of nativism, theorizing that all knowledge is acquired through **life experience**, impressing itself on a mind and brain that are **blank** at the time of birth. Major proponents of empiricism were Thomas Hobbes, John Locke, David Hume, and George Berkeley.

Johannes P. Müller, Hermann L. F. von Helmholtz, William James, and Wilhelm Wundt

Johannes P. Müller and Hermann L. F. von Helmholtz conducted scientific, organized studies of sensation and perception. As the first psychologists to attempt this kind of study, they showed that it was possible to study actual physical processes that work to produce mental activity.

William James was the founder of the world's first psychology laboratory. **Wilhelm Wundt**, a student of Helmholtz, published the first experimental psychology journal and is known as the father of modern psychology. Together, James and Wundt helped bring psychology into its own, separating it from philosophy. The method of psychological study called introspection grew out of their work.

Sigmund Freud

An Austrian doctor, Freud developed a number of theories regarding human mental processes and behavior. He believed the **subconscious** to hold numerous repressed experiences and feelings that drive behavior without the individual's awareness, and that these subconscious motivators could lead to severe personality problems and disorders. He particularly stressed sexual desire as a motivating force. Freud developed the method of **psychoanalysis** to help discover the hidden impulses driving individual behavior. Freud's psychoanalytic theory proposed three major components to an individual's psychological makeup:

- **Id**—driven by instinct and basic drives
- **Ego**—most conscious and producing self-awareness
- **Superego**—strives for perfection and appropriate behavior

The **ego** acts as mediator between the **id** and **superego**, which function in opposition to each other.

Review Video: Sigmund Freud
Visit mometrix.com/academy and enter code: 473747

Carl Jung

A student of Freud, Jung eventually developed different theories regarding the workings of the human mind. With an intense interest in both Eastern and Western philosophy, he incorporated ideas from both into his psychological explorations. He developed the theories of **extroversion** and **introversion**, as well as proposing the existence of the **collective unconscious** and the occurrence of **synchronicity**.

Ivan Pavlov and B. F. Skinner

Ivan Pavlov and B. F. Skinner both built on Watson's theories of behaviorism. This work came about largely as a counter to the growing importance of introspective techniques to psychological study. Believing **environment** strongly influenced individual behavior, Pavlov and Skinner searched for connections between outside stimuli and behavioral patterns. Pavlov's experiments proved the existence of **conditioned response**. His most famous experiment conditioned dogs to salivate at the sound of a ringing bell. Skinner went on to build further on these ideas, developing the "Skinner box," a device used to develop and study conditioned response in rats.

Gestalt Psychology, Social Psychology, and Modern Psychology

Gestalt psychology is a theory developed by **Max Wertheimer**. In **Gestalt theory**, events are not considered individually but as part of a larger pattern. **Social psychology** is the study of how social conditions affect individuals. **Modern psychology**, as it has developed, combines earlier schools of psychology, including Freudian, Jungian, behaviorism, cognitive, humanistic, and stimulus-response theories.

Divisions of the Human Lifespan

Developmental psychologists divide the human lifespan into stages and list certain developmental milestones that generally take place during these stages:

- **Infancy and childhood**—this is the most rapid period of human development, during which the child learns to experience its world, relate to other people, and perform tasks necessary to function in its native culture. Debate exists as to which characteristics are inborn and which are learned.
- **Adolescence**—this period represents the shift from child to adult. Changes are rapid and can involve major physical and emotional shifts.
- **Adulthood**—individuals take on new responsibilities, become self-sufficient, and often form their own families and other social networks.
- **Old age**—priorities shift again as children become adults and no longer require support and supervision.

Types of Learning

Psychologists define learning as a **permanent change in behavior**. Learning is divided into three basic categories, based on how the behavioral change is acquired:

- **Classical conditioning**—this is a learning process in which a specific stimulus is associated with a specific response over time.
- **Operant conditioning**—this is a learning process in which behavior is punished or rewarded, leading to a desired long-term behavior.
- **Social learning**—this refers to learning based on observation of others and modeling others' behavior.

These three learning processes work together to produce the wide variety of human behavior.

Factors Involved in Social Psychology and Effects on Various Groups of People

Social psychology studies how people **interact** as well as why and how they decide whom to interact with. The ways people react with each other are defined in several ways, including:

- **Social perception**—this describes how we perceive others and their behavior as we make judgments based on our own experiences and prejudices.
- **Personal relationships**—close relationships develop among people for various reasons, including the desire to reproduce and form a family unit.
- **Group behavior**—people gather into groups with similar beliefs, needs, or other characteristics. Sometimes group behavior differs greatly from behavior that would be practiced by individuals.
- **Attitudes**—individual attitudes toward others develop over time based on individual history, experience, knowledge, and other factors. Attitudes can change over time, but some are deeply ingrained and can lead to prejudice.

Chapter Quiz

Ready to see how well you retained what you just read? Scan the QR code to go directly to the chapter quiz interface for this study guide. If you're using a computer, simply visit the bonus page at **mometrix.com/bonus948/fsot** and click the Chapter Quizzes link.

Communications

Public Speaking

Speech communication instructors often refer to public speaking as a "transaction" to indicate the important active roles of both the speaker and audience. Too often, people consider speech-giving as a process in which one person actively provides information while another group of people passively receives information. Instead, the ideal public speaking relationship is one in which the speaker presents a message and the audience presents feedback. Even when the audience is not given an opportunity to speak, they provide feedback in the form of attention or inattention. By referring to public speaking as a transaction, instructors emphasize the roles and responsibilities of both speaker and audience. In general, speech communication instructors would define a **transaction** as any communication in which information passes from speaker to listener and vice versa.

Purpose of Studying Public Speaking

There are a number of reasons for studying public speaking, but the most commonly cited are social, intellectual, and consumer motives. People need to learn to speak in public in order to function in society and to manage relationships, administrate social events, and minimize conflict. Intellectually, a study of public speaking gives insight into human thought, ethics, and persuasion. Public speeches can generate emotions and ideas in listeners as well as influence their existing thoughts and feelings. It is also important to study public speaking not only to improve one's own speaking skills, but to improve one's ability to analyze and interpret the speeches of others. Students need to be able to understand the forum of public expression, the rhetorical vocabulary, and the various methods of thinking critically about speech.

Basic Methods for Studying Public Speaking

An effective speech communication teacher will incorporate different pedagogical modalities into his or her instruction so that students receive exposure to a wide range of different methods. Students should practice giving different kinds of speeches in both formal and informal settings. Some of the different types of speeches include technical lectures, extemporaneous speeches, and entertaining monologues. Students should get some practice interpreting and analyzing different kinds of public speech, such as advertisements, political speeches, public service announcements, editorials, or other forms. It is also valuable for students to become familiar with acclaimed historical speeches.

Goals of Public Speaking

For most people, the obvious goals of public speaking are political victories and support for social movements. Both are common motives of public speech, but they are not the only recognized intention of public communication. Public speech is often used to define an individual or a community. For instance, people may use speeches to describe particular attributes of themselves or of the group to which they belong. People also use speeches simply to disseminate information. Speeches can be used to inspire other people to action. Famous addresses like the "I Have a Dream" speech of Martin Luther King, Jr. exemplify this kind of speech. Finally, public speaking can be used to introduce arguments and to debate controversial questions in a community. The presidential debates before the general election are a good example of this.

Speeches

Purpose of an Informative Speech

When one is delivering an **informative speech**, his or her primary goal is to instruct the audience on a particular subject. If the speech is effective, the audience members will leave with more knowledge and understanding. College lectures are great examples of informative speeches. Although informative speeches may be entertaining, the humor or "color" of the speech should not distract from the overall intention, which is to disseminate information. Informative speeches often contain specific statistical data and an organized set of arguments and supporting evidence. Many informative speeches contain mention of counter-arguments, including rebuttals.

Impromptu Speech

An impromptu speech is one delivered "off-the-cuff"; that is, one delivered with a minimum amount of preparation and in an informal style. Not everyone is capable of delivering an effective impromptu speech. Most people can give a successful **impromptu speech** only if the topic is one on which they have discoursed before or if they are extremely familiar with their topic. Of course, we all make impromptu speeches as a matter of course in our daily lives. Every time you are asked to give your opinion on a subject or to explain an idea, you are in effect making an impromptu speech. By studying speech communication, however, people can learn the elements of effective impromptu speeches and improve their ability to deliver them.

Extemporaneous Speech

An extemporaneous speech combines elements of preparation and improvisation. When one is delivering an **extemporaneous speech**, he or she is drawing on prepared research but not reading directly from a sheet of paper nor reciting the speech from memory. An extemporaneous speech is more conversational and informal than a written speech and is therefore more appropriate for casual gatherings. The colloquial and informal nature of an extemporaneous speech can be extremely helpful in cultivating a good rapport between speaker and audience. To deliver an effective extemporaneous speech, however, the speaker must be extremely familiar with his or her source material.

Eulogy

A **eulogy** is a speech that praises a particular individual and highlights his or her best qualities. Eulogies are often given at funerals as the speaker remembers the deceased in a positive light. Eulogies are not the appropriate form for criticism or objective analysis of a person's life. On the other hand, a eulogy may fail if the audience finds it so excessively laudatory that it is not believable. In some cases, a eulogy of sorts may be given in praise of a particular event, community, or culture. Typically, a eulogy is delivered to an audience that is already disposed to think favorably of the subject. The speaker is typically someone who has extensive personal experience with the subject of the eulogy.

Introductory Speech

It is common for a **speech of introduction** to precede a keynote speech, a presentation, or a public performance of some kind. For instance, a symphony director will often give a brief speech of introduction before a concert. The best introductory speeches do not simply list the achievements or characteristics of the person or event that is to follow. Rather, they engage the interest of the audience and whet their appetite for what is to come. A good speech of introduction should not include any criticism of what is to follow. It is always a good rule of thumb for the introductory speaker to confer with those who are to follow so that his or her message can be as appropriate as possible.

Welcoming Speech

A welcoming speech is often given at the beginning of a convention, meeting, or special event of some kind. Typically, the welcome will be delivered by a representative of the group or organization putting on the event. For instance, the chairman of a professional organization administering a business convention might deliver a speech of welcome to convention attendees. **Welcoming speeches** are typically light on substance and primarily provide an overview of the events to follow. Also, a welcoming speech typically includes a message of thanks to the organizers and administrators of the event. The speaker often indicates his or her personal goals for the event and may tell the audience how to make their questions and comments known to the event administrators.

Memorizing and Reading a Speech

When delivering a speech, the speaker may need to decide whether to memorize or read the text. There are advantages to each approach. When a speech is memorized, the speaker can make eye contact with the audience and use his or her hands to make illustrative gestures. Memorized speeches run the risk of sounding overly rehearsed, however, and the speaker may falter if he or she loses track of the speech. Some speakers prefer to read their speeches, often because they prefer to have a copy of the speech for reference. If the speaker plans to read his or her speech, he or she should become extremely familiar with the speech so it is not necessary to read every word from the paper. Regardless of whether a speech is memorized or read, the speaker should practice delivery to increase fluency.

Purpose of a Persuasive Speech

Persuasive speeches are designed to change the minds of the audience or motivate the audience to action. The precise goals of a persuasive speech are dependent on the particular cause promoted by the speaker. Moreover, the methods employed in a **persuasive speech** will depend on the subject matter and the speaker's rhetorical style. Some speakers employ a dry, data-driven style when making a persuasive speech. They hope to overwhelm their audience with the strength and breadth of information. Other speakers seek to beguile their audience by amusing and entertaining them. This kind of speech is appropriate for general audiences and non-technical subjects. When a persuasive speech is being delivered to an audience of experts, or is centered on a complex issue, it must include cogent reasoning and supportive data.

Purpose of an Entertaining Speech

The only goal of some speeches is to entertain and amuse the audience. Standup comedy is a type of **entertaining speech**. Many speeches that also contain information or persuasive content are primarily entertaining. The keynote speakers at conferences and conventions often cloak their arguments in witty anecdotes and jokes. Obviously, serious subjects are not appropriate content for entertaining speeches. However, many speakers will introduce some elements of an entertaining speech to first capture the attention of the audience and then persuade them to engage seriously with the weightier elements of the speech.

Importance of Having Specific Purposes for a Speech

The first step in preparing a speech is knowing the specific purpose of that speech. This enables the speaker to focus on what is important and to research efficiently for relevant material. The specific purpose of a speech might be informing the audience on a particular point, changing a few minds on a particular subject, raising some money, or simply entertaining the audience. It is a good idea to make the specific purpose of the speech explicit in the speech. Although you do not want to beat your audience over the head with your intentions, there should be no question as to what the speech is meant to accomplish. In general, the specific purpose of a speech is defined in terms of the desired reaction from the audience.

Elements of a Presentation

Over the last few years, the presentation has emerged as the most common speech form in the United States. Members of the business community frequently give presentations, but this form is also common to academic lectures, community discussions, and religious gatherings. One of the defining characteristics of a **presentation** is that it includes some form of media beyond simply a speaker. It is common for a speaker to include slide shows, photographs, brochures and handouts, short videos, and audio samples in a presentation. Because presentations are often designed to be given over and over again to different audiences, they may be complex, detailed, and highly coordinated.

Basic Presentation Aid

One of the defining characteristics of a presentation is the use of **presentation aids**. These aids can include supplementary audio or visual materials that elaborate or reinforce their presentation points. Currently, the most popular presentation aids are slide show presentations, a software program that allows speakers to assemble a collection of slides to accompany their speech. Speakers also frequently include video samples in their presentations. In business, tables and charts are frequently used to illustrate the points of a presentation. In the classroom, a teacher might use handouts or overhead projector transparencies as presentation aids. Basically, any media used by the speaker to supplement his or her spoken message is considered a presentation aid.

Increasing Importance of the Presentation in the United States

Most speech communication experts believe that presentations will increasingly become the most popular form of public communication. This is largely because the citizenry of the United States has been raised on television and radio commercials, and they are very familiar with multimedia presentations. For many people, a simple speech is boring. Presentation aids such as audio and video are often necessary to hold the interest of modern-day audiences. In the future, the most successful persuasive speakers will undoubtedly be those who can apply the traditional elements of direction and suggestion to a presentation containing enough multimedia to engage the interest of the audience.

Premise of Audience Analysis

In the study of speech communication, **audience analysis** is simply the practice of examining the characteristics and background of the audience in order to tailor a speech appropriately. For instance, one would want to know the general age, socioeconomic status, culture, and gender of the audience while preparing a speech. The type of speech appropriate to a group of elementary schoolgirls will be quite different from that appropriate to a group of older men, even if both speeches are on the same subject. The prejudices and pre-existing opinions of these two groups will be extremely different and thus, a speaker must tailor and deliver his or her message to each group in very different ways to be effective.

Primary Factors of Audience Analysis

When a seasoned public speaker conducts an audience analysis, he or she focuses on a few specific characteristics of the audience. For one thing, the speaker wants to know the audience's background as it relates to him or her and the subject matter of the speech. Although much of audience analysis consists of determining the approximate ages and socioeconomic backgrounds of the audience, this is primarily because such information enables the speaker to estimate the audience's opinions and degree of familiarity with the subject matter and speaker. A speaker who is well-liked by the audience can employ a different rhetorical strategy than one with whom most of the audience disagrees.

Importance of Remembering the Audience's Capacity to Act

When developing a speech, one should always remember the characteristics and capabilities of the audience. This is especially important when producing a persuasive speech. It does not make sense to encourage the audience to take an action they are not capable of taking. For instance, a politician would be foolish to make an impassioned plea for votes to a bunch of elementary school students, all of whom are years away from voter eligibility. When developing a persuasive speech, then, it is essential to remember the capacity of the audience to act.

Audience Attitude

It is important for a speaker to gauge the attitude of the audience before delivering his or her speech. **Attitude**, because it is more subtle than age, ethnicity, or belief system, can only be determined through direct observation. Thus, if a speaker is able to observe the audience before delivering the speech, he or she can benefit greatly. Observing the audience beforehand can provide clues to what kind of general mood the audience is in, whether good or bad. If the audience is in a hostile mood, the speaker may want to avoid trying to joke with them. An audience that seems jovial and engaged, on the other hand, should not be alienated with strident rhetoric or harsh words. The job of the speaker is to establish and maintain a good rapport with the audience.

Beliefs

To accurately assess what an audience might be thinking, one must understand that audience's core beliefs. Strictly defined, **beliefs** are the facts, ideas, and opinions that the audience holds to be true. Objectively, some of these beliefs may actually be untrue. However, to deliver an effective message, a speaker must take into account the sum total of the audience's beliefs. If the purpose of the speech is to adjust the beliefs of the audience, the speaker must appeal to either the reasoning skills or the emotions of his or her listeners.

Facts and Opinions

When considering the convictions of an audience, it is good to distinguish between facts and opinions. **Facts** are those convictions that can be proven in an objective sense. Scientific assertions, for instance, are considered facts. **Opinions**, on the other hand, cannot necessarily be supported by hard data. People often hold opinions for rather arbitrary individual reasons, such as those based on personal experience. The fact that communities hold collective opinions must also be considered when making a speech. In general, it is easier for a speaker to adjust beliefs or convictions based on opinion than those based on fact.

Fixed and Variable Beliefs

When describing the beliefs of an audience, speech communication instructors often distinguish between fixed and variable beliefs. The primary difference between the two is that **fixed beliefs** are harder to change. Typically, fixed beliefs have been held throughout an individual's life and most likely reinforced by his or her experience. **Variable beliefs**, on the other hand, may have been recently acquired and therefore may be less established in the individual's mind. A speaker is more likely to change variable beliefs and should therefore focus his or her attention on these. Variable beliefs are especially vulnerable to change when they are based on opinion rather than fact.

Fundamentals of Preparing a Speech

To successfully prepare a speech it is best to follow a basic set of established steps. By following these steps, the speaker or speechwriter can more efficiently develop an organized and effective presentation. The first step in preparing a speech is to select a subject, if the topic has not been predetermined. Next, the speaker should articulate to himself or herself the key ideas and arguments to be included in the speech. As he or she begins to formulate these ideas and arguments, it is important to take into account the characteristics of the intended audience. At this point, the speaker should begin gathering materials for the speech, whether through research or brainstorming. The next step is to outline the speech, and finally, write a draft of the speech. It is always a good idea to practice delivering the speech and to make revisions or adjustments where necessary.

Select a Subject for a Speech

Perhaps the most important component of an effective speech is an appropriate and interesting subject. When selecting a subject for a speech, one should look for a topic that is engaging to a general audience. While it is important for the speaker to have some familiarity with the subject, it is not necessarily a good idea to speak about a subject on which he or she is an expert. Too often, an expert delivering a speech to a general audience dwells too much in details and specificities, which has a tendency to bore the audience. It is a good idea for the speaker to have a passing familiarity with the subject, so that he or she will be able to find good research materials and judge what will be interesting to a general audience. However, the speaker should also make sure to emphasize the aspects of the subject that are relevant to the lives of the audience members.

Creativity Can Be Used to Select a Speech Topic

Sometimes it can be difficult to come up with a topic for a speech. All the "good topics" may seem to have already been covered, or there may be no one single subject on which a potential speaker has enough information to be effective. Effective speakers develop creative ways to come up with new speech topics. Being creative, however, does not mean sitting back and waiting for inspiration to strike. Creative speakers work proactively to develop new topics. They list their areas of interest and are constantly considering everything they see and read in terms of how it could be developed into a speech. Most creative speakers discard more ideas for speeches than they ever use.

Creative Analysis of a Speech Topic

After a speaker has decided upon a topic for a speech, the next move is to conduct a creative analysis of that topic—simply a detailed exploration of the topic. To begin with, the speaker assembles as much information as he or she can within the amount of time available. This may include interviews, books, and old periodicals. Experienced speakers will have a good working knowledge of the public or school library and will be able to acquire diverse basic materials in a short period of time. After all this information has been assembled, the speaker will sort through it, looking perhaps for an entry point for his exploration. An interesting narrative, a point of local interest, or a previously overlooked angle on the subject may all be ways for the speaker to engage the interest of the audience on a given subject.

Preparation Phase

During the **preparation phase** of speech composition, a speaker will begin to organize his or her research material. Once the speaker has decided upon the basic angle and structure of the speech, he or she may need to acquire more research materials for elaboration and support. Of course, it may take the speaker a while to find the appropriate flow of ideas. Speakers should not be discouraged by numerous blind alleys or false starts during the preparation phase. Even when it seems that progress is not being made, the speaker should remember that each false start eliminates a possible point of entry, bringing the ultimate goal closer.

Incubation Phase

During the **incubation phase** of creative speech analysis, the speaker actually does not engage in any direct work on the speech. Instead, the speaker allows his or her subconscious to mull over the content of the speech. Even though it seems like no work is being done during this period, the incubation phase is actually very important, as it is during this period that the most creative thinking on the subject occurs. Also, the incubation phase gives the speaker a chance to freely imagine the speech, associate various ideas, and try unique combinations. Many speakers say their most unique and powerful ideas often occur to them when they are doing something totally different than speech preparation.

Illumination Phase

After the incubation phase, the speaker should have a solid structure as well as a number of creative ideas for the speech. In the succeeding **illumination phase**, he or she will apply the ideas gained during the incubation phase to the basic outline constructed during the preparation phase. It is very common for a speaker to feel a burst of enthusiasm during the illumination phase, as he or she discovers the unique ways in which his or her original ideas will elaborate and improve upon the original structure. The illumination phase is still basically a brainstorming phase. Speakers are still experimenting with new ideas and combinations of materials.

Verification Phase

The fourth and final part of the creative analysis of a speech topic is the **verification phase**. During this phase, the speaker looks over his or her notes carefully. Occasionally, some of the ideas that seemed so brilliant during the incubation and illumination phases turn out to be inappropriate or implausible. Other times, a careful examination of the speech will uncover holes in the reasoning of the argument or reveal the necessity of adding or removing a particular part of the speech. The verification phase of creative speech analysis can be seen as a final polishing of the materials gathered and organized during the first three phases.

Necessity of Managing Creativity During the Development of a Speech

For the process of creative speech analysis to be effective, a certain amount of discipline needs to be brought to bear on the creative instinct. This is one reason why the process of creative speech analysis includes four distinct phases. By adhering to a set procedural pattern, the speaker will limit the amount of time spent in any one area and will move along toward completion at a predictable pace. Also, by following an organized analysis process, it is easier to avoid the procrastination that commonly occurs during the creative process. As much as possible, a speaker should try to work at specific times without interruption to allow the creative subconscious to do its work.

Basic Message Units in a Speech

In every speech, the content is divided into what are called **basic message units**. A basic message unit has two parts: the point the speaker is trying to make and the evidence or supporting material he or she has assembled. In order to be complete, a message unit needs to have both components. Otherwise, the speaker will be making points without offering any reasoning or evidence, or he will be giving factual information and argumentation without connecting the dots to make a larger point. The point stated by the speaker needs to be a complete and discrete thought. The supporting material must be pertinent and sufficient to convince a reasonable person.

Value of Making a Logical Analysis of a Speech Topic

A speaker should always perform what is known as a logical analysis before presenting his or her speech. This is simply an analysis of the message units that make up the speech, as well as the connections between these message units. To be effective, the logic of any speech must progress in a systematic and discernible manner and should include ample evidence and supporting materials. Speakers often create a brief outline for their speech, in which they sketch the basic structure of the speech's logic, leaving out the supplementary material. In any case, it is essential to make sure the logical skeleton of a speech is sturdy before focusing on other aspects.

Assess the Logic of a Speech Topic

As the speaker reviews his prepared speech and performs a logical analysis, he needs to be constantly asking himself whether each point and piece of supporting material is essential. Everything included in the speech should be there for a clear and explicit reason or else it must be considered superfluous. The speaker must also determine whether all of the evidence clearly and directly supports the points it is intended to support. Finally, the speaker must make sure every point in the speech follows a proper order, progressing logically to the speech's climax and ultimate conclusion.

Errors of Reasoning

Faulty Attribution of Causation

One of the most common errors of logic one can make in a speech is the **faulty attribution of causation**. This occurs when the speaker erroneously assumes that just because one thing followed another, the second thing was caused by the first. For instance, I may grab my umbrella on the way out the door before it starts raining, yet once it starts raining I cannot claim that bringing my umbrella caused the rain. If a speaker describes a major historical or social event and suggests such an event had only one cause, they are likely committing faulty attribution of causation. Major social and historical movements are simply too complex to be attributed to a single cause. At the very least, a speaker must provide detailed substantiation for any assertions of causation.

Circular Reasoning

A common logical error in speeches is **circular reasoning**. A chain of logic is described as circular when the assumptions made at the beginning of the argument depend on the conclusion of the argument being true. For instance, imagine a speaker declaring that the Tigers baseball team will certainly lose their playoff series. As evidence for this claim, the speaker declares that the Tigers always lose their playoff series. This reasoning clearly does not hold up. In order to believe the Tigers will lose their playoff series, we have to assume they always lose their playoff series, which we do not really know yet, and which depends on their performance in the upcoming playoffs series. In other words, the claims made by the speaker depend on the speaker's assumptions.

Contradictory Argument

Occasionally, a speaker will fall victim to the logical error known as the **contradictory argument**. A contradictory argument is one in which the speaker introduces information that directly contradicts his main argument. For the most part, this error should be easy to avoid. After all, a speaker will be careful not to include information that undermines his main point. Speakers do, however, sometimes include inconsistent arguments in a speech, and this can be highly detrimental to their purpose. Contradictory argument is especially problematic in a persuasive speech, in which the speaker is attempting to persuade the audience from their pre-existing opinions and hoping to sell them on the merits of an alternative view.

Use of Expository Supporting Material

Most speeches include expository supporting material. The word *expository* comes from the same root as *expose* and refers to information that sheds light on areas about which the audience may know little. Some of the common forms of expository information are examples, analogies, and narratives. **Expository supporting material** is distinguished from argumentative supporting material in that it strives to remain as objective as possible When a speaker claims to be providing objective and impartial information, he or she will be held to that standard by the audience. For this reason, it is especially important for speakers who use expository supporting material to verify their sources.

Use of Examples, Both Real and Hypothetical

Successful speakers are likely to use both real and hypothetical examples in the course of a speech. Real examples are appropriate in speeches describing a particular historical or social topic that is grounded in reality. For instance, it would not be appropriate to use a hypothetical example in an argument about the Revolutionary War since there are plenty of real examples to illustrate points regarding that conflict. In more general speeches, however, it may be necessary to use a hypothetical situation as an example. When describing the possible results of some decision, for instance, a speaker might invoke the case of some hypothetical person as a means of dramatizing his or her argument. In general, real examples are treated with more respect by an audience and should be used whenever possible.

How a Good Speaker uses Examples

A good speaker knows that examples can be effective because they provide concrete case studies through which the audience can assess the arguments of the speech. Examples are also good for humanizing an abstract speech. For instance, an audience may have a hard time listening to a speech about water conservation, but if the speaker introduces examples of how drought can affect individual people, they will be more likely to stay engaged. A good speaker includes examples that are appropriate and interesting, but which do not distract from his or her main points. Also, examples should not dominate a speech; they should simply add interest to the body of the speaker's message.

Analogies in a Speech

An effective speaker will often elaborate and clarify his or her ideas with analogies. An **analogy** is simply an extended comparison between two things. For instance, a speech on economics might describe a current downturn in the economy as it relates to the Great Depression. In other words, the speaker is drawing an analogy between a current problem and a known historical event. The important thing to remember about an analogy is that the two things being compared will probably not be identical in all respects. The speaker should take care to indicate this and should not make claims that suggest the analogy is perfect. On the other hand, an effective analogy can be a useful predictive tool and can give the audience a way of engaging with the subject.

Narratives in a Speech

Speakers often incorporate narratives into their speeches as a way of engaging interest and indirectly making a point. A **narrative** is simply a story. Narratives can be either fiction or nonfiction. As with examples, narratives tend to have more impact on an audience when they are true. However, an artfully told fictitious narrative can also captivate an audience. Recent scientific research suggests that audience members are mentally programmed to pay attention to information when it is presented as a story. That is, the human mind is naturally receptive to a narrative. Good speakers take advantage of this tendency by delivering information in the context of a narrative.

Statistics in a Speech

Speakers often use **statistics** to provide numerical evidence for their assertions. Basically, a loose definition of statistics is any information that contains numbers. To be effective, statistics must be clear and accurate. Statistics can have a great deal of sway over an audience, since they carry with them the impression of objectivity and mathematical truth. That being said, audience members should keep in mind that statistics are often highly subjective. For instance, by manipulating sample size, information taken into consideration, and scope of a statistical survey, a speaker can present information to support his point no matter how incorrect it is. Audience members should always be wary of statistics and should press the speaker to provide more information on the origin and methodology behind any statistics he or she uses.

Numbers in a Speech

There are a few different ways to use numbers in a speech. One way is to use numbers as markers of evaluation. When we say a person weighs 120 pounds, for instance, we are using numbers to evaluate their weight. In a similar way, numbers can be used as a basis for comparison. By comparing the prices of two dishwashers, for instance, we obtain an important piece of information we can use in making a consumer decision. Numbers can also be used to make illustrative points. For instance, speakers often cite various statistics in support of an argument. It is important to emphasize that, although numbers suggest impartiality, they are calculated by human beings, who are highly subjective and whose intentions should be rigorously questioned.

Eyewitness Testimony in a Speech

Many speakers incorporate eyewitness testimony into their speeches to great effect. Of course, this kind of supporting material is only appropriate for certain kinds of speeches. For instance, when delivering a speech about the Battle of the Bulge, it might be very useful to quote some soldiers who fought in the battle. On the other hand, eyewitness testimony seems less appropriate to a speech about climate change, which is so widespread that no one person could view its entire effect globally. When using **eyewitness testimony**, it is important to establish the credentials of the person being quoted. Also, a speaker should take care to indicate the particular vantage point of the eyewitness, so the audience can consider his or her testimony in light of that point of view.

Expert Testimony in a Speech

Whenever possible, speakers attempt to incorporate **expert testimony** into their speeches. Any time a speaker can quote a well-known authority who agrees with his or her point of view, he or she will be eager to do so. Most members of an audience will probably feel relatively uninformed compared to the speaker and will be ready to listen to anyone who may be considered an expert. Of course, testimony is only expert and appropriate when it comes from an expert in that particular field. For example, most people would be less inclined to take seriously the political views of an expert in basketball than they would if those views came from a respected public servant. Nevertheless, an audience should remain skeptical about persuasive arguments, even when they are made by experts. The standards of logic required of experts apply to everyone else as well.

Ethics in Public Speaking

To be effective as a public speaker, one needs to maintain a high degree of ethics. This is true not only because of the inherent virtues of ethical behavior, but also because an audience will not trust a speaker whom they believe to be unethical. To promote good ethics as a public speaker, one should always be as honest as possible. One should also try to promote the interests of the audience whenever appropriate. It is important and ethical to give members of the audience responsibility for making up their own minds, rather than attempting to browbeat them into submission with one's argument.

Title of the Speech

It is very important to settle on a clear and appropriate title for a speech early on in the preparation process. The title should make explicit the central idea or concept to be discussed in the speech. The title should also indicate the intention of the speech. For instance, if the intent of the speech is to inform the audience about a particular subject, the title should clearly state the name of the subject. If the intention of the speech is to persuade the audience, the title should indicate the main arguments to be made by the speech. To be effective, a title should be succinct, clear, and, if possible, engaging.

Difference Between Immediate Aim and Ultimate Aim When Making a Speech

On occasion, a speaker will have a slightly different purpose for giving a speech than is apparent from the speech itself. In the field of speech communication, this is known as the distinction between **immediate aim** and **ultimate aim**. An example would be a particular speech intended to be a small part of achieving a long-term goal. A prominent businessman, for example, might make a speech about ethics in public policy. Whereas on its face the speech might seem to be a simple address about local community issues, it might be also be part of the businessman's plan to develop his reputation in advance of a political campaign. The immediate aim of the speech in this instance is to inform, while the ultimate aim is to advance the political ambitions of the speaker.

Location Should Dictate the Characteristics of the Speech

When preparing a speech, one should always keep in mind the occasion for which the speech is intended, as this will help determine what kind of speech is appropriate. Individuals who have gathered together for a summer picnic, for instance, will not be interested in hearing a long and complicated speech. A short, humorous address would be more appropriate for this setting. A convention of professors, on the other hand, will be receptive to a more substantive speech that might also include relevant technical information. On rare occasions, a speaker may decide it is necessary to deliver a speech not entirely appropriate for the setting; however, this should only be done when it is absolutely necessary.

Time Limits Influence the Preparation of the Speech

When preparing a speech, one must be aware of exactly how much time is available for presenting the material. The time limit will greatly influence the content of the speech. It is rarely possible, for instance, to effectively discuss a complicated subject in a short period of time. Nor will it be possible to hold an audience's interest over a long period of time without having a wealth of information and ideas. Giving an effective persuasive speech in particular requires sufficient time. This is especially true when one is trying to convert an audience's opinion on a subject with which they are unfamiliar or on which they already have firm opinions. Generally, it takes a strong argument, elaborated through a number of points, to alter an opinion already agreed upon by most members of the audience.

Elements of Setting a Speaker Should Consider When Preparing a Speech

When preparing a speech, a speaker should take into account any idiosyncrasies of the speech format or setting. For instance, in some situations a speaker will have specific guidelines and rules for his or her speech. When giving an address to the members of a particular religious or cultural group, for instance, one might need to abide by specific rules. Another thing to consider is the placement of the speech in the overall event. For instance, if other speeches are to follow, one might want to make sure there will be no overlap in speech content. Also, if the speech is to be given directly after a dinner, one should be aware that audience members will be less likely to pay close attention to the details of the speech. Finally, a good speaker will be aware in advance what the physical setting for the speech will be. That is, he or she will know beforehand such details as whether or not the speech is to be given standing or sitting and whether a podium will be available.

Research Required Preparing for a Speech

To adequately prepare for delivering a speech, one needs to assemble all pertinent information and create a complete outline. One of the reasons why it is a good idea to select a familiar topic for one's speech is that less research will be required. At the very least, one should know where to look to find the information necessary to deliver an informative and comprehensive speech. Speakers may need to consult with experts in their given subject or peruse newspapers, magazines, and books for extra information. Many local and school libraries have extensive databases for performing research, and a thorough internet search can often provide vast amounts of helpful material.

Composing a Speech Outline

Creating a detailed, comprehensive outline is the first step before actually writing the first draft of a speech. After assembling all the necessary material and information for the speech, the speaker can then begin organizing the main points of the speech and the arguments and evidence supporting his or her ideas and claims. It is important that all secondary ideas and claims also support the speech's main idea or claim. One should always introduce the most important claim, or thesis, at the beginning of the speech. The speaker can then spend the rest of the speech building a case for this thesis and elaborating other related points. When composing an outline, remember that the finished speech will ideally be much more colorful and engaging. An outline is not meant to entertain, but rather to clearly and succinctly indicate the organization of the speech.

PRACTICING SPEECH DELIVERY

Excellent speech delivery does not just happen. It is the result of extensive practice. After the speaker has outlined and drafted the speech, he or she needs to practice delivering it. Practicing a speech serves a number of purposes. For one thing, the speaker might not detect weak points in the speech until he or she actually speaks the words aloud. In addition, it is helpful to record oneself practicing the speech and then play back the tape to identify weaknesses in the delivery. It is often a good idea to practice delivering a speech in front of friends or family and have them critique the performance. Perhaps the most important point is that practice delivering the speech allows the speaker to further familiarize him or herself with the material, thus increasing the level of comfort and fluency in delivery.

METHODS FOR CULTIVATING SELF-CONFIDENCE WHILE GIVING A SPEECH

Most people struggle with some degree of anxiety when they are required to speak in public. One of the best things a person can do to reduce speech anxiety is to present a confident image. Naturally, one should always practice delivering a speech several times beforehand. Through repetition, the speaker becomes familiar with the appropriate gestures and rhythms of the speech, which gives rise to increasing confidence in his or her ability to deliver. Another good way to build confidence is to make eye contact with the audience during speech delivery. A forthright, steady gaze from the speaker connotes a feeling of confidence. Finally, confidence can be communicated through posture and body language. Standing up straight and emphasizing key points with hand gestures is a great way to communicate self-confidence.

ESSENTIAL POINTS OF SPEECH EVALUATION

There are a number of things to look for when evaluating the quality of a speech. All effective speeches share a few essential characteristics, such as a good introduction—one that engages the audience and introduces the main idea or argument of the speech. The introduction also establishes the tone of the rest of the speech. The body of the speech should include clear exposition of ideas and appropriate supporting material. The conclusion of the speech should reinforce the main idea or claim and solidify audience understanding. The presentation of the speech should be appropriate to the audience and setting and should be fluent in its delivery.

BASIC ELEMENTS OF SPEECHMAKING

To master the speechmaking process, one should clearly understand a few basic elements. The **central figure** is the speaker, the one delivering the speech. The speaker brings a self-conception as well as a conception or impression of the audience's general identity. In the study of speechmaking, the audience is sometimes referred to as the **receiver**. Like the speaker, the audience members will have a self-image as well as an impression of the speaker. The setting in which the speech is delivered is known as the **situation**. The speaker uses various channels of communication, including words and gestures, to communicate his or her message. The audience members will deliver their responses to the speech both verbally and through body language. This response to the speech is called **feedback**.

THE MESSAGE OF A SPEECH

The message of a speech is communicated not only with the words being spoken but also through the speaker's self-presentation. In other words, the quality of the speaker's voice and his or her body language contribute to the message as well. The message of the speech is generally considered to have three basic components: structure, content, and presentation. The **structure** of the speech is the order in which information is delivered. To be effective, a speech must have a logical and coherent structure. The **content** of the speech is the information it contains. Even an entertaining or persuasive speech must have good content. Finally, the **presentation** of a speech is the style in which it is delivered to the audience. Different kinds of speeches require different presentation styles. The most important thing is to match the presentation to the intention of the speech.

Most Important Attributes of a Speaker

To be an effective speaker, one must have a clear intention, a good attitude, and extensive knowledge of the subject of the speech, as well as a degree of credibility with the audience. The speaker should fully understand the intention of the speech, even if that intention is not directly expressed in the speech. Sometimes a speaker will have a hidden motive or a long-term goal that cannot be expressed in the speech. To establish credibility, the speaker should possess a solid working knowledge of the subject of the speech. When the speaker is fluent in the subject he or she is discussing, the speech will flow more naturally and the speaker will be able to tailor his or her message to the audience's level of understanding. Referring to a speaker's "attitude" simply means his or her self-conception; that is, the image the speaker has of himself or herself. If a speaker has a positive self-image, he or she is more likely to deliver an effective speech.

Characteristics of the Speech Listener

The individual or groups of individuals who listen to a speech bring their own characteristics to bear on the quality of the speech. For one thing, listeners will always have their own intentions. That is, they will always be seeking to obtain something from the speech, whether it is information or entertainment. Listeners will also have varying degrees of skill, meaning that some groups will be better at understanding complex messages. Listeners will also bring their pre-existing attitudes toward the speaker and the speaker's subject. To deliver an effective message, a speaker needs to perform an audience analysis to determine the characteristics of his or her listeners.

Basic Kinds of Feedback

Feedback is the response of the audience to the message delivered by a speaker. Although feedback is typically thought of as verbal responses to the message, it also includes body language, attention or inattention, and participation in dialogue after the speech. To be effective, a speaker must be attuned to all these kinds of feedback. In other words, he or she must monitor the audience throughout the speech to identify signs of boredom or engagement. The feedback a speaker receives while delivering his speech is called **immediate feedback**. The feedback the speaker receives after delivering the speech is called **delayed feedback**. Delayed feedback usually takes the form of critical comments, praise, or questions. A practiced speaker will use feedback to improve subsequent speeches.

Importance of Selecting a Subject Appropriate to the Time Limits of the Speech

Many speakers handicap themselves from the start by selecting a subject that is either too expansive or too narrow for their needs. To be effective, a speech subject must be appropriate for the amount of time available for giving the speech. Obviously, a half-hour speech can go into much more detail and tackle a wider range of issues than can a five-minute speech. A very short speech should have only one main idea, whereas in a longer speech the speaker may have time to deliver several important points and give supporting information for each. Although the best way to determine the appropriate subject for the time limit is to gain experience as a public speaker, beginning speakers can nevertheless help themselves by considering the parameters of a speech as they begin to consider possible subjects.

Tailoring the Subject of a Speech So That It Is Appropriate to the Audience

When deciding on the subject of the speech, the speaker must take into account the characteristics and ability level of the audience. The speaker should be aware of the audience's expectations. That is, whether they expect to be informed, entertained, or persuaded. Audience members may be annoyed if a speech has a drastically different tone from the one they were expecting. For instance, an audience expecting a serious speech will be impatient with a speaker who spends a great deal of time trying to make them laugh. In some cases, it may be necessary to thwart the expectations of the audience, as for instance when a serious moral point must be made instead of providing sheer entertainment.

Qualifications of the Audience

When deciding upon the subject matter of a speech, the speaker should take into account the audience's general intelligence level and subject-related knowledge. A speech will be ineffective if it is either too elementary or too advanced for the audience. If the speaker is unfamiliar with the knowledge base of the proposed audience, he or she should take steps to determine this knowledge before preparing the speech. For an unschooled audience, it is a good idea to focus on the most basic and important principles of a given subject. For an audience of experts in a given field, however, it is important to provide information that will be stimulating and informative.

Defining the Purpose of the Speech

In preparation for making a speech, it is important to strictly define the purpose of the speech. Without a firm idea of the intention of the speech, it will be too easy for the content to miss the mark. To begin with, the speaker should consider his or her own intentions as well as the intentions of the audience. As much as possible, the intentions of the speaker and those of the audience should be made to overlap. One should define the central argument or idea to be expressed in the speech and take care that this argument or idea is consistent with the intention of the speech. It is also important that the title of the speech indicates the intention as well as the central theme of the speech.

Difference Between an Idea and a Claim in a Speech

The goal of a speech is to disseminate information or persuade the audience. In other words, a speaker will either deliver **ideas** or make **claims**. A speaker who is delivering ideas is expressing information and opinions for their own sake, and not necessarily trying to change the minds of the audience. Informative speeches are usually on subjects about which the audience is not expected to know very much. The purpose of such a speech is to increase the knowledge of the audience rather than to convert them to any particular viewpoint. When a speaker makes claims, on the other hand, he or she is introducing opinions that may or may not be held by the members of the audience. The intention of this type of speech will be to provide arguments and evidence to support the speaker's claims.

Process of Phrasing the Main Idea of the Speech

It is important when giving an informative speech to lay out the **main idea** in a manner comprehensible to the audience. The main idea of an informative speech should be presented near the beginning of the address and therefore should not require an audience to understand any concepts that will be explained later in the speech. The audience should be able to understand the gist of the main idea before the speaker goes on to elaborate. In the preparation of a speech, the speaker should define the main idea early on, so that he or she can procure evidence and supporting arguments appropriate to that main idea. Too often, speakers introduce evidence and arguments not directly supportive of the main idea of the speech. This causes confusion among the audience and waters down the effect of the speech.

Process of Phrasing the Main Claim in a Speech

When a speech is designed to present or advance a particular viewpoint, the speaker will need to pay special attention to the phrasing of the speech's main claim. The **main claim** should be phrased in such a way that it will be comprehensible to a general audience and will not offend casual listeners with a harsh or controversial tone. The degree of intensity appropriate to the claim will depend on the audience. A more strident tone can be used with an audience of like-minded individuals, whereas a diverse group of uncommitted listeners requires a more evenhanded tone. When constructing the main claim of a speech, the speaker should be sure to present only ideas that can be supported by available evidence and reasonable argument. If the main claim of a speech is far-fetched or unsupportable, even the more rational elements of the speech may be dismissed by a skeptical audience.

Fundamental Qualities of a Well-Organized Speech

All well-organized speeches have certain qualities in common. For instance, a well-organized speech is comprehensible, meaning it can be understood by all members of the audience. A well-organized speech also has a formal unity, which means all of its parts contribute to the main idea. A unified speech has no extraneous parts. A well-organized speech is also comprehensive—it covers all the issues an audience member would expect to be addressed by a speech on the given subject. Finally, a well-organized speech does not have any repetition. Every major point should be covered in its entirety, but no points need to be repeated once they have been clearly delivered.

Process of Speech Organization

The process of speech organization entails selecting the elements that will comprise the speech, placing them into a coherent order, and arranging the supporting material for each message unit. During the organization process, a speaker will often summarize each message unit in a simple sentence. This gives the speaker simple building blocks that can be easily rearranged. In general, a speech should include a coherent introduction, body, and conclusion. The introduction should engage the interest of the audience and summarize the main points to be made. The body should contain the central points of the speaker's argument, as well as the supporting evidence. The conclusion should summarize the argument and give the audience food for thought.

Outline for a Proof Speech

Speech communication instructors often refer to a proof speech. This is a common type of speech, in which the speaker introduces his or her argument and then attempts to prove it. **Proof speeches** follow a consistent pattern. In brief, a proof speech has four components: introduction, argument, development, and conclusion. A speech that follows this pattern allows the audience to become acquainted with the thrust of the speaker's arguments before substantiation is offered. The lengths of the various components of a proof speech will vary, depending on the speaker's interests and the knowledge level of the audience. For instance, an audience already familiar with the subject matter may not require as much supporting material to be convinced.

Impromptu Speech Pattern

Any relatively informal speech on a light subject can be referred to as an impromptu speech. An impromptu speech may be given on very short notice and will therefore give evidence of much less preparation. Even so, impromptu speeches tend to follow a similar pattern. There are four basic steps in a typical impromptu speech: an engaging introduction, a brief overview, elaboration, and summary. Notice that the four components of an impromptu speech directly parallel the components of a proof speech. The only real difference is that the delivery will be looser and the style of delivery will endeavor to be more entertaining. An impromptu speech often begins with a humorous or intriguing anecdote and often ends with a light touch as well.

Problem-Solving Pattern of Speech-Making

In a problem-solving speech, the speaker outlines a particular problem, attempts to diagnose the cause, and then suggests a potential solution. **Problem-solving speeches** are at their heart persuasive speeches, since they attempt to convince the audience of the merits of adopting a particular strategy to solve a given problem. To be effective, however, a problem-solving speech needs to follow a logical pattern. These speeches typically begin with an introduction and a definition of the problem in question. The speaker will then summarize the possible causes of the problem and discuss some of the possible solutions. Following this, the speaker will make a case for one of the solutions and provide supporting evidence and argumentation. Finally, the speaker will attempt to rebut some of the possible counterarguments to the proposed solution.

Appropriate Outline for a Call-to-Action Speech

When speech communication instructors describe a call-to-action speech, they are referring to a speech that intends to inspire the audience to follow some recommended course of action. A **call-to-action speech** has five typical components: engaging the audience, describing why the audience should want to change something, explaining the best way to change, describing the positive consequences of making the change, and directly indicating how change can be made. It is not really possible to rearrange the steps in a call-to-action speech. Unless the argument is delivered in this order, the speech will likely be ineffective. It is important to end by outlining the positive consequences of change and making an emotional plea, as this leaves the audience on a high note, which is most likely to translate into direct action.

Body Language in Public Speaking

Posture in Public Speaking

Many speakers fail to recognize the significance of proper posture in the delivery of a speech. As much as words or gestures, a speaker's posture transmits information about his or her attitude, credibility, and confidence. To present a message effectively, a speaker should stand up as straight and tall as possible. Slouching forward or bending over one's notes indicates a lack of interest and preparation. This kind of advice may seem trivial, but an audience will subconsciously pay closer attention to anyone whose posture indicates command and authority. Effective speakers pay close attention to their own posture and make sure that poor posture does not disrupt the transmission of their message.

Facial Expression in Public Speaking

The facial expressions made by a speaker can have a significant impact on the effectiveness of message delivery. The facial expressions of the speaker can either reinforce or contradict his or her words. If the words being spoken are amusing or colorful, it is appropriate for the speaker to be smiling and have a relaxed facial expression. If the speaker is addressing a serious subject while grinning, however, the audience will most likely discount what he or she is saying. A speaker needs to match his or her facial expressions to the subject matter and to the expectations of the audience. A large audience can expect the facial expressions of the speaker to be slightly exaggerated, while a small audience may be put off by what seems like a leering or grimacing speaker.

Eye Contact in Public Speaking

Speakers should never underestimate the importance of eye contact during message delivery. For one thing, it is very difficult for an audience member who is making eye contact with the speaker to lose interest. An effective speaker will often shift his or her gaze around the room, making eye contact with as many people as possible. Under no circumstances should a speaker look up in the air, stare at his or her notes, or fix his or her eyes on some point in the distance. At the same time, the speaker should not constantly move his or her eyes around the room, as this may be perceived as anxious behavior. Eye movements should be calm, regular, and smooth.

Gestures in Public Speaking

A public speaker should make sure that his or her gestures are in harmony with the subject matter of the speech and the expectations of the audience. Many people are in the habit of either moving their hands frequently during speech or keeping their hands stationary. Both of these approaches are only appropriate in certain circumstances. When delivering a speech to a large audience, or delivering a speech with a high emotional content, a speaker may be advised to incorporate wide, energetic gestures. These kinds of motions are not appropriate for a more somber subject, however. And although gestures can amplify the meaning of the speaker's words, they should never become a distraction from the message of the speech.

Proper Way to Use Notes During a Speech

Many speakers will require notes, but they should rely on these notes as little as possible during delivery of the speech. For one thing, notes tend to prevent a speaker from making effective eye contact and using his or her hands expressively while speaking. Also, speakers who become reliant on notes may not be able to orient themselves in a speech if something goes wrong with their notes. Notes should only be used as a reference point of last resort. They should be kept down in front of the speaker, preferably out of view of the audience. They should not be held and should be on as few pieces of paper as possible, to prevent excessive shuffling during a speech. Finally, a speaker who requires notes should carefully look them over before a speech to make sure they are understandable and arranged properly.

Skills Required for Making a Speech

To deliver a successful speech, an individual needs to have acquired certain skills. For one thing, the speaker must understand in depth the topic about which he or she is speaking. He or she must also be able to address the topic from a number of different points of view and to answer any questions the audience might have after the speech. More generally, a successful speaker must have an air of authority, so the audience will pay attention and trust his or her words. A speaker should also have what is known as rhetorical sensitivity, or the ability to adapt his or her message to different audiences. Successful speakers know that a given style of speaking may be very effective with one audience and ineffective with another. A successful speaker will be able to modulate his or her voice and gestures appropriately.

State Apprehension as a Component of Speech Anxiety

To some extent, everyone grapples with speech anxiety. The fear of embarrassment or public disclosure can be overcome only with significant practice at public speaking. There are a couple of different kinds of speech anxiety. **State apprehension** is defined as speech anxiety that is only felt in specific situations. For instance, an individual who is comfortable talking in class but becomes anxious when required to speak informally with peers is experiencing state apprehension. Many people experience state apprehension in relation to delivering formal speeches in front of a group. State apprehension has both physical and mental symptoms, including vocal tics, sweaty palms, and a trembling voice.

Trait Apprehension as a Component of Speech Anxiety

Some people experience speech anxiety to a greater degree than others. Those aspects of speech anxiety that are unique to an individual are known as **trait apprehensions**. For instance, someone might have an aversion to public speaking because of a past experience. People who have an unnaturally high level of trait apprehension tend to avoid situations in which they will be required to speak to a large group. The good news for these individuals is that trait apprehension can be overcome with experience. Unfortunately, however, this means practicing public speaking until it becomes natural.

Interpretation of Speech Anxiety

Speech anxiety is a common malady but not one that should cause a person to lose heart. Even the most successful speakers have a bit of anxiety when delivering a message. In a way, this anxiety is a positive thing, because it focuses the attention and encourages concentration. Speech anxiety is a natural response to confronting an uncertain and unfamiliar situation. Research suggests that those who suffer from severe speech anxiety are often the most effective public speakers. Also, most speakers report that the anxiety they feel before delivering a speech is much greater than the anxiety they feel when actually in the process of speaking.

Using Speech Anxiety Productively

The abundance of nervous energy felt before delivering a speech can be used to the speaker's advantage. For one thing, many people find that speech anxiety sharpens their senses and focuses their concentration on the task at hand. Human beings are naturally inclined to focus their attention when they perceive a threat. The good thing about speech anxiety is that the attention is sharpened even though the threat is not significant. Many accomplished speakers use speech anxiety to increase their level of excitement and dynamism while delivering a speech. Indeed, many speakers say that without speech anxiety, they would not be able to achieve the rhetorical effects that have made them successful speakers.

Four Basic Channels of Public Communication

Normally, speech delivery is considered a simple transmission of words by one person to a group. However, this is only one of the channels through which information is delivered during a speech. In the technical language of speech communication, the speaker's words are said to pass through the **verbal channel**. At the same time, the speaker's tone of voice indicates his or her attitude through the **aural channel**. Some speakers use visual aids, which transmit information through the **pictorial channel**. Finally, a speaker transmits information about his or her attitude and self-image through gestures and facial expressions. This transmission is said to pass through the **visual channel**.

IMPORTANCE OF PHYSICAL SETTING IN THE DELIVERY OF A SPEECH

The physical setting in which a speech is delivered exerts significant influence over the expectations of the audience and should therefore be taken into account by the speaker beforehand. For instance, an audience that is required to stand during a speech will have less patience for a long-winded and complex oration. On the other hand, if the audience is seated in soft, plush chairs, they may be too relaxed to pay attention to a serious lecture. When the subject of a speech requires a fair amount of technical detail, it is a good idea for the audience to be seated in upright chairs and for the room to have sufficient light. In any case, the speaker should consider how the physical setting will influence the mood of the audience and should adjust his or her speech accordingly.

HOW SOCIAL CONTEXT CAN INFLUENCE THE DELIVERY OF A SPEECH

When speakers consider the characteristics of the environment in which they will deliver their speech, they sometimes neglect to consider the **social context**. The social context is the set of relationships between the members of the audience and the speaker and between the members of the audience themselves. The speaker should know beforehand how he or she stands in relation to the audience. For instance, a speaker may be recognized as an expert, an entertainer, or an intriguing fraud. Also, the speaker should understand how the members of the audience stand in relation to one another; they could be friends, colleagues, or strangers, for instance. The information gained by this consideration of social context should inform the construction and delivery of the speech.

HOW COMMUNICATION RULES CAN INFLUENCE THE DELIVERY OF A SPEECH

Sometimes a speech will be delivered in a particular environment or to a particular group that is governed by specific communication rules. For instance, a speech delivered in church is unlikely to be followed by a question-and-answer period. As another example, some debating societies have strict rules for the presentation and critique of a speech. In more informal situations, some groups will have different expectations for speaker behavior. For instance, a gathering of senior citizens is unlikely to respond well to coarse humor. In other words, communication rules may be explicit or implicit. While preparing a speech, the speaker needs to address the formal considerations that will influence his or her message.

Concepts of Oral Interpretation

BASICS OF ORAL INTERPRETATION

Although oral interpretation is a type of public speaking, it is very different than the delivery of a speech. For one thing, oral interpretation does not require the speaker to have written his or her own words. On the contrary, an **oral interpretation presentation** is a reformulation and expression of words written by someone else. In a sense, oral interpretation is a public and social form of storytelling. The work being interpreted may be a dramatic text, a work of prose, or a poem. Before the advent of radio and television communication, oral interpretation was the predominant form of information and entertainment. It is still very prevalent, although much more oral interpretation occurs through other media than in person.

SELECTING A TEXT FOR ORAL INTERPRETATION

Perhaps the most important step in oral interpretation is selecting a proper text. Works of prose, poetry, and drama are acceptable texts for oral interpretation. It is important to choose a text that is appropriate for the audience. For instance, storytellers often take fairytales as their text, this is appropriate for an audience of children but may be too simplistic for an adult audience. Also, it is important to make sure the text is of an appropriate length given the time constraints. An effective oral interpretation may require significant dramatic pauses and periods of nonverbal communication. All of these features should be taken into account when determining whether a text is the right length.

Composite Recital

In the form of oral interpretation known as **composite recital**, two or more people will interpret various texts. All of the texts interpreted by the performers will have some common thread, whether it is the author, theme, cultural background, or subject matter. Typically, an introductory speech precedes a composite recital. In this speech, the unifying thread will be presented and the various pieces to be interpreted will be introduced. In a typical composite recital, all of the performers will be grouped together on a stage and will take turns interpreting their material. Oral interpretation presentations usually require minimal set dressing.

Choral Speaking

In the form of oral interpretation known as choral speaking, a group of people joins their voices together to pronounce a single text. Perhaps the most famous example of choral speaking is the dramatic chorus in Greek drama. Only texts with a regular meter or rhythm can be used in choral speaking; other, more varying texts are too difficult to recite in unison. Different kinds of poetry have been incorporated into choral speaking with great results. Sometimes an individual speaker will deliver the verse and the group as a whole will deliver the chorus. In other cases, each individual will read a line and then the group as a whole will read the refrain.

Basics of Reader's Theatre

Reader's theatre is a form of group oral interpretation in which two or more individuals present a dramatic interpretation of a literary work. The presentation of reader's theatre is similar to that of a play, except the text is a work of prose or poetry rather than of drama. Also, reader's theatre typically has little set direction and scenery. Participants in reader's theatre often use elements of pantomime to suggest props. Because there are so few accessories in reader's theatre, the presenters tend to make exaggerated movements and display broad emotions. Reader's theatre is similar to the run-through performed by actors during the rehearsal of a play.

Dramatic Texts in Reader's Theatre

On occasion, the participants in reader's theatre will use a work of drama rather than one of poetry or prose. Obviously, works of drama lend themselves to oral interpretation and therefore will require much less use of suggestion to indicate costumes and scenery. On the other hand, plays often have elaborate set directions, which may be beyond the scope of reader's theatre. When this is the case, the participants should either select another text or should include an introductory speech in which the potentially confusing aspects of the presentation are explained. In a more formal presentation, the participants may hand out a program that gives this information.

Folklore

Any story passed on by word of mouth until it becomes ingrained in a culture may come to be known as **folklore**. In other words, folklore is the set of narratives that circulate among the members of a community through oral interpretation rather than through writing. Various categories of folklore include legends, jokes, fairy tales, and fables. Even though people usually associate folklore with a bygone age, there is a great deal of modern folklore as well. Although most scholars declare that folklore must be fictitious, it is often based on themes and issues common to everyday "real life." For instance, there is a great deal of folklore surrounding the figure of Davy Crockett. Even though most of this folklore is exaggerated or untrue, it is based on events that actually happened to a real person. Many scholars concentrate solely on the characteristics of folklore in various cultures.

Review Video: Myths, Fables, Legends, and Fairy Tales
Visit mometrix.com/academy and enter code: 347199

Folklore in Performance

Because it is an oral exercise, the creation and dissemination of folklore is by definition an act of performance. Folklore is traditionally allied with storytelling, though there are other ways in which it can be delivered. For instance, one of the most common forms of folklore at present is joke telling. Whenever someone tells a joke to a friend, he or she is engaged in a form of performance. This performance can be subjected to as much scrutiny and evaluation as a formal dramatic presentation. Indeed, all of the elements that define a successful performance (vocal control, nonverbal communication fluency, rapport with the audience) are essential to the delivery of folklore.

Storytelling

Storytelling is the craft of using words, gestures, and sounds to convey a narrative to an audience. At one time in human history, storytelling was the predominant form of information, entertainment, and self-knowledge for communities. Societies defined themselves based on the stories they told about themselves. By studying the stories that have been told in the past, scholars can gain insight into which qualities were particularly valued by a culture and the particular issues that caused the most anxiety for those people. Many people assume that storytelling is a dying art, though in fact it continues to thrive in various media. Television, movies, and radio, for instance, all use traditional elements of storytelling to develop powerful narratives.

Storytelling in Performance

Storytelling as a type of oral interpretation remains a popular form of entertainment even in this modern age of computers and televisions. Storytelling requires a narrative, which means it must have characters and a plot. Outside of these requirements, the storyteller has a great deal of creative freedom. Many storytellers incorporate sound effects and simple props into their performances. In any case, a speech communication instructor can assess a storytelling performance in the same way as he or she would any other oral interpretation. The success of the performance will depend on the fluency, preparation, and rhetorical skills of the storyteller.

Oral History

Oral history is any account of past events that is transmitted through the human voice rather than through writing. In the distant past, many cultures developed their self-identity primarily through oral history because they did not have the means to maintain a written history. At present, many historians focus on oral histories that are tape-recorded or videotaped. Many historians claim that oral history is a good way to give a voice to members of a society who, because of their marginal status, would otherwise not be able to make their voices heard. Also, oral history lends a human element to large, formerly impersonal historical events.

Oral History in Performance

Because it is a serious source of scholarly information, it sounds strange to speak of oral history as performance. However, in the broad sense of the word "performance," meaning any presentation involving speech and other forms of communication to an audience, it is clear that oral history fits the definition. Indeed, oral history is an important supplement to written history because information can be conveyed through the speaker's tone of voice and vocal mannerisms that cannot be expressed through printed language. Oral historians make a point of emphasizing those aspects of vocal performance that differentiate oral history from other forms of record-keeping.

Principles of a Text

Theme and Mood

To present an effective oral interpretation of a piece of literature, one must be able to discern the predominant theme and mood of the work. To discover the **theme**, one must read the text in its entirety and consider the general point the author is trying to get across. Even if the selection to be interpreted is only a portion of the entire work, one needs to understand how the selection fits into the work as a whole. This comprehensive reading should also reveal the mood of the piece. The **mood** is essentially the emotional content of the text.

Naturally, the predominant mood of the text will have an enormous impact on the interpretation. Note that the mood of a text can change.

Characterization

When interpreting a work of literature, one is often required to assume the point of view of a character in the text. To do this effectively, or to provide appropriate emotional emphasis in the portrayal of a given character, one needs to pay special attention to the author's use of characterization. **Characterization** is simply the way the author describes a character. Characterization may be direct, as in descriptions of the character's appearance and personality, or it may be indirect, in which the character is revealed through his or her actions or the ways in which other characters react to said character. It is important not to take whatever a character says about himself or herself at face value because authors often create "unreliable narrators," or characters whose words are not necessarily to be trusted.

Structure

Structure is a combination of plot elements used to give shape and form to a text. These basically include the beginning, middle, climax, and ending. With experience, a reader will develop a sense of the structure of a literary work. This sense of structure is invaluable when developing an oral interpretation. A sophisticated reader will be able to identify the climax, or most intense emotional point, in the text. Identifying the text's climax allows the reader to structure his or her interpretation to properly emphasize this peak dramatic moment. A reader should also be able to identify when an author is attempting to build tension in the text. The interpreter will want to convey this mounting emotion in his or her delivery.

Dialogue

If a selection for oral interpretation includes dialogue, the interpreter will have to make some important decisions about how he or she will handle this dialogue. For instance, the interpreter might decide to use different voices for the different characters in a conversation. Also, the interpreter will need to practice adjusting his or her voice to accurately represent the various moods of the characters involved in the dialogue. It is important for a speaker to understand these characters' motivations as well, as this information will allow him or her to produce a more sophisticated, nuanced interpretation of the words. Conversations have their own rhythms, frequently increasing and decreasing in tension. A good interpreter will be able to capture these rhythms in his or her presentation.

Diction

Diction is the unique style in which an author uses words and expressions. To interpret a work of literature effectively, one must understand both the denotative and the connotative meanings of the words an author uses. If necessary, the interpreter should look up all questionable words in the dictionary. Most importantly, the interpreter needs to understand how to properly pronounce each word. A dictionary will provide pronunciation guides as well as definitions. Besides understanding the pronunciation and definition of each word in the text, the interpreter also needs to know which words deserve special emphasis. Identifying key words in the text allows the interpreter to convey the appropriate meaning and correctly reflect the author's diction.

Punctuation

Although it is easy to pay little attention to it in a literary text, punctuation is an important element in oral interpretation. For instance, punctuation such as periods, colons, semi-colons, dashes, spaces, and spaces between sections of text all require pauses of varying duration. Also, when posing a question, it is typical to lift the voice to a higher register at the end of the sentence. Quotation marks in a sentence, of course, indicate that a character is speaking. In the case of such direct quotations, the interpreter will have to decide whether or not to use a different voice to represent each character who speaks.

Point of View in the Oral Interpretation of a Work of Prose

In the interpretation of a work of prose literature, it is especially important to have a sense of the point of view. The **point of view** is simply the perspective from which the story is told. For instance, in first person point of view, the story is told by one of the participants. First person perspective is distinguished by words like "I," "me," and "mine." When a story is told from the third person point of view, however, the narrator stands outside the story. Such a text is often told from an omniscient point of view, meaning the narrator knows everything, including the thoughts of all the characters. A limited omniscient point of view refers to a narrator who only knows certain information.

Treatment of Rhythm in the Oral Interpretation of Poetry

In the oral interpretation of poetry, one needs to be conscious of the rhythms and repetitions of the poem. Poetry is almost always written in a meter, or rhythm. Rhyming poetry will have what is known as a rhyme scheme, or a pattern of rhyming that occurs in the last word of each line. Also, many poems frequently repeat a single word, phrase, line, or set of lines. An interpreter needs to pay attention to these repetitions and vary his or her reading of the repeated words. The enunciation of the repeated words should evolve throughout the performance, so that the audience gets a sense of progress within the interpretation.

Technique of Emphasis in the Oral Interpretation of Poetry

In the oral interpretation of poetry, it is essential to recognize which words in a line deserve special emphasis. Too often, interpreters simply emphasize the last word in each line. Not only does this give their performance a repetitive and boring quality, it is also incorrect in cases where the line does not end with a comma, semi-colon, or period. When there is no punctuation at the end of a line of poetry, the interpreter should continue reading to the next line with no special emphasis. It is only through close study of the language and punctuation of a poem that an interpreter can learn the proper points of emphasis.

Oral Interpretation of Dramatic Works

Occasionally, a single individual will attempt the oral interpretation of a dramatic work. The obvious advantage of doing so is that the text has been designed for public performance, so the language and points of emphasis should be fairly clear. On the other hand, works of drama may call for elaborate staging and costumes beyond the scope of an individual oral interpretation. The interpreter will have to study the text to determine whether it can be adapted for oral interpretation. If too much action is called for in the stage directions, or if understanding the text depends on the presence of other characters, the interpreter would do well to look for another text.

Condensing Selections for Oral Interpretation

For a literary selection to be of an appropriate length for oral interpretation, it may be necessary to condense or cut the work. When editing a selection, it is important to leave all text that is essential to the meaning. For instance, when condensing a selection from a work of prose, it is a good idea to trim any references to characters or events that do not appear in the selection, unless these references have bearing on the meaning of the selection. The best rule of thumb is to always review the selection after the condensed version has been performed. If it still makes sense and conveys the same thematic meaning as the original, then the process of condensing the work can be considered successful.

Writing an Introduction to an Oral Interpretation Presentation

In some cases, an oral interpretation presentation will be preceded by a short introduction. If a selection is being taken from a larger work, or if a selection requires some context in order to be understood, it will be especially important to provide some guidance to the audience. There are a few key components to this kind of introduction. First, the presenter should outline the selection, including the major characters, back-story, and any other information necessary to understand the selection. A speaker will likely explain why he or she has picked that particular selection and why it might be of interest to the audience. If the selection has any relevance to current events or to the lives of the audience members, this information would be meaningful to an introduction.

Necessity of Practicing for an Oral Interpretation Presentation

It may seem obvious, but it is absolutely essential to practice before an oral interpretation presentation. Practice begins with learning the text inside out, but it is not complete until the performance has been fully rehearsed several times. During these rehearsals, the performer should be timed to make sure his or her delivery does not exceed the time constraints. If possible, the performer should rehearse in front of an audience (perhaps of friends or other performers) so he or she can practice making good eye contact and directing his or her voice to the different parts of the room. Multiple rehearsals also give the performer a chance to experiment with different deliveries and gestures.

Analysis and Interpretation of Dramatic Presentations

During the preparation for a dramatic presentation, the director and the crew will need to analyze and interpret the text. The director must identify the central character, or protagonist, as well as the supporting characters and the main conflict in the text. The director should also identify the mood and theme of the play, as these factors will influence all of his or her other decisions, from casting and staging to vocal emphasis and lighting. The director should outline the general structure of the play in order to bring the action to its appropriate climax and resolution.

Analysis of Rhythm

One of the aspects of drama that receives less attention than it should is rhythm. Every play has a natural **rhythm**, or periods of intense action followed by lighter action. To avoid overtaxing the audience, a dramatist has to mix moments of high and low intensity. Typically, a play will have several small climaxes before reaching its most dramatic point, the major climatic scene toward the end of play. A period of resolution, known technically as the denouement, usually follows the climax. During the analysis of a play, the director and his or her staff should pay close attention to the rhythm of the text so they can bring that same rhythm into the dramatic presentation.

Analysis of Character

During the planning phase of a dramatic presentation, the director and his or her staff should pay close attention to the relationships between the various characters. Each actor should note the attitude of his or her character toward all the other characters in the play. In some cases, the relationships between even distantly-related characters will change subtly during a performance. The director needs to be able to point out these slight changes to the actors so they can be conveyed in the performance. Also, a dramatic performance will convey the unique relationships between characters, such as that of a father and son or brothers.

Benefits of Group Oral Interpretation

There are a number of advantages to performing group oral interpretation. First, it encourages more than one person to familiarize themselves with the text. Also, group members can motivate one another to higher achievement. It is easier for a group to perform works having more than one character since it can be very difficult for one person to express all the different voices required by some texts. Group interpretation is also a good venue for people to gather and share their various ideas of interpretation and of literature. Finally, rehearsals tend to be more productive when there are other people present to critique one another's performances.

Use of Scripts in Choral Speaking

Typically, all of the participants in choral speaking use a script during the performance. Each participant should indicate on his or her script those lines that he or she will be required to speak. If there are any stage directions, these should be indicated on the script. It is a good idea to print the text in a double-spaced format and to number the lines so the cast can easily find their places. Additionally, the scripts should be distributed in advance of rehearsal so cast members can become familiar with where their lines occur throughout the script.

Motion and Position in Choral Speaking

For a choral speaking performance to be effective, the cast members need to practice speaking in unison. Only by beginning and ending each word at the same time can they achieve the clarity necessary to be understood. Also, if the cast is required to make any synchronized motions, these should be practiced as well. The intended effect will be successful only if the motion is performed precisely in unison. Finally, the director of a choral speaking group needs to organize the group by voice. Typically, any soloists will be positioned toward the front of the group. Those with deeper and stronger voices are usually placed in the back.

Memorization for an Actor

To be truly expressive, an actor needs to memorize his or her lines. This is in large part because the actor's concentration needs to move from the recitation of the mere words to the development of nonverbal communication methods and interpretation of character. If an actor is looking at cue cards or holding a copy of the script, he or she will not be able to gesture or move freely about the stage. Furthermore, he or she will not be able to make eye contact with the other actors or with the audience. It is most important to memorize lines before rehearsals begin in earnest. Even if an actor forgets some of his or her lines and requires a prompt during rehearsal, it is still better to start working without a script as soon as possible.

Motivation for an Actor

An actor's **motivation** does not mean his or her reason for participating in the play. Rather, it refers to the actor's identification of the motivations of the character he or she is playing. To effectively interpret a role, an actor needs to understand why the character behaves as he or she does. Without the right motivation, an actor will not be able to demonstrate effective emotion. Even the nonverbal aspects of a character's interpretation are dependent on the character's mood and motivation. Therefore, in order to transmit the right thematic message to the audience, the director and the actors need to have a good sense of each character's motivation.

Establishing Character Background for an Actor

Actors often talk about developing a character's background, or back-story. By this they mean establishing what the character's life and history were prior to the point at which the play begins. By understanding where a character is "coming from," an actor can gain insight into that character's motivation and emotional range. Sometimes this information can be discerned from the author's description of the character for instance, if a character is handicapped, it might be assumed that he or she has been in an accident in the past. Actors also get information from the character's dialogue and behavior. The director and actors need to collaborate to establish character background in order to accurately determine the characters' motivations.

Vocal Control

To effectively interpret his or her role, an actor must have excellent **vocal control**. An actor needs to be able to pronounce words clearly, so that every member of the audience will be able to understand the dialogue. In some cases, an actor may need to incorporate a regional dialect and have it be both credible and comprehensible. Some characters have particular vocal mannerisms, like a stammer or a lisp, which must be interpreted accurately. Finally, an actor must be able to convey the appropriate emotion with his or her voice at different times during a play. An actor who has a sense of his or her emotional vocal range can thereby save his or her most exaggerated vocal techniques for the climactic sections of the play.

Projection

Actors often refer to the vocal quality of **projection**, by which they mean the level of force in volume with which words are delivered. To perform in front of a large audience, an actor needs to have enough projection so that everyone in the audience can hear and understand all the lines. Actors cultivate strong abdominal muscles and lungs so they can maintain their ability to project. Also, actors constantly work on combining clarity of expression with volume. A specific technique that actors use to increase the quality of projection is called **pointing**. This is the technique of emphasizing particular words in a sentence, either by pausing before them or extending their enunciation. Pointing helps the actor's words to be understood.

How an Actor Handles Nonverbal Communication

An actor can handle nonverbal messages during a dramatic presentation in a number of different ways. It is important for the gestures to be appropriate, consistent, and tailored to the audience. Any nonverbal communication used must be appropriate to the character being portrayed; in other words, the gestures and vocal techniques need to be such that they seem right for the character. Also, a character's mannerisms must remain consistent from the beginning of the play to the end of the play. Finally, the ways in which an actor uses nonverbal communication must be expressive enough to be seen by everyone in the audience. When performing for a small audience, an actor can get away with more subtle nonverbal communication than he or she can when performing for a large audience.

How Movement Is Used in a Dramatic Presentation

There should be no random movements during a dramatic presentation. That is, all the positioning of the actors should be choreographed ahead of time. The entrances and exits of the characters are usually indicated in the text, but the proxemics may be at the discretion of the director. A sophisticated director can convey information about the characters and their interrelationships through their positioning onstage. At all times, however, the director needs to keep in mind the necessity of making the actors visible to the audience. Positioning should be one of the main focuses of rehearsal, and the director should experiment with different arrangements.

Basic Parts of the Dramatic Stage

A basic dramatic stage includes a single floor and an arch that extends from one side to the other. The section of the stage closest to the audience is referred to as downstage. The section of stage farthest away from the audience is known as upstage. When the stage directions call for movement to the right or left, this means from the perspective of the actors. Although most of the major set directions are included in a dramatic text, a director will have to come up with supplementary directions. These supplementary directions are known as **blocking**.

Choosing an Appropriate Dramatic Script

When selecting a dramatic script for presentation, a producer needs to keep in mind the makeup of the audience. For instance, when a work is to be presented to a group of children, it should not deal with mature or violent themes. One of the best places to find a dramatic text is the local library. Most libraries have numerous anthologies containing famous plays. Once a play has been chosen, the producer needs to procure playbooks for all the members of the cast and crew. It may be necessary to pay royalties to the author or publisher of the play.

Process of Holding Auditions for a Dramatic Presentation

When holding auditions for a dramatic presentation, directors should have a basic idea of what type of actor they prefer for each role. At the same time, they should keep an open mind. Sometimes an actor will give a unique performance during the audition, thus changing a director's mind about what he or she needs for a given role. If an audition is **open**, that means anyone is allowed to show up and try out. A **closed** audition means only invited actors are allowed to attend. If particular qualities or abilities are required of an actor to fill a given role, such as the ability to sing or play an instrument, these should be made known before the audition.

Typical Policy for Making Casting Decisions

When making casting decisions, directors adhere to a general policy. First, everyone who participates in an audition fills out a form with contact information. This audition form should also include space to indicate any conflicts of interest that might interfere with an actor's ability to appear in the dramatic presentation. During the audition itself, actors may read from a script or be asked to improvise. Sometimes actors will be instructed to prepare a short scene ahead of time. If an actor is going to be required to sing or dance during the presentation, these skills should be tested during the audition. Usually, a committee that includes the director and producers makes its casting decisions once all the auditions have been completed.

Feedback During Rehearsal

During rehearsal of a dramatic presentation, it is essential that the director and producers provide constant and specific feedback to the cast and crew. Rehearsals are a valuable opportunity for everyone involved in the performance to experiment with different techniques, so it is important for the director to let the actors and crew know what is working and what is not. In some cases, it may not be appropriate to give feedback immediately. To provide a venue for feedback, the director will set up regular meetings with each member of the cast and crew. By the time the dress rehearsal and first performance take place, the director should have already fully reviewed and approved the performances of the cast and crew.

Responsibilities of the Student Director and Stage Manager

A student director (also known as assistant director) helps make the director's job easier. He or she may transcribe notes dictated by the director during rehearsal, may help to implement the director's blocking plan, and may coordinate activities with the costuming, lighting, and sound departments. The stage manager has a number of practical responsibilities, including overseeing construction of the set and making sure that any set changes can be accomplished quickly. He or she is also responsible for organizing and managing the crew. A stage manager needs to be intimately familiar with the light and curtain cues in the play and must also have contingency plans in case things go wrong.

Responsibilities of the Business and House Managers

In a dramatic presentation, the business manager is responsible for overseeing all financial aspects of the performance. These include ticket sales, the cost of promotions, and the costs of production. In the case of professional presentations, the business manager also handles wages paid to cast and crew. The house manager, on the other hand, is responsible for handling the admittance and seating of the audience members. The house manager runs a crew of ushers, who help audience members find their seats. Ushers also clean up the auditorium after each performance. The house manager is responsible for maintaining the heat or air conditioning system in the auditorium as well.

Necessity of Makeup, Costumes, and Props

To be performed professionally, a dramatic presentation needs makeup, costumes, props, and crews. Makeup is necessary to counterbalance the effects of bright stage lighting. The members of the makeup crew will need to practice applying makeup to each cast member before the first performance, so they can get a good idea of what makeup scheme is appropriate. Costumes are important for fostering believability in the performance. The costume crew acquires the necessary wardrobe and makes sure it fits the cast. The props crew is in charge of acquiring, caring for, and storing all the movable items used in a performance.

Media and Mass Communication

Development of Radio Communication

At one point in American history, radio communication was the most important means of mass communication. The first commercial radio station began broadcasting in 1920. At first, radio was not very popular, because most people could not afford home receivers. As these devices began to become more common in American homes, however, programming expanded and the radio became a source of information and entertainment. In 1941, the first FM station began broadcasting, allowing signals to be transmitted over long distances with a very small amount of static. Although radio communication has been somewhat superseded by television and the internet, it is still an invaluable source of information and entertainment for millions of people

Relationship of Radio to Other Forms of Mass Media

When it was first introduced, radio was the most important form of mass communication. Unlike telegraphs, radios could deliver complex messages about events as they happened. Also, radio allowed for dramatic use of the human voice and special sound effects. In general, radio is a more personal medium than telegraph communication. Eventually, however, the ability of television to transmit images and sound allowed this medium to supersede radio as the primary form of mass communication. Nevertheless, radio remains the predominant medium for the transmission of music and continues to be an important vehicle for the transmission of news.

Development of Radio Networks

One of the most important periods in the history of radio communication was the development of radio networks. Radio networks first developed as a way to offset the costs of maintaining radio towers and transmission equipment. Radio networks began to sell commercials to businesses that wanted to advertise. These businesses would pay the radio station for the right to air their advertisements. Various radio stations joined together in networks and gave one another permission to air each other's shows. In this way, radio stations around the country standardized programming and made radio a viable business. Each station was able to produce a smaller amount of better programming.

Development of Motion Pictures

The first motion pictures were developed by Thomas Edison and his associates in 1893. After a few years of tinkering, motion pictures were introduced to the general public and were immediately popular. Many stores offered "nickelodeons," in which patrons could watch a brief presentation for a nickel. Around 1910, a small film industry began to develop in Hollywood, California. In 1912, the first full-size theaters were introduced. In the mid-1920s, sound was added to motion pictures, which had previously been silent or accompanied by live music. By 1929, all new films had sound.

Significance of Motion Pictures

Motion pictures have played an important role in the economic and social life of the United States. Perhaps the first example of the effect of the movies was during the Great Depression, when motion pictures continued to portray images of success and wealth in spite of the widespread poverty beyond the theater. It was at this point that people began to note the escapism inherent in the movie-watching experience. Since then, movies have proven to be a powerful medium for exploring real events, including tragic ones. Two good examples of this are the newsreels of battle footage from World War II and the many powerful movies that have been made on the subject of the Vietnam War.

Development of Television Communication

Television is such an entrenched part of daily American life that some might forget that it has really only been part of the culture for the past sixty years. Although the first television broadcasts took place in 1939, it was only after World War II that television truly burst onto the American scene. At first, televisions were extremely expensive and signals were only broadcast in black and white. Also, when televisions were first introduced, radio communication was still the most popular medium. Over time, however, televisions became smaller and less expensive and better quality programming became available. After approximately a decade, television supplanted radio as the most popular form of mass communication in the United States.

News Coverage

Because of its ability to deliver visual images and sound, television has proven to be an excellent medium for transmitting news. Many people get the majority of their information from television broadcasts. Television transmission has allowed people to get global news and learn about life in even the farthest reaches of the world, which they might otherwise never be able to see or visit. At the same time, many television news programs seek to provide in-depth analysis and evaluation of local, state, federal, and global issues. Television has proven to be an excellent medium for interviews and documentaries as well.

ENTERTAINMENT

For most people, television is primarily a source of entertainment. Comedies, sports, dramas, game shows, and reality programs are among the most popular forms of television entertainment. Perhaps the most venerable form of television entertainment is the soap opera, so named because the first programs targeted housewives and were sponsored by soap companies. Some television programs air at a regular time for years on end, while others, such as miniseries, are only on the air for a limited time. Television executives determine which entertainment shows they will continue broadcasting by evaluating Nielsen ratings, which measure how many viewers are tuning in to each program.

RELATIONSHIP BETWEEN TELEVISION AND BUSINESS

Over time, television has become a big business. Television stations make most of their money by airing commercials. Although television stations must pay for their transmission equipment, their primary expenditure is for the development of programming. Television networks, similar to radio networks, developed as a way to share the costs of program development. Broadcast television, which is available simply with the use of an antenna, is free to the general public. Cable television, on the other hand, must be purchased by subscription. The advent of cable television in the 1950s allowed television stations to fund special-interest programming for a limited audience.

MEDIA'S ROLE IN INFORMING THE PUBLIC

The mass media plays a central role in informing the general public about local and global events. When most people think about information disseminated through the media, they think about news programming. But there are a number of other venues through which information is transmitted to the public. For instance, nature documentaries and talk shows inform the general public on issues that are perhaps less immediately pertinent to their lives. The federal government uses channels of communication such as radio and television to broadcast emergency messages and to promote governmental policies. Magazines and newspapers can also disseminate detailed information on behalf of government agencies.

MEDIA'S ROLE IN CHANGING ATTITUDES AND BEHAVIOR

Although the precise power of the media is a matter of controversy, it is beyond question that the major media outlets have an ability to persuade the general public. To take the most obvious example, advertisements on television clearly have a positive effect on sales. Many of the ways in which the media can influence attitudes and behavior are more subtle, however. For instance, the media can influence popular opinion simply by providing information about a particular subject. One indication of the media's influence on behavior is shown simply in the fact that people commonly choose to spend time watching television or listening to the radio rather than doing other things.

MEDIA'S ROLE IN ENTERTAINING THE PUBLIC

In public surveys, people cite entertainment as the number one reason for engaging with mass media. This data is produced by Nielsen ratings, which indicate that people watch sports, comedy, and drama programming much more frequently than news. Moreover, the line between information and entertainment is often blurred. For instance, many documentaries that purport to be informative are also quite entertaining. Indeed, the inherently entertaining nature of mass media communication makes such media a powerful tool for engaging an audience in educational and informative programming. Many people acquire a broad knowledge of the world through television and radio without ever realizing they are engaged in a process of education.

DEVELOPMENT OF THE INTERNET AND ITS EFFECT ON COMMUNICATION

Although the internet has been around for approximately 20 years, it did not truly become part of the mainstream media until the mid-1990s. Today it is ubiquitous within American culture and is an integral part of the way people communicate with one another. Instantaneous forms of communication such as email, instant messaging, blogging, and video blogging and conferencing have all become available to people who formerly would have had no access to them. The result is that it is now possible to communicate with people around the globe at virtually any time. The internet has brought formerly isolated geographic areas into contact with other parts of the world and has provided forums for members of every special-interest group in existence. At the same time, many critics charge that the instantaneous communication afforded by the internet has impoverished communication on the local and community level.

MEDIA

Mass communication is defined as the one-way transmission of messages to a large, diverse audience. Radio, television, and the internet are the typical vehicles for mass communication. Some people include print media as a component of mass communication, although others declare that mass media requires almost instantaneous transmission. One of the signature qualities of mass media communication is that it can be reproduced and replayed in exactly the same way more than once. In other words, since it has the capability of being recorded, it can be played more than once and for more than one audience.

USE OF A MEDIA DIARY

Many people would be shocked to realize just how much time they spend engaged with mass media. Spending a half-hour here, forty-five minutes there in total can add up to a huge chunk of time. One way to gain control over the time spent engaged with mass media is to maintain a media diary. A **media diary** is simply a daily catalog of the amount of time devoted to different forms of media. For instance, a student might want to keep a media diary listing the amount of time spent listening to the radio, watching television, or surfing the internet. It might also be a good idea to include activities such as watching movies and playing video games. Students should record how much time they spend in each one of these activities and then calculate it as a percentage of their total free time.

USE OF A MEDIA EVALUATION FORM

Another way to keep track of individual media intake is through the use of a media evaluation form. Unlike a media diary, which simply indicates how much time was spent with various media, a **media evaluation form** keeps track of the quality and content of the media that is consumed. For instance, a media evaluation form will include a list of the various television programs the individual watched during the week, along with a brief summary and evaluation of the programs. Many people are shocked to discover how much time they spend every week engaged with programming they do not particularly enjoy. The use of the media evaluation form is a great way to streamline media intake because it encourages an individual to devote time only to content he or she most enjoys.

MEDIA'S ABILITY TO SPUR PUBLIC CONVERSATION

One of the key roles of the mass media is to inspire and shape public dialogue. For instance, the news media's coverage of a political issue can set up debate. Many people have alleged over the years that the news media in the United States has a particular political bias. Some people claim it has a liberal bias, while others claim it is a conservative bias. Perhaps the safest criticism one can make of the news media is that it has an inherent interest in conflict, because controversy and disagreement is more interesting to viewers. Most critics of the mass media agree that it is influenced in large part by the desire to sell advertising space.

MEDIA'S ABILITY TO FRAME DISCUSSION

One of the media's greatest responsibilities is to frame public discussion in a fair and objective way. In other words, the media is charged with reporting the news in a way that gives ample space to all reasonable points of view and does not ignore pertinent facts on either side. The role of the media in influencing discussion in a society has led some critics to refer to news outlets as "information gatekeepers." It is important that there be vocal critics of the news media, to identify and remedy problems of objectivity to a certain degree, all citizens are responsible for casting a skeptical eye on the news media and for making sure these media enable free and fair discussion.

Importance of Applying Critical Analysis Skills to the Media

When the news media is free and unfettered, it is essential for all citizens to maintain a skeptical attitude and apply critical analysis skills to informative programming. Television viewers should keep in mind that the way a subject is photographed can influence the way it is perceived. For instance, individuals who are photographed in shadow tend to seem more dangerous or malevolent. Most people are good at critically appraising commercials but do not necessarily apply the same skills to avowedly informative programming. Viewers should remember that a persuasive element exists in every communication, no matter how impartial, and so should remain alert to signs of bias.

General Feedback is Offered to the Media

The providers of mass media communication receive general feedback from a number of different sources. Television companies, for instance, are constantly organizing focus groups to view and offer feedback on new television shows and commercials. Sometimes networks will arrange for a focus group to be composed entirely of members of a particular demographic, as for example women or African-Americans. Perhaps the most famous example of general feedback for the mass media is the Nielsen ratings, which are used to determine how many people watch a particular television program. The providers of mass communication use all of this general feedback to refine and tailor their messages to the audience.

Personal Feedback is Offered to the Media

The media receives a great deal of personal feedback from individuals in the general public. Any time a person writes or calls a television or radio station to convey his or her response to a program, he or she is giving personal feedback. Many television and radio programs explicitly call for audience participation, which is to say they ask for personal feedback to use as content in their programming. In a way, consumers provide personal feedback to the media in their choice of purchases, since these consumer decisions indicate which television and radio advertisements are effective. Individual voices actually do play a great role in affecting the quality of the content of media presentations.

Programming Process for Radio and Television

Radio and television programming are primarily a matter of economics. Networks want to schedule their most expensive and most popular programming at the times when the most people are likely to see or hear it. For radio this means during the morning and afternoon, when people are likely to be in their cars, whereas for television this means the early evening hours. New television dramas and comedies are usually introduced twice a year. Networks usually produce ten to fifteen new episodes in each television season. A show may have two seasons in a year and during the remaining weeks reruns will be broadcast. Traditionally, news programs are broadcast in the early morning, at noon, around dinnertime, and in the late evening.

How Media Outlets are Funded

In large part, television and radio networks are funded by commercials. The Nielsen ratings indicate how many viewers watch a particular television program. The more viewers a program receives, the more expensive is the advertising space during the program. Every year, the Super Bowl marks the most expensive four hours of programming on American television, with some 30-second advertising slots going for more than one million dollars. There are alternatives to advertising-funded television and radio, such as public television and radio stations, which are primarily funded by viewer donations and contributions from grant organizations. Also, some small public access television stations are funded by their local government.

Use of Commercials in Mass Communication

Nearly all programming on radio and broadcast television is funded by commercials. Cable and satellite television receive part of their funding from distributors but are in large part also funded by advertising. Commercials are generally more expensive when they run during programs with a large viewership. Businesses also like to position their advertising during programs that attract viewers who are likely to buy their products. So, for instance, one is likely to see a lot of truck commercials during football games, since presumably a large number of males are watching. Similarly, commercials during the weekdays are often for products preferred by senior citizens and housewives, who are more likely to be watching television at this time.

Advances in Mass Communication Have Changed the Legislative Process

In the past fifty years, the legislative process has been subtly modified by advances in communication technology. Television first made it possible for the president to speak face to face, as it were, with the American public. This meant he could push his legislative agenda without having to spend as much time currying favor among members of Congress. Perhaps the most important change has been the introduction of C-Span, a network that televises all the proceedings in the US Senate and House of Representatives. This has made members of Congress even more conscious of their appearance and has led to much more grandstanding and many more public displays on the floor of the legislature. Also, the acceleration of the news cycle has put perhaps unfair pressure on Congress to move quickly on legislative decisions.

Internet's Effect on Politics

The Internet has influenced politics in unpredictable ways. For one thing, it has made it possible for citizens to acquire political information from sources other than the traditional mainstream media. In the past, many people have complained about the prejudices of the news media, but now people are easily able to get news from sources that share their same personal ideologies. Many people complain, however, that this "hyper-partisanship" of many Internet news sources has polarized the country. Another area in which the internet has radically changed politics is in campaign financing. Candidates can now solicit donations over the internet, which has led to amazing increases in the amount of money available to popular candidates.

Communication Media Affects the Political Campaign Process

Advances in communication technology have drastically altered the political process. Before the advent of television, political candidates could only reach large audiences on the radio or by delivering addresses to enormous crowds. The development of broadcast television made it possible for presidential debates to be transmitted to the entire country. At the same time, candidates began to pay much more attention to the visual elements of presentation. With the introduction of the first 24-hour cable news networks, it became more and more important for ambitious politicians to supply ready-made news events. This has spawned the omnipresent, continuous cycle of political news and campaign coverage. Many critics complain that the incessant need for fresh news by the cable networks has devalued political discourse in the United States, even as these networks provide information to many more people than were reached in the past.

Radio Drama

Vocal Techniques Used in Radio Drama

Some of the best oral interpretation of famous stories and plays has been done over the radio. For oral interpretation to work on the radio, however, the performers must have excellent vocal control. For one thing, they need to be able to indicate excitement or nervousness with their rate of speech. An excited speaker tends to talk more quickly. Radio drama performers also have to indicate their emotional state by varying the volume of their voice. For instance, in many radio dramas a speaker will almost whisper during the most dramatic parts, because the audience will then be forced to listen more intently to what he or she is saying.

Preparing a Radio Drama

A great deal of effort goes into the preparation of most radio dramas. Not only do the performers need to become familiar with their roles and practice the performance, but the producers need to decide on the appropriate sound effects to accompany the performance. Like television programs and movies, radio dramas have directors, who are responsible for organizing the actors and overseeing the general interpretation of the text. Typically, a director will go through the text before auditions are even held, so he or she can get a good idea of the particular themes that should be emphasized in the performance.

Rehearsing a Radio Drama

It is just as important to rehearse a radio drama as it is to rehearse a scene in a movie, a television program, or a play. The director of a radio drama usually organizes a rehearsal right after the parts have been cast, so the group can run through the entire script together and get a general idea of the direction in which they are heading. During this rehearsal, members of the cast make notes on their scripts. In subsequent rehearsals, the director will probably interrupt the cast in order to offer suggestions and make corrections. It is typical to do a final rehearsal a short time before the premiere presentation.

Sound Effects in a Radio Drama

Radio dramas have famously been enlivened by the use of sound effects. Sound effects serve a number of purposes in the presentation of a radio drama. For one thing, they can be used to differentiate between scenes. Often, a bit of background noise helps to establish a new scene in the minds of an audience. For instance, a scene might begin with the sound of shuffling feet and low conversation, to indicate that the action is taking place in a hallway or on the street. Sound effects also add depth to a radio drama. Instead of just listening to the human voice, the audience hears a variety of noises that advance the action, from ringing telephones to slamming doors. Because radio only transmits through the medium of sound, radio drama producers have become extremely creative with the incorporation of sound effects.

Video Production Terms

Basic terminology used in video and film production includes the following:

Angle—the viewpoint from which the camera shoots the action.

Establishing shot—a shot from a long distance, used to establish the setting in the mind of the viewer; often a shot of the building in which the action takes place.

Close-up—a shot in which the camera only focuses on one person; extremely close shots are referred to as tight close-ups and extreme close-ups.

Dolly—a platform on wheels that allows a camera to remain stable while moving; used primarily in action scenes or when there is a change in perspective during a shot.

Medium shot—a camera perspective in which an individual is framed to the waist; a medium shot contains enough width for two people; sometimes used to frame people as they walk or run.

Long shot—a camera perspective in which several people can be included from head to foot; a long shot is often used to establish a conversational group at the beginning of a scene.

Wide angle—a camera perspective that has an extremely broad horizontal distance.

Reverse angle—a camera perspective in which the object being shot is seen from a perspective that is the opposite of the previous shot.

Pan—a filming technique in which the camera is turned horizontally on an axis; often used when the subject is in motion, as for instance when a character is walking.

Tilt—a camera technique in which the camera is moved up and down vertically on an axis; sometimes used to shift the frame from an individual's feet to the individual's head.

Cut—sometimes called a take; a transition from one scene to another.

Zoom—to move closer to or farther away from the subject with the camera.

Fade—a gradual dissolution of the scene; most often, movies and television shows use a fade to black.

Dissolve—a gradual transition between scenes, in which the first scene is slowly replaced by the second scene.

Wipe—a transition between scenes in which one moves in as the other moves out, with no overlap.

Over the shoulder shot—a classic camera perspective in which one individual is seen from the perspective of a point over the shoulder of another person.

Preparation of a Camera Shot Sheet

One of the most important tasks of a television or film director is to prepare a camera shot sheet. A **camera shot sheet** is a detailed set of instructions that the various camera operators must follow during filming. For each shot, the director should list what is to be framed, the type of lens to be used, the length of taping to be expected, and the sound requirements. All this information needs to be condensed into a format small enough for all the camera operators to carry around during shooting. It is very important that the sequence of shots be accurate, so the camera operators can spend their time preparing for their next shot.

Roles of Producer and Director in a Television Production

The **producer** of a television program has a variety of different roles. Perhaps most generally, the producer can be called the overall manager of the production. He or she arranges the financial backing, hires the crew, and assigns a director to the project. Once the production is underway, the producer acts as a liaison between the financial backers and the director. The producer may also have a role in assisting publicity. A television production's **director** is hired by the producer to interpret the script, cast the parts, and to manage the crew that will film the program. The director is responsible for creating an interpretation that is acceptable to the producer.

Roles of Associate Director, Floor Manager, and Production Assistant in a Television Production

An **associate director** has several tasks on the set of a television production. For one thing, the associate director is usually in charge of directing the background action. That is, he or she makes sure future shots are being set up while the director concentrates on what is being filmed at present. The associate director also tries to keep the director organized and on schedule. The associate director is often responsible for managing the logistics of production as well. The **floor manager**, meanwhile, is responsible for organizing the facilities that will be used in the production and for maintaining the operation schedule. A **production assistant** typically takes care of the finer details of production, from the making of cue cards to set design.

Microphones, Switchers, and Mixers in a Television Production

A variety of specialized equipment is required for television production. For one thing, television requires the use of hidden microphones. The most common microphone used on a television set is one suspended from a long horizontal pole, called a **boom mic**. The boom mic allows the microphone to be suspended above the performer but out of sight of the camera. Television production also requires the use of a **switcher**, which is a mixing panel that allows scenes to be placed end to end on a videotape. Finally, television production requires the use of a **mixer**, which is an electronic board on which various sources of sound and video can be spliced together.

Phases of Television Production

Television production includes four basic phases: preproduction planning, rehearsal, productions, and postproduction. During **preproduction planning**, the director familiarizes himself or herself with the script, and a production assistant arranges for the facility and the production equipment. The cast and crew are also hired at this stage. During the **rehearsal phase**, the actors and director figure out their roles and do the blocking. During the **production phase**, the program is filmed. Finally, during the all-important **postproduction period**, the program is edited and mixed. Also during this period, corrections are made, art and music are added, and any necessary dubbing is performed.

Use of a Personal Media Inventory

A personal media inventory is a record of one's media intake over a given period of time. A comprehensive personal media inventory would include categories for television, radio, movies, Internet, recorded music, and any other form of mass media. Most people are very surprised when they realize how much time they actually spend engaged with media. In particular, many people are shocked to realize just how much television they watch each week. One way to gain control over the amount of time one spends with mass media is to catalog this activity in a personal media inventory.

Computers and the Internet

Transform passive reading into active learning! After immersing yourself in this chapter, put your comprehension to the test by taking a quiz. The insights you gained will stay with you longer this way. Scan the QR code to go directly to the chapter quiz interface for this study guide. If you're using a computer, simply visit the bonus page at **mometrix.com/bonus948/fsot** and click the Chapter Quizzes link.

Computers and Information Systems

Basic Computer Parts

The system unit is where the main computing parts are located. It is often shaped as a tower and contains the central processing unit, which processes the information; and the random access memory, which temporarily houses information. It will typically contain drives such as a CD/DVD drive, a floppy disk drive, and a hard disk drive. Cables connect the other components to the main unit. A mouse allows the user to point to and select items. Some people use a track ball instead. A keyboard allows users to input information like letters, numbers, and characters. It has function keys, a numeric keyboard, and navigation keys. Users control the computer with its many functions. A monitor displays information in text and graphic form. A printer allows users to print documents as well as information from the screen. Speakers allow users to hear music, dialogue, and other sounds. A modem gives the user access to the internet.

Networks and Networking

Many businesses possess computer networks that provide a wide variety of functions. A **local area network (LAN)** gives a group of nearby computers networking capability. For instance, they can share files, games, printers, and so forth. This can be inexpensive and easy to set up. They can be wired or wireless and can be connected to each other when networking needs grow. When it grows so large that it might go across cities or even countries, the company can make a **wide area network (WAN)** to connect their systems. The Internet itself is a WAN. The employees can usually go on the Internet from the network. A **virtual private network (VPN)** gives employees remote access to the network. The business can also have an **intranet** with internal web servers that let employees distribute confidential information to each other. This may include an internal email system as well as instant messaging and other forms of communication. To access this information, employees must be logged into the network. Many companies have a wide variety of computer systems.

Basic Troubleshooting of Computer Problems

Not every computer problem requires a call to the IT department. Users can do some simple troubleshooting on their own first. They should write down everything they do, as well as any error messages they receive, in case the problem needs to be escalated. The first thing to do is make sure all the cables and cords are properly connected. They should make sure the outlet or surge protector has power and that the monitor and speakers are on. A simple closing and reopening of a program or restarting the computer in general is often enough to fix the problem. The company may have a source where they list updates and/or identified issues. If the computer or program is frozen, users should press Control/Alt/Delete (Option/Command/Esc on a Mac) to access the task manager where they can select and end the task that is giving them problems. A "non-system disk or disk error" message may mean the user needs to remove a CD, flash drive, DVD, or floppy disk before booting up. If the user can't get the computer to shut down, he can hold down the power button to do it. He can also run antivirus software to scan for problems.

Bits, URLs, Bytes, Browsers, USB Flash Drives, Bandwidth, and CD-ROM Drives

In computing, a **bit** signifies the basic unit of information. It is generally 0 or 1. When bits are combined in groups of eight they make a **byte**. A **URL** stands for uniform resource locator and is the web address of a website. This will bring users to their desired website. A **browser** is the program most people use to navigate the internet. Internet Explorer and Google Chrome are two common web browsers. **USB flash drives** are small portable drives that can be used to store information such as Word files. They can be connected to the USB ports on desktop computers, laptops, and other devices. **Bandwidth** is the bit-rate of resources of data communication. It describes the speed of the network. A **CD-ROM** drive can access, read, and play CDs.

Laptop Computers

Laptops are used very often in business. They are produced from companies such as Dell, Toshiba, and Acer. They are very useful and allow a business professional to take all the features of his computer wherever he goes, including on business trips. Business professionals commonly use them for communication. They will email people and also use them for video conferencing. They can use them for word processing such as writing business letters. They can use them to create and show presentations to clients, customers, or business partners. They can use them to store business information. Especially for someone who travels a lot, this can be very important. Smartphones can also do a lot, but they cannot compare to a full computer. Laptops provide this convenience for many in the business world.

PDAs

Personal digital assistants (PDAs) are like small computers, similar to smartphones without the phone capability. For the most part they have been replaced with smartphones. They provide a wealth of information and give the user connection to the internet. They typically contain a calendar, schedule, listing of contact information, notes program, and calculator. They made it easy for business professionals to carry information and access the internet before smartphone became widely available. They range greatly in features, brands, and price. Most also allow for a form of portable memory to carry information. Some people still use them.

Smartphones

Smartphones are very commonly used in business. First, they allow people to make and receive phone calls while on the go, which is especially valuable for someone who is rarely at his or her desk. Business professionals can also contact others through a wide variety of functions such as texting, email, and video calls. They can conduct videoconferencing while on the go. Smartphones also allow business professionals to access information online. They can show off their websites to clients, for instance. They can access social media where they can post things about the business. There are many apps that may be useful for business professionals. They can access the GPS while on a business trip, or check the weather when planning an outdoor event. They can use it to set reminders and alarms or manage their schedules. They can use it to carry presentations. There are many smartphones, including the popular iPhone series, and Android-based phones.

Hardware and Computer Peripherals Utilized in Business

Memory storage devices allow users to store data. These come in many different sizes and connect in different ways. Some companies may get an external hard drive to provide more space. Flash drives make it easy to share information between people or carry files on the go. There are a number of devices used to connect to the Internet. Modems allow this. Routers create networks that pass and direct data. Scanners create digital copies from physical ones. For instance, companies can scan in receipts to cut back on paper and have a secure digital file. Printers are used to print documents. Other common peripherals include the keyboard, which is used to input data; the mouse, which allows people to select items; and the microphone and camera, which allow for video conferencing.

Computer Viruses

Computer viruses are programs that "infect" computers and spread from one to another. They will interfere with the computer, sometimes allowing hackers to steal information or damaging the computer or its programs. They are often spread without the user realizing it in ways such as email attachments, instant messaging, or internet downloads. It is important for users to protect themselves against computer viruses. Programs like AVG and Norton Antivirus can scan and protect computers against viruses and should be updated regularly. It is important for users not to download files unless they are certain the source is secure. Some viruses will send out emails to a user's address book with the virus, so even if something is from a trusted source, it still might not be safe. Users should keep up to date on the most recent viruses and remove any as soon as they can.

Security Measures When Using Technology

With the prevalence of identity theft, scams, and online fraud, it is important for businesses to protect themselves when using technology. One measure is to use **password protection**. Access to sensitive information should be protected by passwords. These passwords should not be easy to crack and should never be shared. In some cases, there should be multiple passwords. Businesses also encrypt their information. This is where the messages are encoded or changed so they can only be read by the correct users. Even if someone intercepts the message, he or she will not be able to interpret it. Another strategy is the use of **firewalls**. These control the traffic in and out of a network. These can protect against threats online, blocking harmful programs and also blocking others from looking at sensitive data. Most businesses have a firewall to protect them. Businesses also use **antivirus software** to protect against viruses.

Software Often Utilized in Business

Word processing programs allow users to create, read, edit, and manipulate documents. Database management software allows companies to manage their databases. It both manages and analyzes data. There are a lot of specialized programs that allow users to forecast sales and get other data. Spreadsheet software allows users to make spreadsheets and tables and calculate information. Excel is a popular one. Companies also use presentation programs to create, edit, and view presentations. There are a number of software programs related to communication. These allow for email as well as video conferencing and other forms of communication. Many companies have specific programs for accounting and operations. These can help a company manage its business more effectively. Within each of these categories are a wide range of software choices.

Word Processing Software

Word processing software allows users to create, read, edit, save, and format documents. These are often based in text, but may have images as well. They may have tables and other features. They are used very frequently in business for everything from business letters to resumes to company reports and more. The formatting options in the modern programs are vast and allow for great customization of documents. They also allow a lot of shortcuts to make it quick and easy to create a document as well as tools to make a quality document, such as a spelling and grammar checker. There are a number of word processing programs, and Microsoft Word (from Microsoft Office) is one of the most widely used. Other popular programs include WordPerfect (Corel Corporation), Writer (OpenOffice by Apache), and Pages (Apple Inc.).

Database Management Software

Decision support systems are popular. These computerized information systems help managers make decisions. They are interactive and take data, business models, and other information such as sales data to calculate valuable information. They might compare sales numbers, project revenue, or project the consequences of different moves, for instance. A database management system (DBMS) is another system that lets users create, store, change, and view information from a database. They range greatly in size as well as technical specifications and may be organized in a relational, flat, network, or hierarchical manner, with relational being the most common. They preserve the data's integrity. Structured Query Language (SQL) is the standard interface.

Spreadsheet Software

Spreadsheet software allows users to create spreadsheets, making it easy to view information. These programs allow for calculations and manipulations of the data. For instance, a business professional can calculate payroll deductions or average sales results. Microsoft Excel is one of the most common spreadsheet software programs used today. It has columns (denoted by letters) and rows (denoted by numbers), and the current cell is called the Active Cell, which is denoted by the letter of the column and number of the row. It is useful to know the basic Excel formulas for calculations. First, a user starts with the equal sign and then the formula. For instance, if he wanted the D4 cell to be the sum of C1 and C2, then he would put in the formula =C1+C2. Users can also make a similar formula with subtraction (-), multiplication (*) and division (/). They can put more than one of these in a formula. Also, to add a range of values, users can use the SUM function. For instance, SUM(B1:B3) adds the values of B1, B2, and B3.

Traditional Software

With traditional, or **closed-source software**, the software owners do not allow others to see or modify their code. This is the case with many of the large programs like Microsoft Office. Companies may prefer it because they do not want anyone changing or stealing their code. Users might like knowing exactly what a program will contain when they get it and not worry about changes to the code. There are disadvantages for users, however. Users cannot go into the code to add or disable features. When the code is open-source, people can look through and fix bugs, but this is not possible with closed-source.

Open-Source Software

Open-source software is software that has the source code available to people for viewing, modification, and enhancement. Individuals can go in to the source code and take out things they do not like or add code to create additional features. It is advantageous because people can make improvements or disable parts of the code they do not wish to utilize. People can also spot errors in the code. They can adapt it for their own needs and then pass it on, so others can take advantage of the new features and altered programming. It also helps teach individuals how to program and understand code. Many companies choose not to do open-source code because they do not wish others to change their programs.

Common Computer Operations Utilized in Business

One very useful computer operation is **file management**. Companies typically have a lot of files, and they need to be able to manage, sort, store, and access them efficiently. For instance, an insurance company will have a wide range of files for its different clients. There are many file management programs that allow companies to easily manage their files. **Network operations** involve the management and maintenance of a telecommunications network. Computers allow users to communicate with each other in various ways such as email. Companies also use computers for **data backup**. They can send information offsite so that even if something catastrophic happens to the first source of data, the data will remain secure in another location. There are also specific **shutdown procedures** that make everything easy and logical. It is important to close all programs and then use the Shut Down button located on the Start menu.

Techniques to Input Data on Computers

There are many special function keys and shortcuts that allow users to perform a myriad of functions on the computer. The Tab key moves the cursor to the following tab stop. The Insert key changes the inputting between the overtype mode, in which it overtypes existing text; and insert mode, in which the existing characters are forced one forward to make room for the new character. The Home key moves the cursor to the start of the line or to the start of the document if the text cannot be edited. There are a number of key combinations that make it easy to perform tasks. Many of these use the Control (Ctrl) key (or the Command key on a Mac), which is combined with another key to perform a function. Some of the popular ones are Copy (Ctrl and C), Undo (Ctrl and Z), Cut (Ctrl and X), Paste (Ctrl and V), Select all (Ctrl and A), New browser window (Ctrl and N), Terminate application or restart computer (Ctrl and Alt and Delete), Find (Ctrl and F), and Save document (Ctrl and S). Users can also access special features on the computer such as the spell checker through the Review tab, Proofing group, and Spelling & Grammar option.

Find and Replace Functions on Computers

The Find and Replace functions allow a user to find one or more characters in a document and then (if the user chooses) replace it with a different characters or characters. The user can go through the document to view every time the characters appear, or just replace them all. To access it, users can either click on the Find icon (the word or magnifying glass) or press down Control (Ctrl) and the letter F. The user will then type in the characters to be searched for and can choose options such as matching case and whole words only. They can click on Find or Enter. They can then go to Replace (which might show up right away or be in its own tab, depending on the computer program) and type what is to replace the item. The user can specify whether to replace one or all of them at the same time.

Techniques to Format Documents

There are many options to format a document in popular word processing programs such as Microsoft Word. A user can change the font style and size in the drop-down box in the Home tab. He or she can go to the paragraph option to justify text, change line spacing and change indentation. He can click the appropriate icon to create a numbered or bulleted list. The page layout page has a number of options. In the page setup section, a person can click on the columns tab to make columns. He can change the margins and orientation from the tabs of the same name. In the page background section, he can add a watermark or change page colors or page borders. When he clicks on the icon, he will be taken to an easy-to-understand menu that provides options such as type and thickness of border. The Insert tab allows users to insert a variety of elements such as tables, pictures, and clip art. They can insert a page break, blank page, or cover page in the pages section. There is also a header and footer section where these can be inserted and formatted.

Making, Formatting, and Modifying Tables on Computers

It is simple to make, format, and modify a table in Microsoft Word. Users should go to the Insert tab and click on the Table icon, where they can specify the size of the table. It has some built-in templates for tables such as a calendar, a matrix, and a tabular list. Users can also draw a table to customize it to their exact specifications by using the Draw Table option. Once the table is created, the user can go to the table tools design tab to specify things like banded rows, banded columns, table style, shading, and borders. Users can type in the tables. They can go to the layout section under table tools to make further formatting changes such as changing cell margins and text direction, managing properties of tables, inserting rows and columns, specifying height and width, and more. It is very flexible and allows users to modify the text and format to whatever they want.

Chapter Quiz

Ready to see how well you retained what you just read? Scan the QR code to go directly to the chapter quiz interface for this study guide. If you're using a computer, simply visit the bonus page at **mometrix.com/bonus948/fsot** and click the Chapter Quizzes link.

FSOT Practice Test #1

Want to take this practice test in an online interactive format?
Check out the bonus page, which includes interactive practice questions and much more: **mometrix.com/bonus948/fsot**

Job Knowledge

1. What is the most efficient way to send another person a copy of an e-mail you are writing without letting the primary recipient know?

a. Add a cc
b. Forward it
c. Add a bcc
d. Send it through postal mail

2. An instructor lists all student grades on a particular test. The most common grade is an 86, attained by 13 of the 22 students. What is 86 considered?

a. The mean
b. The average
c. The range
d. The mode

3. Where is the U.S. banking system regulated?

a. On the local level
b. On the state level
c. On the federal level
d. On both the state and the federal level

4. During which president's administration were Medicare and Medicaid started?

a. Lyndon Johnson
b. Franklin Roosevelt
c. Herbert Hoover
d. Theodore Roosevelt

5. What is the main way the U.S. government controls our money supply?

a. Changes in interest rates
b. Raising taxes
c. Striving for high economic growth
d. Regulating inflation

6. The economic systems of the United States and Russia are both most closely tied to which of the following?

a. The government
b. Their geography
c. Historical events
d. Technology

7. The European Union's first treaties focused on building:

a. A common market
b. Environmental stability
c. Humanitarian values
d. Solidarity

8. How is a database best defined?

a. A tool for collecting and organizing information
b. An accounting program for keeping track of revenue and expenses
c. An index describing a company's departments
d. A listing of computer software

9. What is a true statement about motivating people?

a. People have to be self-motivated.
b. People are always motivated by money.
c. Fear of losing a job is a good long-term motivator.
d. All people are motivated by the same things.

10. An employer makes a rule that employees speak only English on the job. What law is this most likely to violate?

a. Immigration Reform and Control Act
b. Title VII
c. Civil Rights Act of 1991
d. Anti-Discrimination Act

11. Which is a true statement about noncitizens living in the United States?

a. They are illegally residing here.
b. They can receive Social Security benefits.
c. They are not eligible for food stamps.
d. They do not contribute to the U.S. economy.

12. Which two countries made efforts to curb overpopulation in their countries in the late 20th century?

a. Great Britain and Mexico
b. Nigeria and China
c. Iran and Great Britain
d. Nigeria and Great Britain

13. Who led Poland as president from 1990 to 1995?

a. Vaclav Havel
b. Nicolae Ceausescu
c. Lech Walesa
d. Helmut Kohl

14. Which group was responsible for a large part of the terrorism in Northern Ireland throughout most of the last half of the 20th century?

a. Al-Qaeda
b. Independent Muslims
c. IRA
d. Catholics

15. Weak organizational, financial, and political governments are at risk for:

a. Insurgency
b. Immigration
c. Failed states
d. Loss of military

16. Which 1992 treaty established the euro as the single currency for Europe?

a. General Agreement on Trade and Tariffs
b. European Union Treaty
c. Maastricht Treaty
d. World Trade Organization Agreement

17. In the 1980s, some Latin American countries took up neoliberalism. What was the main idea of this economic model?

a. Government dependence and monopolization
b. Free markets and privatization
c. Denationalization and taxation
d. Industrialization and regulation

18. Which country put the first satellite in space in 1957?

a. Russia
b. United States
c. Germany
d. Korea

19. Which word is best defined as the unlimited power to govern?

a. Oligarchy
b. Communism
c. Absolutism
d. Patriarchy

20. How many Federal Reserve banks are in the United States?

a. 1
b. 2
c. 12
d. 27

21. Which phrase, coined during the Cold War, best describes a First World country?

a. A stateless nation
b. An impoverished and unstable country
c. An industrialized but not democratic country
d. An industrial democracy

22. In 2002, President George W. Bush cited certain countries as being part of an "axis of evil." Which country was NOT part of that description?

a. Iran
b. Iraq
c. North Korea
d. Afghanistan

23. What was the Patriot Act created to confront and work against?

a. Terrorism
b. Weapons of mass destruction
c. Free trade
d. Global warming

24. Which freedom is NOT covered by the First Amendment to the Constitution?

a. Freedom of the press
b. Freedom from cruel and unusual punishment
c. Freedom of assembly
d. Freedom to petition the government

25. Which amendment guarantees a speedy trial in the United States?

a. Fourth Amendment
b. Sixth Amendment
c. Eighth Amendment
d. Fourteenth Amendment

26. Which is a phrase used to describe irresponsible and inflammatory reporting by the press?

a. Propaganda
b. Penny press
c. Free speech
d. Yellow journalism

27. How long is the elected term for a member of the Senate?

a. 3 years
b. 4 years
c. 5 years
d. 6 years

28. What is a term used for a person who flees a nation for political freedom?

a. Prisoner of war
b. Nonresident alien
c. Immigrant
d. Refugee

29. Which is NOT a constitutional responsibility of the president of the United States?

a. Negotiating treaties with Senate approval
b. Recommending legislation
c. Choosing chairpersons for standing committees of Congress
d. Seeking counsel of cabinet secretaries

30. Which government body has the least influence on foreign policy?

a. Congress
b. State Department
c. Defense Department
d. National Security Council

31. Which factor is least likely to be considered to affect a country's gross domestic product (GDP)?

a. The size of its workforce
b. The amount of its capital
c. Technology in place
d. Education of its workforce

32. Most political theorists, regardless of ideology, believe that __________ benefits all countries economically.

a. Multistate structures
b. Population control
c. Free international trade
d. Interest groups

33. What is the most likely result when the minimum wage is raised?

a. A decrease in saving
b. A decrease in inflation
c. An increase in saving
d. An increase in inflation

34. What is the most important component to a successful market economy?

a. Price
b. Government
c. Banks
d. Demand

35. An athlete will buy the same amount of spinach each week regardless of its price. What can be said of spinach and the athlete?

a. The athlete's purchases are dependent on her income's elasticity.
b. The athlete considers spinach a low utility purchase.
c. The athlete has an inelastic demand for spinach.
d. The athlete has an unlimited demand for spinach.

36. A city in California charges a fine of $49 for each mile a speeder is driving above the speed limit. Tina received a $882 fine for speeding. How many miles per hour above the speed limit was she traveling?

a. 16 mph
b. 24 mph
c. 20 mph
d. 18 mph

37. A book retails for $35.00. A book store marks it 15% off, today only. Those with frequent buyer cards get an additional 10% off when they show their card at the register. What will the book cost a frequent buyer today?

a. $26.25
b. $26.78
c. $29.75
d. $31.50

38. Which of these is the least biased sampling technique?

a. A politician interviews every 8th grade student in the district to get the opinion of youth on a new policy.
b. A business directs users to leave anonymous reviews online.
c. A principal goes through the school directory and calls every 5th family to request opinions on a policy change.
d. A political commercial asks voters to call in with ideas for reform so that he can get a better understanding of what his constituents want.

39. The check for a $10,000 lottery win has 32% deducted for taxes. What is the amount of the check?

a. $3,200
b. $6,800
c. $9,680
d. $9.968

40. Given the histograms shown below, which of the following statements is true?

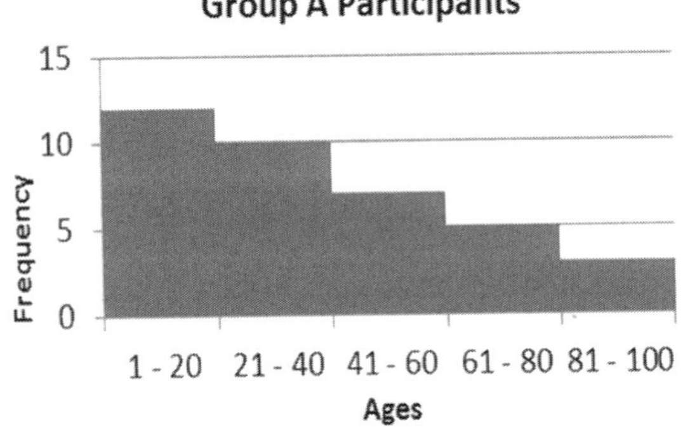

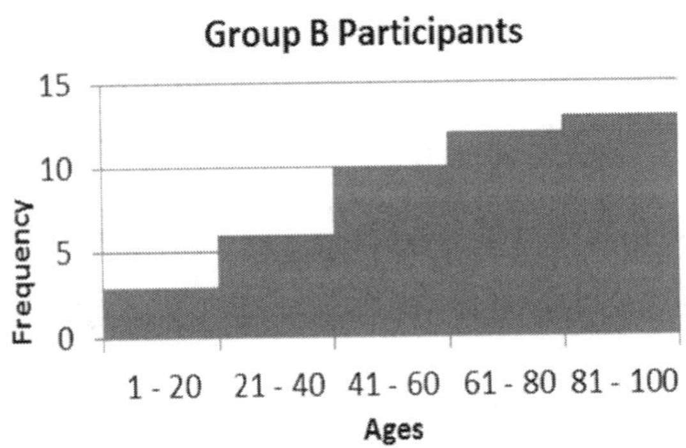

a. Group A is negatively skewed and has a mean that is less than the mean of Group B.
b. Group A is positively skewed and has a mean that is more than the mean of Group B.
c. Group B is negatively skewed and has a mean that is more than the mean of Group A.
d. Group B is positively skewed and has a mean that is less than the mean of Group A.

41. A man spends one-fourth of his day at school, one-twelfth of his day eating and doing errands, and one-half of his day working at his family business. How much of his day is left for sleeping?

a. 4 hours
b. 5 hours
c. 6 hours
d. 8 hours

FSOT Practice Test #1

42. What is a true statement about the subject line in an email?

a. Most people do not bother reading it.
b. It should be just one or two words.
c. It is not necessary on most business emails.
d. It should convey what the message is about.

43. When speaking to a heterogeneous audience of adults, to whom should planned remarks be targeted?

a. To the middle part of the group
b. To the most educated of the group
c. To the least educated of the group
d. To the least educated for the first half, to the most educated for the remainder

44. Which leader was NOT part of the Allied Big Three who met for the Yalta Conference during World War II?

a. Winston Churchill
b. Franklin D. Roosevelt
c. Douglas MacArthur
d. Joseph Stalin

45. Which word describes a way to separate a computer network from viruses and outside networks?

a. Bug
b. Filter
c. Firewall
d. Encryption

46. Which country has the problem of trying to unify 250 different ethnic groups?

a. Nigeria
b. China
c. Iran
d. Mexico

47. Which part of a computer is considered to be its brain?

a. Central processing unit (CPU)
b. Random access memory (RAM)
c. Operating system (OS)
d. Universal resource locator (URL)

48. In order to add the fractions 5/7 and 3/8, what must first be found?

a. Lowest common denominator
b. The greatest common factor
c. A multiple of 5
d. The lowest factored numerator

49. What is a true statement about individual employees' goals?

a. They should be difficult for the employee to attain.
b. They should be aligned with the organization's goals.
c. They should be set up by a manager.
d. There should be consequences for not attaining them.

50. The Immigration Reform and Control Act (IRCA) of 1986 required employers to:

a. Permit employees to speak their native language
b. Give hiring preference to people born in the United States
c. Verify that all employees can legally work in the United States
d. Give hiring preference to individuals born outside the United States

51. Which of the following countries contributes the least amount of trade to the US?

a. China
b. Japan
c. Mexico
d. The United Kingdom

52. Which of the following contains the greatest amount of digital information?

a. Megabyte
b. Gigabyte
c. Terabyte
d. Kilobyte

53. The term "Brexit" refers to which nation leaving the European Union in 2020?

a. The United Kingdom
b. Belgium
c. Denmark
d. Brazil

54. An NFT is a form of data stored within a digital database called a blockchain that tracks all transactions of the data. What does NFT stand for?

a. Non-fiduciary trade
b. Non-fungible token
c. Near-flawless transaction
d. Network form trade

55. Which Supreme Court case enforced the civil rights of citizens to not incriminate themselves?

a. Marbury v. Madison
b. Miranda v. Arizona
c. Youngstown Sheet and Tube Company v. Sawyer
d. United States v. Carolene Products Company

56. Which US president is credited with paving the way for formal diplomatic relations with the People's Republic of China?

a. Gerald Ford
b. Ronald Reagan
c. Richard Nixon
d. George Bush

57. What judicial system did America borrow from England?

a. Due process
b. Federal law
c. Commerce law
d. Common law

58. To be President of the United States, one must meet these three requirements:

a. The President must be college educated, at least 30 years old, and a natural citizen
b. The President must be a natural citizen, have lived in the U.S. for 14 years, and have a college education
c. The President must be a natural citizen, be at least 35 years old, and have lived in the U.S. for 14 years
d. The President must be at least 30 years old, be a natural citizen, and have lived in the U.S. for 14 years

59. What petition needs to be filed to request that the Supreme Court hear a case?

a. Writ of certiorari
b. Writ of habeas corpus
c. Writ of mandamus
d. Writ of attachment

60. The Animal and Plant Health Inspection Service, the Food and Nutrition Service, and the Forest Service are members of which department?

a. The Department of Health and Human Services
b. The Department of Agriculture
c. The Department of the Interior
d. The Department of Transportation

Situational Judgment

1. Your supervisor asks you to perform a duty that you have never done before. You are confident that you can accomplish the task but are busy with other time-sensitive work. Select the BEST response and the WORST response.

a. Tell your supervisor that you are busy right now but will get to the task later today.
b. Tell your supervisor that this request is outside of your scope of practice.
c. Tell your supervisor that you have not performed this task before and might have questions during the process.
d. Tell your supervisor that you will get started on it right away.

2. You notice that your coworker stays logged into her desktop computer with personal health and financial information visible to customers and colleagues passing by. The computer is in a high-traffic area, and when your coworker leaves for a break, the computer is unattended. Select the BEST response and the WORST response.

a. Log your coworker out of the computer, and inform her of your actions when she returns.
b. When your coworker returns, talk with her about the security risk associated with staying logged into an unattended computer.
c. Immediately inform your supervisor of her transgression.
d. Close the visible customer information screen on the computer, and wait for your coworker to return.

3. You are the team leader for a new project in the workplace. Your teammates offer an idea on how to accomplish your latest task, but the plan is not achievable at this time due to current logistics. Select the BEST response and the WORST response.

a. Tell your coworker that you appreciate his idea and will take it into consideration going forward.
b. Tell your coworker that the idea can't be implemented.
c. Tell your coworker that changes may need to be made before the idea can be implemented.
d. Tell your coworker that although you appreciate his enthusiasm, you are the leader, and you have to make all of the decisions.

4. Your supervisor implements a new policy that you do not agree with. You believe that the policy is detrimental to the department and business. Select the BEST response and the WORST response.

a. Refuse to participate in the new policy, and voice your concerns immediately.
b. Stop by your supervisor's office to talk about your concerns privately.
c. Bring up your concerns at a department meeting where other coworkers can help debate the issue.
d. Follow the new policy without objection.

5. You are stationed in a foreign country that is experiencing civil unrest. You are unfamiliar with the culture of the community and want to meet some of the community members and learn about their culture. Select the BEST response and the WORST response.

a. Schedule a meet-and-greet event between your team and the community.
b. Accept a volunteer community outreach position within your organization.
c. Read the local newspaper and watch the daily news.
d. Organize an open-house event when community members can visit your facility.

6. Your facility is hiring new employees, and you are called to conduct an interview with another manager. The other manager is asking the female applicant questions such as these: "Can you tell us about your personal life? Do you have any small children that will be a hindrance to your job performance?" Select the BEST response and the WORST response.

a. Politely interject with a different line of questioning.
b. Whisper to the manager that he can't ask those kinds of questions.
c. Immediately ask to speak to the other manager outside the interview room.
d. Allow the other manager to continue, but don't record the applicant's answer.

7. You are the manager of a small group of individuals. You notice that morale is low in your department, with many staff members complaining of long hours and low pay. Several staff members are threatening to quit. Select the BEST response and the WORST response.

a. Organize a department meeting where staff members can discuss their issues.
b. Send a memo asking staff to email you with their problems and opinions.
c. Offer "take 5" meetings daily, during which you can have real-time discussion with staff.
d. Tell the staff that you will reevaluate the current workflow and salary guidelines at the end of the fiscal year.

8. You are the manager of a small department, and you have the opportunity to promote one member of your staff to supervisor. Which of the following employees should be promoted first? Select the BEST response and the WORST response.

a. An employee with the most seniority in the department but is frequently tardy
b. An employee who is new to the company but is reliable and punctual
c. An employee who is a new graduate but has taken on extra responsibility and performed the job duties well
d. An employee who has worked for the department for several years and offers new ideas and solutions to problems

9. You are a team leader in your department. Your supervisor has added a significant number of tasks to your workload, all of which are time sensitive. Select the BEST response and the WORST response.

a. Prioritize the tasks, and work on the most important ones first.
b. Delegate some of the tasks to your most responsible team members.
c. Tell your supervisor that you have too many projects due at once and you can't take on the new tasks.
d. Tell your supervisor that you may need an extension on the projects' due dates.

10. Your department is performing at a deficit due to wasteful allocation of funds and materials. Your current projects include a weekly newsletter sent to hundreds of customers, purchasing office supplies, and other general office work. Your manager asks you to look for ways to save money on supplies in your current projects. Select the BEST response and the WORST response.

a. Instead of sending paper newsletters to your customers, send email notices.
b. Decrease your newsletter release from weekly to twice per month.
c. Instead of printing important emails, scan them into your desktop computer.
d. Stop purchasing office supplies for the office, and ask employees to supply their own.
e. Evaluate other vendors for better pricing on office supplies.

11. A customer has waged a complaint against you for rudeness and aggression. You don't think that you did anything wrong, as the customer was rude to you first and you responded in kind. Select the BEST response and the WORST response.

a. Offer to apologize to the customer personally.
b. Apologize to your supervisor.
c. Make no efforts to apologize, as the customer was rude to you first.
d. Tell your supervisor that the customer was rude to you and you lost your temper.

12. A customer group is coming into your office to learn about a new piece of equipment that your company is now producing. Your supervisor asks you to lead the presentation to the group. Select the BEST response and the WORST response.

a. Use technological terms and scientific jargon.
b. Use lay terms for most of the presentation, but highlight any critical technical terminology.
c. Use lay terms for the entire presentation.
d. Offer a hands-on demonstration if possible.
e. Conduct a lecture-based demonstration with time for questions at the end.

13. You are responsible for paying the invoices in your department, and you've noticed that the printing costs for your department's promotional materials have increased significantly each month. You have used other printing companies at your previous employer that offer more competitive pricing. Your coworker, who is in charge of the printing account, says that your supervisor's family member works at the more expensive printing company, and that's why your company uses them. Select the BEST response and the WORST response.

a. Report your supervisor for an ethics violation.
b. Present your supervisor with information about the other less-expensive printing companies.
c. Tell your supervisor that you've noticed an increase in printing costs and ask if you can investigate other options.
d. Continue paying the invoices without questioning the cost increase.

14. You are employed by a relief organization that offers daily living supplies to the community at a discounted price. A mother approaches you saying she can't afford the high price of your organization's baby supplies. She is $2 short on her purchase. Select the BEST response and the WORST response.

a. Ask your supervisor if the customer can be offered credit or a discount.
b. Pay the $2 difference yourself.
c. Manually change the price of the item to $2 less than the sticker price, as this is a small amount of money for essential items.
d. Apologize to the customer, and state that the price can't be changed.

15. Your department is undergoing diversity training as a facility-wide initiative. You don't see the value in diversity training, as you have completed similar training at your previous employer just a few months ago. Select the BEST response and the WORST response.

a. Don't attend the training session, as it would be redundant to complete the training a second time.
b. Ask your supervisor if you may skip the training because you've already completed a similar course.
c. Attend the required diversity training.
d. Ask for more information on the diversity class curriculum.

16. You are in the break room having lunch with a group of coworkers. After a few minutes, some of the group starts speaking in a foreign language and laughing. You feel uncomfortable because you can't understand the conversation and worry that they are making fun of you or the rest of the group. Select the BEST response and the WORST response.

a. Ignore the conversation.
b. Interrupt the conversation, and tell the coworkers that it is rude to speak in a language that the rest of the group doesn't understand.
c. Speak with one of the coworkers privately, and tell him or her that speaking in another language makes the rest of the group feel left out.
d. Start your own conversation with the remaining coworkers.

17. You are a new employee at a foreign embassy. Your job responsibility includes handling classified documents in a small office setting. You find your coworker looking over your shoulder, possibly attempting to read a classified national security-related document. Select the BEST response and the WORST response.

a. Quickly put away the document.
b. Tell your coworker that the document is classified.
c. Inform your supervisor of the possible security breach.
d. Report your coworker for a security violation.
e. Ask another coworker about the office's security policy.

18. Your facility has an equipment reprocessing room in which types of equipment are sanitized, tested, and prepared for future use. Hazardous chemicals are used to clean these machines, but you see that your coworker is not using any personal protective equipment. Select the BEST response and the WORST response.

a. Tell your coworker that the cleaning chemicals can be hazardous and offer personal protective equipment to wear.
b. Ask your supervisor to post signs reminding employees to use personal protective equipment.
c. Offer to help, and put on your own protective equipment as an example of the proper procedure.
d. Allow the coworker to continue.

19. You are working in a government facility based in the United States. Part of your job includes transporting large pieces of equipment from one area to another. While pushing an exceptionally heavy machine around a corner, the machine's wheel breaks off, causing the machine to suddenly stop moving. The quick twisting motion, combined with the machine's sudden stop, causes pain in your back. Select the BEST response and the WORST response.

a. Report the equipment as inoperable, and send it to the repair ward.
b. Fill out an incident report, and give it to your supervisor.
c. Seek medical care for your injury.
d. Return to work and see if the pain improves later.
e. Go home and rest.

20. Your team is asked to reorganize your department's equipment room. The equipment room is small and difficult to walk through due to pieces of equipment and boxes of supplies stored there. Your coworker begins to remove equipment and boxes from the room and piles them in front of the doorway to make more room for you to work. Select the BEST response and the WORST response.

a. Work as quickly as possible so that you can clear the doorway sooner.
b. Immediately remove the equipment from the doorway.
c. Tell your coworker that you can't completely block a doorway, and remove one of the boxes to clear a small path.
d. Continue moving boxes as needed because it won't take more than a few minutes to complete your task.

21. You are employed in a facility that uses types of gases that are stored in cylinders. While walking through another unit, you see pressurized E cylinders of oxygen propped against a wall, whereas others are laying on the ground. Select the BEST response and the WORST response.

a. Leave the cylinders as they are.
b. Put the cylinders that are on the ground in a tank holder.
c. Find tank holders for all of the cylinders.
d. Inform your supervisor that some oxygen cylinders are unsecured.
e. Tell the unit's employees that some of their cylinders need to be secured.

22. You are the leader of a small team in a foreign embassy. Some of your team members practice a religion in which they must pray several times a day at specific intervals. You are shorthanded today and would prefer that these employees work without their usual prayer breaks. Select the BEST response and the WORST response.

a. Tell the employees that you are too shorthanded today to take breaks.
b. Ask the employees if they could alter their prayer schedule so that not all employees are away at once.
c. Offer the employees a quiet place to pray that is close by so that they are not away for too long.
d. Allow the employees to take their usual prayer breaks with no modifications.

23. You are stationed at the front desk of a foreign embassy. Your job entails checking and recording visitors' and employees' identification information, logging their entrance and exit times, and giving directions as needed. A visitor, whom you've met several times before, is running late for his appointment and is irritated that you are stopping him for an identification check. Select the BEST response and the WORST response.

a. Tell him that you do recognize him and wave him through.
b. Apologize for the inconvenience, and tell him that although you do remember him well, you are required to log his identifying information at every visit.
c. Tell him that your job requires you to log his identifying information, and you will report him if there is any further argument.
d. Record his identifying information, and then speak with your supervisor to ensure you are following proper procedure.

24. You work in an area that handles and disposes of hazardous chemicals. During orientation, you were instructed to wear gloves and a splash mask when handling the chemicals, as they can be dangerous to your health. Lately, you've noticed that your department has not been stocking the protective equipment that you need to perform your job. You notified your supervisor, who stated that due to budget constraints in the department, she is trying to stop nonessential purchasing. She says the chemicals aren't that dangerous and to be careful. Select the BEST response and the WORST response.

a. Bring personal protective equipment from home.
b. Continue to work while being extra cautious with the chemicals.
c. Tell your supervisor that you can't complete your job without the splash mask and gloves.
d. Report the issue to your facility's safety team.
e. Ask the supervisor in a neighboring department if you might use some of their personal protective equipment today since your department ran out.

25. You are working at the front desk of a foreign embassy when an employee enters. She looks ill and is sweating. She says she feels lightheaded and promptly loses consciousness. You can tell that she's hit her head from the sound of her falling to the floor. What should you do first? Select the BEST response and the WORST response.

a. Splash water on her face, and call for another employee's assistance.
b. Activate the emergency response system.
c. Move her out of the vestibule and over to a quieter area for further assessment.
d. Immediately call her supervisor to report the incident.
e. Check to see if she is breathing and has a pulse.

26. You are a new employee stationed in a foreign country that is experiencing civil unrest. An act of terrorism is carried out with many casualties and injured civilians. You are called along with the rest of your facility to help assess and move victims into the medical tents. The situation is chaotic, and you have no specific instructions from your supervisor. Select the BEST response and the WORST response.

a. Wait for specific instructions from the medical team.
b. Look for the most severely injured people, and move them to the medical tents first.
c. Move the people closest to you over to the medical tents first.
d. Ask a coworker with more seniority to help you assess victims.

27. You are a new member of your facility's disaster response team. You are on your way home when you receive an automated phone call from your facility's emergency response system. The call says that a mass casualty disaster has taken place at your facility, and you are asked to report back to the building immediately and meet in the front parking lot. Once you return to the building, what should you do first? Select the BEST response and the WORST response.

a. Report to the parking lot, and ask a coworker what needs to be done.
b. Report to the parking lot, and find your emergency coordinator.
c. Begin work immediately by assessing the situation and taking action.
d. Call your supervisor, and ask how you can help.

28. A new employee has reported for work, and your supervisor asks you to escort her to the department and make her feel welcome. Select the BEST response and the WORST response.

a. Say hello to the employee and offer a handshake. Then, introduce yourself and escort her to the department.
b. Greet the employee with a warm hug, and tell her you are delighted she's joining the team. Then, take her to the department.
c. Say hello to the employee and wait for her to initiate a handshake. Then, escort her to the department.
d. Greet the employee with a handshake, and tell her you'd be happy to show her around.

English Expression

Questions 1 through 15 pertain to the following passage:

1

A nuclear nonproliferation treaty was signed in 1968 to attempt to stop the spread of nuclear technology. The United Nations was instrumental in (1) ensuring that the text of the treaty conveyed what it meant to—that the United States and other so-called nuclear states (France, United Kingdom, the then–Soviet Union, the (2)Peoples Republic Of China) could not provide nuclear weapons to nonnuclear states—those states that did not have them. The treaty was signed by over sixty countries, but some refused. (3) Israel, Pakistan, India, and North Korea have admitted to having nuclear weapons but won't agree to abide by the treaty.

2

(4) The first pillar ensures safety with all nuclear weaponry presently in possession of countries in the treaty. Those countries that have signed the treaty agree that they will not receive, create, or otherwise get or use another country's help to acquire nuclear weapons. They vow that they won't use those nuclear weapons they may already have (5) excepting to protect (6) their self.

3

The second pillar of the treaty says that those (7) nuclear weapons' countries should work toward disarmament, meaning (8) therefore, that they are to eliminate those weapons that they may already have. This part of the treaty may be difficult to enforce and (9) implying international trust that all countries will eventually work toward that end. Since the treaty asks countries to negotiate this pillar in (10) Good Faith, it may make enforcement procedures difficult as the treaty is presently written. Still, countries signing the treaty have agreed that disarmament is an ultimate goal.

4

The third pillar of the treaty allows for (11) peacetime use of nuclear energy. Compliance (12) about this part of the (13) treaty; means that countries are still able to use the nuclear energy they presently have, but not as part of nuclear weaponry. Nuclear materials (14) that are generally considered to be ingredients for nuclear weapons (e.g., uranium, plutonium) should be carefully overseen.

The United Nations was instrumental in (1) ensuring that the text of the treaty conveyed what it meant to—that the United States and other so-called nuclear states (France, United Kingdom, the then–Soviet Union, Peoples Republic Of China) could not provide nuclear weapons to nonnuclear states—those states that did not have them.

1. Which of the following is the most correct?

a. ensuring
b. assuring
c. insuring
d. reassuring

FSOT Practice Test #1

The United Nations was instrumental in ensuring that the text of the treaty conveyed what it meant to—that the United States and other so-called nuclear states (France, United Kingdom, the then-Soviet Union, the (2) Peoples Republic Of China) could not provide nuclear weapons to nonnuclear states—those states that did not have them.

2. Which of the following is the most correct?

a. Peoples Republic Of China
b. People's Republic of China
c. Peoples Republic of China
d. People's Republic Of China

(3) Israel, Pakistan, India, and North Korea have admitted to having nuclear weapons but won't agree to abide by the treaty.

3. Which sentence best joins the previous sentence with the one following?

a. Here are the names of the countries.
b. All of these countries cite the same reasons.
c. There are a variety of reasons.
d. They won't sign the treaty.

(4) The first pillar ensures safety with all nuclear weaponry presently in possession of countries in the treaty. Those countries that have signed the treaty agree that they will not receive, create, or otherwise get or use another country's help to acquire nuclear weapons. They vow that they won't use those nuclear weapons they may already have excepting to protect their self.

4. Which sentence best introduces this paragraph?

a. The nuclear nonproliferation treaty comprises three parts, or pillars.
b. The nuclear nonproliferation treaty is made up of pillars.
c. The nuclear nonproliferation treaty is multi-faceted.
d. The nuclear nonproliferation treaty is three-tiered.

They vow that they won't use those nuclear weapons they may already have (5) excepting to protect their self.

5. Which of the following is the most correct?

a. excepting
b. accepting
c. except
d. accept

They vow that they won't use those nuclear weapons they may already have excepting to protect (6) their self.

6. Which of the following is the most correct?

a. their self.
b. their selves.
c. them self.
d. themselves.

The second pillar of the treaty says that those (7) <u>nuclear weapons' countries</u> should work toward disarmament, meaning therefore, that they are to eliminate those weapons that they may already have.

7. Which of the following is the most correct?

a. nuclear weapons' countries
b. nuclear weapons countries
c. countries with nuclear weapons
d. countries with nuclear weapons'

The second pillar of the treaty says that those nuclear weapons' countries should work toward disarmament, meaning (8) <u>therefore, that</u> they are to eliminate those weapons that they may already have.

8. Which of the following is the most correct?

a. therefore, that
b. therefore that
c. that
d. OMIT phrase

This part of the treaty may be difficult to enforce and (9) <u>implying</u> international trust that all countries will eventually work toward that end.

9. Which of the following is the most correct?

a. implying
b. implies
c. applying
d. applies

Since the treaty asks countries to negotiate this pillar in (10) <u>Good Faith</u>, it may make enforcement procedures difficult as the treaty is presently written.

10. Which of the following is the most correct?

a. Good Faith
b. good faith
c. "Good Faith"
d. "good faith"

The third pillar of the treaty allows for (11) <u>peacetime</u> use of nuclear energy.

11. Which of the following is the most correct?

a. peacetime
b. peaceable
c. peacelike
d. peaceful

Compliance (12) <u>about</u> this part of the treaty; means that countries are still able to use the nuclear energy they presently have, but not as part of nuclear weaponry.

12. Which of the following is the most correct?

a. about
b. among
c. with
d. over

Compliance about this part of the (13) <u>treaty; means</u> that countries are still able to use the nuclear energy they presently have, but not as part of nuclear weaponry.

13. Which of the following is the most correct?

a. treaty; means
b. treaty, means
c. treaty. Means
d. treaty means

Nuclear materials (14) <u>that are</u> generally considered to be ingredients for nuclear weapons (e.g., uranium, plutonium) should be carefully overseen.

14. Which of the following is the most correct?

a. that are
b. which are
c. are
d. OMIT the underlined portion

15. Which sentence could best be used as a final sentence of this passage?

a. The three pillars of the treaty combine for a strong program among those who have signed.
b. The treaty is ultimately meaningless, since not all nuclear materials are being overseen in this way.
c. The three pillars contain essentially the same information and should be combined into one.
d. The three pillars of the treaty ensure that there are no nuclear problems in our world.

Questions 16 through 37 pertain to the following passage:

1

Most journalists would agree that print newspapers today are in survival mode. The past decade has been an unsettled one for national and local papers, as online technology has provided (16) enhanced opportunity's" for readers to get news that is usually (17) free, extensive, and available at any time of the day or night. Add our (18) countries' current poor economic conditions to the equation and publishers of most large national newspapers don't need to read quarterly figures. They know that the (19) circulation figures for print newspapers continue to fall.

2

Since they employ so many people in a variety of capacities, newspaper publishers have a dilemma that is (20) not going to only get worse with time. They know that their reading audience is moving to online content. Although most of (21) there older readers are still loyal to the print edition of the newspaper, the number of new, younger readers is in decline. These tech-savvy readers get almost all of their news through the electronic (23) media their computers cell phones and handheld devices. News executives, many of them not completely comfortable with technology themselves, must figure out a way to be successful in this easily accessible electronic world.

3

Advertising online may not have the impact a print advertisement can have. Think of (25) a full page advertisement in (26) The New York Times or USA Today. A well-placed print ad is often difficult for readers (27) to ignore it. The opposite tends to be true with online advertising—savvy readers can click past an ad in a second. Advertisers are still gauging the effectiveness of placing their ads on online (28) newscites.

4

Some newspapers have experimented with charging a (29) fee for access to their online news sites. Successful (30) subscription, based online newspapers have content that is (31) both unique or valuable. Since many reputable websites offer their news at no charge and update it constantly, it is difficult for most newspapers to compete online. (32) Subscribers' seem to have no reason to pay for (33) his newspaper's content.

5

News is big business. Publishers and owners of print newspapers must figure out ways to (35) keep their readers loyal, produce revenue, and stay viable in (36) todays' changing world. Most newspaper executives know that the window of time (37) to adopted to the changing market narrows each week.

The past decade has been an unsettled one for national and local papers, as online technology has provided (16) enhanced opportunity's" for readers to get news that is usually free, extensive, and available at any time of the day or night.

16. Which of the following is the most correct?

a. "enhanced opportunity's"
b. enhanced opportunity's
c. "enhanced opportunities"
d. enhanced opportunities

The past decade has been an unsettled one for national and local papers, as online technology has provided enhanced opportunity's" for readers to get news that is usually (17) free, extensive, and available at any time of the day or night.

17. Which of the following is the most correct?

a. free, extensive, and available
b. free extensive and available
c. free, extensive, and available,
d. free extensive, and available

Add our (18) countries' current poor economic conditions to the equation and publishers of most large national newspapers don't need to read quarterly figures.

18. Which of the following is the most correct?

a. countries'
b. country's
c. countries
d. countrys'

They know that the (19) circulation figures for print newspapers continue to fall.

19. Which of the following is the most correct?

a. circulation figures for print newspapers continue
b. circulation figures for print newspapers continues
c. circulation figure for print newspapers continue
d. circulation figure for print newspapers continues

Since they employ so many people in a variety of capacities, newspaper publishers have a dilemma that is (20) not going to only get worse with time.

20. Which of the following is the most correct?

a. not going to only get worse
b. not only going to get worse
c. only going to get more worse
d. only going to get worse

Although most of (21) there older readers are still loyal to the print edition of the newspaper, the number of new, younger readers is in decline.

21. Which of the following is the most correct?

a. there
b. their
c. theyre
d. they're

22. The writer wants to add this sentence to the paragraph:

They must solve their problem before their company is no longer viable.

The best place to put this sentence would be after the sentence ending with:

a. . . . moving to online content.
b. . . . younger readers is in decline.
c. . . . cell phones, and handheld devices.
d. . . . in this easily accessible electronic world.

These tech-savvy readers get almost all of their news through the electronic (23) media their computers cell phones and handheld devices.

23. Which of the following is the most correct?

a. media their computers cell phones and handheld devices
b. media, their computers, cell phones, and handheld devices
c. media: their computers, cell phones, and handheld devices
d. media: their computers, cell, phones and handheld devices

Advertising online may not have the impact a print advertisement can have. Think of a full page advertisement in *The New York Times* or *USA Today*. A well-placed print ad is often difficult for readers to ignore it. The opposite tends to be true with online advertising—savvy readers can click past an ad in a second. Advertisers are still gauging the effectiveness of placing their ads on online newscites.

24. Which of the following sentences would provide the best introduction to paragraph 3?

a. Many newspapers contain advertisements of different sizes.
b. A logical place to gain revenue is advertising.
c. Advertising is big business.
d. Don't count out advertising.

Think of (25) a full page advertisement in *The New York Times* or *USA Today*. A well-placed print ad is often difficult for readers to ignore it.

25. Which of the following is the most correct?

a. a full page advertisement
b. a full, page advertisement
c. a full-page-advertisement
d. a full-page advertisement

Think of a full page advertisement in (26) *<u>The New York Times</u>* or *USA Today*. A well-placed print ad is often difficult for readers to ignore it.

26. Which of the following is the most correct?

a. The New York Times
b. The New York Times:
c. The New York Times,
d. The New York Times—

Think of a full page advertisement in *The New York Times* or *USA Today*. A well-placed print ad is often difficult for readers (27) <u>to ignore it</u>.

27. Which of the following is the most correct?

a. to ignore it
b. to ignore them
c. to be ignored
d. to ignore

Advertisers are still gauging the effectiveness of placing their ads on online (28) <u>newscites</u>.

28. Which of the following is the most correct?

a. newscites
b. news sites
c. news sights
d. newsites

Some newspapers have experimented with charging a (29) <u>fee for access to their</u> online news sites.

29. Which of the following is the most correct?

a. fee for access to their
b. fee for accessing to their
c. fees for assess to their
d. fee assessing to their

Successful (30) <u>subscription, based</u> online newspapers have content that is both unique or valuable.

30. Which of the following is the most correct?

a. subscription, based
b. subscription based
c. subscription-based
d. subscription based,

Successful subscription, based online newspapers have content that is (31) <u>both unique or valuable</u>.

31. Which of the following is the most correct?

a. both unique or valuable
b. both unique, or valuable
c. both unique, and valuable
d. both unique and valuable

(32) <u>Subscribers'</u> seem to have no reason to pay for his newspaper's content.

32. Which of the following is the most correct?

a. Subscribers'
b. Subscriber's
c. Subscribers
d. Subscriber

Subscribers' seem to have no reason to pay for (33) <u>his</u> newspaper's content.

33. Which of the following is the most correct?

a. his
b. her
c. their
d. its

34. What is the best place to put this additional sentence?

That's why the next year will be crucial to this market.

a. Before Sentence 1
b. After Sentence 1
c. After Sentence 2
d. After Sentence 3

Publishers and owners of print newspapers must figure out ways to (35) <u>keep their readers loyal, produce revenue, and</u> stay viable in todays' changing world.

35. Which of the following is the most correct?

a. keep their readers loyal, produce revenue, and
b. keep their readers loyal produce revenue and
c. keep their readers loyal, produce, revenue, and
d. keep their readers, loyal produce, revenue and

Publishers and owners of print newspapers must figure out ways to keep their readers loyal, produce revenue, and stay viable in (36) <u>todays' changing world</u>.

36. Which of the following is the most correct?

a. todays' changing world
b. todays changing world
c. today's changing world
d. to-day's changing world

Most newspaper executives know that the window of time (37) <u>to adopted</u> to the changing market narrows each week.

37. Which of the following is the most correct?

a. to adopted
b. to adapted
c. to adapt
d. to adopt

Questions 38 through 45 pertain to the following passage:

1

Cronyism (38) was best described like when a person in (39) an authoritarian position gives a job to a loyal friend or social contact simply because of (40) their relationship to each other. Many times the person hired or appointed is not particularly qualified to perform the job and learns the duties once in (41) place—on-the-job-training.

2

Cronyism is a problem for business and government because the most qualified (or even a marginally qualified) person is (42) overlooked with regard to a position in favor of an administrator's or (43) managers' buddy with zero experience in that line of work. This friend, or crony, usually won't perform the duties of the job with any efficiency or skill and (44) the company, business, or organization can suffer as money and time is wasted and the job is not being done as well as it could be.

3

Some historians cite President John Kennedy's appointment of his longtime friend Robert McNamara as secretary of defense as a classic case of cronyism. McNamara had no experience at all in foreign affairs or defense strategies, yet was given this highly influential and important appointment by his friend. Robert McNamara is often mentioned as the person directly responsible for getting the United States involved in the war in Vietnam—

Cronyism (38) <u>was</u> best described as when a person in an authoritarian position gives a job to a loyal friend or social contact simply because of their relationship to each other.

38. Which of the following is the most correct?

a. was
b. were
c. is
d. are

Cronyism was best described as when a person in (39) <u>an authoritarian position</u> gives a job to a loyal friend or social contact simply because of their relationship to each other.

39. Which of the following is the most correct?

a. an authoritative position
b. a position of authority
c. a position
d. the know

Cronyism was best described as when a person in an authoritarian position gives a job to a loyal friend or social contact simply because of (40) <u>their relationship to each other</u>.

40. Which of the following is the most correct?

a. their relationship to each other.
b. each's relationship to the other.
c. ones' relationship with the other.
d. the relationship one has with the other.

Many times, the person hired or appointed is not particularly qualified to perform the job and learns the duties once in (41) <u>place—on</u>-the-job-training.

41. Which of the following is the most correct?

a. place—on
b. place. On
c. place; on
d. place on

Cronyism is a problem for business and government because the most qualified (or even a marginally qualified) person is (42) <u>overlooked with regard to a position</u> in favor of an administrator's or managers' buddy with zero experience in that line of work.

42. Which of the following is the most correct?

a. overlooked with regard to a position
b. overlooked with a position
c. overlooked during a position
d. overlooked for a position

Cronyism is a problem for business and government because the most qualified (or even a marginally qualified) person is overlooked with regard to a position in favor of an administrator's or (43) <u>managers'</u> buddy with zero experience in that line of work.

43.Which of the following is the most correct?

a. managers'
b. managers
c. manager
d. manager's

This friend, or crony, usually won't perform the duties of the job with any efficiency or skill and (44) <u>the company, business, or organization</u> can suffer as money and time is wasted and the job is not being done as well as it could be.

44. Which of the following is the most correct?

a. the company, business, or organization
b. the company business, or organization
c. the company—business—or organization
d. the company; business; or organization

Some historians cite President John Kennedy's appointment of his longtime friend Robert McNamara as Secretary of Defense as a classic case of cronyism. McNamara had no experience at all in foreign affairs or defense strategies, yet was given this highly influential and important appointment by his friend. Robert McNamara is often mentioned as the person directly responsible for getting the United States involved in the war in Vietnam—(45)

45. Which ending to this sentence provides the best conclusion to the passage?

a. a war that is said to be a disastrous event in our country's history.
b. a war that was fought for many years.
c. a war that many people today may not understand.
d. a war that has cronyism to thank for its inception.

FSOT Practice Test #1

Questions 46 through 53 pertain to the following passage:

1

The United States Coast Guard (46) was founded in 1790 as the branch of military service responsible for safeguarding the country's sea-related interests. (47) It was originally created to protect the U.S. (48) from smugglers, and to enforce tariff and trade laws. While this may seem like a job for the Navy, the Navy's purpose is very different from that of the Coast Guard. The Navy's job is (49) to engage in combat, defend the seas from threats to the U.S. and its interests worldwide. The United States Coast Guard is actually a part of the Department of Homeland Security and is considered a federal law enforcement agency. The mission of the department is to protect and to enforce laws on US coastlines and in ports and to safeguard other interests within American waters.

2

In addition to enforcing maritime (50) law, we need to recognize that the United States Coast Guard also serves as a guardian of the environment. This includes stopping waste and other types of pollution from being dumped into the ocean, preventing and helping to clean up oil spills, and even preventing introduction of species of marine life that could threaten the balance of existing environments. (51) This is a real important job for the Coast Guard because there would not be much of a coastline to protect if the seas were too polluted to entertain or to sustain life.

3

(52) Performing in a single day, the United States Coast Guard personnel save 12 lives, respond to 64 search and rescue cases, keep 842 pounds of cocaine off the streets, service 116 buoys and fix 24 discrepancies, screen 720 commercial vessels and 183,000 crew and passengers, issue 173 credentials to merchant mariners, investigate 13 marine accidents, inspect 68 containers and 29 vessels for compliance with air emissions standards, perform 28 safety and environmental examinations of foreign vessels, board 13 fishing boats to ensure compliance with fisheries laws, and (53) explore and investigate 10 pollution incidents.

The United States Coast Guard (46) <u>was founded in 1790</u> as the branch of military service responsible for safeguarding the country's sea-related interests.

46. Which of the following is the most correct?

a. NO CHANGE
b. was founded in 1790,
c. were founded in 1790
d. will have been founded in 1790

(47) <u>It was originally created</u> to protect the U.S. from smugglers, and to enforce tariff and trade laws.

47. Which of the following is the most correct?

a. NO CHANGE
b. It was originally established
c. The branch was originally created
d. Originally, it was created

It was originally created to protect the U.S. (48) from smugglers, and to enforce tariff and trade laws.

48. Which of the following is the most correct?

a. NO CHANGE
b. from smugglers, and enforce
c. from smugglers, and to promote
d. from smugglers and to enforce

The Navy's job is (49) to engage in combat, defend the seas from threats to the U.S. and its interests worldwide.

49. Which of the following is the most correct?

a. NO CHANGE
b. to engage in combats and defend the seas
c. to engage in combat, and defend the seas
d. to engage in combat and defend the seas

In addition to enforcing maritime (50) law, we need to recognize that the United States Coast Guard also serves as a guardian of the environment.

50. Which of the following is the most correct?

a. NO CHANGE
b. law, also serving the United States Coast Guard
c. law we need to recognize that the United States Coast Guard serves
d. law, the United States Coast Guard also serves

(51) This is a real important job for the Coast Guard because there would not be much of a coastline to protect if the seas were too polluted to entertain or to sustain life.

51. Which of the following is the most correct?

a. NO CHANGE
b. Truly, this is not an important
c. This is a critical
d. This is a truly, valuable

(52) Performing in a single day, the United States Coast Guard personnel save 12 lives...

52. Which of the following is the most correct?

a. NO CHANGE
b. In one single day
c. Accomplishing in a day
d. In an average day

Performing in a single day, the United States Coast Guard personnel save 12 lives ... board 13 fishing boats to ensure compliance with fisheries laws, and (53) explore and investigate 10 pollution incidents.

53. Which of the following is the most correct?

a. NO CHANGE
b. investigate 10 pollution incidents
c. explore, and investigate 10 pollution incidents
d. explore to investigate 10 pollution incidents

54. Select the best order for the following sentences to create a well-organized paragraph.

Sentence 1: However, telecommuting does have some drawbacks.
Sentence 2: Companies can also save money by lowering overhead costs because off-site employees do not require office space, lighting, heating/cooling, and other expenses.
Sentence 3: The employee, obviously, can save time and money by staying home and may be able to have a more flexible schedule to work around children's school days or other responsibilities.
Sentence 4: Telecommuting has many advantages both to the employee and the employer.

a. 4,3,2,1
b. 2,3,4,1
c. 4,2,3,1
d. 3,1,2,4

55. Select the best order for the following sentences to create a well-organized paragraph.

Sentence 1: Historically, there have never been any legal regulations in the United States to control power plants' emissions.
Sentence 2: Power plants in America source half of their energy from coal.
Sentence 3: The emissions from coal-fired power plants include arsenic, lead, mercury, and many other poisonous air pollutants.
Sentence 4: However, the EPA has developed such regulations with laws such as the Disposal of Coal Combustion Residuals that are continually updated and amended.
Sentence 5: Death, respiratory illnesses like asthma, and developmental disabilities in children are all attributed to these types of air pollution.

a. 2,1,3,4,5
b. 2,3,5,1,4
c. 4,5,2,3,1
d. 3,5,2,1,4

56. Select the best order for the following sentences to create a well-organized paragraph.

Sentence 1: Vladimir Ilyich Lenin founded the communist Soviet Union and was succeeded by Joseph Stalin.
Sentence 2: Stalin died in 1953, with the blood of perhaps 20 million people on his hands.
Sentence 3: Stalin's totalitarian regime aimed to industrialize the country, in part by forcing the migration of peasants to the cities.
Sentence 4: He murdered thousands of farmers who resisted forced migration, and his program for turning over the countryside to collectives resulted in massive famines that killed millions.

a. 1,2,3,4
b. 1,3,4,2
c. 1,4,2,3
d. 1,4,3,2

57. Which of the following is the most correct?

a. When there is no dominant or majority party, disparate parties must join together to create a coalition government.
b. When there is no dominant or majority party: disparate parties must join together to create a coalition government.
c. Disparate parties must join together to create a coalition government. When there is no dominant or majority party.
d. When there, is no dominant or majority party, disparate parties must join together to create a coalition government.

58. Which of the following is the most correct?

a. Some comparative political scientists focus on granular, on the ground research, which they use to create general theories.
b. Some comparative political scientists focus on granular, on-the-ground research. Which they use to create general theories.
c. Some comparative political scientists focus on granular, on-the-ground research, which they use to create general theories.
d. Some comparative political scientists focus on granular, on-the-ground research; which they use to create general theories.

59. Which of the following is the most correct?

a. The Mexican constitution arranges the government in much the same way as that of the United States, which was drafted on February 5, 1917.
b. The Mexican constitution, which was drafted on February 5; 1917, arranges the government in much the same way as that of the United States.
c. The Mexican constitution which was drafted on February, 5 1917, arranges the government in much the same way as that of the United States.
d. The Mexican constitution, which was drafted on February 5, 1917, arranges the government in much the same way as that of the United States.

60. Which of the following is the most correct?

a. In 1995, russians elected very conservative and communist candidates, and in 1996, Yeltsin won reelection only because he was supported by a coalition of wealthy businessmen.
b. In 1995 and in 1996, Russians elected very conservative and communist candidates. Yeltsin won reelection only because he was supported by a coalition of wealthy businessmen.
c. In 1995, russians elected very conservative and communist candidates and in 1996. Yeltsin won reelection only because he was supported by a coalition of wealthy businessmen.
d. In 1995, Russians elected very conservative and communist candidates, and in 1996, Yeltsin won reelection only because he was supported by a coalition of wealthy businessmen.

61. Which of the following is the most correct?

a. However; Jiang also promoted the Special Economic Zone program and worked to get China admitted to the World Trade Organization.
b. However: Jiang also promoted the special economic zone program and worked to get China admitted to the World Trade Organization.
c. However, Jiang also promoted the Special Economic Zone program and worked to get China admitted to the World Trade Organization.
d. However, Jiang also promoted the Special Economic Zone program. He also worked to get China admitted to the World Trade Organization.

62. Which of the following is the most correct?

a. Great Britain does not have a written constitution; instead, it relies on historical precedent and case law.
b. Great Britain does not have a written constitution, instead; it relies on historical precedent and case law.
c. Great Britain does not have, a written constitution; instead, it relies on historical precedent and case law.
d. Great Britain does not have a written constitution, instead, it relies on historical precedent and case law.

FSOT Practice Test #1

63. Which of the following is the most correct?

a. Gorbachev had three goals; perestroika, or industrial reform, democratization, and glasnost, or openness to the rest of the world.
b. Gorbachev had three goals: perestroika, or industrial reform; democratization; and glasnost, or openness to the rest of the world.
c. Gorbachev had three goals—perestroika, or industrial reform, democratization, and glasnost, or openness to the rest of the world.
d. Gorbachev had three goals. Perestroika, or industrial reform; democratization; and glasnost, or openness to the rest of the world.

64. Which of the following is the most correct?

a. Ernesto Zedillo became known as the accidental president of Mexico; he only became the PRI candidate after the murder of Luis Donaldo Colosio.
b. Ernesto Zedillo became known as the "accidental president" of Mexico because he only became the PRI candidate after the murder of Luis Donaldo Colosio.
c. Ernesto Zedillo became known as the accidental president of Mexico because he only become the PRI candidate after the murder of Luis Donaldo Colosio.
d. Ernesto Zedillo became known as the "Accidental President" of Mexico; because he only became the PRI candidate after the murder of Luis Donaldo Colosio.

65. Which of the following is the most correct?

a. In the socialist and communist systems the government owns the vast majority of the means of production.
b. In the socialist and communist systems the government own the vast majority of the means of production.
c. In the socialist and communist systems, the government owns the vast majority of the means of production.
d. In the socialist, and communist systems, the government own the vast majority of the means of production.

Written Essay

You will have 30 minutes to write an essay on an assigned topic. Sample topics are provided below. Choose one.

As you create your essay, you should present and support your point of view. Your writing will be evaluated on the quality of the writing and not on your opinion. A good essay will have an organized structure, clear thesis, and logical supporting details. Ensure that you are presenting your topic in a way that appeals to your target audience. Use clear and appropriate word choice throughout. Ensure that grammar, punctuation, and spelling are correct. Your response can be of any length.

1. The issue of how to deal with student loan debt in the United States has grown more contentious in recent history as the outstanding balance for federally owned student loans has grown beyond one trillion dollars. Some argue that cancelling student loan debt across the board is unwise or simply unfair, while others claim it is a necessary and vital part of creating a well-educated and stable society. Some instead argue that the real crisis is that the cost of higher education is unsustainable and needs to be reevaluated at a fundamental level. Is erasing student loan debt a viable option? Explain your rationale.

2. The Russian invasion of Ukraine in early 2022 was a major shock to the world, both in terms of the brazenness of the unprovoked attack, but also the tenacity of the Ukrainian resistance against such a daunting opposition. However, despite near universal condemnation among Western nations of Russia's actions, no other nations militarily intervened, recognizing that aggressive direct intervention could potentially escalate the conflict to nuclear levels. Are economic sanctions and arms dealing sufficient forms of intervention in a foreign conflict when direct military intervention is not viable? Should the United States engage in foreign intervention at all when not directly threatened or compelled by treaty?

Answer Key and Explanations #1

Job Knowledge

1. C: "Bcc" means "blind carbon copy." When an email is sent this way, the original recipient does not know who else may be getting it. Sending a cc means that all recipients know who is getting a copy. Forwarding an email is a way to send it to someone else without letting the intended recipient know, but it is not the most efficient way.

2. D: The mode is the value that occurs most often in a listing.

3. D: The U.S. banking system is one of the most regulated banking systems in the world, with regulations within each state and the federal government.

4. A: Although many programs were introduced under Franklin Roosevelt's New Deal, the Medicaid and Medicare programs were started by Johnson.

5. A: The Federal Reserve System raises and lowers the prime rate to regulate the nation's money supply.

6. B: The waterways of the United States are closely tied to its ability to transport the goods that are able to be grown year-round within the country. This greatly affects the economy. The U.S. government has a laissez-faire policy as it applies to the economy. Russia's geography means that there is a short growing season. The country has a very small coastline and waterways that do not connect. Their economy is defined by their geography.

7. A: The EU is committed to the environment, humanitarian values, peace, stability, European solidarity, and a common market. The first two treaties shared a common theme. The Treaty of Paris, 1951, created a common steel and coal market between the original members. The Treaty of Rome, 1957, built the European Economic Community (EEC). These treaties both focused on creating a common market.

8. A: Among the choices listed, a database is best defined as a tool that is used for collecting and organizing information. The other choices are all potential uses for a database, but choice A is the best general definition.

9. A: Good managers will set up an environment where people will be motivated to work.

10. B: Title VII prohibits intentional discrimination and practices with the effect of discriminating against individuals because of their race, color, national origin, religion, or gender.

11. B: Noncitizens are able to receive Medicaid, food stamps, and Social Security benefits. They contribute to the economy by working, paying taxes, and buying products.

12. B: In an attempt to keep the population down, China instituted a one-child policy. Nigeria has the largest population in Africa. The government has provided more access to birth control and encouraged families to limit themselves to four children.

13. C: Lech Walesa was the president during this time. Helmut Kohl was the German chancellor. Ceausescu was a Communist dictator. Havel was elected president of the Czech Republic in 1989.

14. C: The Irish Republican Army (IRA) was a paramilitary organization wanting Northern Ireland's independence from Britain. Al-Qaeda is a Muslim terrorist group.

15. A: Insurgency is a military struggle involving guerilla warfare of small rural bands. Insurgents can hold to different causes or ideologies. While it is commonly thought to be caused by ethnic or religious differences, weakened governments are more likely to see insurgency.

16. C: The Maastricht Treaty was signed in the Netherlands and created both the European Union and the euro as its currency.

17. B: Neoliberalism is an economic model encouraged by the United States which encourages free markets and private ownership of businesses.

18. A: Germany developed rocket technology and the United States put a man on the moon in 1969.

19. C: In absolutism, the ruler is sovereign. Kings often said that they governed by divine right and were responsible to only God. Patriarchy is a social organization where descent follows the male line. An oligarchy is a small group of people who control a government. Communism is where a communist party holds power alone.

20. C: There are Federal Reserve banks in (1) Boston; (2) New York; (3) Philadelphia; (4) Cleveland; (5) Richmond; (6) Atlanta; (7) Chicago; (8) St. Louis; (9) Minneapolis; (10) Dallas; (11) Kansas City; and (12) San Francisco.

21. D: A stateless nation is one that wants statehood but does not have it (Kurds in the Middle East). An industrialized but not democratic country is how a Second World country is usually described. An impoverished and unstable country is a description of a Third World country.

22. D: In 2002, the United States was involved with nation building in Afghanistan.

23. A: The Patriot Act was specifically formed to combat terrorism.

24. B: The First Amendment covers freedom of the press, petitioning the government, and assembling peacefully. "Cruel and unusual punishment" is covered in the Eighth Amendment.

25. B: The Fourth Amendment outlaws unreasonable search and seizure. The Eighth Amendment protects against excessive bail. The Fourteenth Amendment states the rights of citizenship.

26. D: Free speech means that people can generally say what they want to. Propaganda is misinformation and half-truths about something. "Penny press" is the phrase used to describe the early newspapers published in the United States.

27. D: Senators are elected for a term of 6 years.

28. D: Although an immigrant or a nonresident alien can be a refugee, the term for people who flee for political reasons is "refugee."

29. C: Chairpersons for standing committees of Congress are chosen by leaders of the majority party.

30. A: Although Congress must agree to pay for foreign policy dictated by the president, it does not decide foreign policy.

31. D: The education of the workforce generally does not affect GDP. The size of the workforce implies that there are people who are ready and willing to work. The amount of capital means that there is a sufficient number of factories and assets available to create goods and services. Technology includes the skills and knowledge people have to direct and enable the workforce.

32. C: While many Communist regimes limit international trade, liberals, Marxists, social democrats, and conservatives support the idea of free international trade. Mercantilists do not support free international trade, but mercantilism is not a widely respected ideology.

33. D: Raising the minimum wage ultimately causes a rise in the rate of inflation, since employers' labor costs are raised. Employers pass this increase on as higher prices for their goods and services.

34. A: Price determines what goods will be produced, who will be producing them, and how they will be produced. Banks and demand are both affected by price. Government is not a big part of a market economy and is more a part of a command economy.

35. C: An inelastic demand is not very sensitive to changes in price. "Utility" means satisfaction or usefulness, which is not affected if the athlete buys the same amount of spinach every week.

36. D: To find the number of miles per hour over the speed limit, divide the fine by the cost for each mile over the speed limit: $882 \div 49 = 18$ mph over.

37. B: To find the correct price, first subtract 15% from the price of the book:

$$\$35.00 - 5.25 = \$29.75$$

Then subtract 10% from the discounted price:

$$\$29.75 - \$2.97 = \$26.78$$

Choice A is incorrect because the 2 percent figures cannot be added together. Choice C is just 15% off the original price. Choice D is just 10% off the original price.

38. C: Choice A represents convenience sampling since it is limited to one age. The pool of 8th grade students may not represent the opinions of all youth in the district. Choice B is biased because participants are self-selected rather than randomly selected. It may be that customers who have a strong opinion are more likely to respond than those who are more neutral, and this would give a skewed perspective of opinions. In choice C, families are randomly selected, so the sampling technique is not biased. Choice D, like choice B, is biased because participants are self-selected rather than randomly selected.

39. B: Multiply \$10,000 by 0.32 to get \$3,200. Subtract this amount from the total winnings:

$$\$10{,}000 - \$3{,}200 = \$6{,}800$$

40. C: Data is said to be positively skewed when there are a higher number of lower values, indicating data that is skewed right. Data is said to be negatively skewed when there are a higher number of higher values, indicating that the data is skewed left. Group A is positively skewed because there is a higher number of low scores. Group B is negatively skewed because there is a higher value of high scores. Since Group B generally has higher scores than Group A, Group B has a mean that is more than Group A.

41. A: In a 24-hour day, one-fourth of a day is 6 hours. Subtract this from 24 to get 18 hours. One-twelfth of his day is 2 hours. Subtract this from 18 to get 16 hours. One-half of his day is 12 hours. Subtract this from 16 to get 4 hours.

42. D: A subject line is an important part of an email and should contain a strong clue about what the message is about.

43. A: The group will be made up of people with varying education levels, attitudes, prior knowledge, and interests.

44. C: Douglas MacArthur was Roosevelt's general who advised him during this time but was not one of the Big Three. Winston Churchill was the British prime minister, Roosevelt was the ailing U.S. president, and Joseph Stalin was the head of the Soviet Union.

45. C: A firewall protects a computer from other computers and viruses. Encryption is a way to send something so that it can be read by only the recipient. A filter screens incoming messages. A bug is a problem with a computer.

46. A: Regional and ethnic cleavages have been a political struggle for the government of Nigeria. Although English is the official language of Nigeria, the country is made up of a variety of languages and cultures. Religious influences also vary. Most citizens align themselves with Muslim, Christian, and indigenous African beliefs.

47. A: The CPU is the most important part of the computer. RAM is the type of memory a computer uses. A URL is part of a web address. The OS is software used by the computer.

48. A: The denominator is the number on the bottom of a fraction. The denominator must be the same to add fractions, so before adding, the least common denominator must be found.

49. B: Goals should closely align with what the company or organization is trying to do. Although employees are usually rewarded for reaching their goals, they are not typically penalized for not reaching them. They should be set by the employee and should be attainable—but not necessarily difficult.

50. C: The law requires employers to ensure that those they hire are legally permitted to work in the United States.

51. D: The United Kingdom is a major trade partner with the US, bringing in over 100 billion dollars in trade annually, but it is significantly overshadowed by China, Japan, and Mexico.

52. C: A terabyte is equal to 1 trillion bytes (1×10^{12}) of digital information.

53. A: The term "Brexit" refers to the mixing of the two words "British" and "exit." Major contentions of this withdrawal include trade agreements and disagreements over the state of the border of Ireland.

54. B: A non-fungible token, or NFT, allows a digital file to be completely and verifiably unique. Because the file is stored in a blockchain, the file can always be proven to be the original version, even if other copies of the file are made.

55. B: The Supreme Court ruled that statements made in interrogation are not admissible unless the defendant is informed of the right to an attorney and waives that right. The case of Miranda v. Arizona was consolidated with Westover v. United States, Vignera v. New York, and California v. Stewart.

56. C: Contemporary China, also known as the People's Republic of China, was established in 1949. Nixon became the first US president to travel to the nation when he visited in 1972. He is credited with forming the basis for modern diplomacy with China.

57. D: America is a common law country because English common law was adopted in all states except Louisiana. Common law is based on precedent and changes over time. Each state develops its own common laws.

58. C: The President must be a natural citizen, be at least 35 years old, and have lived in the U.S. for 14 years. There is no education requirement for becoming President. Truman did not have a college education, but most Presidents have degrees.

59. A: A writ of certiorari is filed if a case is lost in appeals or the highest state court. The writ of certiorari is a request for the Supreme Court to hear the case, but it does not guarantee the case will be heard.

60. B: The Animal and Plant Health Inspection Service, the Food and Nutrition Service, and the Forest Service are agencies in the Department of Agriculture. The Department of Agriculture ensures food safety, works with farmers, promotes trade, and protects natural resources.

Situational Judgment

1. Best: C. Worst: B. Telling your supervisor that you have not performed this task before and may have questions about it demonstrates good communication skills and offers the supervisor insight on your comfort level regarding the new task. Telling your supervisor that you will get started right away is not the best answer because the employee in this vignette is currently "busy with other work" that was previously assigned and might need to be completed first. Similarly, option A is not the best answer because telling your supervisor that you're "busy" is never a good approach. However, the worst answer is B. Telling your supervisor that the task is outside of your scope of practice is rude and insubordinate.

2. Best: B. Worst: C. It is never appropriate to alter a coworker's workspace, as you are unfamiliar with her current work plans. Closing her screen or logging her out of the computer could result in loss of work or other mistakes. Therefore, waiting until your coworker returns and then discussing the problem with her is the best option. The worst option is C, to immediately discuss the problem with the supervisor, as this is a small security infringement and no imminent danger is present. It is best to first discuss the issue with the coworker rather than involving a supervisor.

3. Best: A. Worst: D. It is always good business practice to express appreciation for workers that go above and beyond expectations and offer new ideas and suggestions, no matter how feasible they are. This level of engagement makes a workplace run more smoothly. Although option C is similar to A, the main difference is in the execution. Telling a coworker that changes need to be made before the idea can be implemented leads the worker to believe that the idea will be implemented, when in reality, it will not. The worst answer is D. Team leaders are not dictators and must not behave as such. Team leaders must take a collaborative approach and listen to any and all ideas from their team.

4. Best: B. Worst: A. When conflict happens in the workplace, it is always appropriate to discuss the matter privately. This allows for the free exchange of ideas without outside interjection. The worst option is A. To refuse to participate in the new policy and voice your concerns immediately is a knee-jerk reaction that is rarely helpful. Refusal to follow directions is insubordinate and in many facilities, insubordination may end in termination.

5. Best: B. Worst: C. If you are unfamiliar with the culture of a community, especially one who is experiencing civil unrest, it is most beneficial to participate in company-approved events that provide you with support from coworkers as well as structured, safe interactions with the community. If the area is dangerous, it is best to visit with an existing group who knows the area and its culture. Scheduling meet-and-greet and open-house events may be useful in meeting the community as well; however, these don't provide you with support and safety from coworkers who have familiarity with the culture. Option C is the worst answer, as reading the local newspaper may offer you news stories about the civil unrest; it will not reveal as much about the culture as an immersive, firsthand experience.

6. Best: A. Worst: D. A polite redirection of the interview is best in this situation. Asking personal questions such as marital status, how many children an applicant has, and other sensitive information is illegal and potentially discriminatory. This line of questioning must be stopped immediately; therefore, option D is the worst answer.

7. Best: C. Worst: D. Your department is in turmoil. Offering daily 5-minute meetings with staff provides an immediate response to a problem within the department. When morale is low, productivity suffers. Therefore, it is good business practice to take immediate action and begin the communication process. Option A is an appropriate action to take but is not as timely as an immediate meeting with the staff. Option B is also not a wrong answer, but it takes the personal touch out of the interaction. Face-to-face discussion is always better than a memo, as tone and emotion are rarely accurately conveyed in writing. The worst answer is D, as this prolongs the unrest in the department.

8. Best: D. Worst: A. This employee has several years of experience at this company and offers solutions and new ideas. This employee would be more successful in management than a new graduate who has minimal experience or a new employee who is not as experienced. The worst answer is A. Seniority is not the only factor that should be taken into consideration when offering a promotion. This employee is frequently tardy, which may indicate a lack of interest in the job or simply poor time management skills, both of which are not conducive to a successful managerial position.

9. Best: B. Worst: C. Delegating some of the projects to responsible team members ensures that all of the projects will be completed in a timely manner. Although prioritizing is helpful, it is more beneficial to prioritize which tasks you need to complete personally and then delegate other less-important projects to your team members. Option C is the worst answer, as you have been assigned tasks that must be completed regardless of your busy schedule.

10. Best: A. Worst: D. If your department is having financial difficulties, immediate action is needed. Sending email notices rather than paper newsletters is a quick and easy way to reduce costs, as you are eliminating the need for any paper use on that project. Reducing the publication of the newsletter is also helpful but does not have as much of an impact as stopping paper use completely. Options C and E are also helpful but not quite as impactful as stopping paper use completely. Option D is the worst choice, as it is not good practice to require employees to incur the expense of bringing their own office supplies when other actions can be taken first.

11. Best: A. Worst: C. In customer service situations, it is good practice to apologize to the customer for your part in the altercation. This can go a long way to "save" a sale and potentially prevent the business from losing a customer. The worst option is C. Customer service agents must take ownership of their mistakes and make every effort to rectify them, even if they are not fully to blame for the altercation.

12. Best: B. Worst: A. The audience for your presentation is a group of customers who may be interested in purchasing the new equipment. They are likely laypeople who have no prior knowledge of technical terminology or scientific jargon. Therefore, it is important to use lay terms whenever possible but highlight and explain any important technical jargon that is critical for the understanding of how the product works or its application. Option A is the worst choice, as these customers may be confused by the technical jargon, which can lead to confusion and a lack of interest in the product.

13. Best: C. Worst: A. Open communication is critical in the workplace. Speaking to your supervisor about the cost increase and possible solutions shows enthusiasm and initiative. Option A is the worst choice because you are basing your assessment of the situation on hearsay from your coworker. It is best to discuss the problem with your supervisor first and then, if there is an ethical issue, report it to the proper chain of command in your unit or organization.

14. Best: A. Worst: C. Although option B is a kind gesture, your generosity may be abused in the future. Therefore, other options should be considered first. Option A allows for you to attempt to rectify the situation in a fair manner. Many stores and organizations do offer discounts or credit in certain situations, and it is acceptable to ask a supervisor for guidance. The worst option is C. Changing prices without permission is considered theft.

15. Best: C. Worst: A. The director has stated that the diversity training is a facility-wide initiative, which indicates that attendance is required of all employees. The worst answer is A. Skipping a required training without giving prior notice or without giving a valid reason for the absence is unacceptable and could be grounds for termination in some instances.

16. Best: C. Worst: B. It is considered rude to speak in a foreign language in front of other non-fluent members of a workplace. Speaking with a coworker privately about the issue shows maturity and tactfulness. The coworker might not realize that he or she is making other colleagues uncomfortable and should be given the benefit of the doubt. Option B is the worst option, as interrupting the conversation is a rude gesture in itself, and it can also be considered confrontational. It is not acceptable workplace behavior to instigate a potential altercation when a more tactful approach can be taken.

17. Best: A. Worst: D. It is unknown if the coworker was actually reading the document, so it is best to simply put the document away. At that point, you can speak to the coworker about the classified nature of the document and inform your supervisor of any possible security breach. Option D is the worst answer because it is unknown whether the coworker read the document; reporting him or her is premature.

18. Best: A. Worst: D. Politely correcting a coworker in a hazardous situation is an appropriate course of action. Offering to help while performing the task correctly is also an appropriate choice, but clear, direct instructions in a dangerous situation are preferred. The worst answer is D. If a situation is potentially unsafe, immediate action is required.

19. Best: B. Worst: D. After any work-related injury, it is important to immediately fill out an incident report. This should take place before any other intervention, including labeling the equipment as "broken." Once a report is filled out, your facility's human resources department or your supervisor will instruct you on further actions to take, including seeking medical care. Unless the situation is life-threatening or critical, medical care should be sought out after receiving instructions from your workplace. The worst option is D. Ignoring the incident and continuing with your workday is dangerous and can result in further injury.

20. Best: B. Worst: D. The Occupational Safety and Health Administration (OSHA) requires that all exits remain clear at all times. Boxes and equipment should never block an exit, even for only a few minutes. The worst answer is D. A blocked exit is a safety hazard and could cause injury or death in an emergency situation.

21. Best: C. Worst: A. E cylinders of oxygen are pressurized and highly combustible. If they topple over or are struck, they could explode, causing facility damage and personal injury. All gas cylinders must be secured at all times. Therefore, the worst answer is A.

22. Best: D. Worst: A. Although the employer can ask for concessions, these employees are not required to give them. Practice of religion is protected under federal law, and these employees have a right to continue to take their prayer breaks as they have done previously. The worst answer is A. It is unlawful to require employees to work with no breaks, whether that time is taken for prayer, meals, or other activities.

23. Best: B. Worst: A. Apologizing for any inconvenience is good business etiquette. Your job requires you to check the visitor's identification, log the information, and record the in and out times. Therefore, you must follow these steps with every individual every time unless told otherwise. You may choose to check with your supervisor after the encounter to ensure that you are following proper procedure, but you should first perform your job duties as previously instructed. Although both options A and C are poor choices, A is the worst choice. Waving him through without logging any information can be a potentially serious security breach. C is also a poor choice as it is a confrontational and unprofessional way to conduct your job responsibilities, but you are still logging his information as required. This is better than simply waving him through the security checkpoint, possibly putting employees and the facility at risk.

24. Best: D. Worst: B. Because you have already brought the issue to your supervisor, and she is unwilling or unable to help, it is time to follow the chain of command and make a formal complaint. The worst answer is B. The chemicals are known to be hazardous to your health, and you must not be in contact with them without the proper personal protective equipment in place. If you are unable to obtain a splash mask and gloves from other sources (such as your home or another department), then work must cease until the stocking issue is resolved.

25. Best: E. Worst: C. Whenever a medical emergency takes place and someone loses consciousness, the first thing you should do is assess the person and make sure he or she has a pulse and is breathing. This is important because to call for help, you have to describe the situation. Treating a pulseless person is different from treating a fainting victim. The next best answer is B, activating the emergency response system. This should take place shortly after you assess the severity of the emergency. The worst answer is C. This woman has hit her head and could have a cervical spine injury, so moving her may cause further injury. You should never move an accident victim of any kind unless there is immediate danger to his or her safety.

26. Best: B. Worst: A. You have been asked to assess and move victims to the medical tents. That is enough instruction to begin working. Choice A is the worst choice because waiting for more specific instruction from the medical team wastes valuable time when trying to transport critically injured civilians. Therefore, option A is the worst answer. Moving the most severely injured patients first ensures quicker access to medical care and can help prevent more casualties.

27. Best: B. Worst: C. When managing a crisis, it is important to take instruction from the leader who is managing the situation. Option C is the worst answer because taking it upon yourself to begin working without instruction can result in confusion, mistakes, and chaos. The emergency coordinator will give instructions based on the severity of the situation and will determine what actions need to take place first. They will then assign tasks to individuals.

28. Best: A. Worst: B. When greeting colleagues, it is best to take a warm but professional approach. Saying hello, introducing yourself, and offering a handshake is an appropriate greeting for a professional situation. Hugging a new acquaintance is never appropriate, as you don't know the other person's comfort level with that type of personal touch. Option B is the worst answer because hugging is not a socially appropriate greeting in the professional setting. Although C and D are also appropriate greetings, they aren't as comprehensive or welcoming as option A. Option A offers a handshake, an introduction, a greeting, and a personal escort to the department. Options C and D do not include all of these components.

English Expression

1. A: The word "ensuring" means "making certain," and it is used correctly in this sentence.

2. B: "Of" is not capitalized in this country's official name (nor would it be in a title), and "People" is in its possessive form.

3. B: The sentence that follows implies that each of these non-signing countries provides the same reason for not signing.

4. A: The sentence provides a meaning for the word "pillar," which is introduced at the beginning of the next sentence and used within the rest of the passage.

5. C: "Except" means "but" or "only" in this instance.

6. D: This sentence is talking about the countries involved with the treaty, so "themselves" is used.

7. C: "Nuclear weapons' countries" is awkward phrasing and should not be used here. There is no possessive form when the phrase is converted to "countries with nuclear weapons."

8. D: This phrase can be omitted without changing the meaning of the sentence.

9. B: The sentence is written in the present tense. "Applies" means "pertains to" or "relates to." This is not the meaning conveyed in this sentence.

10. B: "Good faith" is a phrase meaning "with fairness and trust." It is not presented in quotes or capitalized, since it is an accepted English-language phrase.

11. D: The sentence infers that nuclear energy should be used only for good.

12. C: Countries comply "with" an agreement or treaty—meaning that they will uphold what they have signed.

13. D: This part of the sentence does not need a semicolon, comma, or period, since it is not a clause or phrase.

14. D: The phrase can be omitted and the sentence does not lose its meaning.

15. A: The pillars are only as effective as those who have signed them.

16. D: There is no indication that the phrase is a quote, so quotation marks should not be used here. The plural of "opportunity" is "opportunities."

17. A: The words "free" and "extensive" should be separated by a comma, and so should "extensive" and "and." There should not be a comma after "available," since it is not part of the list.

18. B: The passage is referring to one country (the United States), and the noun "country" is in the possessive form here—apostrophe *s*.

19. A: Since "figures" is the subject of the sentence (it must be "figures" and not "figure," since it refers to more than one newspaper), "continue" must align with that word. "The figures continue" is correct but not "The figures continues."

20. D: "More worse" is considered to be bad grammar. Using "not only" implies that there will be a "but" to complete the thought, which is not the case here.

21. B: The word refers to the newspaper's older readers—the possessive form. "There" means "in that place." "Theyre" is not a word. "They're" is the contracted form of "they are."

22. D: The sentence ties up the paragraph and is best used to conclude it.

23. C: The colon after "media" indicates that the words that follow will further explain it. These items are listed, so there should be a comma after each one.

24. B: The sentence provides an overview of the solution to the problem. Sentence A provides a fact about print advertising, which is not really what the paragraph is about. Sentence C provides a statement that does not address the main idea of the paragraph—that advertising may not work as well online as it does in a print paper. Sentence D infers that advertising may work well online, which contradicts what the paragraph seems to state.

25. D: The words "full-page" are hyphenated to form an adjective phrase describing "advertisement."

26. A: There are only two newspapers listed and they are separated by "or." They do not have to be additionally separated by a comma or any other punctuation mark.

27. D: The word "it" is not needed here, since it is clear from the sentence that "ignore" is referring to "ads." Adding "it" or "them" is incorrect grammatically. "To be ignored" implies that the readers will be ignored, changing the meaning of the sentence.

28. B: "News sites" is short for "news websites." This is the only acceptable spelling.

29. A: The fee is charged for readers to gain access to the site. "Assess" means to evaluate or review something. The -ing form of either word is not grammatically correct here.

30. C: The words "subscription based" describe "online newspapers." The words must be joined with a hyphen to form an adjective phrase that is read together. The commas are not necessary.

31. D: The word "both" means that the words following will go together. The conjunction "or" can't be used here, as it means "either." There is no need for a comma, since there are only two adjectives listed to describe the content.

32. C: The plural form of "subscriber" is used with "seem." There is no apostrophe, since the word is not in the possessive form.

33. C: The subject of the sentence is plural: subscribers. The pronoun "their" is plural.

34. D: The sentence provides a summary and conclusion to the passage, so should appear at the end of the piece.

35. A: The phrases "keep their readers loyal" and "produce revenue" are part of a list of ways newspaper owners will try to save their business. The listed phrases must each be separated by a comma.

36. C: The noun "today's" is in the singular possessive form, with "changing world" further describing "today."

37. C: "Adapt" refers to what the news executives have to do. "Adopt" is not used correctly here. The present tense is used in the sentence, so the verb "adapt" should correctly be used in the present tense.

38. C: The sentence is written in the present tense, and the noun "cronyism" is written in the singular form.

39. B: An authoritarian position is a strict position. The person appointing another to a job must be in a position of authority—one that will allow him or her to make such appointments or hires.

40. A: This response provides the most succinct way to make this point.

41. A: The dash is used here to add words, almost as an afterthought. A semicolon is used to join two simple sentences. The words appearing after "place" cannot stand alone, so they cannot be considered a simple sentence.

42. D: The person is not noticed for a particular position—he or she is overlooked for it. Other responses indicate complicated or confusing ways to say this.

43. D: The singular form of "manager" is used in this sentence, and this is made possessive by adding an apostrophe *s*.

44. A: Each item on the list is separated by a comma.

45. A: The end of this sentence provides a reason why McNamara's decision to enter the war may not have been one an experienced official may have made. It provides a conclusion to the article by giving an example of how cronyism can backfire.

46. A: Choice B is wrong because the comma is not necessary. Choice C is incorrect because the singular subject of *United States Coast Guard* needs the singular verb *was*. Choice D is incorrect because it uses the future perfect verb tense but the event was completed in the past.

47. C: This is the best answer choice because the vague pronoun *It* has been replaced with a specific noun.

48. D: This is the best answer choice as it removes the unnecessary comma. Choice B incorrectly removes the infinitive signifier *to* from the sentence. Choice C changes *enforce* to *promote*, which alters the author's meaning from the laws being upheld to the laws being advertised.

49. D: Choice A uses a comma instead of a conjunction. Choice B makes *combat* plural, which is unnecessary. Choice C adds a comma that is not needed in the sentence.

50. D: Choices A and C utilize a dangling modifier, since *we* are not the ones enforcing maritime law. Choice B is missing a subject.

51. C: Choice A is incorrect due to using an adjective (real) rather than the adverb (really). Choice B is incorrect because it negates the statement. Choice D is incorrect because of the comma between the adverb and its object. Choice C is a concise and grammatically correct introduction to the sentence.

52. D: Answer choices A and C incorrectly introduce the clause with participles. Choice B is redundant (both *one* and *single*), as well as possibly implying that the Coast Guard performs this exact list in one day, rather than on average.

53. B: *Explore* and *investigate* are synonyms, so it is redundant to use both terms. Thus, answer choices A, C, and D are incorrect.

54. A: Sentence 4 should begin the paragraph in order to introduce the main topic that will be supported by evidence in the following sentences. Sentence 2 belongs after Sentence 3 because it uses the term "also," which indicates that it is a secondary or follow-up point to an idea before it. The negation of Sentence 1 belongs at the end of the paragraph to create an opposing line of thought to the other three sentences.

55. B: Sentence 2 should begin the paragraph in order to introduce the main topic that will be supported by evidence in the following sentences. Sentence 5 belongs after Sentence 3 because it uses the phrase "these types of air pollution," which indicates that it is referring to something described beforehand. The negation of Sentence 1 belongs at the end of the paragraph to create an opposing line of thought to the other three sentences. Sentence 4 must be the final sentence because it directly contrasts with the idea of Sentence 1.

56. B: Sentence 1 should begin the paragraph because it introduces Stalin as the main subject of the following sentences. Sentence 4 comes next because it details the migration of peasants into cities; this is then further explained in Sentence 3, when it says that those peasants resisted and were killed for their rebellion. Sentence 2 comes last because it describes Stalin's death.

57. A: Choice B incorrectly uses a colon. Choice C incorrectly breaks the sentence into two pieces leaving the second half as a fragment. Choice D incorrectly inserts a comma where it is unnecessary.

58. C: Choice A incorrectly removes the hyphens between "on-the-ground research." Choice B incorrectly breaks the sentence into two pieces leaving the second half as a fragment. Choice D incorrectly uses a semicolon.

59. D: Choice A incorrectly rearranges the sentence. As written, it appears as though the United States was drafted in 1917. Choice B incorrectly uses a semicolon. Choice C has improper placement of commas.

60. D: Choice A does not capitalize "Russians." Choice B incorrectly rearranges the sentence. It reads as though Russians elected candidates in 1995 and 1996, rather than define when Yeltsin was reelected. Choice C incorrectly splits the sentence and forgets to capitalize "Russians."

61. C: Choice A incorrectly uses a semicolon. Choice B incorrectly uses a colon and does not capitalize the proper noun "Special Economic Zone program." Choice D incorrectly splits the sentences which makes it less concise.

62. A: Choice B incorrectly rearranges the comma and semicolon. Choice C incorrectly inserts an unnecessary comma after "have." Choice D does not include the necessary semicolon before "instead" to separate two independent clauses.

63. B: Choice A incorrectly inserts a semicolon where there should be a colon and removes necessary semicolons after "reform" and "democratization." Choice C incorrectly removes necessary semicolons after "reform" and "democratization." Choice D incorrectly establishes a fragment by splitting the sentence into two.

64. B: Choice A disjoints the sentence by adding a semicolon and removes necessary quotation marks around "accidental president." Choice C incorrectly switches between verb tense and removes necessary quotation marks around "accidental president." Choice D incorrectly adds a semicolon and improperly capitalizes "accidental president."

65. C: Choice A incorrectly removes the necessary comma after the opening prepositional phrase. Choice B incorrectly removes the necessary comma after the opening prepositional phrase and uses the improper form of "own" to match the subject. Choice D inserts an unnecessary comma and does not have subject-verb agreement.

FSOT Practice Tests #2 and #3

To take these additional FSOT practice tests, visit our bonus page:
mometrix.com/bonus948/fsot

How to Overcome Test Anxiety

Just the thought of taking a test is enough to make most people a little nervous. A test is an important event that can have a long-term impact on your future, so it's important to take it seriously and it's natural to feel anxious about performing well. But just because anxiety is normal, that doesn't mean that it's helpful in test taking, or that you should simply accept it as part of your life. Anxiety can have a variety of effects. These effects can be mild, like making you feel slightly nervous, or severe, like blocking your ability to focus or remember even a simple detail.

If you experience test anxiety—whether severe or mild—it's important to know how to beat it. To discover this, first you need to understand what causes test anxiety.

Causes of Test Anxiety

While we often think of anxiety as an uncontrollable emotional state, it can actually be caused by simple, practical things. One of the most common causes of test anxiety is that a person does not feel adequately prepared for their test. This feeling can be the result of many different issues such as poor study habits or lack of organization, but the most common culprit is time management. Starting to study too late, failing to organize your study time to cover all of the material, or being distracted while you study will mean that you're not well prepared for the test. This may lead to cramming the night before, which will cause you to be physically and mentally exhausted for the test. Poor time management also contributes to feelings of stress, fear, and hopelessness as you realize you are not well prepared but don't know what to do about it.

Other times, test anxiety is not related to your preparation for the test but comes from unresolved fear. This may be a past failure on a test, or poor performance on tests in general. It may come from comparing yourself to others who seem to be performing better or from the stress of living up to expectations. Anxiety may be driven by fears of the future—how failure on this test would affect your educational and career goals. These fears are often completely irrational, but they can still negatively impact your test performance.

Elements of Test Anxiety

As mentioned earlier, test anxiety is considered to be an emotional state, but it has physical and mental components as well. Sometimes you may not even realize that you are suffering from test anxiety until you notice the physical symptoms. These can include trembling hands, rapid heartbeat, sweating, nausea, and tense muscles. Extreme anxiety may lead to fainting or vomiting. Obviously, any of these symptoms can have a negative impact on testing. It is important to recognize them as soon as they begin to occur so that you can address the problem before it damages your performance.

The mental components of test anxiety include trouble focusing and inability to remember learned information. During a test, your mind is on high alert, which can help you recall information and stay focused for an extended period of time. However, anxiety interferes with your mind's natural processes, causing you to blank out, even on the questions you know well. The strain of testing during anxiety makes it difficult to stay focused, especially on a test that may take several hours. Extreme anxiety can take a huge mental toll, making it difficult not only to recall test information but even to understand the test questions or pull your thoughts together.

Effects of Test Anxiety

Test anxiety is like a disease—if left untreated, it will get progressively worse. Anxiety leads to poor performance, and this reinforces the feelings of fear and failure, which in turn lead to poor performances on subsequent tests. It can grow from a mild nervousness to a crippling condition. If allowed to progress, test anxiety can have a big impact on your schooling, and consequently on your future.

Test anxiety can spread to other parts of your life. Anxiety on tests can become anxiety in any stressful situation, and blanking on a test can turn into panicking in a job situation. But fortunately, you don't have to let anxiety rule your testing and determine your grades. There are a number of relatively simple steps you can take to move past anxiety and function normally on a test and in the rest of life.

Physical Steps for Beating Test Anxiety

While test anxiety is a serious problem, the good news is that it can be overcome. It doesn't have to control your ability to think and remember information. While it may take time, you can begin taking steps today to beat anxiety.

Just as your first hint that you may be struggling with anxiety comes from the physical symptoms, the first step to treating it is also physical. Rest is crucial for having a clear, strong mind. If you are tired, it is much easier to give in to anxiety. But if you establish good sleep habits, your body and mind will be ready to perform optimally, without the strain of exhaustion. Additionally, sleeping well helps you to retain information better, so you're more likely to recall the answers when you see the test questions.

Getting good sleep means more than going to bed on time. It's important to allow your brain time to relax. Take study breaks from time to time so it doesn't get overworked, and don't study right before bed. Take time to rest your mind before trying to rest your body, or you may find it difficult to fall asleep.

Along with sleep, other aspects of physical health are important in preparing for a test. Good nutrition is vital for good brain function. Sugary foods and drinks may give a burst of energy but this burst is followed by a crash, both physically and emotionally. Instead, fuel your body with protein and vitamin-rich foods.

Also, drink plenty of water. Dehydration can lead to headaches and exhaustion, especially if your brain is already under stress from the rigors of the test. Particularly if your test is a long one, drink water during the breaks. And if possible, take an energy-boosting snack to eat between sections.

Along with sleep and diet, a third important part of physical health is exercise. Maintaining a steady workout schedule is helpful, but even taking 5-minute study breaks to walk can help get your blood pumping faster and clear your head. Exercise also releases endorphins, which contribute to a positive feeling and can help combat test anxiety.

When you nurture your physical health, you are also contributing to your mental health. If your body is healthy, your mind is much more likely to be healthy as well. So take time to rest, nourish your body with healthy food and water, and get moving as much as possible. Taking these physical steps will make you stronger and more able to take the mental steps necessary to overcome test anxiety.

Mental Steps for Beating Test Anxiety

Working on the mental side of test anxiety can be more challenging, but as with the physical side, there are clear steps you can take to overcome it. As mentioned earlier, test anxiety often stems from lack of preparation, so the obvious solution is to prepare for the test. Effective studying may be the most important weapon you have for beating test anxiety, but you can and should employ several other mental tools to combat fear.

First, boost your confidence by reminding yourself of past success—tests or projects that you aced. If you're putting as much effort into preparing for this test as you did for those, there's no reason you should expect to fail here. Work hard to prepare; then trust your preparation.

Second, surround yourself with encouraging people. It can be helpful to find a study group, but be sure that the people you're around will encourage a positive attitude. If you spend time with others who are anxious or cynical, this will only contribute to your own anxiety. Look for others who are motivated to study hard from a desire to succeed, not from a fear of failure.

Third, reward yourself. A test is physically and mentally tiring, even without anxiety, and it can be helpful to have something to look forward to. Plan an activity following the test, regardless of the outcome, such as going to a movie or getting ice cream.

When you are taking the test, if you find yourself beginning to feel anxious, remind yourself that you know the material. Visualize successfully completing the test. Then take a few deep, relaxing breaths and return to it. Work through the questions carefully but with confidence, knowing that you are capable of succeeding.

Developing a healthy mental approach to test taking will also aid in other areas of life. Test anxiety affects more than just the actual test—it can be damaging to your mental health and even contribute to depression. It's important to beat test anxiety before it becomes a problem for more than testing.

Study Strategy

Being prepared for the test is necessary to combat anxiety, but what does being prepared look like? You may study for hours on end and still not feel prepared. What you need is a strategy for test prep. The next few pages outline our recommended steps to help you plan out and conquer the challenge of preparation.

Step 1: Scope Out the Test

Learn everything you can about the format (multiple choice, essay, etc.) and what will be on the test. Gather any study materials, course outlines, or sample exams that may be available. Not only will this help you to prepare, but knowing what to expect can help to alleviate test anxiety.

Step 2: Map Out the Material

Look through the textbook or study guide and make note of how many chapters or sections it has. Then divide these over the time you have. For example, if a book has 15 chapters and you have five days to study, you need to cover three chapters each day. Even better, if you have the time, leave an extra day at the end for overall review after you have gone through the material in depth.

If time is limited, you may need to prioritize the material. Look through it and make note of which sections you think you already have a good grasp on, and which need review. While you are studying, skim quickly through the familiar sections and take more time on the challenging parts. Write out your plan so you don't get lost as you go. Having a written plan also helps you feel more in control of the study, so anxiety is less likely to arise from feeling overwhelmed at the amount to cover.

Step 3: Gather Your Tools

Decide what study method works best for you. Do you prefer to highlight in the book as you study and then go back over the highlighted portions? Or do you type out notes of the important information? Or is it helpful to make flashcards that you can carry with you? Assemble the pens, index cards, highlighters, post-it notes, and any other materials you may need so you won't be distracted by getting up to find things while you study.

If you're having a hard time retaining the information or organizing your notes, experiment with different methods. For example, try color-coding by subject with colored pens, highlighters, or post-it notes. If you learn better by hearing, try recording yourself reading your notes so you can listen while in the car, working out, or simply sitting at your desk. Ask a friend to quiz you from your flashcards, or try teaching someone the material to solidify it in your mind.

Step 4: Create Your Environment

It's important to avoid distractions while you study. This includes both the obvious distractions like visitors and the subtle distractions like an uncomfortable chair (or a too-comfortable couch that makes you want to fall asleep). Set up the best study environment possible: good lighting and a comfortable work area. If background music helps you focus, you may want to turn it on, but otherwise keep the room quiet. If you are using a computer to take notes, be sure you don't have any other windows open, especially applications like social media, games, or anything else that could distract you. Silence your phone and turn off notifications. Be sure to keep water close by so you stay hydrated while you study (but avoid unhealthy drinks and snacks).

Also, take into account the best time of day to study. Are you freshest first thing in the morning? Try to set aside some time then to work through the material. Is your mind clearer in the afternoon or evening? Schedule your study session then. Another method is to study at the same time of day that you will take the test, so that your brain gets used to working on the material at that time and will be ready to focus at test time.

Step 5: Study!

Once you have done all the study preparation, it's time to settle into the actual studying. Sit down, take a few moments to settle your mind so you can focus, and begin to follow your study plan. Don't give in to distractions or let yourself procrastinate. This is your time to prepare so you'll be ready to fearlessly approach the test. Make the most of the time and stay focused.

Of course, you don't want to burn out. If you study too long you may find that you're not retaining the information very well. Take regular study breaks. For example, taking five minutes out of every hour to walk briskly, breathing deeply and swinging your arms, can help your mind stay fresh.

As you get to the end of each chapter or section, it's a good idea to do a quick review. Remind yourself of what you learned and work on any difficult parts. When you feel that you've mastered the material, move on to the next part. At the end of your study session, briefly skim through your notes again.

But while review is helpful, cramming last minute is NOT. If at all possible, work ahead so that you won't need to fit all your study into the last day. Cramming overloads your brain with more information than it can process and retain, and your tired mind may struggle to recall even previously learned information when it is overwhelmed with last-minute study. Also, the urgent nature of cramming and the stress placed on your brain contribute to anxiety. You'll be more likely to go to the test feeling unprepared and having trouble thinking clearly.

So don't cram, and don't stay up late before the test, even just to review your notes at a leisurely pace. Your brain needs rest more than it needs to go over the information again. In fact, plan to finish your studies by noon or early afternoon the day before the test. Give your brain the rest of the day to relax or focus on other things, and get a good night's sleep. Then you will be fresh for the test and better able to recall what you've studied.

Step 6: Take a Practice Test

Many courses offer sample tests, either online or in the study materials. This is an excellent resource to check whether you have mastered the material, as well as to prepare for the test format and environment.

Check the test format ahead of time: the number of questions, the type (multiple choice, free response, etc.), and the time limit. Then create a plan for working through them. For example, if you have 30 minutes to take a 60-question test, your limit is 30 seconds per question. Spend less time on the questions you know well so that you can take more time on the difficult ones.

If you have time to take several practice tests, take the first one open book, with no time limit. Work through the questions at your own pace and make sure you fully understand them. Gradually work up to taking a test under test conditions: sit at a desk with all study materials put away and set a timer. Pace yourself to make sure you finish the test with time to spare and go back to check your answers if you have time.

After each test, check your answers. On the questions you missed, be sure you understand why you missed them. Did you misread the question (tests can use tricky wording)? Did you forget the information? Or was it something you hadn't learned? Go back and study any shaky areas that the practice tests reveal.

Taking these tests not only helps with your grade, but also aids in combating test anxiety. If you're already used to the test conditions, you're less likely to worry about it, and working through tests until you're scoring well gives you a confidence boost. Go through the practice tests until you feel comfortable, and then you can go into the test knowing that you're ready for it.

Test Tips

On test day, you should be confident, knowing that you've prepared well and are ready to answer the questions. But aside from preparation, there are several test day strategies you can employ to maximize your performance.

First, as stated before, get a good night's sleep the night before the test (and for several nights before that, if possible). Go into the test with a fresh, alert mind rather than staying up late to study.

Try not to change too much about your normal routine on the day of the test. It's important to eat a nutritious breakfast, but if you normally don't eat breakfast at all, consider eating just a protein bar. If you're a coffee drinker, go ahead and have your normal coffee. Just make sure you time it so that the caffeine doesn't wear off right in the middle of your test. Avoid sugary beverages, and drink enough water to stay hydrated but not so much that you need a restroom break 10 minutes into the test. If your test isn't first thing in the morning, consider going for a walk or doing a light workout before the test to get your blood flowing.

Allow yourself enough time to get ready, and leave for the test with plenty of time to spare so you won't have the anxiety of scrambling to arrive in time. Another reason to be early is to select a good seat. It's helpful to sit away from doors and windows, which can be distracting. Find a good seat, get out your supplies, and settle your mind before the test begins.

When the test begins, start by going over the instructions carefully, even if you already know what to expect. Make sure you avoid any careless mistakes by following the directions.

Then begin working through the questions, pacing yourself as you've practiced. If you're not sure on an answer, don't spend too much time on it, and don't let it shake your confidence. Either skip it and come back later, or eliminate as many wrong answers as possible and guess among the remaining ones. Don't dwell on these questions as you continue—put them out of your mind and focus on what lies ahead.

Be sure to read all of the answer choices, even if you're sure the first one is the right answer. Sometimes you'll find a better one if you keep reading. But don't second-guess yourself if you do immediately know the answer. Your gut instinct is usually right. Don't let test anxiety rob you of the information you know.

If you have time at the end of the test (and if the test format allows), go back and review your answers. Be cautious about changing any, since your first instinct tends to be correct, but make sure you didn't misread any of the questions or accidentally mark the wrong answer choice. Look over any you skipped and make an educated guess.

At the end, leave the test feeling confident. You've done your best, so don't waste time worrying about your performance or wishing you could change anything. Instead, celebrate the successful completion of this test. And finally, use this test to learn how to deal with anxiety even better next time.

Review Video: Test Anxiety
Visit mometrix.com/academy and enter code: 100340

Important Qualification

Not all anxiety is created equal. If your test anxiety is causing major issues in your life beyond the classroom or testing center, or if you are experiencing troubling physical symptoms related to your anxiety, it may be a sign of a serious physiological or psychological condition. If this sounds like your situation, we strongly encourage you to seek professional help.

Additional Bonus Material

Due to our efforts to try to keep this book to a manageable length, we've created a link that will give you access to all of your additional bonus material:

mometrix.com/bonus948/fsot